JOHN L. HULTENG

Stanford University

ROY PAUL NELSON

University of Oregon

The Fourth Estate

An Informal Appraisal of the News and Opinion Media

SECOND EDITION

HARPER & ROW, PUBLISHERS, New York
Cambridge, Philadelphia, San Francisco,
London, Mexico City, São Paulo, Sydney

1817

Sponsoring Editor: Philip Leininger
Project Editor: Beena Kamlani
Production: Delia Tedoff
Photo Researcher: Mira Schachne
Compositor: ComCom Division of Haddon Craftsmen Inc.
Printer and Binder: The Murray Printing Company
Cover Design: Wanda Lubelska Design

THE FOURTH ESTATE: An Informal Appraisal of the News and Opinion Media, Second Edition

Library of Congress Cataloging in Publication Data
Hulteng, John L., 1921–
    The fourth estate.

    1. Mass media—United States.   2. Press—United
States.   I. Nelson, Roy Paul.   II. Title.
P92.U5H8   1982   001.51   82-23206
ISBN 0-06-042991-7

Contents

Chapter 14
For Immediate Release 380

Chapter 15
Curbs and Limits on the Media 421

Chapter 16
The Pear-Shaped Silhouette 447

Index 461

Preface

The communication of ideas and information can be a simple process or an exceedingly complex one. A casual conversation with friends is one kind of communication; reading a newspaper or watching a television news broadcast is quite another.

In the first instance, the one-to-one relationship allows each party to evaluate the information exchanged. Chances are, you know your friends well enough to have evaluated their trustworthiness as bearers of news; you also have some ideas about their motives and are aware of their personal biases that may affect how they pass on information or transmit an opinion.

But very likely you are not in as good a position to assess the information or ideas that come to you from one or another of the mass communication media. You probably do not know much about the way these media work or why they function as they do.

Yet all of us are very heavily dependent on these channels of information from the time we leave the formal educational system. Once we are out of school, teachers and textbooks are no longer primary sources of information or ideas for us. The average adult learns new concepts or new information largely from the media of mass communication. Even the ideas and news items picked up in conversation very likely came originally from one of the mass media.

These channels shape our knowledge of events, of persons, of ideas. They provide us with the bases for our judgments and opinions. The men and women who operate the communication media are intellectual gatekeepers who let through some facts and ideas and hold back others. Sometimes the picture presented by the channels of information is a true and complete one. Sometimes it is as misleading and distorted as the image in a fun-house mirror.

This makes it important that all of us find out how these media function, what pressures affect them, what motives activate those who staff them.

We need to know their limitations and their possibilities. Most particularly, we need to be aware of their possibilities. For as consumers of the products that the mass media produce, we are important to those media. If we as customers insist on good service, we can have it. But we cannot ask for good service if we do not know enough about the media of mass communication to tell whether they are serving us well or poorly.

That is why this book was written. Its purpose is to help readers become more understanding and more discriminating consumers of the products that the mass media thrust at us every day, and nearly every hour, of our lives.

John L. Hulteng
Roy Paul Nelson

Chapter 1
The Media and Society

If a person is deprived of a continuous flow of fresh air, death swiftly follows. In very much the same way, a people's liberties and freedoms weaken and die when they lose a continuous flow of honest and uncensored news about the community, the nation, and the world.

Dictators and other unscrupulous rulers have always been quick to sense this fundamental truth and to act on it. Rigid control of the newspapers and radio was one of the first and most urgent objectives of Adolf Hitler in Germany and Juan Peron in Argentina. Cuba's Fidel Castro and Uganda's Idi Amin were equally prompt in gaining control of all the media in their nations, and martial law was imposed and maintained in Poland through virtually total control of all communication media.

Once the press is under control, the people are no longer exposed to anything other than the doctored propaganda the state permits them to read, hear, or watch. Behind this intellectual curtain, totalitarian forces can consolidate their hold on a nation.

The media of information thus constitute the jugular vein of a free political system; strike there decisively, and the wound is mortal. This importance of the information media to the survival of democratic freedoms stems from a basic concept of representative government: if, and only if, the people are fully and accurately informed, they will be able to choose their governors wisely.

If the media provide the people with a continuing and complete picture of what is happening in the world, and particularly with an accurate account of the way their elected representatives conduct the public business, then the people will know how to register their judgment at the polls when election day comes. If the people do not have a true picture, they have no sound basis for election-day decisions and may be swayed by misinformation, fear, or propaganda.

An eighteenth-century legal philosopher, Jeremy Bentham, saw the value of press publicity for the public business:

> Without publicity on the entire governmental process, no good is permanent; under the auspices of publicity, no evil can continue. Publicity, therefore, is the best means of securing public confidence.

HOW THE CONSTITUTION MAKERS VIEWED IT

A similar awareness led Thomas Jefferson to make his often-quoted comment on the role of the press in a democracy:

> Were it left to me to decide whether we should have a government without newspapers, or newspapers without a government, I should not hesitate a moment to prefer the latter.

He and others of the Founding Fathers saw to it that the First Amendment to the Constitution contained a guarantee against government interference with the freedom of the press. They put that freedom on a par with freedom of speech and freedom of religion. That equality is worth noting, for it underlines the original concept of press freedom in American society: It was to be a freedom belonging to the people, as were freedom of speech and freedom of worship; it was not intended to be the right of only a privileged few.

As with some other ideas embodied in the Constitution, this concept has never been fully realized. At no time in our history has freedom of the press been equally available to all citizens except in theory. Perhaps reality was nearer this ideal in the post-Revolutionary period, when an occasional pamphlet or a weekly newssheet could be launched with very little capital, and when population centers were small. But even then, as now, the channels of communication were utilized by a relatively small number of persons; for economic and other factors tended to limit the access of most citizens to the means for disseminating information to the public.

How much greater is the economic limitation today, when television stations, newspapers, and magazines are enormously costly enterprises. In the late 1970s the *Kansas City Star* was sold to Capitol Cities Corporation for $125 million, and the Gannett newspaper group paid $370 million for eight newspapers owned by the Booth chain of Michigan. Television stations command equally impressive prices, and even small community weekly newspapers change hands at figures ranging from $100,000 to $1 million or more.

Today's channels of communication are also relatively few in number, considering the size to which our national population has grown. There are now around 1750 daily newspapers, two-thirds of them owned by groups or chains; nearly 8000 weeklies, many of them also under group ownership; 8500 radio stations; and 900 or so television stations to serve more than 220 million Americans. Most citizens, despite First Amendment guarantees, have scant practical access to freedom of the press. For that reason all citizens need

to monitor the performance of the news media knowledge-
ably and critically.

WHO SETS THE STANDARDS?

Over the years, various means have been tried or proposed
to ensure quality performance by the information media.
Some of the means will be examined in detail in a later chapter. In a practical sense, however, there are only two general
quality controls operating on the media today: the con-
sciences of those who own and run the media, and the expressed demands of consumers. And only one of these is very
effective.

Most consumers of the mass media products make their
needs known only rarely and inexactly. When they do express preferences, it is more likely with respect to the entertainment features of the media than to the character of the
news content. In the competitive market of the information
media, the working of consumer preference typically favors
the shoddy product over the quality one. This leaves the burden of maintaining responsible standards of performance
very much on the shoulders of those who direct and operate
the media of information—the owners and their hired representatives.[1]

Whether or not a given community is well served by its
local broadcasting station or newspaper often depends on the
accident of inheritance or a marketplace purchase. If the
owner, however the ownership came about, wants to run a
responsible broadcasting property or a balanced newspaper,
that is what the community will get. If the owner wants to
milk the medium for profits and ignore the obligation to inform the public, that is what will happen.

[1]In its obituary editorial on the death of Arthur Hays Sulzberger, publisher
of the *New York Times, The Wall Street Journal* observed (December 16,
1968): "Around newspaper city rooms and press rooms it is traditional to
underrate the role of publishers in the making of a newspaper. But the truth
is that no newspaper can be greater than the vision and integrity of the man
who makes the ultimate decisions."

If the lack of quality in the media products becomes too obvious, the consumers theoretically might rebel and encourage competitors to enter the market. But this seldom happens, particularly in relation to substantial broadcasting or newspaper operations. In many cases, readers or viewers simply are not aware that they are the victims of bad journalism; they are not familiar enough with the media to recognize signs of superficial newscasting or biased reporting. Even if consumers sense that they are poorly served and attempt to encourage corrective competition, the odds against their effectiveness are steep. In very few instances in recent years has a competitor, even with widespread community support, been able to encroach successfully on the market of an established daily newspaper or television station. In the field of radio, the competitive situation is more fluid, making the growth and contraction of stations' markets more rapid.

In the last analysis, it is usually the media owners and their staffs who determine whether a community enjoys responsible journalism or suffers mediocrity.

WE HAVE BEEN LUCKY—SOME OF THE TIME

Fortunately for all of us, many of the media decision makers have responded in at least some degree to the central ethic of journalism: that the people be informed.

To be sure, the early years of American newspaper journalism were marked by biased and partisan reporting. "Yellow" sensationalism colored the news toward the close of the nineteenth century and into the early decades of this one. And in today's media—both print and broadcast—there is distressing evidence of subordination of the public interest to the merchandizing of the news at a level of the lowest common denominator. But through all of these periods some individual journalists have shown extraordinary dedication to the basic mission of the press, and in recent decades this dedication has been more the norm than the exception.

Joseph Pulitzer, one of the makers of American journalism, saw his responsibility clearly as he guided his *New York World* and *St. Louis Post-Dispatch:*

> We are a democracy, and there is only one way to get a democracy on its feet in the matter of its individual, its social, its municipal, its national conduct, and that is by keeping the public informed of what is going on. There is not a crime, there is not a dodge, there is not a trick, there is not a swindle, there is not a vice which does not live by secrecy. Get things out in the open, describe them, ridicule them in the press, and sooner or later public opinion will sweep them away.

Katherine Graham, one of the owners of the *Washington Post,* put Pulitzer's credo into practical application when she showed the courage to back up her reporters and editors who uncovered the Watergate scandal and helped drive President Richard M. Nixon from office in disgrace. In the same spirit, Edward R. Murrow used his television program as a platform to expose the character-assassination tactics of Senator Joseph R. McCarthy at a time when the Wisconsin demagogue had clouded the nation with fear and distrust.

There have been many other journalists who sensed and fulfilled their obligations as clearly as did Pulitzer, Graham, and Murrow, and they have not all been big-city practitioners by any means.

Hazel Brannon Smith, Mississippi publisher of the small weekly *Lexington Advertiser,* persisted in informing her readers accurately about the integration movement in the South, despite the bitter opposition of the White Citizens' Councils and most of the important business interests of her community. She followed in the tradition of publisher J. N. Heiskell and editor Harry Ashmore of the *Little Rock Gazette,* who put that paper behind the move to bring black children into previously all-white schools even though most of their readers opposed the policy. In California, 85-year-old Thomas Storke won the Pulitzer Prize for his *Santa Barbara News-Press* by having the courage to publish a documented exposé of the John Birch society in one of the strongholds of that right-wing organization. A few years later an even tinier

California publication, the *Point Reyes Light,* won the 1979 Pulitzer award for public service for its unflinching reporting about a dangerously misguided California-based group, Synanon.

But there also have been editors and publishers who were indifferent to the role of the press in society, or who deliberately abused their control of the channels of communication in order to wield political power or fatten their fortunes.

The national chain of newspapers owned by William Randolph Hearst, Sr., reflected his personal biases not only in the columns of editorial opinion, but also in the news columns, where readers assumed they were getting undistorted reports. Harry Chandler, one of the early builders of the *Los Angeles Times,* blatantly used that paper to further his financial dealings in Southern California and to conduct a bitter war against unionism. Although Hearst and Chandler are now long gone, their tradition was continued into relatively recent times by figures like William Loeb, whose *Manchester* (New Hampshire) *Union-Leader,* in the words of press observer Thomas Griffith, used "political venom" to skew "New Hampshire's politics and even the state's closely watched presidential primary."

Other present-day decision makers are also sometimes deficient in adherence to the journalistic ideal, though less dramatically and less culpably than the Hearsts and Loebs. In a number of small towns today the local editors deliberately follow a comfortable "don't rock the boat" policy in covering home-town news. They thus avoid antagonizing advertisers or officials and keep the profit margins sound. But they also neglect their ostensible reason and chief obligation for being: informing the people fully and honestly.

In the broadcast media considerations other than public service may also determine decisions. Much news on radio and television is too brief to provide the information the public needs. Often, particularly in times of crisis or disaster, the rush to get on the air leads to the dissemination of sketchy or inaccurate information, and in the hotly competitive broadcast industries a scramble for ratings results in the jazzing up of newscasts and over-emphasis on dramatic developments. Yet, as in print journalism, there are exemplary efforts as well, including the measured, balanced reporting of a Roger Mudd and the aggressive investigatory work of the CBS "60 Minutes" crew.

In short, the picture in the media now, as it has always been, is a spotty one. The controls are uncertain, and it is usually the media owner's sense of integrity and responsibility that determines how good or how bad the service will be. It is this haphazard quality that makes observers and critics of the press agree on the increasing need for readers and viewers, the consumers of the media, to exert more knowledgeable and effective influence on the level of performance of the channels of mass communication.[2]

WINDOWS AND SOCIALIZERS

While the primary focus of this book is on the functioning of the news media as indispensable catalysts of the democratic system, it should be noted that these media perform numerous other functions as well, some of them of great significance to us all.

They serve, for example, as our windows on the world beyond our immediate range of vision. They bring us tidings of innovations, discoveries, and new applications of existing knowledge. They bring us warnings of dangers developing abroad, in distant sections of our own country, or in corners of our community. We are heavily dependent on the media for these glimpses of what is happening outside our immediate neighborhood. We flick on the radio each morning for news of what happened while we slept, we search the newspapers and news magazines for reports of new medical cures

[2]Additional background on the development of the press and its role in American society can be found in the excellent journalistic history *The Press and America,* Fourth Edition, by Edwin and Michael Emery, Prentice-Hall, Englewood Cliffs, N.J., 1978.

"Search me, Boris. All I know is what I read in 'Izvestia.'"

Source: Drawing by B. Tobey; © 1982 The New Yorker
Magazine, Inc.

or economic survival tactics, we watch a television documentary for insight into social systems different from our own. Without these views through the windows of the media we would be cut off, wondering and fearful in a world full of menacing unknowns.

The media of mass communication also serve as socializing agencies, partly through the news they purvey and partly through the other information they disseminate. We learn, particularly from television, about developing fads, about modifications in manners and morals. Conduct that is depicted in the news reports or in the entertainment segments of the broadcast media becomes more and more acceptable and is gradually assimilated by the general public. Our perception of institutions and other persons is often shaped by the manner in which they are shown to us through the news or in "sitcom" (situation comedy) plots.

This socializing influence can be constructive. It has helped to further integration in this country (albeit after a slow start) by showing as a daily commonplace the gradually increasing involvement of blacks and other minorities in all aspects of contemporary society.

But the socializing function, combined with the windows-on-the-world function of the media, can also produce less fortunate results. For example, the news report as it is perceived by the reader or viewer often seems to be crowded with disasters, crimes, accidents, and violence. These are aberrations, departures from the norm, and thus they are legitimately part of the news; we need to be informed about them. But the end impression conveyed through the media packaging formats may be gravely distorted.

A plane crash causing several deaths is undeniably a part of the news: It belongs on the front page and on the television newscast. Yet the readers and viewers who get a vivid impression of the crash see or read nothing about the hundreds of other planes that flew routinely and safely to their destinations that same day. It is also not front page news that 99.9 percent of Americans went about their business in law-abiding fashion on a given day. It *is* news that one among those millions opened fire with a rifle on a crowded downtown street, killing or wounding nine persons before being himself shot down by the police.

It is news when an earthquake measuring 5.1 on the Richter scale jolts three small towns in Southern California. Understandably, the fact that natural disasters did not occur that day in any other part of the country goes unreported.

Consider, however, what results when these several unquestionably legitimate news reports are combined within the limited format of the day's newspaper front page or the nightly television newscast. Because these unhappy events take up so much of the space or time in the news media, the reader or viewer is left with the impression that there are troubles and disasters all about, that the world is becoming a dark and crumbling place. An unwarranted sense of overall apprehension is generated. The news report has not been inaccurate, but the reality has been distorted in a way that can affect the outlook of an entire society, particularly since that society has been conditioned to accept the media's version of the world outside as accurate and complete.

Thus, while the window and socializing functions of the news media constitute valuable and necessary aids to personal adjustment in a complex and often bewildering existence, they can also sometimes lead us to unfortunately warped perceptions. We need to be intelligent consumers of the news media and the only way we can achieve this is to find out as much as possible about the media and the way they perform.

Chapter 2
What Is News?

During his visit to America in 1979, Pope John Paul II addressed a gathering of 400 reporters at the United Nations. "You are indeed servants of the truth," he told them. "You are its tireless transmitters, diffusers, defenders." Most journalists, not only that 400, would like to think that the generous papal assessment of their role was an accurate one. But they acknowledge that the news they deal in and diffuse to the public is something less than the truth. News and truth are sometimes very nearly the same, but more often they are different; the degree of difference varies from event to event and from journalist to journalist.

Before we look at the news and information media in detail, we must first attempt to understand the commodity that they peddle to the public. What is news? How close is it to truth and reality? How is it altered in the news-gathering and news-dissemination processes?

Journalism textbooks contain numerous definitions of news. Two are particularly useful in the context of this book:

1. News is anything that interests you and that you did not already know.
2. News is whatever the reporter and editor decide is news.

These suggest the essential dimensions of news as it is disseminated by the media of mass communication. It is possible, of course, to be much more detailed and technical about the components of news; some writers catalog the 10, or 15, or 20 components of newsworthiness (consequence, conflict, suspense, proximity, and the like). But no reporter sits down at the typewriter or the video display terminal with such a catalog handy, checking off the items as they are packed into the paragraphs. Nor does an editor gauge a reporter's story or an Associated Press (AP) dispatch against a checklist to determine whether it should go on the air or into the paper. Most of the decisions about news— whether the reader's or viewer's decision to pay attention to a story, or the journalist's decision to emphasize a certain aspect of that story—are made by intuition.

WHAT'S NEW AND INTERESTING

Consider that first definition above: News is anything that interests you and that you did not already know. Both elements are typically present in an item of news a person selects from the smorgasbord of each day's newspaper or television newscast. But they may not be present in equal degree. If a story deals with something that deeply interests one, it will get close scrutiny even though it may not include very many truly *new* bits of information. But even if everything in another story is new, it may be skipped if the *topic* is not of interest.

Newspaper photographers call this an "enterprise shot," a photograph used more for setting a mood than for journalistic reasons. Dreaming up an idea for a photograph to go with a hot-weather story can be a problem. What is there left to say? Oregon photographer Peter Haley, came up with this idea for the *Ashland Daily Tidings.* His close-up photograph becomes something of a symbol. It ran large on the front page for impact.

A person's interest can be generated in a number of ways. The story may deal with a subject that has directly to do with one's trade or profession; it may appear to offer help in a personal situation (e.g., a father might be drawn to a story about a community approach to drug experimentation among teen-agers); or it may offer vicarious experience (a suspenseful rescue, or an achievement in sports).

The most newsworthy story of all, of course, is one about the person receiving the news. No matter how flatly written it may be, no matter how prosaically dull to others, a story that is about you, yourself, will earn your close and repeated attention. Look at your family scrapbooks, or the bureau drawers where fading newspaper clippings are carefully folded away. There you will not learn about the first heart transplant, or the landing of men on the moon. Instead there will be wedding stories, obituaries, and the account of a family member being promoted to first assistant cashier.

THE DECISION MAKERS

Before the consumer of news has an option to ignore or pay attention to a given item, others have screened the choices. This is the meaning of the second definition: News is whatever the reporter and editor decide is news. Events by the billions take place every day. A microscopically tiny fraction of these become news—because someone decided they were newsworthy.

A newspaper's city editor or a television news director drawing up the day's assignment sheet makes some of these decisions even before the event takes place. A reporter or a camera crew may be sent to cover a City Council meeting, but no one will be sent to get an account of the Fortnightly Club's panel discussion on the energy crisis. The decision may be made simply because there are not enough reporters and cameras to cover both events, so one must be picked as more important than the other. Or the decision may be made that the club meeting would not be of enough general interest.

The reporter who covers the City Council meeting also

makes decisions. During the meeting a dozen items come up for discussion. The reporter picks out three or four as being important and of interest and includes them in the story. Other items may be tallied in a final paragraph beginning, "In other business . . ." while some may be ignored altogether. Thus, some events of the evening become the stuff of news, while others subside to gather dust in the official records. The reality of the City Council meeting is one thing; the news of that meeting reported through the media pipelines may be more or less than the reality, but it is certainly *different from* the reality.

In some cases the decisions made by the news gatekeepers—the reporters and cameramen on the scene and the editors back at the station or the newspaper—may not be ones that a citizen observing the meeting might have made. Most of us have participated in an event about which we later read in a newspaper or see briefly depicted on television, and in all probability we snort: "That wasn't the way it really happened!"

Walter Lippmann, in his *Public Opinion* published in the 1920s, wrote that ". . . each of us tends to judge a newspaper, if we judge it at all, by its treatment of that part of the news in which we feel ourselves involved." This, of course, applies equally to television news today.

Where the observer's recollection of an event differs from the news report, there has in some instances been a failure somewhere in the flow of the news. The reporter may have missed a significant point, or jotted down a wrong figure, or misspelled a name; the cameraman may have focused on a trivial incident and missed a more significant one.

In a good many other cases, however, the difference may be in priorities. The persons who participate in an event quite naturally remember best their individual parts, which to them loom above all else. But the reporter covering the event as news attempts to be a disinterested party, which gives a very different perspective. The reporter's account, meant to be as balanced and complete as media limitations permit, may barely mention or even ignore the facet of the event in which an individual was directly involved. To that person, now a news consumer, the reality will have been distorted; to the reporter, the report presented was best suited to the needs of readers and viewers generally.

Most journalists, most of the time, do their conscientious best to perceive and report news fully and accurately. They hew as closely to truth and reality as they can, functioning as disinterested observers. But their success is inevitably affected by their emotional and intellectual orientation, and by the nature of the media in which they work. To a considerable extent, the mechanics of news reporting, writing, and editing determine the shape of the news as it is presented through the media.

DISTILLING THE ESSENCE

A news report—whether transmitted by newspaper, magazine, or television—is necessarily an abstraction or condensation of the original event. For example, when a presidential candidate makes a 5000-word speech before a national television audience, some persons will have sufficient time and interest to watch all of it. Most of us, however, will get our impressions of the speech at second or third hand.

A television newscast later that evening may show excerpts totaling a couple of minutes of the original half-hour speech; a commentator may sum up in another 60 seconds or less what were—in the commentator's judgment—the salient points covered by the speaker.

Next morning's newspaper may offer a somewhat fuller report, perhaps as many as 700 words in a summary story studded with pertinent quotations from the speech. The headline written for the newspaper story will attempt to boil it all down to a half-dozen or so expressive words. A radio news bit on the speech may be little longer than the newspaper headline.

A news magazine published three days after the speech may deal with the event much more succinctly than did the newspaper and may also infuse some analysis and evaluation into its report.

By whatever means an individual gains an impression of

the candidate's speech, that impression will differ from the
one produced by witnessing the original event. However, it
should be noted that one might well get a clearer picture
from the reports than from attendance, where attention is
distracted by the surroundings, by the incipient indigestion
induced by the bad luncheon served, by the conversation of
table partners, or by the activities of the persons and equipment reporting the event.

Distilling the central significance of a sprawling, complex event is part of the job of the reporter. A journalist
skilled at the task and impartial in approach can accomplish
this without violating the meaning of an event or the theme
of a speech, even though the version presented is inevitably
different from the original. If the reporter is inexpert, or has
an axe to grind, the nature of the event may be significantly
misrepresented in the process of condensing it into news.

Consider the following case.

An assistant philosophy professor at the University of California at Los Angeles was dropped from her position by action of the Board of Regents of the university. She was both
black and an avowed Communist sympathizer. The news account of the dismissal appeared in two different daily newspapers under these headlines:

MARXIST PROFESSOR   UC REGENTS FIRE
ORDERED DISMISSED   BLACK PROFESSOR

The difference in emphasis in the headlines was reinforced in the stories. That difference is of obvious importance. Each headline establishes a frame of reference within
which the reader views the reported events. Why two different editors chose to focus on different aspects of the same
incident cannot be determined just on the face of the matter.
It is impossible to tell from a distance whether an honest difference in news judgment was involved, or whether a deliberate attempt was made to put a special slant on the story.
But the difference in approaches certainly affected the attitudes of readers toward the news.

That same event, as covered by a television crew, might have been shaped in a different fashion. The TV reporters would very likely have been frustrated in getting usable film footage. The Regents' meeting would probably have been closed to the media, with someone appearing for the group afterward to read a formal statement before the cameras and microphones. On the other hand, there would have been some lively footage of the professor's supporters waving their placards and shouting angry slogans as they picketed outside the building where the meeting was held. Thus, when the producer of the evening news looked over the several minutes of film in order to select the 20 or 30 seconds that would actually show the event on the air, the choice might well be the action scene, with just a fleeting glimpse of the person reading the Regents' statement. Those responsible for putting together television news programs are well aware that one way to heighten viewer interest is to keep as much activity on the screen as possible. They prefer such active scenes to "talking head" interludes.

The end result—emphasizing the action in one aspect of the event and minimizing the more sedate presentation of the other—may give the viewer as distorted an impression of the event as did the two contrasting headlines above. In both instances, the condensation inherent in packaging the news affects the nature of the version presented to the public.

SOMETIMES LAST COMES FIRST

Certain conventions, resulting to some extent from media time and space limitations, govern the way in which news is packaged for presentation to the consumer, whether in newspapers or over the air.

Once the events to be covered in the news have been selected, there is not enough space in the paper, or time on the air, to present even these in complete detail, so the report is condensed, as noted above. But there are also other differences between the original event and the news report

of it. The event on which a news account is based originally
took place in a known time span, with a specific beginning
and a definite end. But a reporter writing for the paper or
the newscast usually presents elements in an order different
from the one in which they occurred.

A news story in a newspaper might begin:

> An eight-year-old South Chicago youngster was killed today
> when a driverless car rolled down a hill and into a crowded
> school playground.

Not often would a reporter present such a story chronologi-
cally, as it happened, telling first how a driver parked his car
on a hillside to go into a neighborhood store, then how the
worn-out hand brake gave way, how the car gathered momentum as it rolled down the hill, how passers-by shouted
warnings in vain, how the eight-year-old ran from one end
of the playground toward the other, and how the car broke
through the chain-link fence and struck him down.

On the other hand, some stories have such strong elements of pathos or humor that the reporter decides their significance can best be brought out by using the chronological
sequence and a climactic ending. The news magazines frequently take this tack, to heighten interest and create an anecdotal or suspenseful mood. But in most cases of "spot"
news (recent, fast-breaking events) reported for a newspaper
or the broadcast media, a beginning sentence (called a "summary lead") of the kind quoted above would be preferred.
Following that lead sentence, the story would be filled out
with additional details, usually arranged in order of descend-
ing importance. This would be particularly true of a newspaper account, which might end not with the climax of the
news event, but with such information as the home addresses
of the participants or similar wrap-up details. This story form,
with the major element of the news first and less important
material following, is the "inverted pyramid" style of news-
story construction. It is still widely used for much spot news
for two reasons.

First, this approach helps the consumer decide quickly

whether to read the newspaper story or listen to the television news item. Readers do not read everything in the newspaper; viewers do not attend to every item in the newscast. The quick, capsule identification of the news to be reported enables the reader or viewer to decide whether the story is of particular interest.

Second, for the newspaper the inverted pyramid story form also has a another useful feature. A newspaper is put together rapidly, over a brief period of time. Changes are made up to the last minute. When a story needs to be shortened to make room for another news item, the makeup editor knows that the last couple of paragraphs contain the least important elements of the story and can be lopped off without serious damage. The essential points will still be intact in the earlier paragraphs.

The inverted pyramid form, for all its usefulness, is something of a literary corset. Its sequence is artificial rather than natural. If it is utilized unvaryingly for every story, the effect on the news consumer is wearying.

Both newspaper reporters and broadcast journalists are aware that a chronological, narrative approach will generate greater interest, provided the topic itself is inherently interesting. Thus, for news events with dramatic human interest, in recent years both writers and editors have been turning more and more often to an anecdotal format, telling the story from beginning to end, even though it takes more newsprint space or air time than the inverted pyramid. It is still true, however, that for most of the top stories of the day the inverted pyramid formula, giving the most important elements first, is the one used.

THAT CRUCIAL FIRST IMPRESSION

Another journalistic packaging convention that can affect the presentation of the news is the newspaper headline, or its broadcast counterpart. The headline is more significant in the print media than it is for radio and television. On the broadcast media the anchor's introductory reference to the story to come represents the equivalent of the newspaper headline and summary lead combined ("Fighting continued today in southern Lebanon . . ." or "More oil companies reported big profits today . . ."). That opening sentence helps to shape the viewer's perception of the news account, just as the headline helps to determine how the reader will approach the news story below.

But the nature of the newspaper headline is more rigidly prescribed by space limits and convention than is the newscaster's opening observation; so the headline's impact on the reader is more aggravated, and more aggravating.

Most headlines, for example, are written in the present tense, even though the story itself is in the past tense. People are not already dead in the world of headline writers: they *die,* now, right before our eyes. Sometimes, in order to fill out space, the headline writer adds a "when": Tuesday, say. Then the headlines read as if somebody has "put the finger" on somebody else: JOE BLANK DIES TUESDAY, when the fact is that poor Joe Blank has already gone to his reward.

Headlines must be as brief as possible, since they have to fit into very limited space. All nonvital words such as "a," "the," and "and" are dropped; initials are used as abbreviations (ICBM for intercontinental ballistic missile, FCC for Federal Communications Commission); quotations and sources are telescoped (PRESIDENT: AID SOCIAL SECURITY). The result can be lack of precision at best, misdirection or misrepresentation at worst.

Consider this headline:

SCHOOL SUPERINTENDENT BANS BLACK AUTHORS

The story that followed mentioned only two books—*Soul on Ice,* by Eldridge Cleaver, and *Dutchman,* by LeRoi Jones— removed as texts for a black studies course in a city's high schools. They were banned because they contained, in the superintendent's opinion, "unbridled obscenity and pornography," not because they were written by blacks. Seventeen other books by blacks remained on the reading list. The headline, squeezed down to fit, conveyed a distorted impression that all black authors had been banned. For the hasty reader who did not bother to read the whole story, that was the only impression left.

Other instances of misleading headlines are more amusing than consequential. Consider a few examples (they are very easy to find):

MOTHER OF 16 SEEKS DIVORCE TO GET RELIEF

That describes, it turns out, not a woman pestered by her husband but a mother who has discovered that she can get her family on the welfare rolls only if there is no employed man in the house.

CHAMPION DAIRY
ANIMALS SHOWN BY
BORING FARMER

VIRGIN WOMAN
GIVES BIRTH
TO TWINS

These two make more sense when you get into the stories and discover that Boring is a town in Oregon, Virgin a town in Utah.

CITY MAY IMPOSE MANDATORY TIME FOR PROSTITUTION turns out to refer to a change in the sentencing policy of the court, not a municipal requirement for extralegal hanky panky.

Such inadvertencies are relatively harmless; the misrepresentation is ludicrous, short-lived, and inconsequential. But other distortions caused by the headlines can be much more significant.

The head PRESIDENT TRAILING IN POLLS conveys an instant impression to the reader. The story that follows may point out that the poll was financed by the President's opponent; it may turn out to be an unscientific "straw" vote not truly deserving to be called a poll; the actual margin by which the candidates differ may be trifling. All of the information may be put in proper perspective if a person reads the entire account, but very many readers skim the headlines and skip the full story; for them the headline may affect their way of looking at the campaign, even their decision about which way to vote.

The editors who write headlines are, of course, aware of the damage their efforts can inflict on the reality of the news. They try hard to whittle and fit the words, yet also to convey a fair representation of the story below the headline. But the problem persists, as it does to a somewhat lesser extent in the broadcast equivalent of the headline. The brief initial impression conveyed to the reader or viewer can importantly affect the way in which the remainder of the news item is perceived.

A LONG AND COMPLEX PROCESS

As we have seen, the reporters and camera crews who actually gather the stuff of the news make the basic, and perhaps the most crucial, gatekeeping decisions about the version of reality that will eventually reach the consumer. But other persons, like the newspaper headline writers, also shape the news as it proceeds through the media pipelines. For both newspapers and broadcast media there are intermediary editors who have an opportunity to modify the reporter's copy or the camera crew's film or tape before it goes to the public.

On a newspaper, the city editor and the copy desk editor may alter the reporter's story (with editing pencil or on a video display console, depending on the degree to which electronic devices have taken over in that particular newsroom). They may cut out a superfluous phrase here, clarify an obscure point there, perhaps even rewrite an entire paragraph to bring out some half-buried meaning. They may also decide that the reporter gave too much space to the story and trim it accordingly.

In a radio or television news department, a news director will perform similar functions, editing copy or scanning film footage to determine which segments will go on the air and which will end up as "outtakes" never seen outside the station.

These secondary gatekeepers can obviously have an important influence on the final news account. In some infrequent instances, even the top-ranking figures in the media hierarchies may be involved. The newspaper publisher, or the station manager, may intervene to order a certain story killed altogether, for reasons of news judgment or management policy. At each stage along the way the mechanics of the communication process and the individuals who do the processing impose changes on the account of the original reality. The men and women who make these changes have individual backgrounds, attitudes, biases, and reactions. As professionals, the news gatherers and editors try to keep their own attitudes and prejudices out of the picture, but inevitably these factors color their judgments.

At the end of the communication line, we, as readers and viewers, also color the final version of the news account according to *our own* biases and backgrounds, selectively perceiving elements in the news that accord with our individual views of the world and ignoring those that conflict with our beliefs and hopes.

To appreciate the implications involved, let us accompany a hypothetical news item through the communication process from the event to the final form of its description to the public.

A college president announces that fraternities and sororities will be abolished on the campus. The reporter who covers the story is a student who works as a part-time correspondent for the newspaper. As he writes the story he must try to keep his own reactions under control, even though he is a fraternity member and deplores the decision.

At the newspaper downtown, the editor who scans the reporter's story has a dozen others to weigh against it that day and decides to trim it, thus cutting out some of the explanation that accompanied the college president's announcement.

Many types of readers find this story before them that evening—the outraged alumna whose happiest memories were of the old Sigma Zeta house, the teen-ager who had been planning to enter the college next fall, the gas station attendant who has built up a grudge against the hot-rod college students who roar in and out of the station, the restaurant owner who wonders what this might do to the profitable homecoming weekend business each fall, and so on and on.

The communication of news and ideas to a mass audience, through media structures, is an intricately complex process. At every step there are possibilities for alterations that affect the way in which the account will be perceived by the final receiver—the reader, listener, or viewer—who is surrounded by personal frameworks of learned attitudes and unconscious biases. Perhaps the true wonder is that the ultimate perception has even a glancing resemblance to the original reality.

HOW TRUE ARE THE FACTS?

Given the complexity of the communication processes utilized by the mass media, and taking into consideration the institutional, human, and mechanical frailties we have just discussed, what is the consumer to believe about the reliability of the information served up by the newspapers, the television newscasters, and the weekly magazine pundits? How factual are the "facts," how dependable the judgments, how complete the picture?

For answers it is necessary to probe a little further into the ways in which news is gathered and written and into the motivations of the men and women who staff the channels of information. A brief historical background will be helpful at this point.

The thinkers who developed the libertarian philosophy on which the concept of a free press is based—John Milton in the seventeenth century, Thomas Jefferson in the eighteenth century, and John Stuart Mill in the nineteenth century—were thinking in terms of ensuring a free exchange of information and opinion.

Milton argued in the *Areopagitica* that men would be able to recognize the truth and distinguish it from falsehood so long as there was an "open market place of ideas." Jefferson envisioned the public interest being safeguarded in a society where there were numerous newspapers free to express themselves without government censorship, and with every citizen able to read them and piece out an impression of reality from their various offerings. Mill emphasized the need for every man to be able to express his opinion, so that others could benefit from the clash of views and refine their own understanding of the truth on the basis of such interchange.

As this philosophy developed, it rested on two basic assumptions. First, that there would be numerous channels through which information and opinion could be disseminated. Second, that it would be relatively easy for the average citizen to obtain information and opinions from those channels *and* to make use of the same channels to pass his own ideas on to his fellows.

These conditions have not been completely met in any society, in any age. But during the early history of journalism in this and in other countries, there were periods when there did exist many channels—in the form of newspapers, newsletters, and irregularly issued pamphlets. And it was not too difficult for a determined individual to make use of such a channel to disseminate his views, since neither substantial investment nor specialized skill was required.

But as society became more complex and populations grew, the means by which men could communicate ideas and information to one another became costly enterprises and dwindled in number, as was noted in Chapter 1. The channels of communication came under the control of a very few, and the conditions assumed by the architects of the libertarian theory of the press became more and more difficult to realize.

Thus, although its constitutional basis was not altered, the concept of press freedom had to undergo some internal modification. The notion of social responsibility was grafted onto it.

It was recognized that the free clash of ideas in an open marketplace, as contemplated by the philosophers, was not very likely to take place automatically when the avenues of communication were under the control of a relatively small handful of persons. It followed, then, that those who did have the media of information under their control had not only freedom but also responsibility—a responsibility to society to employ these media in the public interest.

To be sure, this concept of social responsibility was not self-enforcing. No watchdog agency was established to keep the editors honest. But the idea was a powerful and pervading one, and it gave rise to some of the ground rules by which the media more and more tended to abide.

OBJECTIVITY: IDEAL OR MYTH?

The ethic of objectivity as an ideal of reporting is one such ground rule. In the "free and open encounter" of ideas pictured by Milton and Mill, objectivity was not a necessary consideration. Amid the clash of various versions of an issue or event, the outlines of the truth would gradually become clear. But the new social responsibility theory contemplated a situation in which there might be only a few—or perhaps only one—version being circulated; in those circumstances it becomes vital that this single version be as near the truth as possible. The man who runs the only wheel in town had better run an honest one.

So during the first half of the twentieth century the ethic of objectivity made its way into most newsrooms, winning more wholehearted acceptance in some than in others. Most reporters and editors strove as best they could to discover and report the news in undistorted form, and to confine expressions of opinion to the editorial page.

Even the best-intentioned journalist would acknowledge, however, that objectivity is an unattainable ideal. (Bill Moyers, press secretary for President Lyndon Johnson, publisher for several years of the Long Island newspaper *Newsday,* and a television journalist, once declared that "of all the myths of journalism, objectivity is the greatest.")

As our earlier examination of the communication process suggests, a completely undistorted report would not be likely to survive all the way through *any* channel, whether back-fence gossip or *New York Times*. But journalists have rationalized that if we keep trying for a truly objective news report, we ought at least to come close. That is a reasonable, pragmatic stance, and if honestly lived up to it would provide the consumer of the mass media product with some assurance that the goods are relatively unadulterated.

Or would it? Even before it had been fully enshrined, the ethic of objectivity had come under question from thoughtful persons both inside and outside the news field. Their concern was not with objectivity as a guide for journalists. What they questioned was whether objectivity was *enough*. If a reporter or editor presented the news as faithfully as possible, with as little distortion as possible, had the obligation to society been met? Or should something more be expected?

After World War II a national Commission on Freedom of the Press conducted an inquiry into the ways in which the media of information functioned. Among their conclusions was this: "It is no longer enough to report *the fact* truthfully. It is now necessary to report *the truth about the fact.*" The commission members and others contended that unswerving adherence to the ethic of objectivity might actually result in misleading the public.

Suppose a reporter carefully and accurately reports what a cabinet officer says in a speech. The reporter has been true to the ethic of objectivity. But suppose that the cabinet officer was uttering deceptive falsehoods. The report of what he said may have been a factual report—but was it truth?

Elmer Davis, for many years a radio reporter and later director of the Office of War Information during World War II, once observed that "Objectivity is all right if it is really objective, if it conveys as accurate an impression of the truth as can be obtained. But to let demonstrably false statements stand with no warning of their falsity is not what I would call objectivity."

To meet such objections as those raised by Davis and the

Commission on Freedom of the Press, reporters and editors began to apply the social responsibility concept in a new way. It was called, variously, "interpretive reporting," "backgrounding the news," or "explanatory writing." As James Reston of the *New York Times* put it: "You cannot merely report the literal truth. You have to explain it."

The proponents of this new approach had no trouble documenting the points they made.

HOW INTERPRETATION HELPS

It was quite true that news sources had become sophisticated about managing the news—that is, presenting only those facts about an issue, a personality, or an event that would make the most favorable possible impression. Government officials, corporate spokesmen, public relations experts had all become adept at exploiting news situations for special ends. If reporters and editors functioned only as hygienic, impartial channels for transmitting to the public the pronouncements, propaganda pitches, or half-truths put out by news sources, they would be guilty of the very offense that Davis had been warning about.

Moreover, the day-to-day, common garden variety of news had indeed been growing more complicated and difficult to understand, as Reston suggested. The issues involved often stretched far beyond the experience of the average news consumer, who clearly could use some help in placing the facts in meaningful perspective. Interpretive reporting offered one way of providing such help.

A skillful interpretive reporter can add depth to a story and to the reader's understanding, not by resorting to fiction or opinion, but by presenting the basic facts either with supplemental information, or in a helpful context. Sometimes such interpretation involves personifying the elements of the news story, so that the reader or viewer can immediately identify with flesh-and-blood individuals rather than being obliged to grasp abstract issues or forbidding statistics.

For example, in the winter of 1979–1980 the following

conventional summary lead was written for a news story dealing with one of the issues of the day:

> Soaring fuel oil prices are causing increasing deprivation and suffering for the state's poor, a Massachusetts legislator charged today. He urged the Carter administration to act to remedy the situation "without delay."

But a somewhat different approach was taken to the same topic in another account written at about that same time:

> In her two-room apartment in a Boston tenement, 73-year-old Hattie Wilson huddled on a sofa. She was wearing two dresses, a coat, a muffler, and a stocking cap.
>
> On her feet were two pair of men's wool socks and some worn bedroom slippers. Still, she was shaking with cold. The thermometer outside read 18 degrees above zero. Inside the apartment, it was somewhere between 40 and 45.
>
> For Hattie Wilson, the "heating or eating" dilemma the politicians argued about was no abstraction. She was doing little of either. . . .

The writer of the second version managed to dramatize the news situation in personal terms, and very likely arrested the reader's attention more fully than would the first version. This made the story more meaningful to the reader, as the advocates of interpretive reporting urge.

Similar personification of large issues to make them more understandable and more immediate is a staple of television news coverage. If there is a strike, for example, the camera crew will inevitably interview some of the pickets to get their reactions. This serves a double purpose—it puts the news event into personal terms with which the viewer can identify, and it provides some action footage for the screen. Unfortunately, such personalization of news on TV is often so superficial and hasty that it does not adequately serve the central purpose of interpretation.

Sometimes interpretive reporting involves not personification, but the combining of several related elements to explain the meaning of a development in the headlines, as in this instance:

> Two major New York banks today raised the prime rate, the
> interest fee charged to the banks' best customers, to a record
> 21 per cent. Officials of the housing industry immediately
> warned that the reflected impact of the move would have
> "devastating" effects on the availability of money for home
> mortgages. "It's going to be harder than ever before," said one
> industry spokesman, "for the average family to buy a home."

The writer of that lead made use of definition of an unfamiliar term (prime rate) in order to make the news understandable, and also drew in a related news aspect to explain the
effect of the interest rate change in terms that would be immediately meaningful to the reader. Such interpretation
serves the public effectively and is increasingly evident in
the work of both print and broadcast journalists. Yet it should
be noted that there are pitfalls involved in interpretive reporting. The obligation to interpret the news, to bring out
the half-obscured truth or significance behind the reported
events, often confronts the journalist with a staggering assignment. The search for truth has eluded philosophers for
centuries, but the reporter must come up with a definitive
version before air time or press deadlines.

DEPARTING FROM THE ETHIC

In attempting to respond to the challenge, journalists sometimes come up not only with legitimate forms of interpretation—personification, sequence, combination, and setting—
but also with opinion. And that involves a considerable departure from the ethic of objectivity.

As has been pointed out, even the best-intentioned journalist confronts a task that is formidable enough just in trying
to adhere to the ideal of objectivity. Under the rubric of interpretive reporting, that same journalist must now obtain
an accurate report of an event, then add to it an overlay of
interpretation that will make the report meaningful; he must
somehow reveal "the truth about the fact," as the Commission on Freedom of the Press phrased it. There is perhaps

little wonder that in the process some reporters stray over the boundary and wind up opinion mongering, an activity they are theoretically supposed to shun.

Even the proponents of interpretive reporting recognize this hazard. One of the earliest advocates of the new approach was Lester Markel, at that time Sunday editor of the *New York Times:*

> There is a vast difference between interpretation and opinion. And the distinction is of the utmost importance. Three elements, not two, are involved in this debate. First, news; second, interpretation; third, opinion. To take a primitive example:
>
> To say that Senator McThing is investigating the teaching of Patagonian in the schools is *news.*
>
> To explain why Senator McThing is carrying on this investigation is *interpretation.*
>
> To remark that Senator McThing should be ashamed of himself is *opinion.* [1]

Markel intended that simplification to clear the air. But even in its own terms it contains disturbing ambiguity. How can one explain *why* Senator McThing is doing his thing without suggesting motives? And does that not veer into the realm of opinion?

This suggests how delicate and demanding is the job of the interpretive reporter. There certainly are some news writers (perhaps many) who are experienced, well-informed veterans who could accept this kind of tightrope assignment and bring it off in a fashion that would enhance the reader's understanding of a difficult aspect of the news. But the cult of interpretive reporting is a widely appealing one, for it offers the chance for creative self-expression usually denied to a reporter functioning as a passive channel for the transmission of news facts. Thus many reporters—not only the seasoned experts—are tempted to try their hands at it, and some

[1] Quoted in the *Bulletin of the American Society of Newspaper Editors,* April 1, 1953.

of them simply do not have the judgment or the informa-
tional background that would equip them to do a responsible
job of explaining the meaning of the news.

Consider the following newspaper lead, written by a respected wire service correspondent:

> For months Senator Ted Kennedy of Massachusetts has teased
> politicians and the public with his "will he—won't he" act. But
> now the indications are more and more numerous that he defi-
> nitely will enter the 1980 presidential primaries in an effort
> to take the nomination away from an incumbent president.
>
> Earlier this week, Kennedy let it be known "inadvertently"
> that his mother and other members of his family no longer
> were opposed to his candidacy. And today he sent encouraging
> signals to Draft-Kennedy committees in two southern states.
> Said one of the senator's aides: "You might say it's all but offi-
> cial."
>
> If it is all but official, the senator from Camelot faces a formi-
> dable challenge. President Carter can wield all of the leverage
> of his office, and he is likely to do just that. He has the loyalty
> of party officials in the South and parts of the Midwest, al-
> though his hold is less certain in the Northeast, which is Ken-
> nedy country. Still, most observers feel, party regulars in any
> section will shrink from denying a second term nomination to
> a sitting president.

In the space of just a few sentences, the reader is asked
to take several items on faith. Who is "one of the senator's
aides" who signals that the announcement is all but official?
Who are the "most observers" who feel that party regulars
will hesitate to deny a sitting president the renomination
prize? So far as the reader knows, these are all faceless ano-
nymities. Do they exist at all, or did the writer make them
up to give his story greater authenticity? And what about the
use of "inadvertently" in quotes? Is the writer not in effect
winking at the reader and implying that the Senator engi-
neered the revelation deliberately? Is this fact, interpretation, or the writer's opinion?

In this instance the writer was a highly regarded journalist with an established reputation. Many readers would pre-

sumably be willing to trust him, to accept the reality of the quoted aide, and to believe that the reporter really did sound out some well-placed observers. They might even go along with the expression of opinion, on the ground that the writer's background qualified him to offer it.

EVERYBODY IN THE ACT

So far so good. But suppose it had not been an established expert who wrote that story. When the techniques of interpretive reporting begin to extend through all of the news columns, and when everyone from the gray-haired Washington correspondent to the police-beat cub reporter gets into the act, the possibilities for trouble are numerous. How much trust is the reader justified in extending to journalists who dilute the ethic of objectivity with the doctrine of interpretation?

Some editors do not believe that the trust should be extended very freely. James S. Pope, then editor of the *Louisville Courier-Journal,* observed: "Objectivity is a compass for fair reporting, a gyroscope, a little secret radar beam that stabs you when you start twisting news to your own fancy; news-column interpretation, as interpreted by far too many of its practitioners, is a license to become a propagandist, an evangel, a Crusader under a false flag."[2]

It is probably true that most journalists feel, with Pope, that objectivity still has very real meaning. Most also regard interpretation as a delicate, demanding art to be practiced with care and only by those whose experience and judgment qualify them to undertake it. Some thoughtful observers of the media wonder whether even reputable and established veterans can employ the techniques of interpretive reporting without significantly tampering with the integrity of the news.

Consider the efforts of that elite, thoroughly experienced band of journalists assigned to cover the presidential

[2]In a speech at the University of Michigan on March 24, 1959.

election campaigns every four years. These correspondents deal daily with faceless informants, "sources close to . . .", and trends based on "most observers" or "the consensus of party pros." By their reporting they in large measure establish public perceptions of the horse-race aspects of a campaign. By their speculations and analyses they help to establish what percentage of votes will constitute a victory, an upset, or a setback in a specific primary. They create front-runners, and then record the exact moment when those same front-runners are seen to falter. In the judgment of Theodore H. White, author of the "Making of the President" books, "The reporting of 40 or 50 senior political correspondents can determine the outcome of an American presidential election. They've become as important as the 100 senators of the U. S. Senate."[3]

It is disquieting to reflect on the implications of such power being vested in a small corps of unelected journalists, however seasoned and well-intentioned they may be. It is even more alarming to think of reporters at all levels of competence eagerly trying their hands at interpretive journalism. We who are the consumers of the products of the news media can be grateful that many editors and managers still hold with Pope that objectivity is a worthwhile ideal and that interpretation ought to be left to those who have demonstrated their competence and earned seniority.

Media consumers have some obligations of their own, however. Since interpretation is a part of contemporary journalism, it follows that readers and viewers ought to exercise intelligent discrimination in accepting the mass media products that are served up each day. They ought to take the trouble to find out enough about the local newspaper and television newscast to judge how much trust to put in the reliability of the media when they venture into interpretation of the news.

Comparing versions of a news event as reported through

[3]Quoted in Robert W. Merry, "The Press as Pawnbroker in the Presidential Sweepstakes," *The Quill,* January 1980.

several different channels can help to reveal bias in a given medium. Knowing the credentials of reporters and newscasters can provide a basis for evaluation of their performances as journalists.

Some abuses of the concept of interpretation can be spotted on their face by an alert observer. Consider the following newspaper lead:

> DETROIT—Barbara Hoffa got married Saturday. Her father, President James R. Hoffa of the Teamsters Union, gave her away without batting an eye before a wedding crowd that packed the church.

At the time this story appeared, Hoffa had been under investigation by Congressional committees and was facing court action for alleged misuse of union funds. The press had been sniping at him for some time, and the habit of referring to him in denigrating terms had apparently become standard. The phrase "without batting an eye" is irrelevant to this story. If the reporter had wanted to indicate that the father of the bride was calm and unflustered, these adjectives could have been used. The expression used was a gratuitous piece of negative interpretation that leaves the reader with an unfavorable impression of the person thus described. Its use in this fashion should have put the reader on notice that the publication was less than meticulous in its adherence to objective standards.

As a general rule, most journalists and news channels try to be scrupulous in their use of background or interpretive material, and when such reportage is well done its inclusion in the overall report is unquestionably beneficial to the consumer of news. It provides a clearer understanding of the bewildering glut of facts in each day's flow of information. Interpretive reporting has added a new and valuable dimension to the service that the news media can provide us, but it must be *within* the ethic of objectivity, not a substitute for it.

Chapter 3
The Electronic Media:
Always with Us

When Walter Cronkite intoned his final "And that's the way it is" in March 1981 and slipped out of the CBS anchor's chair, the momentous occasion was witnessed by one of the largest television news audiences in the medium's history.

For nearly two decades Cronkite had headed the front-ranking television news team. A nationwide poll had identified him as "the most trusted man in America." He had dealt virtually as an equal with presidents and foreign heads of state and had been credited by some with single-handedly bringing together those once-implacable foes, Prime Minister Menachem Begin of Israel and President Anwar Sadat of Egypt.

Now he was turning his summit seat over to his successor, Dan Rather, and the passing of the torch was recorded with the kind of massive media attention usually reserved for presidential transitions. There were newsmagazine cover stories, columns of newspaper space, summaries of reactions from abroad, and even extensive coverage on the rival networks, ABC and NBC.

The flood of ink and the generous allocations of air time were probably justified, for in many ways this was a benchmark episode for the television news industry. For one thing, it underlined the significant role that television news had come to play in American life; more than half of all U.S. citizens were getting most of their news from television (although there were significant differences among viewers according to age and education levels). The point was reinforced in terms of that common denominator of success and importance—money. Rather's salary was to be $8 million over a five-year contract. That rate of pay is approximately eight times the salary of the President of the United States.

But there were other facets of the transition worth noting. Cronkite was one of the last of the generation of journalists who came to television from print; he had been a reporter and war correspondent for 11 years for United Press. Rather, like many of his contemporaries, came directly into broadcasting from college (although he did work briefly and on a part-time basis for the *Houston Chronicle*). Whether for good or bad, the training and traditions of the new breed differ from those of the Murrows, Collingwoods, Sevareids, and Cronkites of an earlier era.

The attention to the succession at CBS also signaled the importance of news in television programming. Once a loss-leader, the nightly news slot had become a money-maker and a showcase for both the networks and the local stations. That other denominator of broadcasting success, the Nielsen rating, placed a news documentary show, "60 Minutes," consistently among the top ten television offerings and periodically at the very head of the list. Fred Friendly, a media critic and former CBS News president, observed of television programming: "The news is the one thing networks can point to with pride. Everything else they do is crap, and they know it."[1]

From its ragged and uncertain beginnings after World War II, by the time of Cronkite's retirement television had grown into one of the major information media—the dominant medium, in the estimate of some experts. Touching 99 percent of U.S. households, it "educates" the nation's children more pervasively than the school system, helps set the agenda for public discussion, and often plays a king-maker role (or a regicide one) in national elections.

Our concern in this book is with the news and information aspects of television, not with its entertainment function. We examine the ways in which television news is brought to us and the ways in which it affects our lives as America moves through the 1980s.

AT THE NETWORK LEVEL

Television in the United States must be viewed on two levels—the network and the local station. Consider first the networks.

News flows into a television network from a number of sources. The major U.S. wire services, Associated Press and United Press International, feed in thousands of words of news copy. This copy is usually not used as it is in newspapers in the form in which it comes to the network. Instead it provides grist for a staff of the network's own writers, who prepare the script that will be read on the air by the anchor, and sometimes by the correspondents, too.

Much of the content of a network news broadcast is in the form of film or videotape. On an average day, each major network will generate or acquire several hours of film and tape. Some originates with the network's correspondents scattered around the country and the world, some is fed to the network from affiliated local stations that have covered

[1]Quoted in "On the Record," *Time*, January 14, 1980, p. 74.

news in their localities, and some is occasionally bought from freelancers. Only a small fraction of the film and tape will be put on the air that same day; the rest will be discarded by editors or will survive as "outtakes," footage filed unused.

Film or tape is of obvious importance to television, a visual medium. Producers are reluctant to include in the news program stories that are unaccompanied by film or tape footage and must be read by the anchor against a static background (the "talking head").

Yet getting the desired action can be very costly. To equip, service, and maintain a typical three- or four-person camera and reporting crew in the field in the United States will very likely cost the network between three-quarters of a million and a million dollars a year. When the crew is assigned abroad, particularly in a war zone, the costs go up sharply.

Network film teams have to be able to move quickly from one news scene to another, as events dictate. Major news centers are always covered, but special situations such as a natural disaster, a presidential visit to Europe, or a continuing story like the Iranian hostage crisis of 1979–1981 call for concentrated—and expensive—coverage.

Of course, not all news seen on the air is same-day material. Each network maintains an extensive library of footage used in earlier stories, or unused scenes that have been stockpiled in the probability that their subject matter or personages will someday be at the top of the news. These files are drawn on regularly to amplify the spot coverage that may be available in a breaking story. For example, when a world figure dies, on very short notice, an obituary documentary can be pieced together from such files.

To transmit visual footage to the production headquarters in New York, the networks rely on leased cables or on satellite relay, both of which add to the operating costs. Some feature stories can be covered and fed to headquarters by less expensive means, but spot coverage has to be moved by the fastest method available.

At network headquarters, this massive daily flow of news

in words and pictures is processed by a large and highly skilled staff. A typical half-hour network news broadcast is the end product of the efforts of hundreds of journalists and technicians working under intense pressures of deadlines and timing.

Heading the organization will be the producer, who oversees the work of others on the staff. The producer also makes the major decisions about what stories in the day's news flow will get a slot on the program and how much air time should be allotted to each; a minor story may get 30 seconds to a minute, an important one 3 or 4 minutes. A major news break or world crisis might get half or more of the approximately 22 minutes available in a half-hour newscast (the other 8 go to commercials, lead-ins, and credits).

The assignment editor functions much like a newspaper's city editor, deciding which correspondents and film crews will cover the stories breaking that day. As copy and footage come in, they are edited to conform with the producer's overall plan for the newscast, with adjustments being made from time to time in the broadcast day as the relative importance of stories changes.

When it is finally time to put the show on the air, the director takes over, coordinating the various elements involved—script, film, tape, graphics—and blending them all into a finished production.

SUBTLE SHADING

Graphics are increasingly important in television news. Modern studio equipment allows the director to enhance the basic film and script ingredients with many kinds of visual material. Still shots, bar graphs, drawings, maps, and symbols can be used as backdrops for the anchor or as corner inserts while film is running. Split screens, expanding or shrinking inserts, "wipe" shots that give the impression of turning pages—these and many other special effects contribute dynamism and action to the newscast even when film or tape is not available.

Graphics can significantly affect the way in which the news report—both oral and visual—is perceived by the viewing audience. For example, the drawing chosen as backdrop to a story on oil prices might be a sketch of an oil well derrick, a fairly neutral choice. If, instead, the sketch was of a service station gas pump, the viewer would be led to see the story in terms of the price of gasoline and its impact on the consumer's pocketbook. If the sketch was of a man in Arab dress, the role of OPEC would be suggested and the viewer would be influenced subtly to blame the rising costs on factors abroad. A montage of U.S. oil company logos would tend to link the price increases to corporate profits in the viewer's mind.

Graphs or charts are frequently used as visual supplements to television news stories. Their influence on the viewer's perception of the news can be considerable. That same story on oil prices might be accompanied by a chart showing that regular gasoline prices had moved up six cents a gallon over the last three months, say from $1.28 to $1.34. If the chart scale showed only the price range from $1.25 to $1.50 as the frame of reference, the rise would look steep. But if the scale of the chart was from $1.00 to $2.00, the increase would appear much more moderate.

Television network graphic designers try to create visuals that will make the story more meaningful and understandable to viewers without skewing or distorting their perception of it. This calls for a skillful hand and an unbiased approach, a combination not always achieved.

STAGE FRONT

The work of the various backstage figures—technicians, producers, writers, editors, camera crews, and graphics experts—is little sensed by the viewers of a television newscast. For them, the only important personages are the on-screen anchors and correspondents.

Anchors and correspondents work from carefully-timed scripts. Writers prepare the script for anchors, although sometimes an anchor will edit or rewrite the copy to some degree. Correspondents normally write their own copy on the scene.

Television journalists on camera generally do not read from a script but from a prompter positioned just above the camera. They can thus appear to be looking directly at the viewer as they read. Some shuffle sheets of script as they proceed, glancing down occasionally to suggest that they are reading from last-minute copy. In some fast-breaking story situations, when there is no time to process copy for the prompter, they may indeed be dependent on written script.

Most television news stories have a standard format. There is an introduction delivered by an anchor, with a lead-in line to the correspondent: "Ed Bradley is at the scene of the crash. . . ." Then comes the body of the story, consisting of several scenes with the voice of the correspondent heard explaining the action on the screen and filling in additional facts. The typical closing segment is a shot of the correspondent against a backdrop associated with the story scene or theme (e.g., the White House, the briefing podium at the State Department, or the site of a ministers' meeting in Europe). Such a "stand-up" ends with the correspondent shifting the action back to network with a uniform cue line: "Robert Simon, CBS News, Tel Aviv."

The anchors and correspondents are the stars of television news. Through daily exposure in the nation's living rooms they become celebrities, recognized wherever they go and often by their presence creating news as well as reporting it. They also reap impressive financial rewards.

Dan Rather's $8-million contract put him in a very select bracket occupied by only a few (Walter Cronkite among them). But other network salaries reported in 1980 by *The Wall Street Journal* were nonetheless impressive. Network anchors, other than the megastars, earned about $650,000 a year, and top correspondents received from $250,000 to $300,000. At big-market individual stations the major on-screen personages also did very well; a New York station paid its weatherman $300,000 and its chief sportscaster $400,000.

Salaries trailed off sharply for smaller-market stations. A Salt Lake City anchor earned about $35,000 and one in Waco, Texas, $24,000.[2]

THE WORK DAY

A typical work day leading up to a nightly television network newscast might actually have begun the previous day when producers made assignments to correspondents and camera teams around the country and the world. Film began arriving in the morning hours, by cable or satellite, and the flow continued right up to air time.

Producers, directors, and editors convened several times during the day to map out and then later revise the schedule for the broadcast, allocating times to stories and requesting appropriate script from the writers, graphics from the art department, and file footage from the library. Directors, editors, and anchors timed the various segments that are welded together to form the telecast. (The anchor might have taken part in one or all of the planning sessions.) At the final meeting, held only an hour or so before the broadcast time, the show's shape was already fairly definite. Late-breaking developments are accommodated even during the actual broadcast, as editors feed bulletins to the anchors. Live coverage is rare on network news, though it is used frequently on local newscasts.

The final product, the network nightly news, is a smoothly coordinated program, precision-machined so that viewers are seldom conscious of the intricate and complex efforts that go into its production.

THE HOME FRONT

The effort and expense of a television network news program has no impact on an audience until it is fed out through local commercial stations. There are more than 700 of these.

[2]*The Wall Street Journal,* May 15, 1980, p. 1.

Each of the three major networks owns five large-market local stations (tagged "owned-and-operated") and they, of course, carry the parent network's programs. No single entity—network, corporation, or individual—may own more than five VHF (very-high-frequency) commercial television stations, according to Federal Communications Commission (FCC) rules (the limit is seven if two are in the less sought-after UHF—ultrahigh-frequency—category).

In addition, about 200 other local stations are affiliates of each network—they can air the network's programs and they receive part of their revenues from the network. The 100 or so remaining commercial stations, the independents, contract with program producers or with one of the minor networks for news programs to supplement those locally produced.

ABC, CBS, and NBC compete with each other aggressively to mount a network news show that will attract the largest number of viewers and will therefore justify the network in charging advertisers high prices for the few commercial spots spaced through the program. Although each of the networks may have about as many affiliates as the others, it is the total number of viewers watching a given news program that determines its audience rating, advertising revenue, and profitability. For many years CBS dominated network competition, largely thanks to Walter Cronkite's aura and to a top-notch staff of correspondents. NBC, first with the team of Chet Huntley and David Brinkley and later with John Chancellor as anchor, had a firm grip on second place. ABC ran a weak third.

But as the 1980s began, the battle was a good deal closer. The three networks were bunched in the rating reports, and the order was shifting from week to week rather than remaining static. ABC, with its "World News Tonight" crammed with action and electronic gimmickry, had moved up past NBC and from time to time even nudged CBS out of the top slot.

Paying ABC the ultimate compliment, the other two networks revamped their formats to include some of the action and wizardry combination that had given "World News Tonight" such ratings momentum.

All three networks were exploring the possibility of expanding the evening news to one hour, provided that local affiliates could be persuaded to give up that much more prime time. The network news executives were spurred by an advertising agency study that had predicted that by 1990 the broadcast networks might lose more than 25 percent of their viewing audiences to competitors such as cable and satellite offerings.

THE STAR FACTOR

Except for feature and enterprise stories, the raw material available to the competing networks—the news of the day—is pretty much the same for all three: Between two-thirds and four-fifths of the stories covered on an average network evening telecast will also appear on the other two networks that day. So viewers tend to select the program to watch by the *ways* in which the news is covered. That often boils down to which telecasters viewers trust and are attracted to. It isn't surprising, then, that the networks raid each other for proven or promising talent. CBS, as the long-time leader, has suffered most from raiding, and ABC has been the most aggressive raider. (When ABC offered Barbara Walters a record-setting million dollars a year, the network's officials openly expected the dynamic and photogenic Walters to pep up the network news show's rating.)

This competition is reflected in the news-gathering tactics of the network correspondents. An NBC correspondent was poised one evening in front of the flood-lit White House to tape her "stand-up" to be broadcast later. She had an exclusive report on the announcement of an important new presidential appointment. A few steps away was the CBS White House correspondent, awaiting *her* turn to pose before the portico, and she overheard the NBC scoop. She managed to verify it and pass it on in time for CBS to air the announcement ahead of NBC.

Frank Reynolds (left) and Ted Koppel act as anchors for ABC's coverage of the 1980 Democratic National Convention at New York City's Madison Square Garden. In recent years ABC has become a more aggressive network for news than it had been in the past. (*Source:* Photograph reproduced by permission from ABC Television Network.)

When footage is transmitted by satellite, all of the network producers sometimes can tune in their competitors' transmissions and thus preview each other's film and juggle their own newscasts accordingly.

The battle for places and points is likely to continue, since network news has become a richly profitable element of overall programming and the stakes are thus far higher than in the earlier, loss-leader days.

A DIFFERENT MIX

In addition to the network news shows and documentaries, the local stations air newscasts of their own, some of them

AN OPEN LETTER TO TELEVISION WRITERS AND PRODUCERS FROM THE

"Clean Up TV"
CAMPAIGN

REGARDING SYNDICATED TV PROGRAMS!!

During the past several months thousands of churches and millions of individuals from every state in the Union have voiced their concern regarding the presentation of immoral, excessively violent, and profane television programs.

The nation-wide "Clean Up TV" Campaign and the resulting parallel programs by hundreds of other groups which it has generated, have now made it clear that the public is far more upset over such presentations than many within the television industry were originally willing to admit.

After months of preliminary planning the almost explosive results which the Campaign was able to generate within a few weeks of its beginning, on March 16, 1980, came as a shock to many national sponsors. When more than 6,000 Churches of Christ almost immediately agreed to take part, and when, within just the first three months, nearly half a million individuals signed a solemn pledge to boycott companies sponsoring immoral presentations for a period of one year, if necessary, it became clear that by enlisting similar action by hundreds of other concerned groups, these figures could be multiplied many times over. We announced to the media at the June 17, 1980 news conference that these initial efforts were only the tip of the iceberg. The increasing number of groups now taking parallel action and other developments of the past several months we have now clearly demonstrated the total accuracy of that statement.

Still another indication of this fact is the major national opinion survey published in the June 1, 1981 issue of Time Magazine which revealed that a whopping 60% of the American public now feel that television "presents a permissive and immoral set of values which are bad for the country."

While we are thankful for the numerous published reports stating that the new fall television season is now being cleaned up to a remarkable degree, one point should remain crystal clear: That is, that "lip service" to common decency will not be enough. The Fall monitoring period is now about to begin. If sponsors do not live up to their recently stated commitments and the Networks choose to defy the obvious concerns of the public, a far more massive Campaign with its resulting boycotts will be launched near the first of the year. If such action becomes necessary several additional groups, representing millions of additional people who are now quietly waiting to see the present outcome, will also launch major parallel programs to oppose such material.

During the coming months the "Clean Up TV" Campaign will also be moving into a second major phase designed to deal with syndicated programs. Although we do not question your right as television writers and producers to provide the networks with any material you choose, we do want to make it clear that we have no intention of providing financial support to companies whether national or local who support immoral, excessively violent or profane presentations.

While you have every right to decide for yourselves what you will or will not produce, you have no right whatever to expect morally decent people who are offended by indecent programs to financially support your decisions unless they feel these decisions are morally acceptable.

During the coming weeks the Campaign will be in contact with every local television station in the nation. Each of them will be asked to carefully consider the negative effects of such presentations before they are accepted for syndication. We believe the events of the past several months have indicated that the majority of local stations are far more sympathetic to the moral concerns of the public than the networks have thus far demonstrated.

While we respect the right of local stations to decide for themselves what they will or will not broadcast and have therefore not resorted to legal action or to censorship, (as has been falsely charged) we do intend to fully exercise our Constitutional rights in expressing our concern publicly and in encouraging every morally decent person in the nation to refuse to buy the products of both national and local sponsors who are willing to undermine the moral fabric of the country for money.

We are keenly aware that the really big profits in television lie usually in the syndication of programs rather than in the original production of such material. If necessary, therefore, we intend to oppose the presentation of locally syndicated immoral material with even greater vigor than was true of our original efforts with network presentations.

During the coming months, if such material continues to remain a problem on a locally syndicated basis, the thousands of churches taking part in the Campaign will be asked to see that local sponsors are contacted and asked to refrain from such advertising. This will be encouraged by letter writing and telephone campaigns to such sponsors in preparation for a nation-wide series of local boycotts.

We believe local sponsors are even more sensitive to the concerns of the community than the multi-billion dollar national corporations which have occupied our initial efforts. Not only do most of them not have the massive financial "cushion" of the giant corporations but many also already share our views.

.Other probable plans include asking participating churches and individuals to run local newspaper ads identifying all such sponsors publicly or to conduct a city-wide direct mail campaign to provide such information to the public.

You, of course, remain completely free to produce the most degrading of material if you choose to do so, but while new shows are still being planned you should be aware that the ultimate syndication of such material will not be financially supported by a sizeable portion of the public.

Although this announcement will undoubtedly be met with a chorus of "censorship" accusations from some within the television industry it is clear that the public is not nearly so naive as those opposing our efforts would apparently like to believe. Thoughtful people will be able to distinguish the difference between "censorship" (which involves authoritative restrictions) and the simple exercise of our basic Constitutional rights to say what we think publicly and to decide from whom we will or will not buy products.

While we remain seriously concerned over the effects of immoral television presentations, we are also deeply grateful for the many fine qualities which have characterized the television industry through the years. We believe television represents one of the greatest developments of the Twentieth Century. We hope you will take renewed interest in helping it to again become a positive and uplifting influence on the nation.

"Clean Up TV" Campaign Committee
Joelton Church of Christ
P.O. Box 218
Joelton, Tn. 37080

Various groups have launched attacks against television programming in recent years. Some of the attacks are designed to catch the attention of viewers and people who might buy the products advertised on offending programs. This one, a full-page ad in *Advertising Age,* goes directly to the people who write and produce the programs. (*Source:* Reproduced by permission of the "Clean Up TV" Campaign of the Joelton Church of Christ, Joelton, Tennessee.)

as much as twice as long as the network offerings. The organization responsible for turning out news programs at the local level is comparable to that of the networks, except that it may be on a smaller scale (though some major-market stations field as many camera teams as a network) and the coverage area is local or regional rather than national and international.

At the station level the news director, as the title suggests, is the operating head of that organization. There are also producers and assistants, directors, assignment editors, film editors, writers, and other counterparts of the network figures whose work was discussed above. The smaller the station, the less elaborate will be the infrastructure and the more doubling-up there will be in job assignments. Some local television reporters function also as directors and producers of their individual segments.

More important than the size differences between network and local news operations are the substantive and qualitative differences in coverage and presentation. A network news show will rarely pay attention to weather and sports news, unless there is a calamitous tornado or a national baseball strike. But both weather and sports loom large on the local newscast every evening. Most of a network newscast will be made up of "hard" news—national politics, foreign affairs, economic developments. But on a local show generous allocations of air time and staff effort go into "soft" news—human-interest features, oddball happenings, humorous stories.

Some local television newscasts are as well-balanced, serious-minded, and professional as a network show. But many others seem preoccupied with the entertainment mission of television. They place heavy emphasis on action, excitement, and gimmickry, and the on-camera personnel seem to have been chosen for their looks and their skills at repartee rather than for journalistic expertise. Frequently, members of the cast engage in informal banter with one another between (or even during) news segments, trying to achieve a friendly rapport with the audience. This "happy talk" is encouraged by news consultant firms, "news doctors" who are brought in to advise station managers how to spice up their news shows and improve ratings.

Anchors at such stations are regularly evaluated in terms of audience reaction to their personalities. This is sometimes determined by multiple-choice "Q tests" filled out by audience members, or by the reactions of a sample audience as tested by measuring changes in skin perspiration of the audience members when a given anchor appears on the screen. A staff member who flunks the Q test or the skin test is soon out of a job.

Many local news programs are advertised as "Eyewitness News" or "Live Action News," and priority is given to news situations that can conveniently be covered in person by the station's reporters ("This is Jay Jones at Stafford County Court House . . .") even if they are not significant news events.

When one TV station attracted attention and audience by buying a helicopter and putting a reporter and camera crew high in the air over rush hour traffic or a fire, the vogue quickly spread. By 1980 more than 70 stations around the country had "Eye in the Sky" coverage (and a helicopter represents a quarter-million-dollar investment). The airborne reporting has certainly added drama to the mix; whether any journalistic purpose was served is questionable. Ron Powers, a television critic, derided the action and happy-talk school as "Eyewitless News." Powers concluded that "Until local television news ceases to exploit the entertainment bias that is conditioned by its host medium . . . it is engaging in a pollution of the worst sort: pollution of ideas."[3]

But to some station managers and owners the jazz-it-up tactics make excellent sense. The action and happy-talk approach often results in higher ratings for the local news shows, and higher ratings quickly turn into cheerful figures on the balance sheet. For a large-market television station, a single rating point increase can mean an additional million dollars in revenue; each of the three owned-and-operated stations in New York earns more than $30 million a year on its news operations. With such numbers on the line, the local news practices that Ron Powers labels "pollution" are likely to be around for a while longer.

COMPLEX RELATIONSHIPS

The financing of commercial television impinges in a number of ways on both entertainment and news programming. The interrelationships are complex.

Networks develop programs themselves (as is the case

[3]Ron Powers, "Eyewitless News," *Columbia Journalism Review*, 16, no. 1 (May/June 1977): 17–24.

with nightly news shows and documentaries) or buy program packages put together by production companies (as with some entertainment programs). The networks function as suppliers of these programs to local stations. It seems logical, therefore, to assume that the local stations pay the networks for the programs that make up so large a part of the local affiliates' stock in trade. But that is not the case. Instead, the networks pay the local stations to carry the network fare. The networks make their money by selling commercial spots to national advertisers. They are in business to sell an audience to advertisers, and the larger that audience, the more the networks can charge for the commercial spots sandwiched in among the program offerings. Such spots are sold on a "cost-per-thousand" basis—that is, a dollars-and-cents charge is made for each 1000 viewers who can be expected to watch the program, *and* the commercials. Thus 30 seconds on a high-rated show in prime time might cost an advertiser $150,000, while 30 seconds on a less popular show would go for $60,000; in both cases the cost per thousand would be roughly the same, with one show having about two-and-a-half times as many viewers as the other.

The local stations make *their* profit by selling their own commercial minutes (or fractions of minutes) to local and national advertisers. Some of those minutes appear in locally produced programs, including newscasts, and some of them are in network programs. The network might sell four or five of the minute or 30-second spots in a half-hour show, then allow local stations to sell one or two remaining spots by contract to a national or regional advertiser. Local stations earn a small part (10 to 15 percent) of their total revenue in direct payments from the networks for carrying network offerings.

In this set of relationships, the importance of reaching and holding large audiences is obvious. As far as the entertainment programs are concerned, this fosters a lowest-common-denominator approach to programming.

THOSE PRECIOUS POINTS

Broadcast programs' audiences are measured in terms of ratings. The most important of these ratings is the one compiled by the A.C. Nielsen Company, which gathers its rating data from a carefully selected sample of U.S. households. The sample is designed to reflect accurately the composition of the entire U.S. television audience. In each sample household, Nielsen attaches a black box, an audimeter, to the family television set to record which channel is tuned in whenever the set is on. Based on the sample from audimeters nationwide, Nielsen reports each week how many viewers tuned in each program offered in the week's schedule. These ratings are pored over intently by network officials, program producers, and—most importantly—advertisers.

A Nielsen rating of 18 means that when that program was broadcast, 18 percent of the households with Nielsen audimeters were tuned in. By extension, assuming that the Nielsen sample is truly representative, 18 percent of the whole national audience was watching.

This assumption of representativeness is a crucial one. Any sampling technique involves some possibility of error. The Nielsen national sample covers fewer than 1200 households, out of 80 million or more. Even if the sample has been chosen with scientific care, there is likely to be a margin of error of a couple of percentage points either way. Thus, the show with an 18 rating actually may have had only 16 percent of the total audience, or it might have had 20. Those differences loom frighteningly large when they are translated into the price of commercial time—a network might be able to charge $120,000 for 30 seconds on a 20-rated show, but only $80,000 for the same time on one rated 16.

To be sure that the sample continues to be as representative as possible, the Nielsen firm replaces about a fifth of the sample households each year. Still, that means that a given block of households might stay on the panel for as long as four years; a significant bias (e.g., a tilt in the sample toward football or soap operas) could carry over for long periods, affecting the fortunes of programs and networks alike. Also, longstanding sample members must inevitably become aware of the vast leverage they have in the ratings game, and it seems likely that some will succumb to the temptation to make deliberately perverse selections.

The most significant impact of the ratings is on the quality of programming. Since success is measured by rating points, the networks tend to choose shows that are likely to pull the largest audiences. These are often flashy rather than solid shows: sitcoms, private-eye action series, and programs that trade on sex and suggestion. Some of this programming philosophy in choosing the entertainment shows spills over into decision making for news and documentaries, hence the happy-talk and action formats at the local level and the increasing attention of the networks to the anchor's star quality and electronic gimmickry.

Source: Drawing by Ron D. Kingsley for the Brigham Young University *Daily Universe.*

NO COMMERCIAL INTERRUPTIONS

One area of broadcasting where commercial concerns and preoccupation with massive audience numbers are not so influential (or at least are not supposed to be influential) is public television. Of the total number of television stations operating in the United States as the 1980s got underway, 25 percent, or about 240 stations, were licensed as public or educational channels.

Two governmental agencies, the Corporation for Public Broadcasting and the Public Broadcasting Service, function as rough equivalents of a national network. Funds appropriated by Congress are received by the Corporation for Public Broadcasting (CPB), which exists to channel the funds to the individual stations through the Public Broadcasting Service (PBS), the distributor for public television programming. The two agencies are supposed to serve as buffers to insulate the public stations from the heavy hand of governmental interference that might otherwise accompany the public funds.

CPB and PBS were both created by the Public Broadcasting Act of 1967: prior to that time most public broadcasting channels had been concerned chiefly with educational offerings and had usually been associated with a college or university. The 1967 legislation sought to create a system of local public television channels that would offer cultural and educational programs not available on commercial stations because they could not command large enough audiences.

As the system developed through the 1970s, funding came from several sources. Congress voted money outright, from a trickle, at first, to more than $100 million a year before the end of the decade. Public stations also drew support from local audiences, who pledged annual gifts to underwrite station operating costs. Additional funds for programming came from industrial corporations. In return for a simple mention at the beginning and end of a program, a corporation would foot the bill, whether for a PBS production or for the purchase of a program or series from the British Broadcasting Corporation. There were, however, complications and drawbacks associated with all three funding avenues.

In practice, it proved difficult to provide effective insulation from political heat for the stations benefiting from the direct Congressional grants to CPB and then on down the pipeline. PBS and station programmers were inevitably aware that such funding could be reduced or cut off at any time if the Congress found public television offerings too esoteric or too controversial. This fostered timidity in program selection.

The solicitation of support from local audiences became a repetitive chore, and the station managers' ingenuity was tested as they tried one approach after another to sugarcoat the hat-in-hand appeals. The audiences grew weary of the recurring "pledge nights" and other gambits—after all, they had turned to public television in part to escape commercial solicitations.

And reliance on the corporate grants also had some unwanted ramifications. As the annual grant support rose to nearly $50 million the roster of big business credits tacked to program offerings became an embarrassment. So many of the subsidies came from major oil firms that some wags tagged PBS the "Petroleum Broadcasting Service." Because the corporations were reluctant to fund controversial programming, their participation in public television's support represented an indirect but significant influence on content—it was easier to accept a "safe" show underwritten by corporate sponsors than to scratch around for the dollars to produce a show on a prickly topic.

As cable systems grew and offered more and more varied fare, some observers began to question whether there really was a need for public television. One of the chief arguments for public television, that it was needed to provide quality programming for small and discriminating audiences who couldn't find what they wanted on commercial channels, was substantially undercut by the diversity increasingly available on cable.

But public television had its stout defenders. The Carnegie Corporation, a respected foundation, produced persuasive reports in 1967 and 1979, advocating, in the first, the creation of a national public television system and, in the second, expanding and strengthening that system. "Public broadcasters," declared the 1979 report, "have the obligation and the opportunity to bring together a fragmented and wounded society." Then in 1980 the Carnegie organization sponsored yet another report calling for the creation of a public television cable network that would carry out the original objectives of public broadcasting and also take advantage of the growth of cable technology.

Among the most faithful of public television's defenders have been the members of its audience, a small but loyal band. Their annual contributions help support the local stations and, through them, PBS programming. Many of the PBS offerings circulated by the system are programs originated by a local public channel.

Critics of public television often belittle the size of the audience for public TV, pointing out that even the most popular programs draw only about 5 percent of the potential audience. Yet 5 percent of the 160 million persons to whom public television is accessible is 8 million, a substantial number. And it is a fact that some of the best efforts of public television—"Washington Week in Review," "The MacNeil/Lehrer Report," and "Wall Street Week"—explore dimensions of the news that are not often taken up on the commercial channels.

RADIO: THE COMEBACK MEDIUM

When television took off explosively on the American market in the years following World War II, it appeared that radio's golden age had come to an abrupt end. The once-flourishing radio networks shriveled, as both talent and advertisers flocked to the glamorous new medium. Local stations scrambled desperately to find a survival formula. And, although it took a few years, find it they eventually did.

Radio in the 1980s is a healthy and growing industry.

From around 3000 stations in 1954, after the full impact of television competition had manifested itself, the industry expanded to more than 8500 AM and FM stations by 1980, when industry analysts claimed that radio was reaching more Americans than any other medium, and the average household had five sets, counting car radios and "walkabout" units.

The resurrection of radio was accomplished by specialization and fragmentation. The radio stations of the 1980s do not much resemble those of the 1930s and 1940s, which were network-oriented programmers with something for everyone. Stations of the new breed aim their offerings at carefully identified segments of the audience—the fans of hard rock, or classical, or country music, or those who want all news, or black news, or talk shows. They can demonstrate to advertisers that commercials on their stations will reach, say, male listeners between 25 and 34, or a mixed audience between 33 and 54. The advertisers' appeals can be targeted precisely, and radio time thus becomes a canny marketing buy.

One California station, for example, had 1980 research data to prove that its average audience member lived in a $93,000 house, ate out 18 times a month, had a MasterCard credit card, and was planning to spend more than $400 in the next five days at Las Vegas gambling resorts. The station, KRXV, beamed its signal to cars traveling Interstate 15, which connects Los Angeles and Las Vegas, and all of its programming was carefully designed to appeal to such travelers. That made it easy for the station's ad manager to peddle the audience to advertisers with something to sell to that category of consumer.[4]

REACHING FOR SPLINTERS

Stations juggle their program formats, with demographic research findings to guide them, seeking a combination that

[4]Reported by Laurel Leff, "As Competition in Radio Grows, Stations Tailor Programs for Specific Audiences," *The Wall Street Journal*, November 19, 1980. p. 48.

will give them access to an audience segment, sometimes a very thin splinter, that will be distinctive enough and attractive enough for advertisers to pay to reach it. Thus radio in the 1980s offers a very broad spectrum of specialized programming.

News is included in the spectrum, but its significance in the station mix varies widely. On some music stations featuring top-40 hits, news may consist of from one to three minutes of headlines on the hour, nothing more. And on some other stations news—national, international, sports, weather, features—may be the sole program ingredient through the entire broadcast day.

On those stations where news is an incidental component of overall programming, it may amount to no more than rip-and-read briefs from a wire service machine or it may be "borrowed" shamelessly from the local newspaper. At an all-news station, on the other hand, the newscasts may be products of a highly professional staff of reporters, supplemented by the reports of one or more of the networks, for networks, as well as individual stations, have also come back on the radio scene.

In 1981 there were 11 American radio networks in operation, with two others waiting in the wings. The American Broadcasting Company operated four of them, NBC had two, and CBS and the Mutual Broadcasting System had one each. Two of the networks, the National Black Network and the Sheridan Broadcasting Network, tailored their offerings to black audiences.

All of the networks were in a sense specialized, just as individual radio stations had become specialists. One, offering a mix of news, sports, features, and special events, was aimed at persons between the ages of 35 to 44. Another provided large blocks of programming, such as a midnight-to-6:00 A.M. talk show, and promised to appeal to viewers between the ages of 12 and 24. The National Black Network offered five-minute newscasts on the hour, from 6:00 A.M. to midnight. They touched on all news areas, but they emphasized events and information of special interest to black audiences.

A COMPETITIVE SCRAMBLE

As the number of radio stations climbed again, and the hunt for profitable audience segments to mine intensified, competition became heated. In 1980 the Los Angeles market had more than 80 radio stations, and 13 of them had a contemporary top-40 format, with all 13 scrambling for the audience such fare would attract. Just about any television station anywhere in the country is likely to be profitable, and some are veritable money machines. But many radio stations are barely surviving as they cast about for the demographic data and the programming formula that will give them a niche in which to flourish.

Radio's role as a news medium in the 1980s is that of the sentinel in the watchtower. Millions of Americans tune in radio news each morning while shaving or breakfasting, seeking assurance that the world has not blown up overnight and an update on weather and travel information to guide their activities for the day. Commuters driving home from work in the evening during "drive time," one of radio's prime times, get a quick fill-in on the day's happenings to hold them until they catch the nightly newscast on television or scan the evening paper. Radio news presents headlines and bulletins; most listeners turn elsewhere for the body of the news.

However, some of those listeners turn not to visual or print media but to National Public Radio, the counterpart of public television. Its showcase offering, "All Things Considered," presents a daily hour-and-a-half package of news, light features, and background reports. *Time* called it "the most literate, trenchant and entertaining news program on radio." And a competitor on the CBS staff conceded that "they have one of the best news staffs around."

National Public Radio, like public television, is financed largely from taxpayer money voted by Congress, with some supplementary support from contributions and grants. With its comparatively miniscule annual budgets ($10 to $20 million) it turns out polished, professional products for a small but discriminating audience.

OVER THE WIRES

When cable television first came on the scene shortly before 1950 it amounted to little more than an extra-powerful antenna. It caught on initially in rural communities unable to receive through-the-air signals because of intervening hills or mountains or simply because the stations were too far away. Some enterprising individual or group would erect a community antenna on the highest ground in the area and then pipe the captured signal to customers through cables very much like telephone lines. There would, of course, be a fee for the cable transmissions to offset the installation and maintenance costs of the antenna and the system of connecting wires. Later, cable systems spread to communities where signals could be received over the air but not as clearly as by cable, and householders paid the cable fee for better reception of existing channels.

But in the 1970s and early 1980s a series of developments dramatically changed the character of cable. The Federal Communications Commission began to relax the restrictions that had at first severely limited the development of cable. Operators were given more freedom to transmit signals, not just those being broadcast in the immediate community, but also additional ones from distant cities. This broadened the fare available to local viewers from, say, 2 or 3 channels to as many as the 12 channels provided for on the VHF band.

Some cable organizations also began to originate programming rather than merely to pass on various broadcast offerings. The first programs were crude—a camera panning a series of weather instruments, back and forth, or a local public affairs panel, starkly produced. But cable programming rapidly grew more sophisticated, providing access channels for various segments of the public previously without a television voice. Pay-television variations came along, offering sports events and first-run movies over the cable system, priced by the offering or on a subscription basis.

Cable horizons widened abruptly when satellites for transmitting communication signals came into use in the

1970s. Then it became possible for a television broadcaster to bounce the station's signal off a satellite poised high over the earth and back down to just about any designated point, overleaping mountains and other interference more impressively than Superman. Cable systems could receive and pass on to their customers a very wide range of programming.

Naturally, cable networks grew up, such as the one founded in 1980 by Atlanta super-station owner Ted Turner. His Cable News Network (CNN) provides 24-hour news coverage primarily designed to be picked up by cable systems anywhere in the country. The network began with a modest budget and a potential audience of fewer than 2 million, but after a year it had found its stride and was reaching 6.3 million U.S. homes.

Other ventures were quickly in the field or on the drawing boards. One, Entertainment & Sports Programming Network, offered 24-hour sports coverage and by late 1981 was reaching more than 12 million American homes. A New York station, WPIX-TV, launched Independent Network News (INN) to beam a daily prime-time national newscast via satellite to any cable system and independent station that wanted the service. After a year of operation, INN's newscasts were being seen by more than 3 million viewers in 51 cities.

Most of the audience of the several fledgling networks were cable customers. But a sizeable number were viewers of the 100 or so independent stations, the ones not linked to the three major networks as affiliates. Now the independents had a way to offer national newscasts of network quality. One executive at an independent, Eric Steffens of KGSW, Albuquerque, New Mexico, said that "now we don't have to be ashamed" when a major national story breaks.[5] A few major network affiliates even use one of the new ventures as supplementary coverage.

Analysts of cable's future in national communication foresaw a rapidly and unpredictably expanding prospect. We will explore some aspects of their vision in a later section.

---

[5] Quoted in "Two Upstarts vs. the Big Three," *Time*, June 1, 1981, p. 81.

NEWS UNDER LICENSE

Aside from the obvious technological differences, the broadcast media—including satellite-cable—are unlike their print-media counterparts, newspapers and magazines, in one fundamental respect. The electronic news and information channels are licensed by an arm of the federal government: Every few years each broadcaster must seek renewal of its license on terms laid down by the Federal Communications Commission. A station operator who for any reason is denied renewal is at that point out of business. The print media, of course, are subject to no such controls. The First Amendment shields them effectively.

Why are the broadcast media thus controlled when newspapers are not? The reason is simple: Control is essential to orderly communication.

Through-the-air broadcasters reach their audiences by the use of a limited number of carrier waves—radio frequencies or television channels. There are 105 different broadcast positions on the AM radio broadcast band[6] and only 12 channels on the equivalent band of television carrier waves in the VHF range that most television sets are primarily equipped to receive. There are approximately 70 more television channel spaces open in the UHF range, but for various technical reasons these have not come into wide use. Cable systems, using overhead or buried wires to carry their signals, could conceivably bring as many as a hundred channels into a single home, but cable was not around when the regulation patterns were set for the broadcast industry.

Within a given through-the-air broadcast pattern (the distance over which a signal can be received clearly), only so many operators can be licensed or their broadcasts would overrun each other. In radio's early days there was an uncontrolled scramble to make use of the through-the-air channels,

---

[6]In the early 1980s, study began on the feasibility of squeezing the spots on the radio frequency band closer together, with the aim of increasing the number of frequencies available for use.

with overlapping signals blotting each other out and filling the ether with an unintelligible babble. Clearly some agency had to be set up to parcel out the right to use a given radio frequency or television channel in each broadcasting region.

Thus, in those helter-skelter early days of radio, the broadcasters themselves requested the federal government to do this, and in the Radio Act of 1927, later replaced by the Federal Communications Act of 1934, the government accepted the charge. The Federal Communications Commission was established and instructed to make sure that the public airwaves were being utilized by the licensees in "the public interest, convenience, and necessity." The act also directed that the commission refrain from censorship of the content of broadcasts.

In the view of the broadcasters, the FCC should act primarily as a traffic policeman to keep people from bumping into each other on the frequencies. But the commission has at least tried, with varying degrees of persistence through the years, to fulfill more completely its responsibilities as set out in the Communications Act.

There have been four ways in which the FCC has attempted to affect the nature of the broadcasting industry by the exercise of its regulatory power.

1. It has sought to ensure that ownership of the licensed radio and television stations not be unduly concentrated. The FCC will permit a single individual or corporation to own a maximum of seven AM radio stations, seven FM radio stations, and seven television stations, and only five of the TV stations may be in the VHF band, which is the commercial range currently being utilized. This restriction has prevented the growth of large chains.

2. It has required that a prospective licensee, or a license holder seeking renewal, provide assurance that the station will devote a "reasonable" amount of its broadcast time to public service broadcasting—that is, news, public affairs, educational offerings, religious programs, and various categories of "sustaining" (not commercially sponsored) material.

This sounds better on paper than it works out in practice.

Only a tiny handful of license renewal applications have ever been denied by the FCC, and these involved flagrant violations of standards. In the average renewal case, a minimal showing of "public interest" effort usually suffices to earn another franchise term. As one television producer put it,

> The FCC does list "news, public affairs and all other programs exclusive of entertainment and sports" in its forms for those who seek licenses or their renewal. And the commission does ask how much time broadcasters propose to devote, in what time blocks, what staff and facilities will be employed, the source (network, recorded or local) and how much local or regional coverage is planned. Yet the FCC neither establishes nor enforces any standards. Stations whose logs are totally deficient in programming under those rubrics regularly win licenses and renewals. . . . Instead of compelling stations to prove that they serve the public interest, the FCC renews their license unless somebody else proves the contrary. The commission's own staff hasn't the resources. The public rarely intervenes because it doesn't know that it can.[7]

Any member of the public, however, does have the right to offer evidence to the commission at the time of a local license renewal if it seems that the licensee is not fulfilling responsibilities. The renewal hearings are publicized locally, and are held within the region in which the station operates, though not often in the home community itself.

One such citizen intervention that finally achieved some result was begun in 1964 in Jackson, Miss. A local group, aided by Dr. Everett Parker of the Office of Communications of the United Church of Christ, complained to the FCC that WLBT-TV in Jackson was discriminating against the black population of the community by blanking out civil rights news, failing to provide coverage of the black community, and making use of pejorative references to blacks.

The FCC at first dismissed the complaints, holding that such a group had no standing before the commission. An ap-

[7]Arthur Alpert, "Your Time Is Their Time," *The New Republic*, October 18, 1969, pp. 17–21.

peal to the United States Court of Appeals won a verdict for the complainants' right to press their case, and they thereupon reentered their action with the FCC in 1965. Once more the FCC dismissed the complaint, on the ground that the alleged discrimination by the station had not been adequately documented.

The determined band of citizens once again turned to the court, and in his final decision before leaving the Court of Appeals to become Chief Justice of the United States, Judge Warren Burger held again for the complainant group, rebuked the FCC for failing to give the complainants a "hospitable reception," vacated the license of station WLBT-TV, and invited new applicants to seek the franchise.[8]

3. The FCC has promulgated a "fairness doctrine," which specifies that any broadcast license holder must grant free time to reply to any individual or organization that has been attacked on the air. Its purpose is to ensure that all sides of a controversy will have equal access to the public airwaves.

4. Finally, the commission administers the "equal time" provision of Section 315 of the Federal Communications Act. In effect, this provision requires that a broadcaster who sells time to one political candidate during a campaign, must be ready to sell an equal amount of time to the candidate's opponent or opponents; if the broadcaster makes free time available to a candidate, he must make equal free time available to the other candidates in that race.

As might be expected, the equal-time provision is more often invoked successfully than is the fairness doctrine. In the case of both provisions, the demand for even-handedness

---

[8]A more recent case of license refusal was making its way through the courts in the early 1980s. The FCC had voted to deny renewal of licenses for three television stations owned by RKO General, Inc., charging that RKO had acted in concert with its parent company, General Tire, to pressure companies into placing advertising with the RKO stations. In late 1981 the U.S. Court of Appeals for the District of Columbia upheld the FCC action in the case of one of the stations, Boston's WNAC-TV, but directed the agency to reconsider the license denial for the two others. The case seemed destined to reach the Supreme Court before being resolved.

comes from the aggrieved party, and candidates are more likely to be aware of their rights than is the average citizen. Moreover, the fairness doctrine is difficult to pin down in practical terms; unless a given program has been monitored or taped, the question of its fairness is almost impossible to determine, and the commission does not have the resources to maintain constant watch on all the broadcast output of approximately 9500 radio and television stations.

Through the years the various forms of FCC control have not been unduly restrictive for most broadcasters. But the industry resented them, nonetheless, and contended that as long as they existed in the law and regulations the potential for a tighter clampdown always loomed.

By the 1980s, there were signs that the FCC itself was beginning to question the need for at least some of the controls. In late 1981 the Commission voted four-against-two to ask Congress to repeal both the fairness and equal time doctrines, an action in keeping with the program of deregulation emphasized by the Reagan administration in various aspects of business and industry.

But strong and vocal supporters of the two doctrines among citizens groups and some well-placed politicians created the prospect of a sharp, protracted struggle before final action on the FCC recommendations.[9]

[9]For detailed descriptions of broadcast news operations and analysis of their effects see: Cole, Barry, ed., *Television,* The Free Press, New York, 1970; Epstein, Edward Jay, *News From Nowhere: Television and the News,* Random House, Inc., New York, 1973; Johnson, Nicholas, *How to Talk Back to Your Television Set,* Little, Brown and Co., Boston, 1970; Mayer, Martin, *About Television,* Harper & Row, Publishers, Inc. New York, 1972; Newcomb, Horace, *Television: The Critical View,* Oxford University Press, New York, 1976; Stephens, Mitchell, *Broadcast News,* Holt, Rinehart and Winston, New York, 1980; Tuchman, Gaye, ed. *The TV Establishment,* Prentice-Hall, Inc., Englewood Cliffs, N. J., 1974.

BOX 3-1

THE ONLY ALTERNATIVE FOR KFAD

BY WALT BRASCH

The news ratings of television station KFAD went out to lunch and didn't return.

This, of course, caused great concern for the station manager who had just bought a new boat to go with his new beach-front house.

Since he didn't like the possibility of spending the rest of his broadcasting career as station manager for a small 500 watt station in Hogshead, Iowa, a shake-up of his staff was in order.

So, one bleak day recently, he called in his news director, and firmly announced that if the ratings didn't improve, there would be two new families in Hogshead.

"But, Boss," pleaded the news director, "we've tried everything we know to boost the ratings."

"Well," snapped the station manager, "you obviously didn't try hard enough." He thought a moment, then asked, "What about story length—haven't they been getting longer?"

"No, sir! We've never run a story longer than ninety seconds, and most of the stories are fifteen or twenty seconds. I fully understand the attention span of our audience, and I don't want to do anything to lose that audience by giving them longer, more in-depth stories."

The above piece is from "Wanderings," a column appearing in the Bonita Newspaper Group. © 1978, 1982 by Walter M. Brasch. Reprinted by permission. Brasch is a professor at Bloomsburg State College, Bloomsburg, Pennsylvania.

"Good. Good. But, that new guy, Smidgkins—
didn't he spend an awful long time on that story about
tax problems with the County?"

"Well, sir, Smidgkins is a new reporter and hasn't
learned all the procedures yet. But, we did manage to
edit his story down to only a little more than a minute."

"But, we are still using the local newspapers,
right?"

"Oh, yes, sir! My reporters—every one of them—
know that the only way to get good television news is
to rewrite from the local papers. It saves a lot of time
and money that way. And it gives us a lot of time to devote our energies to stories of real importance."

"Like that beauty pageant last week," said the station manager enthusiastically. "You guys did one heck
of a good job filming that. In fact, we even got an additional point for that coverage. Loved that coverage!
Real, hard-hitting news coverage. Wish we could have
more like it."

"Thank you, sir. Our reporters spent a lot of time
covering that story. It just seemed to lend itself to our
newsfilm coverage. I sure hated to miss the Senate investigation, though, but since they didn't allow cameras
in the chambers, there wasn't any sense having a reporter there."

"Well," said the station manager reflectively,
"there's nothing wrong with our basic news coverage,
so it has to be our on-air personalities. How long has
it been since Susie Sweetwater changed her hair
style?"

"Oh, about two months, but I think we should let
it stay that way another month or so just to increase
viewer identification."

"In another month or so," said the station manager,
"we may be off the air. How's Susie handling the
slump?"

"Oh, remarkably well. She's done an awful lot of

work just to try to boost the ratings. Just yesterday, for example, she had her fingernails manicured, and bought a new dress. I think she looks good. A lot better than Laura Landfill over at that other station. The technicians certainly have noticed."

"But, she has presented a few special problems to your staff, hasn't she?" asked the station manager.

"Well, sir, our newswriters are getting a bit cramped writing scripts with no more than two-syllable words in them. But, they've adapted remarkably well. In fact, someone even saw Susie trying to read a newspaper last week. She's sure come a long ways since she's been with us."

"What about Hearthrob? Has he been doing anything? You know the coanchor is just as important."

"Well, he has been putting on a little weight, so I sent him over to the spa a couple days ago. It should boost his image immeasurably. I've even gotten him a new make-up artist."

"It's not working, is it?" said the station manager, looking right through his news director. The news director swallowed hard and sadly admitted that not even a transfusion could save Sweetwater's and Hearthrob's careers on KFAD, and concluded that it was time for them to be "put on notice" or, as TV executives say, to "get the shaft."

"I don't understand it," said the news director over and over. "I just don't understand it. Six months ago, they both passed their interviews with the highest marks of any personality in the country. We ran the TVQ test, and the audiences salivated all over their shirts when Susie and Harry did the news together. That was real viewer identification."

"Well, times have changed. We've got to revamp our format immediately, or both of us will soon be shoveling our way into downtown Hogshead. What about ethnic balance? You know how the FCC is. Can we get any more ratings by adding another ethnic?"

The news director shook his head. "We've already got two Blacks, three Chicanos, an Alaskan, an Indian, two Laplanders and a Southern Baptist on the news team. I don't think we can add any more right now."

"OK, what about delivery? Can we laugh it up more on the set? We'd have to keep up the Happy News format or we'll lose every point we've ever earned."

"I think we're at the saturation point on laughter right now. In fact, our on-air people have become so good that Johnny Carson wants them to do a comedy bit on his show next week. I do think, however, that Susie did get carried away when she laughed all the way through that air disaster in the Bahamas."

"The weather segment has been weak. Can we try something there?

"We tried it several ways. As you know, McDonald gave the weather once in a raincoat, and another time with a bathing suit on. I think the viewers liked that. And remember the times he brought the chickens into the studio? You can't do much more than that to get ratings!"

"What about another pie fight? Can't we try it again?"

The news director paused a moment, then reported that the bill for all the cream pies, for the laundry, and for repairing a boom mike and a television camera—both now permanently identified with caked-in meringue—would preclude any further attempts.

"We could try," the news director suggested, "having the on-air people dress in costumes—you know, one night like the English lords and ladies, another night like Civil War soldiers."

The station manager just shook his head, and sadly asked, "How much does a hog weigh?"

"Don't get discouraged, Boss. I know we've been

here all day trying to get a new format, but things aren't all that bad. We'll come up with some radical new innovative way to boost the ratings."

There was a moment of silence, then the news director blurted out his idea. "A journalist!"

"A what?"

"A journalist! That could be the radical new way to get our ratings. We could hire a journalist to give the news."

The station manager was furious. "Don't be ridiculous! A journalist on TV would be a disaster!"

"No, Boss, I mean it. No one else has a journalist on the air. It could be the novelty that sells the station to the advertisers. Imagine our slogan—'Watch KFAD, the station that has the only journalist on the air.' It could be *big* for us."

"Well," said the station manager thoughtfully, "we did have one journalist who applied for a job a couple weeks ago. He claimed to have spent four years with the New York Times, a couple more with Newsweek, and, I think he said something about being with the Christian Science Monitor for a decade or so. Claimed to have won a Pulitzer. I'm afraid I was rather rude to him. I hate to even talk to journalists. It lowers our image just to have them around."

"But, we're desperate, Boss. Let's give it a try. If it works, we go boating. If it doesn't work, then all we've lost is a couple days shoveling after the pigs."

"We'll give it a try," said the station manager, happy to get any kind of a reprieve. Then he leaned back in his overstuffed chair, pushed away from his eight-foot conference table, lit an oversized cigar, and thought a moment. "A journalist ... On TV ... It's radical enough ... It's even revolutionary! ... It might work ... It just might work."

Then, he turned on his personal TV to watch Laverne & Shirley.

Chapter 4
Newspapers:
The Original
Fourth Estate

Of the various news media in existence today, newspapers have the longest tradition. Books came even earlier, but the dissemination of news has not been their chief function. The news-gathering and news-processing methods of the newspaper press have set the pattern for the later-arriving media of radio, newsmagazines, and television. It is thus appropriate that we take a close look at the functioning of the newspaper in present-day America.

Television may have become the primary source of news for many Americans, but newspapers continue to play a significant role in the dissemination of detailed information about what goes on in the community, the nation, and the world. In America today more than 60 million copies of daily newspapers are distributed from newsstands or by home carriers. More millions of copies of weekly or semiweekly newspapers find their way to readers by carriers or through the mails.

The number of newspapers in the United States reached a peak in the early 1920s and has slowly declined since then. But in recent decades the number of dailies has remained fairly constant, fluctuating narrowly around 1750, with arrivals and departures balancing each other. Big-city newspapers have been dwindling, while suburban publications have grown up to take their places in the ranks.

SOME TERMINOLOGY

Like any profession or trade, newspaper journalism has developed a language of its own. While some of it is jargon, and therefore of interest only to newspaper people, some of it is useful to readers.

The newspaper industry has been called the *Fourth Estate.* This goes back to the early days of the British Parliament, with its three estates of man, Lords Spiritual, Lords Temporal, and "Commons." "The gallery in which the reporters sit has become a fourth estate of the realm," wrote Lord (Thomas Babington) Macaulay.

One of the most versatile terms in newspaper journalism is *editorial.* As a noun, it means an essay or article on the editorial page, usually without a byline, that expresses the opinion of the editor or editorial writer on an issue or event that is often controversial. A regular column, supplied by a syndicate, even though it deals with controversy and appears on the same page, is not considered an editorial. Papers usually run their editorials—or *edits,* as they are sometimes called —on the left-hand side of the editorial page, often in wider columns than other material on the page.

As an adjective, *editorial* is used to distinguish the non-business from the business side of the paper. An editorial worker is one who does not work in advertising, circulation, or printing departments. In other words, reporters and editorial writers work on the editorial side. Sometimes newspapers use the term *news-editorial* for *editorial* to show that both news and opinion are involved.

On the news side, a reporter writes a *story,* and yet it is not a story in the classic sense. Technically, it is a *news report.* But newspaper people seldom call it that.[1] Any item of entertainment in the newspaper is called a *feature. Feature* is also a verb, meaning *to give prominence to;* a newspaper, for example, may feature a picture series on its front page.

Some readers have trouble with the significance of the words *publish* and *print. Publish* is the broad term covering all aspects of putting out a publication, including its printing. To *print* something is simply to make multiple impressions from type or plate. A newspaper *publishes* a story, it does not merely *print* it.

Another term commonly misused is *masthead.* A masthead is a box or table, usually on the editorial page, listing top editors and offering such other information about the paper as frequency of publication, place of publication, and the like. The name of the paper, running across the top of the first page, is not the masthead, but the *nameplate* or *flag.*

WHO DOES WHAT

No organization chart can trace precisely a daily newspaper's chain of command. Some departments and some executives defy categorization. Duties overlap. Short cuts develop. And no newspaper's organization exactly resembles the operation of another. Even the titles of top executives vary.

The chief executive officer usually is the *publisher,* who manages the entire operation. On some newspapers, the owner is publisher; on others—especially the big dailies—the publisher is a hired hand, although a very special one. Ideal-

[1]Magazines use "story" for a short piece of fiction, reserving "article" for their news and opinion pieces.

ly, the publisher has a background on both the news-editorial and business sides of journalism.

Two top-level executives answer directly to the publisher: the *executive editor* or the *editor-in-chief* (or simply, the *editor*), in charge of the news and editorial side and the *business manager,* in charge of accepting and soliciting advertising and of printing and circulating the publication. Other executives may work directly with the publisher on public relations, personnel, and other administrative matters.

THE EDITORIAL SIDE

An *editorial page editor*—or *chief editorial writer* on many newspapers—and a *managing editor* work with the editor-in-chief.

The editorial page editor supervises the work of the editorial writers, the editorial cartoonist, and the staffers who edit the syndicated columns and other opinion pieces, select and edit the letters to the editor, and make up the page.

When during a political campaign a newspaper comes out in favor of one candidate over the other, that support represents the thinking of the editorial page editor and the editorial writers. The publisher—the owner, too—may influence the decision. But reporters and other staff members, including those on the ad side, usually play no role in decisions on editorial policy.

The managing editor, who is concerned more with news than with opinion in the paper, works with various subeditors, the most important of which are the *news editor* and the *city editor*. The news editor watches over the process of selecting and editing national and international (but not local) news, copyediting the stories, writing the headlines, and making up the pages. The city editor assigns regular "beats" and special stories to reporters, and also directs photographers. The city editor gets ideas for stories from tips phoned and mailed in, from watching what other papers do, and from a "future book" listing events to be covered.

OWNER

PUBLISHER

EDITOR

BUSINESS MANAGER

EDITORIAL PAGE EDITOR
STAFF

MANAGING EDITOR

PRODUCTION MANAGER
STAFF

ADVERTISING DIRECTOR

CIRCULATION MANAGER
STAFF

COPY EDITOR
STAFF

NEWS EDITOR

CITY EDITOR
STAFF

WIRE EDITOR

MAKEUP EDITOR

STATE EDITOR
STAFF

SUNDAY EDITOR
STAFF

SPORTS EDITOR
STAFF

HOME EDITOR
STAFF

FINANCIAL EDITOR

CHURCH EDITOR

DISPLAY MANAGER
STAFF

NATIONAL MANAGER
STAFF

CLASSIFIED MANAGER
STAFF

The chain of command in a daily newspaper

Reporters keep opinion out of their news stories, and their city editor has little to do with the editorial writers. But the managing editor, representing the news side, often sits in on editorial conferences, primarily to brief the editorial writers on developments in the news.

The city editor and the news editor work closely together. The city editor sends stories to the copy editor (working with the news editor) to have them checked, headlined, and finally fitted into the pages. On the other hand, some of the editors of special sections (the sports editor and the home editor, to name two) have their own little empires and do their own checking, headline writing, and makeup.

Important on newspapers with large out-of-town circulations is the *state editor* or *county editor.* This editor works with both full-time reporters and "stringers." The stringers—or correspondents—turn in stories on a piecework basis, whenever something newsworthy happens in their communities; they often work under an arrangement that pays them by the story or by the published inch. Their "string" is a pasteup, one following the other, of stories written for a particular month.

The *Sunday editor* puts out the locally edited magazine section and, unusual among newspaper editors, buys some material from freelancers. Some newspapers in their Sunday issues offer readers a syndicated magazine section—like *Parade*—in place of, or in addition to, a locally edited magazine. The newspaper's own staff, of course, plays no role in the production of the syndicated magazine.

Other editors on the organization chart hold less vital though still important jobs, supervising smaller staffs than that of the city editor. In some cases they represent one-person departments where they work more as writers than as editors. A large newspaper would also have a number of minor editors not included on this chart: for instance, an entertainment editor, an automobile editor (a holdover from the time automobiles were a novelty), a science editor, an aviation editor.

THE BUSINESS SIDE

The *business manager* shares equal billing with the editor-in-chief. Working directly under the business manager is a *production manager,* in charge of typesetting, platemaking, and printing; an *advertising director;* and a *circulation manager.*

Some organization charts show the production manager directly under the publisher, serving both news-editorial and business departments.

The advertising director supervises the work of three managers: one in charge of display advertising (ads placed mostly by local retailers), one in charge of national advertising (ads prepared by advertising agencies for manufacturers of brand-name merchandise), and one in charge of classified advertising (the want ads).

The circulation manager uses three different methods for distributing the paper: mail, newsstands, and home delivery. The copies that go into the mail may differ from those sold on newsstands. And the copies delivered by carriers may differ from the other two. All the copies published for a certain day make up the *issue* for that day. A single issue may consist of several *editions,* published at different times during the day; editions change slightly as the news day wears on and emphasis shifts. For example, an afternoon paper may put out a "suburban" edition at 1:00 P.M., for distribution to the outlying areas of its circulation district, then a "city final" at 2:00 P.M. for carrier distribution within the city proper, and still later a "market final" carrying the closing stock market quotations and designed to be sold on downtown newsstands.

The chart does not show the subtleties of relationships between departments and executives. Nor does it show how isolated some departments are from others. For instance, most newspapers discourage communication between the advertising and news departments. The advertising department lets the news department know what parts of inside pages are reserved for advertisers; the news department fills in the remaining areas with stories. The contact ends there. The news department does not know what the ads will say or who the advertisers will be.

An organization chart for a weekly newspaper, of course, would be much simpler. It would still show an editor-in-chief and a business manager, but the supporting cast would be much smaller or, in some cases, nonexistent. For instance, there is no need for an editor or a staff to process national and international news—as far as these weeklies are concerned, all news is local.

A few weekly newspapers are so small that a single person serves in both an editorial and a business capacity. On such a paper it would not be unusual for that one person to sell some advertising space while out covering a story, and maybe to sweep out the place after returning.

THE WIRE SERVICES

Much of what goes into a newspaper comes from the outside. Serving the editorial side are two different kinds of organizations: *wire services* (sometimes called "press associations") and *feature syndicates.*

The two major wire services are Associated Press (AP) and United Press International (UPI). AP and UPI use leased telephone wires, satellites, teleprinters, and underwater cables to transmit stories and pictures to their users. It takes less than a minute to flash a bulletin around the world.

The Associated Press evolved from the New York Associated Press, started in 1848. It became a cooperative owned by the member newspapers and broadcast stations it serves, 6500 of them by 1979. Some 2500 people work for AP full-time at more than 180 bureaus around the world. It is the largest of the wire services. For a long time AP was thought to be the more accurate of the American wire services. UPI was livelier. Such a distinction would be hard to document today.

United Press International started as United Press in 1907 for newspapers that could not get AP service or

Placed outside the entrance to the *Lapeer County Press*, "America's largest country weekly," published at Lapeer, Michigan, is this life-size statue by Derek Wernher of a typical reader of the paper. He is the mythical Len Ganeway, who represents "the strength of the people, the importance of the land, the county's firm roots," according to Lynn Myers, editor of the paper. It took about a year for the sculptor to complete his work. Joe Bybee took this photograph.

wanted an alternative. As the number-two wire service, United Press had to try harder. Its reporters scrambled to cover their beats and make their deadlines. They were never happier than when they scooped the AP.[2] In 1958, UP merged with the small, sensation-oriented International News Service (a wire service started by the William Randolph Hearst newspapers in 1909) and became United Press International. UPI, not a cooperative, was owned by the Scripps-Howard organization until it was sold in 1982. About 1700 people work for more than 160 UPI bureaus. Its clients number about 5880.

Other countries have wire services, too, and some antedate those headquartered in the United States Reuters, in England, started in 1815. Agence Havas of Paris started in 1835, became Agence France-Presse after World War II, and was for a time owned by the French government. Russia has TASS, said to have 10,000 subscribers. Wire services in other countries are mostly national, rather than international, and some have cooperative working relationships with the bigger agencies.

The wire services helped originate the objective style that became important to most American newspapers. The early newspapers had been partisan and opinionated, even in their news columns. Serving papers with a variety of points of view, the wire services could not afford to be one-sided. What they sent had to be acceptable to all editors.

---

[2]Some reporters could not take the strain. Joe Alex Morris in his *Deadline Every Minute*, the story of the United Press, tells about a staffer in an under-manned bureau in Raleigh. The poor fellow was trying to run two teleprinters at once. He would punch on one for a while, then run over to punch on the other. When the one going to Atlanta stopped, the man in Atlanta punched this message to Raleigh: WHAT'S THE MATTER? CAN'T YOU PUNCH? The Raleigh man punched back: ONLY HAVE 2 HANDS. The Atlanta man then sent this message to the boss of the man in Raleigh: SUGGEST YOU FIRE THE CRIPPLED BASTARD. Another story has a man quitting UP with this terse letter of resignation: "Pay too low. Hours too long. Life too short." Morris's book was published in 1957 by Doubleday and Company, New York. For a history of the early AP, see Oliver Gramling, *AP: The Story of the News*, Holt, Rinehart and Winston, New York, 1940.

Wire service reporters work like newspaper reporters, but they watch for regional, national, and international stories or angles instead of local ones. However, a local story might have enough human interest to merit transmission to papers all over. What the wire services transmit largely determines the national and international news newspapers carry. A check of the front pages of dailies in several cities for a single day would show a remarkable similarity of stories featured.

Both AP and UPI make New York their headquarters, and most national and international news reports originate there, but major bureaus can be found in Washington, D.C., of course, and in Chicago, Los Angeles, and other big cities in the United States and other countries. Smaller cities have bureaus or offices, too, where news is both sent and received. Computers tie the systems together with newspapers. Big newspapers and broadcast stations pay more for the service than small ones pay. Weekly newspapers, with their local emphasis and less frequent deadlines, do not buy the services.

Several smaller, more specialized wire services supplement what AP and UPI send out. The smaller services, including the *New York Times* News Service, the *Los Angeles Times–Washington Post* News Service, and several others, deal more in feature and interpretive material. Some of the additional services—Copley News Service is one—originated to serve papers that were part of a chain and then expanded to serve others. Various supplemental services specialize in certain subjects, like business or religion.

FEATURE SYNDICATES

While wire services deal mostly with hard, fast-breaking news, feature syndicates deal with entertainment and opinion features. They bring the work of big-name columnists, editorial cartoonists, and comic-strip artists to newspapers at a fraction of what the original material would cost the newspapers themselves.

The idea of a feature syndicate emerged in 1880 with

the formation of the Western Newspaper Union. Shortly afterward some magazine editors began selling their short stories and articles to newspapers for reprinting. In the early 1900s, William Randolph Hearst began his King Features Syndicate, which today is still big in the industry. Scripps-Howard started United Feature Syndicate, another important one. Some individual newspapers developed features that had possibilities for sale to other papers and so formed their own syndicates to distribute them. The *Chicago Tribune* and *New York Daily News* got together for one of the big ones. The *Los Angeles Times* and the *Des Moines Register and Tribune* own important syndicates, too.

One of the liveliest of the feature syndicates—also a relatively new one, founded in 1970—is Universal Press Syndicate, Fairway (Kansas City), Kansas. It was the syndicate that introduced *Doonesbury* to a national newspaper audience. Among its columnists are William F. Buckley, Jr., Mary McGrory, Sylvia Porter, Abigail Van Buren, James J. Kilpatrick, Gary Wills, Jeff Greenfield, and Georgie Ann Geyer.

Syndicated editorial cartoons and comic strips get attention later in this book; the columnists are discussed here. To be syndicated, a columnist has to deal mostly with national or international issues, with universal concerns, or with common foibles. The typical syndicated column runs to about 750 words, and it comes to the subscribing newspaper three times a week. A big newspaper buys a number of columns and uses only those that seem good or appropriate. When several columnists choose to write on the same topic, the paper may include two or three to allow readers to compare them.

While the number of daily newspapers remains pretty much the same each year, the syndicates continue to introduce new columns. It is a good idea, syndicates find, to line up important newspapers first, before advertising a new feature to the trade. A full-page ad in *Editor & Publisher* on March 3, 1979, announced the launching by Universal Press Syndicate of a column by Richard Reeves, who has been called by Edwin Newman "one of the best political reporters in the country." William Safire, the house-conservative columnist with the *New York Times,* says "Reeves is a pleasure to disagree with." The *Boston Globe, Philadelphia Inquirer, Chicago Sun-Times,* and *Miami News* were among the papers starting Reeves off. Reeves, brash and irreverent, at that time had several books to his credit and was writing regularly for *Esquire* and other magazines.

Among the opinion columnists in 1980, Jack Anderson circulated to the most newspapers (950), followed by Art Buchwald (800), James J. Kilpatrick (400), and William F. Buckley, Jr. (350).[3]

Buckley is probably the best-known conservative columnist, but another conservative is crowding him for readership. He is George F. Will, who began a semiweekly syndicated column in 1973. By 1979 the *Washington Post* Writers Group was distributing his column to about 300 newspapers. He also writes a column for *Newsweek.* His column-writing colleague at *Newsweek,* Meg Greenfield, observes that Will has "an interesting Tory mind." Edward S. Shapiro writing in *The American Spectator* speculates that Will may be the true successor to the late Walter Lippmann, probably the most important columnist this nation has produced.

But where Lippmann was stilted, Will is lively. Such readability would not ordinarily be expected from someone with a Ph.D in political science (from Princeton). Shapiro points out that Will is "more concerned with preserving ethical and religious values than with conserving the wealth of the affluent. . . . At the very least, he has helped to rescue conservatism from those who believe that conservatism is more a matter of profits than principles."[4]

Among the columnists, Jack Anderson continues to

[3]Lenora Williamson, "Study Syndicates as 'Opinion Merchants,' " *Editor & Publisher,* May 31, 1980, p. 47. Buchwald is best known as a humor columnist, but much of his humor makes political, economic, or social points.
[4]Edward S. Shapiro, "Book Review," *The American Spectator,* March 1979, pp. 36, 38; the review was of *Pursuit of Happiness, and Other Sobering Thoughts,* Harper & Row, New York, 1978.

make the headlines. A writer for *Washington Journalism Review* calls Anderson "America's foremost investigative reporter [who] obsessively seeks to right wrongs, expose corruption and disclose political indiscretions." Anderson took over the column from his boss, Drew Pearson, in 1969. With a staff of 17, Anderson does much more than produce a daily column. He is also involved in television shows, magazines, books, and other journalistic ventures. His Mormon faith makes him see the world as a battleground where vice and virtue meet. (He is on the side of virtue.) Anderson is not a muckraker, writer Dom Bonafede argues; ". . . while obviously a passionate believer in justice, [he] appears motivated more by the joy of the hunt and the rewards that come with journalistic accomplishment."[5]

Like Buckley and other columnists and journalists, Anderson has tried his hand at novel writing. With Bill Pronzini he brought out *The Cambodia File* in 1980, a story Doubleday advertised as "too personal to ignore," whatever that means. In 1981, Anderson launched his own magazine, *The Investigator.*

How long does it take to write a column? Russell Baker, the cerebral humor columnist distributed by the *New York Times* News Service, spends about four hours doing each of his three columns each week. But he spends a lot of additional time "trying to take in this junk, this garbage, that we all swim in, so I'll have something to put out when I do sit down at the machine." Baker avoids sitting down at the typewriter with a fixed idea in mind. He keeps things spontaneous. He does not want to become predictable.[6]

Some of the most popular columns are those that offer advice. Abigail Van Buren and Ann Landers, sisters with competing columns, continue to lead in that field. And the gossip column is still alive in America. The *New York Daily*

[5]Dom Bonafede, "Jack Muckraker Anderson," *Washington Journalism Review,* April 1980, p. 42.
[6]Quoted by Harry Stein, "Russell Baker," *Esquire,* January 30, 1979, p. 76.

News asked Liz Smith to write one in 1976, and by 1979 it appeared in 70 newspapers. "I thought maybe the gossip era had already passed," she said. "Who could know that we were just on the verge of this era of trivia-tidbit journalism, that it would absolutely deluge us?" All kinds of people feed her information, including those who want themselves talked about. She acknowledges an "intense interest in gossip . . . because we're not beset by anything truly serious except our own selfish seriousness—inflation, gasoline—and those are the kinds of worries people want to forget. Sooner or later, though, as a society we're going to move on to more pertinent things."[7]

Some newspaper columns do not come from syndicates. They deal mostly with local matters, but they can carry information or opinions of national interest as well. Newspaper writers like to launch columns because in them they are freer than in regular news stories, features, or even editorials to say whatever they wish, to shock readers, even, or to entertain them. Some columns are profound, others are mere diversions. A column is a personal piece of writing and is usually left alone by the editor.

Mike Royko is a local columnist working with the *Chicago Sun-Times* (he moved from the *Chicago Daily News* when that paper died in 1978), but much of his material holds such universal interest that it is often distributed nationally by the Field News Service, part of the Field Newspaper Syndicate. He is as important to Chicago as Herb Caen, columnist for the *San Francisco Chronicle*, is to San Francisco. "He is a lowbrow, a boor, ill-mannered, vulgar, the Philistine of the prairie. . . . He calls his readers old bats, coots, crones, bullies, and hacks," observes William Brashler, a novelist and fellow Chicagoan. But "Mike Royko is a nice guy. He is also the best columnist writing today."[8]

---

[7]Quoted by Harry Stein, "Liz Smith," *Esquire*, August 1979, pp. 89, 90.
[8]William Brashler, "The Man Who Owns Chicago," *Esquire*, May 8, 1979, p. 44.

WHAT GOES WHERE

For generations, editors tended to present newspaper fare in an order that rarely varied from day to day or from newspaper to newspaper. On the front page was major local, national, and international news, with no advertising. Then more of the same on the following inside pages, where large ads started to intrude. Near the end of the first section of the paper came the editorial page, with comment and columns. On the first page of the second section was local or regional news, followed by regular departments. A third section offered sports news, another financial and business news, and yet another the comics and the classified advertising.

In recent years, partly to provide better service to their readers and partly to counter the competition of television and magazines, newspapers have shown more variety in look and content. The once rigidly staid *New York Times,* for example, now has special sections titled "Living," "Home," and "Weekend" providing compartmentalized news about entertainment, food, leisure time use, and coping with the problems of living.

Many newspapers have departed from the once-standard pattern of vertical columns of type, punctuated by headlines and occasional pictures, to adopt a magazine look. They use horizontal layout, white space, larger and more numerous pictures, and headlines that say more than the curt labels of old.

Yet many of the former conventions persist. Page one is still the place for the most important news of the day; local and regional news is concentrated in the second section; sports and business have their separate bailiwicks. The front page table of contents that in the past was a terse listing may now be a more exhaustive "news in brief" column, with bright, "teasing" copy meant to lure the reader inside. On page one the upper right corner remains, on most papers, the spot for the top story of the day, and the upper part of any page is considered a more important spot for news than the lower half.

A big-city full-size daily contains several sections, each with several pages, so that members of a family can concentrate on areas that interest them. The several sections also make the bulk of the paper manageable. Big newspapers these days tend to departmentalize the news. As shown here, the *Dallas Morning News,* which calls itself "The Voice of Texas," runs special sections on business, arts, and entertainment, sports, and other subjects.

OWNERSHIP

How the complex organization of the newspaper functions in practice depends in the last analysis on the objectives and values of the owners, the persons who make the ultimate decisions.

In the early days of American journalism, most newspapers, both daily and weekly, were individually owned enterprises, and most functioned in a competitive context, with one or several rivals in the community. Still today many newspapers are individually owned, but they are in a minority. Increasingly in recent decades, as has also been the case with the broadcast media, the ownership of newspapers has been consolidated into the hands of fewer and fewer corporate entities.

In 1940 a few more than 300 of the country's daily newspapers belonged to chains (a chain, or group, as it is sometimes euphemistically termed, is made up of a number of newspapers controlled by a single owner or ownership syndicate). By 1980, nearly 1100 of the 1750 U.S. daily newspapers were owned by groups and chains; they represented more than two-thirds of all newspaper circulation in the nation. And the chains were continuing the takeover of individually owned papers at the rate of about 50 a year.

Part of the groups and chains were made up of newspapers only; others included newspapers, magazines, and broadcast stations; still others were giant conglomerates that owned not only media properties but also a variety of other corporations and businesses.

The Gannett group, one of the nation's largest, is an example of a chain made up only of media-oriented properties. As the 1980s began, Gannett owned 80 daily newspapers, 17 weeklies, 7 television stations, and 6 radio stations. Some of the conglomerates that include newspapers among their holdings also own oil companies, theater chains, and even such unlikely companions as a piano manufacturing concern and a water-bottling company.

Analysts at the *Washington Post* in 1978 conducted a lengthy study of the newspaper business and concluded that within two decades virtually all the daily newspapers in America will be owned by perhaps fewer than two dozen major communications conglomerates. The trend is evident as well in the weekly newspaper field. Between 100 and 150 weeklies change hands each year, and most of them wind up in the fold of some group or chain.

There is also another dimension of the consolidation trend. Competition, which once flourished in the newspaper field, is now all but extinct. If you collect scary statistics, try this one: In about 96 percent of American cities with daily newspapers there is only one newspaper, or else a single newspaper owner with a morning-evening combination. In other words, in only a handful of our cities is there any genuine, head-to-head newspaper competition. And that handful continues to dwindle. The late 1970s and early 1980s saw the demise of such venerable journals as the *Washington Star,* the *Chicago Daily News,* and the *Philadelphia Bulletin,* squeezed by competition from rival papers and from television, and hurt also by the migration of former faithful readers to the suburbs.

The consolidation of ownership and the virtual elimination of effective competition are of profound significance for the newspaper industry, and particularly for the readers who depend on that industry for a flow of complete and accurate news.

The tags "monopoly journalism" and "one-newspaper town" are familiar to most of us. And the connotations they call to mind are mostly bad ones. The spread of group and conglomerate ownership of the press stirs equally unwelcome concerns. Just how justified are these connotations and concerns? Just how bleak is the picture?

NOT TRUE MONOPOLY, BUT BAD ENOUGH

Let us consider first the issue of monopoly journalism. It should be recognized that the one-newspaper or one-ownership town usually does not represent anything like a true monopoly. In addition to the one daily, the citizens are generally also served by one or more weekly newspapers or "shoppers" (free-circulation throwaways consisting mostly of advertising with a sprinkling of local news). Readers also have access to local radio and television channels, various forms of cable service, regional newspapers, and national news magazines. There are, to be sure, a few communities in which one owner controls more than one news medium, perhaps even all of them, on the local scene, which would come close to a true monopoly, at least of the channels through which news of the community could reach the members of that community.

But in the vast majority of the towns and cities embraced by that fearsome 96 percent statistic, the newspaper constitutes only a semimonopoly, considerably tempered by the competition of the electronic and other media. It can still be argued, however, that even the semimonopoly is an unhealthy situation in that it represents a narrowing of the channels through which the citizen can obtain various reports and interpretations of the news. The check-and-balance effect provided by true head-to-head competition is absent. The opportunity for abuse is present, whether or not it is exploited.

Defenders of the one-ownership situation point out that the consequences of monopoly or semimonopoly are sometimes anything but inimical to the public interest. They contend that a monopoly or semimonopoly publisher can *afford* to publish a good paper precisely *because* there is no competition. The paper is more independent of advertiser pressure and other influences than it might be in a hotly competitive situation. Also, the paper likely will have a good profit margin, which should allow increased expenditures for a quality staff and modern facilities. They point to such one-ownership towns as Louisville (with its *Courier-Journal* and *Times* one-ownership combination) as evidence that monopoly journalism can be of superior quality. And they cite the sensational and irresponsible excesses that are sometimes characteristic of newspapers in competitive battle.

Yet, when all this has been entered on the record and duly considered, the fact remains that the *opportunity* for abuse is there once a monopoly has been created. And that

is legitimate cause for concern. There are just too many examples of communities in which a monopoly publisher has
taken advantage of the comfortable situation to lapse into a
shoddy, nickel-nursing mockery of journalism that coldly ignores the public interest, in which the extra profits deriving
from the monopoly go into stock dividends rather than improvement of the newspaper product, and in which independence from external influences is exploited to enhance the
political clout of the publication rather than to defend journalistic principles.

Once a one-newspaper or one-ownership situation has
been established, it can go either way—the potentiality for
improved service may be there, but the opportunity for neglect of responsibility is there, too. On balance, the decline
in the diversity of media voices is bad news for the public.

A BACKWARD STEP, OR THE WAVE OF THE FUTURE?

There is both bad news and good in the spread of chain and
group ownership of American newspapers.

Critics of the development can draw up a weighty bill
of indictment. They point out that chains wipe out individu-
ality among the member papers. Policies tend to be dictated
by corporate headquarters rather than by a local owner.
Howard H. (Tim) Hays, California publisher of the independent *Riverside Press-Enterprise,* has posed the question:

> We wonder whether—if not now at least in the long run—
> editors and publishers who own their own newspapers and live
> with and identify with their readers can't better serve their
> communities and better protect the First Amendment rights
> than can corporate officers in distant cities, however able and
> idealistic some of them may be.[9]

In some cases those distant corporate officers tend to
change the values and objectives of the chain's member pa-

[9]In the 1979 Eric W. Allen Memorial Lecture delivered at the University
of Oregon, February 9, 1979.

pers. Where an individual owner might take risks in order to cover a touchy news situation in the community, the chain owners may insist on soft-pedaling controversial matters in order not to offend local advertisers and jeopardize the publication's profit margin. In some chains and groups, editorial policy on political and other issues is written at headquarters, and individual hired editors and publishers are expected to implement that policy at local levels. The result often is homogenization of the news and editorial products of the chain papers; one member of the group can scarcely be distinguished from another without checking the nameplate.

Perhaps even more ominous is the concentration of control represented by the spread of chain ownership. If the *Washington Post* analysts mentioned earlier are right in forseeing a day not far in the future when virtually all American newspapers will be run by a couple of dozen corporate entities, the implications are chilling. Imagine an edict going out from chain headquarters to beat the editorial drums and tilt the news coverage on behalf of a certain presidential candidate, or against a certain issue pending before the Congress. The exercise of such vast power could be decisive in a nation so dependent on the information networks.

Defenders of the chain and group system tend to dismiss these fears and downplay the alleged drawbacks. They contend that many chain newspapers do a much better job of serving their communities than they had under previous independent ownership. Group executives point to the lists of prizes for public service won by member papers, and to increased expenditure for staff and facilities. In one respect, at least, that last point is well taken. It can be persuasively argued that the swift technological advances in the newspaper industry in recent years paralleled and to a considerable degree resulted from the spread of chain ownership.

For generations the newspaper field was one stubbornly reluctant to change its established ways. Presses and other equipment remained in use, with little updating or modification, for decades, while in most other sectors of American industry change was rapid and constant. Newspaper procedures that had been standard practice at the turn of the twentieth century were still being followed 50 years later. Reporters typed out their stories in the newsroom, then handed the finished copy to editors who worked it over with thick black pencils before sending it down to the composing room. There, Linotype operators sat before their clanking machines, painstakingly setting the copy into small metal slugs; then stereotypers made heavy lead castings of page forms to fit on the massive presses that turned out the finished newspaper.

But in the 1960s and particularly the 1970s the picture changed swiftly and dramatically. Newsroom typewriters were replaced with electronic consoles; reporters punched out their stories on video display screens rather than paper, and stored the finished version in a computer; editors called up the copy from the computer, scanned and modified it on

The city news room of the *Chicago Tribune,* one of the nation's largest and most influential daily newspapers. The paper was founded in 1847. After 1955 and the death of Publisher Robert R. McCormick it moved away from its isolationist and ultra-conservative editorial stands. (*Source:* Johnson, Leo De Wys Inc.)

their own video screens, and, when they were satisfied, instructed the computer to set the story in a form ready to go directly to the new offset presses, with no cumbersome mechanical intermediaries to slow or complicate the process.

The wondrous new equipment and procedures were very costly. Moreover, switching over to the new systems meant that publishers had to write off or sell at sacrifice prices their substantial investments in hot-type and letterpress equipment. Not many individual newspaper owners could round up the cash or borrowed money to finance the extensive change-overs. But the groups and chains, with their economies of scale and their pools of capital, had no problem footing the bill. Many of their acquisitions were of papers whose owners had despaired of finding a way to finance needed updating of their plants and had turned to the chains as the only solution.

Thus, there is some substance to the claim made by chain and group owners that their system made possible a needed technological transformation in the newspaper industry. Many very large newspapers had the means to make the changes on their own, but for most medium-sized publications only the infusion of group capital made the advances economically feasible.

BACK TO SQUARE ONE

What about the contention of the defenders of group ownership that the quality as well as the procedures of newspaper journalism have been improved by the spread of chains? The answer to that question cannot be a simple one. In many of the groups and chains it is possible to detect the homogenization of news and policy, the profits-first emphasis, and the tendency to exploit the leverage of the group's publications for the ends of the ownership rather than public service. But it also must be acknowledged that some of the nation's most respected and admired newspapers are themselves members of a group or chain.

The parent company of the *New York Times,* universally regarded as one of the world's finest newspapers, also owned in 1979 nine smaller daily newspapers, several weeklies, two broadcast stations, several book publishing houses, and a piece of three Canadian pulp mills that provided part of the paper on which the *Times* is printed. Two of the other top-ranked newspapers in the country, the *Washington Post* and the *Los Angeles Times,* are also members of groups that include additional media and other properties.

There is, to be sure, a significant difference between these three groups and, say, the Gannett or Knight-Ridder chains. In each of those three cases, a prestigious flagship newspaper acquired smaller satellite properties and extended to them its own philosophies of excellence and responsibility. In the case of the more typical chain or group a corporate entity controls a number of individual publications and manages them as profitable, efficient enterprises, not necessarily as vehicles for public service.

In sum, it cannot be said flatly that a newspaper owned by a chain or group is automatically and inevitably an inferior publication. There are strong forces at work in the move toward chain or group ownership that tend to lead to a decline in quality and a sense of responsibility. But those forces do not always dominate, as some of the distinguished exceptions among chain members demonstrate.

We are brought back to a point made earlier: In the American news media, quality is ultimately determined by the owner; the integrity and the standards of ownership determine how ably or how shabbily the public interest will be served by a given media property, whether it is an independent individual enterprise or member of a group.

RAISING A SPECTER AT WASHINGTON

Whether on balance it has been for good or bad, the spread of chain ownership has become a focus of concern for those in and out of government who are worried about the future of the press.

Publisher Hays of Riverside, quoted before, feels certain that the chains and groups are likely to keep on growing.

> The acquisition parade is going to continue because most if not all of the groups want more newspapers and because independent owners find that in the long run, given the situation that now obtains, they have almost no alternative to selling, sooner or later, even if later means far down the line.[10]

He and other independent publishers feel that their ranks will keep on diminishing not only because group acquisition represents one means of financing needed modernization of plant, but for other and equally compelling reasons.

There is, for example, the tax situation. Present tax laws make it possible for chains and groups to make use of their profits from existing properties to buy up additional publications and in the process escape significant taxation on those profits. They are thus enabled to offer vastly inflated prices for newspapers on which they have an eye, since they are bidding with cheap dollars. They can easily over-match any individual would-be purchaser who cannot use the tax advantage and must tailor the offer to the realistic market value of the property. This poses an almost irresistible temptation to the independent owner weary of the long struggle, or to second- or third-generation heirs eager to seize the opportunity for a windfall. The prospect was evidently tempting even in the case of two employee-owned newspapers (at Kansas City and Palo Alto, California) that were acquired by chains in recent years.

As the trend continues its seemingly inevitable way, many editors worry that the situation increasingly raises the prospect of some sort of government trust-busting or regulatory move that would represent a threat to press freedom. Some tentative beginnings toward this have been made.

In 1979 Senators Larry Pressler (D.–S.D.) and Robert Morgan (D.–S.C.) introduced legislation designed to guard

[10]Howard Hays, in the 1979 Eric W. Allen Memorial Lecture delivered at the University of Oregon, February 9, 1979.

against takeovers of independent newspapers by chains or conglomerates. A similar measure had been introduced in the House the previous year by Rep. Morris Udall (D.–Ariz.). The Pressler-Morgan legislation would have eased inheritance taxes for the families of newspaper publishers, in order to reduce the pressure to sell out just to be able to pay estate taxes. This would, of course, get at only one of the factors underlying the spread of group ownership. In the wings are other more stringent legislative efforts aimed at breaking up ownership concentrations.

Group and chain owners obviously view any such measures with disfavor. But they are not alone. Most persons familiar with the role of the press in our society are troubled by the prospect of government regulation of any kind, however concerned they may be about the drawbacks of chain and group ownership. If government is to take a hand, most observers of the press would prefer that it be to modify the special tax provisions that now make it possible for the chains and groups to grow at will. Any more direct form of government control of the structure of the newspaper industry would raise the unwelcome specter of interference with the freedom to publish that is central to the functioning of our democratic society.

Chapter 5
Critical Hits and Misses

When a would-be assassin shot President Ronald Reagan outside the Washington Hilton hotel in 1981, the news spread quickly through radio flashes heard in homes and cars, through television bulletins interrupting soap operas, and by word of mouth through telephone calls or shouts across workplaces. In increasing numbers, those who could stayed in front of their television sets through the long afternoon.

During those tense hours a large part of the American population joined in a vigil—watching stunned, despairing, or angry—as anchors and correspondents stayed on the air to relay each new development and to rerun many times the graphic film of the assassination attempt. The reporting was

"Touché!"

uneven and sometimes flawed (all three networks mistakenly confirmed that White House press secretary James Brady had died of his head wounds), but the exhaustive and repetitive coverage made the viewers feel fully involved in the drama. Observed *Time:* "For one draining afternoon, television turned America into a giant newsroom."

That March afternoon demonstrated once again one of the ways in which the resources of television can impressively serve the needs of the public. Eighteen years before the shooting outside the Washington Hilton, television had helped significantly to knit the nation together in the shocked aftermath of the assassination of President John F. Kennedy at Dallas. The saturation coverage then—for days, not just hours—helped the American people through the catharsis of grief. It also very likely prevented the hysteria that might have been incited by rumors of coup and conspiracy, rumors that thorough news coverage stopped almost as soon as they started. The other news media also reported extensively on both assassination episodes, of course. But the immediacy and the visual dimension of television helped to make its impact on the national audience both memorable and decisive.

In another national crisis it was the newspaper medium that best served the public interest. Led by the *Washington Post,* newspaper reporters and editors chipped doggedly away for many months at the rock-hard cover-up of Watergate, until the unlovely rot at its heart was fully exposed and a president had been driven from office in disgrace. Had the pressure not been kept on the story with unrelenting diligence, the conspirators might well have gotten away with the most sweeping scandal in American political history.

Both media—newspapers and television—played a role in combating the demagoguery of Senator Joseph R. McCarthy in the early 1950s.[1] And both also were instrumental in the massive turnaround of American public opinion that eventually led to the repudiation of our country's involvement in the Vietnam war; newspaper correspondents documented the deception and the bankruptcy of our policy in Southeast Asia and television cameras brought the war's savagery and futility into the nation's living rooms.

The great media institutions are awesome in their power and impact when they are fully mustered to cover major news. They are also indispensable in noncrisis times, bringing us news we must have in order to understand our society and our times and function effectively as citizens of our community and inhabitants of earth. As was noted in Chapter 1, the news media are as necessary to us as the air we breathe.

Yet it also the case that no institutions of our society— except, perhaps, for marriage—are more frequently the sub-

---

[1]It should be acknowledged that the same media were to some degree responsible for McCarthy's rise to prominence in the first place by giving automatic and uncritical coverage to his sensational and unsubstantiated charges of Communist infiltration of the American government.

ject of criticism than are the news media. Some of that criticism is informed and on the mark, but sometimes the critics attack imagined faults and overlook genuine weaknesses. They complain about minor or nonexistent abuses but fail to perceive some very real and persistent problems. Many of the uninformed criticisms are repeated often enough to achieve widespread currency and acceptance. Thus, a smoggy mixture of myth and fact accumulates around the media, and it is difficult for the average consumer to distinguish the reality from the illusion.

THE ADVERTISER AS DICTATOR

For example, many newspaper readers are firmly convinced that important advertisers call the tune for editors. Buy enough advertising space, the theme runs, then tell the editor what to keep out of the paper, and what position to take on a controversial issue. After all, the newspaper's chief source of revenue is advertising, and "money talks" (income from subscriptions and newsstand sales represents only about a quarter to a third of newspaper revenue; the rest comes from sale of space to advertisers).

In earlier eras of American journalism, when papers competed fiercely for the advertiser's dollar, this claim had some substance. And even today, in some cities, there is truth in it. But to most daily newspapers in our time, it simply does not apply. Most daily newspapers in this last third of the twentieth century do not have local newspaper competition. The advertiser needs the newspaper more than the newspaper needs the advertiser, since the paper usually represents the most effective way for the advertiser to get a sales message to the potential purchasers in the community. This semimonopoly allows the newspaper to be independent of advertiser pressure, even when it is applied.

But if most dailies can afford to be indifferent to advertiser pressure and to other outside forces, that is not necessarily the case with weekly newspapers or with radio stations.

It is far less costly to introduce competition into the weekly newspaper field, or into a radio market. A group of disgruntled advertisers in a small town could very possibly withdraw enough advertising revenue from the local weekly to put it in serious trouble. If they combined to set a competitor up in business, they might well be able to drive the original publisher out. It has happened in more than one community.

Because they are aware of this possibility, many small-town publishers tend to walk warily with respect to local issues and local advertisers. Generalizations about the press are usually misleading, since it is by no means a monolithic institution, but it is fair to say that there is less editorial crusading on local issues among weekly newspapers than among dailies. Many weeklies carry no editorial comment at all. One important reason for their muted editorial voices is the editors' recognition that they are indeed vulnerable to pressures.

THE ELEVATOR SYNDROME

And there is at least one substantial qualification to be entered to the general assertion that daily newspapers are well armored against advertiser influence.

A wry comment on the newspapers of England once ran:

> You cannot hope to bribe or twist
> Thank God! the British journalist.
> But, seeing what the man will do
> Unbribed, there's no occasion to.[2]

In that vein, some critics of the American press suggest that even though the advertisers may not be able to put any pressure on modern daily newspapers, they really do not have to—the publishers share the advertisers' philosophy anyway and reflect it in their papers.

---

[2]By the English poet, Humbert Wolfe. Quoted in "Queries and Answers," The *New York Times Book Review,* May 7, 1961.

It is true enough that most newspaper publishers tend to be conservative on economic and political issues, as do most business leaders, although in both groups there are notable exceptions, of course. It is also true that the attitudes of a newspaper owner seep out into the staff generally, sometimes by directive, sometimes by a kind of osmosis or as a result of the "elevator syndrome" (employees overhear the publisher's comments as they ride together up and down in the office elevator, and either consciously or unconsciously reflect the overheard attitudes in their own approach to their jobs).

An anonymous employee of the *Louisville Courier-Journal* put into the newsroom suggestion box a list of the persons and institutions that he felt were regarded as "sacred cows" by the news staff simply because the publisher or someone else in management had indicated an interest in them. The note said:

> News sources or topics don't really have to be considered by the publisher to merit special treatment. . . . However, if someone in the editorial chain of command *between* the publisher and the news gatherer believes the publisher has a special interest, the effect is the same on the reporter. Or, if one of the executives in this chain has himself a special interest, that interest is transferred down the line, too. It is rare—although it happens here—for an editor to say "be careful, you know how the publisher feels about this one," but the way stories are edited, the questions asked reporters by editors about them, and sometimes just a tone of voice can quite effectively get across the message that this is "of special concern."[3]

As a counterbalance to this effect, there is the fact that many working journalists—reporters, editors, broadcasters—tend to be liberal rather than conservative in their personal outlook. Though they may strive to keep their own views out of their handling of the news, these views inevitably exert

[3]Quoted by Robert U. Brown in "Shop Talk at Thirty," *Editor & Publisher*, September 13, 1969, p. 72.

some influence, perhaps enough to nullify the ripple effect of the publisher's attitudes.

In any case, both publisher and staff member tend to resist, and resist strongly, any overt attempt by an advertiser or other outside pressure source to influence the handling of the news. They may sometimes arrive at the policy decision the advertiser would prefer, but they usually arrive at the decision for reasons of their own, not because they have knuckled under.

ADVERTISERS AND TELEVISION

Critics are also suspicious about the influence of advertisers on the content of the news reported by television. Their concern stems largely from the well-documented history of advertiser control over the entertainment content of both radio and television. In the early days of both broadcast media, that control was absolute. The entertainment packages were put together by the representatives of advertisers, and anything that was offensive to the corporations footing the bill would be promptly excised or never allowed on the set or in the studio in the first place. Though it is considerably muted, even today such advertiser leverage on entertainment content is still evident in much television programming.

But the critics' suspicion is to a considerable extent misdirected so far as broadcast *news*—particularly at the network level—is concerned. The traditions of independence that characterized the print media carried over into the newer electronic enterprises, and the traditions survived, due in part to the fact that advertisers paid little attention to broadcast news during its early years, when the news was not considered a marketable commodity. By the time news had become an important component of programming, the network news operations had grown strong enough to fend off pressure from advertisers.

There have, to be sure, been cases in which advertisers have managed to affect the content of newscasts in a generalized way. For example, before cigarette advertising was banned from the airwaves there were charges that news of the cancer danger incurred by cigarette smokers had been played down or hushed up on the networks that profited so substantially from tobacco company advertising.

But, as is the case with major newspapers, the network news organizations of today are not very vulnerable to the importunings of even the most powerful advertisers, and the journalists who staff those organizations show few signs of timidity or subservience. The oil companies, despite their vast advertising budgets, got no special handling when the news came out about the large profits they amassed during and after the oil shortages and scares of the 1970s.

The weekly television news documentary "60 Minutes" and its imitators make a practice of poking into embarrassing corners of corporations and government agencies, exposing a dismaying variety of waste, fraud, and corruption, despite the fact that many of the juiciest targets are also big-money advertisers (e.g., chemical companies, realtors, utilities, and hotel chains).

Yet, again as is the case in the newspaper industry, the relative fearlessness and invulnerability of the network newshounds are not always mirrored in individual television or radio stations. Competitive pressure or simply the factor of proximity can sometimes breed in local station managers a sensitivity to advertisers' wishes and interests. This can happen, as an example, in a small community with a workforce that depends on the economic health of a single local industry; problems affecting the town's mainstay may be soft-pedaled even though it would be in the public interest—and certainly in the journalistic tradition—to air them fully.

THE SENSATION-MONGERS

Another frequently voiced complaint of media critics is that both newspapers and television peddle too much sensationalism in their versions of the news. In the competition to sell more papers or earn higher Nielsen ratings, the critics assert, newspaper editors and television news producers dwell overmuch on disaster, sex, and crime, particularly crime. In weighing the validity of this charge against the media it is necessary to consider newspapers and television separately, since different factors come into play. Let us look first at newspapers.

As far as newspapers are concerned, cases to prove the critics' point are no trouble to find. When Carmine Galante, the reputed godfather of New York crime organizations, was riddled with machine gun bullets and shotgun pellets as he sat down to lunch in a Brooklyn restaurant, the New York tabloids played the story for all its gory worth. The *Post*'s front page carried a one-word headline, "GREED!" and a multi-column closeup photograph of the slain mobster, his head twisted at a grotesque angle and blood pooled on the restaurant floor. The *Daily News* ran an even bigger front-page picture, taking up nearly half of the tabloid page. The *News* picture was also of the corpse, taken from a different angle, giving a clearer view of the small river of blood beneath the body.[4] In other cities, too, and not just in tabloids, can be found headlines almost as big and pictures almost as revoltingly graphic.

But the observer who looks over the whole spectrum of American journalism, and not just at the gamiest sectors, is likely to come away with quite a different impression from that of the critics.

Nearly all newspapers carry news of crime (the *Christian Science Monitor,* as a matter of policy, carries hardly any) and stories that center on human interest elements, including sex. But in most newspapers—big city, small town, and community weekly—these stories are only a part of the daily coverage. They are not sensationalized or overplayed in order to sell a few more papers, but are included because they are legitimately a part of the news of the day.

[4]The front pages of July 12, 1979.

As citizens we need to be informed about news of crime. We need to know what crimes are being committed, what the law enforcement officers are doing about them, and how the courts are dealing with persons accused of crimes. If we are not well informed about these matters, we cannot be alert to abuses that may readily develop in the machinery of law enforcement, we cannot be aware of the festering corners of our society in which crime is bred, we cannot be discerning voters when the time comes to pass judgment on those who have been elected to balance the scales of justice on our behalf.

So news of crime, criminals, and the machinery of the law properly belongs in the paper. But it should not be given undue emphasis, or presented in the kind of morbid detail that feeds the fantasies of sick minds. That is sensationalism. In some papers, crime news is indeed given sensationalist treatment, but in most American newspapers there is not as much sensationalism as the casual critics would have us believe.

If we take a ruler and measure out the inches given to crime news in the average newspaper, we discover that it constitutes a very small percentage of the total news. If we were to make a simple content analysis of most crime stories, we find that the language is largely legalistic rather than sensational. Why, then, do typical readers nod in agreement when they hear the charge that the newspapers are full of crime? Why does it seem to them that there is so much of this kind of news?

There are, of course, the horrible examples, the individual papers of which the charge is all too true. But a large part of the answer lies with the readers themselves. Communication is, after all, a two-party process. The newspaper presents news stories; the readers select and read those that interest them. Crime stories interest the average reader greatly. They are sought out, even in the back pages, and pored over. They are remembered when the story on water pollution or tax reform has been forgotten, if it was read in the first place. Even though they may not take up much of the overall news space in absolute terms, and even though they may be presented in straitlaced fashion, crime stories leap up from the pages and into the reader's mind. And because they are selected and given close attention, the reader is left with a distorted impression of the place they occupy in the overall news budget.

Editors are well aware, of course, of the reader's built-in interest in crime and similar news. An editor who had no other purpose than to make a successful newspaper from a cash-register viewpoint would find this a simple matter. Some have done precisely that.

But the fact is that most editors do not take this easy road to success. They include in their papers the crime and human interest news they feel readers need and want to know about. Yet this is usually only a small part of the whole; the editors fill out the rest of their papers with the news of consequence and importance that we must know about if we are to function as citizens, even if that news is of far less interest to us than the crime stories or the human interest features.

If the standard motto in the editorial room really were "anything to sell a few more papers," we would have 1750 sensational sheets rather than a handful.

ALWAYS ACTION

The sensationalism argument against television news coverage is often different from the complaint leveled at newspapers. On television the pictures of slain gangsters are likely to be from a distance, not close up, and the bodies are usually draped in sheets. Moreover, the fleeting glimpse on the television screen is less offensive than the blown-up tabloid picture that stays before you in grim black and white (or perhaps even in bleeding color).

Yet the television news content is often distorted, not specifically toward crime stories but toward action episodes of any sort. Television news producers are always alert for story situations that involve some activity that will make arresting film footage, anything to avoid too many talking-head shots. Walter Cronkite once observed of local television news that "the emphasis is on crime, barn burnings, and jacknifed trailer trucks."

A complex story on local politics that offers no opportunity for anything more active than an official talking from an office desk may get short shrift, while a story of trivial significance in absolute terms may get several minutes because it involves stern-faced officers searching a tenement district with drawn guns—fine photo opportunities. (The Watergate scandal story was a newspaper enterprise through its early painstaking investigative phases; television moved in on it when there were confrontational hearings to film.)

Andrew Kopkind, a critic writing in *Columbia Journalism Review,* describes the news as presented by television as "flashing glimpses of the world . . . of drama, immediacy and passion. . . . " In an evening's newscast, Kopkind writes, the news from Nicaragua "is a picture of a woman weeping in the ruins of her war-torn house. In the American economy it's the interior of a supermarket with a tight shot of the price of hamburger—followed by a peek at a chart showing all the vectors soaring upward. New York during the 1977 blackout is black looters carrying television sets through shattered windows. . . ."[5]

The nature of the medium, the conventions that have grown up within it, and the advice of the news doctors pushing their jazz-it-up formats all combine to produce the bias toward action stories that distorts television news and gives rise to the charge of sensationalism.

The very brevity of television news stories also contributes to an impression of urgency and breathlessness. The scene shifts so rapidly—from a mountainside where an ice avalanche has claimed six climbers, to a factory gate where angry pickets wave their signs and threaten a car entering the plant, to a coroner's office where the body of a tavern shoot-out victim is being brought in—that a feverish and stri-

[5]Andrew Kopkind, "MacNeil/Lehrer's Class Act," *Columbia Journalism Review,* September/October 1979, pp. 31–38.

dent impression is left in the viewer's mind. The world, as television presents it, seems a menacing and uncertain place of crisis and disaster, everywhere you turn.

"YOU SEE IT HAPPENING"

Nonetheless, that picture of the world is one a great many Americans accept as real. In 1981 a national poll conducted by the Gallup organization for *Newsweek* showed the continuation of a trend that has been evident for many years: respondents believe television to be a more trustworthy bearer of the news than other media. Asked to pick which medium they felt was providing the most accurate and unbiased news report, the respondents put network television first, local television second, newsmagazines third, and newspapers fourth.

Press analysts believe that the public perception of the various media is based in part on the impression of greater immediacy conveyed by television, and in part on the viewer's sense of seeing the news happening, without any possible distortion by an intermediary. The impression of immediacy gained by the television viewer (and the radio listener) may indeed be legitimate much of the time, but not always. Some television news shows are seen on tape that was produced several hours earlier, and the news they contain may be less up to date than the version in the paper that arrived on the doorsteps a few minutes ago.

The "you see it happening" impression implanted by television can also be misleading, simply because the viewer does not realize how the "reality" on the screen may have been processed and modified before it got on the air. Readers scanning a newspaper account of an event are well aware that they are reading some reporter's condensed version of what actually happened. The same readers watching a telecast may not be as aware of the judgmental and editing factors that were involved in boiling down that same event to the few scattered glimpses they are now watching. The television version seems more believable because they have seen it with their own eyes.

As we noted earlier, there are numerous ways in which distortions can enter a printed news report. Similar distortions can just as easily occur in television news coverage. Two persons filming the same protest rally, by their selection of the segments on which to focus, can come up with altogether different versions. Yet each of these versions, when it comes on the television screen, will give viewers the mistaken impression that they are "seeing it all happen."

Moreover, television tape or film is as much subject to editing as newspaper copy. Two speakers who addressed the same audience hours apart can be shown in a television report as though they were engaging in head-to-head debate. In television interviewing of news sources, the interviewer may go back on camera, after the person being interviewed is no longer present, to rephrase questions; the new questions will then be spliced into the tape and it will seem to the viewers that the person is answering directly to them, even though in actuality the new questions may be significantly different in purport from the questions to which the source had originally responded. The way in which viewers perceive news film can be conditioned by factors added in the editing booth—visual effects, split-screen juxtapositions, backdrop graphics, or quick cuts from one scene to another, suggesting a causal link between the two.

Another reason that television news may seem more believable than the versions supplied by the other media is the reinforcing impact of the anchor's personality on the viewers. "Uncle Walter" Cronkite was accepted by viewers as wholly trustworthy; if *he* reported it, the story just had to be accurate. Other, less-idolized anchors also have their followings, and by adroit use of their pivotal on-screen role they can shape the impression that a news story makes on the viewers. Some television newscasters have made an art of conveying an extra dimension of the news report by a wry twist of the mouth or a strategic arch of the eyebrow. They can signal to the viewer to "take this with a grain of salt" or whittle down a speaker on the screen with a "Can you believe this guy?" smirk.

SOMETHING (BUT NOT MUCH) FOR EVERYONE

One charge of the media critics lands squarely on target: superficiality.

Both the daily newspaper and the TV newscast are put together to appeal to a very wide range of potential readers and viewers—they are, after all, *mass* media. In addition, their approach is catholic (small c)—the world, the nation, the state, the community, the serious and the comic, the portentous and the trivial are all a part of the sprawling, constantly changing impression of reality that the newspapers and television attempt to provide for their consumers.

Reporters and editors are skilled at encapsulating large events in small segments of newspaper space or a few moments of air time. But despite their skills the end product is inevitably a less-than-complete account of most of the news. Some very few major news events (an assassination attempt, or a national political transition) may be given such extensive coverage by all of the media that even the most intensely interested find out all they want to know. But most news stories, most of the time, are sketched out only in essential outline.

This is true of the newspaper, which may have anywhere from 10 to 30 pages of "news hole"—that is, space allotted to news copy, not to advertisements or headlines. It is even more emphatically true of television. The actual wordage conveyed to the viewer/listener during a half-hour television newscast is the equivalent of about four columns (half a page) of newspaper copy. (Of course, many facets of information in addition to words are conveyed by television; film, backdrop, graphic devices, even the facial expressions of correspondents contribute meanings.) And radio news, in a typical package of five minutes' worth on the hour, amounts only to a rapid-fire recitation of headlines.

The news in outline, as it is provided by television and—

somewhat more fully padded—by newspapers, is probably as much as most consumers want. But to some who have a special stake in the event, and to others who may have considerable expertise in the field involved, the newspaper and television coverage seems shallow and inadequate.

The reader or viewer who has been a participant in a situation reported in the news (e.g., as a speaker at a conference, or as a witness in a trial) rarely feels that the subsequent news coverage provided a full and satisfactory report. Someone who is an economist by profession is impatient with the brevity and lack of precision of a news story on an increase in the rediscount rate or a proposed tax reform. The lodge member who has just been elected Grand Redeemer is outraged when the one-paragraph newspaper account or the 20-second radio report fail to convey the solemnity and significance of his elevation. In each case, the media coverage provided *most* of the consumers of the media products with all they wanted to know about the various events, but in each case the informed person with a special interest found the coverage wanting.

All the media have been trying during recent years to respond to the criticism of superficiality. Newspapers carry more background and interpretive articles; some run regular weekly sections of many pages, under a heading such as "Briefing," to give the in-depth coverage wanted by subgroups of their readers. Network television increased its nightly broadcast time; the 15 minutes that was standard in the 1950s grew to 30 minutes, and as the 1980s began, further growth to an hour was being debated. Occasional documentary reports, some of them 90 to 120 minutes in length, focus intensively on a single topic such as the oil crisis, a new national administration, or the hazards of nuclear proliferation. Many local stations stepped up their community and regional newscasts from a half-hour to an hour. Cable television, including the all-news network CNN, began to provide supplemental news coverage that in part responded to the complaints about the shallowness of news media reporting.

"THE PRELEVANCE [*SIC*] OF ERROR"

The subtitle above appeared as the headline on an article in the *Columbia Journalism Review.*[6] The article took a wry, rueful look at the persistent nemesis of the mass media—the mistake, plain or fancy, human or mechanical.

Errors of all kinds, from trivial to catastrophic, find their way into the end products of the information media. They can be amusing and harmless typographical mistakes (From a wedding story: "The sacred cows were exchanged before the Rev. Francis King.") or they can be grave misrepresentations that damage careers and give rise to multimillion-dollar libel actions.

All the persons involved with the gathering, writing, processing, and production of a newspaper story or a radio news broadcast do their best to avoid letting mistakes show up on the newsstand or on the air. But their best is not good enough, time after embarrassing time.

Some of the mistakes (including most of the inadvertent typos) can be chalked up to the high-speed pace at which news is gathered, written, and presented to the consumer. Despite the introduction of automated equipment, human hands and minds have a role at every step in the process. And even pros err when they hurry under pressure. Gladwin Hill, then chief of the Los Angeles bureau of the *New York Times*, put the newsman's case well:

> Laymen, although they expect their newspapers to be on the doorstep every morning and their radio and television news reporter to chime in on the appointed second, are chronically unable to comprehend the time pressures involved in producing these results. Ask a college professor to write a 1000-word treatise and he will say gladly—in a week, two weeks, a month. In the news business, it is a standard exigency to have to assemble, select, arrange, and indite the material of a 1000-word article *in the time it takes to type it.* One hour would be par for

6Wilbur G. Lewis, "The Prelevance of Error . . ." *Columbia Journalism Review,* Winter 1965, pp. 48–49.

such an operation—several hundred times faster than the one-month schedule available to a college professor or a lawyer writing a brief.

In asking for short-order history, the public underwrites an implicit compromise: the completeness of information, the ruminations and judgments open to the scholar, simply are not humanly and mechanically possible when you are racing the clock.

No competent reporter trifles with accuracy, presents as unqualified fact information about which there is a reasonable doubt, or cites as an authority someone whose competence is questionable without indicating that questionability.

But there are limitations inherent in the compromise of short-order history. There is not time to delve into the lifetime reliability of the farmer who saw the airplane crash; readers are supposed to infer that his account is no more nor less dependable than would be that of the average farmer. The statements of public officials must be assumed, barring arrant implausibility, to be competent. If they are not, that is a problem for the citizenry to rectify; it is not something the press can reform before press time.[7]

Some critics of the press would not accept the whole of Hill's thesis on its face. They argue that the reporter and editor should take whatever time is necessary to eliminate the mistakes and check the reliability of the source of information. But, the journalist responds, completely error-free news would be stale news; the consumer has been accustomed to immediacy, and short-order history inevitably has flaws.

Whatever its cause, the error that finds its way into the newspaper's columns, or into the news broadcast, is doubly dangerous to the medium. It may have tangibly painful consequences, as in a libel damage award to someone injured by the mistaken publication. But almost invariably it is costly

[7]Quoted in Gladwin Hill, "The Press and the Assassination: Dispelling Some Illusions," *Frontier*, March 1966, pp. 17–20.

to the newspaper or the broadcasting station in terms of lost public confidence.

Any reader, listener, or viewer who spots an error—whether it injures that person or not—is from that time on less confident about the accuracy and integrity of the news media. Over time, the cumulative effect can be the development of a dangerous credibility gap.

BEGGING PARDON

For decades the media seemed indifferent to the implications of that credibility gap. On newspapers, errors were acknowledged and corrected only grudgingly, if at all; it was standard procedure to tuck corrections into the far back reaches of the paper, near the classified ads, even though the original mistake might have been printed up front, even on page one.

But during the 1970s the newspapers became much more responsive to readers' sensitivities. Regular correction departments were instituted, positioned consistently up near the front of the paper, and clearly labeled with such tags as "Corrections" or "Fact-Finder." By 1980 three-fourths of large-city newspapers carried such departments, and half of the smaller dailies also had adopted one variation or another. Several dozen of the biggest papers had installed ombudsmen to further protect readers' interests. The ombudsman is an institution imported from Scandinavia, where it is the name for a government officer whose job it is to hear and investigate citizens' complaints about bureaucratic errors or offenses. The American newspaper version is a staff member who receives reader grievances and responds to them, in public and in print.

Radio and television have made fewer efforts to deal with error correction. The evanescent nature of the broadcast report makes it difficult to spot and document instances of error; the newspaper's mistakes are permanently recorded, and the offended reader has the evidence in hand to support the complaint. Still, some local television stations do make an effort to acknowledge and make up for major errors that find their way into a newscast. And even the network news shows occasionally take a few precious seconds to admit and atone for a slip by a correspondent or even an anchor.

Such efforts on the part of the various media were long overdue. Unacknowledged and uncorrected errors had caused destructive erosion of consumer confidence.

THE ONES THAT HURT

Even more destructive are the lapses from accurate reporting that are deliberate rather than inadvertent. Fortunately for the reputations of the media, they are also much less frequent than the typographical error or the unintentional mistake caused by haste and deadline pressure.

One such knowing error sent shock tremors through the entire newspaper industry in 1981 when a Pulitzer Prize, the highest accolade for journalistic achievement, had to be returned when it was revealed that the prize-winning story had been faked.

A reporter for the greatly respected *Washington Post* had won the Pulitzer in the category of feature writing with a compelling and dramatic account of an 8-year-old heroin addict named Jimmy. Several days after the announcement of the award, the reporter admitted to her editors that she had made up the central character in her story. The *Post* apologized to its readers and to the profession through its ombudsman, Bill Green, who wrote three-and-a-half pages of solid copy in the next Sunday edition, tracing the story from its beginnings and apportioning blame not only to the errant reporter but to the various editors up the chain of command who had failed to check the story's authenticity.

The reporter had been so desperately eager to get a page one by-line that she had made up the sensational "facts" in her story; the editors had been so trusting and also so eager for a major story break that they refused to hear alarm bells ringing when the story crossed their desks. For the reporter, wrote *Post* ombudsman Green, "it was personal tragedy. For the *Post* it was inexcusable."[8]

Perhaps because of the consciousness-raising effect of the Pulitzer episode, there were uncovered in rapid succession several other incidents involving deliberate falsification by journalists.

A columnist for the *New York Daily News* (who had also won an award earlier for his reporting, though not a Pulitzer) resigned from the paper after it was disclosed that he had quoted a nonexistent British soldier in reports from the scenes of violence in Northern Ireland. The columnist had used the soldier as a protagonist in his story, quoting him extensively, but when challenged could not substantiate that such a person actually existed.

A few weeks later the management of television station WABC in New York asked three staff members to resign after it turned out that they had concocted several letters that had been used on various shows as communications from viewers. Then the National News Council, an agency set up to monitor press performance, issued a report criticizing as unfair and reckless yet another Pulitzer Prize–winning story, this one published by New York's weekly *Village Voice*. The Council report found the article "to have been marred by the overuse of unattributed sources, by a writing style so colored and imaginative as to blur precise meanings and by such reckless and speculative construction as to result in profound unfairness" to the person described in the story.[9]

In early 1982 it was discovered that even the great, gray *New York Times* had nodded. An article published in the paper's Sunday magazine about guerillas in Cambodia was revealed as partly plagiarized and partly fabricated.

[8]The full report of the ombudsman appears on pages 12 to 15 of the *Washington Post*, Sunday, April 19, 1981.

[9]The council report was quoted in an Associated Press dispatch printed by numerous newspapers on June 12, 1981. The text of the report was later published in *Columbia Journalism Review*, September/October 1981, pp. 85–86.

"YOU CAN'T BELIEVE . . ."

The reverberations of these various incidents, one reinforcing another, echoed for weeks, even months in the professional journals and in the writing of press critics. The damage they inflicted on the credibility of the news media was suggested when some partisans attempted to make the case that the several exposures, particularly the one involving the *Post,* should cast doubt on the validity of the reporting of the Watergate scandal. If the *Post* lied so blatantly in this case, they asserted, it probably also lied about Nixon.

While few members of the reading and viewing public were likely to buy that line of reasoning, a great many did seize upon the several embarrassing revelations as support for the generalized feeling that "You can't believe anything you read in the papers" (or "see on TV").

Spokesmen for the news media, while acknowledging the several lapses exposed in 1981 and 1982, claimed that this was aberrant coincidence. Such deliberate faking or distorting of the news happens only very rarely, they said, and it should not be considered as typical of the performance of the overwhelming majority of journalists. Unfortunately for the media apologists, the string of incidents that began with the Pulitzer bombshell had been preceded by several other somewhat similar instances that had not been widely noted when they first occurred but now were getting a second look.

In September, 1980, the Portland *Oregonian* published an exclusive interview with Governor Dixy Lee Ray of Washington. When Governor Ray complained that the account was inaccurate, an investigation disclosed that the reporter's tape recorder had malfunctioned, and that rather than take the time and trouble to go back to the governor he had tried to reconstruct the interview from memory, putting into the governor's mouth words she had never uttered. It might have been his word against hers, except for the fact that the governor had been running *her* tape recorder during the interview, and it worked. A month later the paper published a retraction that began on the front page and went on inside for a total of 51 column inches, acknowledging that quotations attributed to the governor in the interview had been "false, fabricated, and distorted."[10]

Some months earlier, the *Los Angeles Herald Examiner* published a photograph to illustrate a story about the exploitation of mentally retarded prison inmates. The picture showed a young man seated on the floor in the corner of a bare room, his head bowed on his knees. In the background were several blurred white-coated figures. The reader was left to infer that the scene was that of a prison hospital ward. Later it turned out that the picture was deceptive in all respects. The blurred men wearing white coats were not doctors or attendants but some *Herald Examiner* staff members. And the forlorn "inmate" huddled on the floor was a copyboy. The picture had not been taken in a prison but posed in the paper's newsroom.[11]

And in April 1981, not long before the Pulitzer scandal, a television talk show host who also doubled as a newspaper columnist, admitted that he had helped to fake an interview with a psychic who purportedly had predicted the assassination attempt on President Reagan four weeks before it happened. Actually, the talk show host confessed, the interview with the psychic had been taped the day after the shooting and then doctored to make it appear that it had been aired four weeks earlier. "I have committed the cardinal sin," he acknowledged.[12]

Despite the damning chain of episodes, however, there probably was justification for the claim by news media spokesmen that deliberate faking by journalists is rare. The eight cited instances must be viewed in perspective. Over the same time span there were many thousands of other stories that were reported as honestly and accurately as the ca-

[10]The retraction was published in the *Oregonian,* October 19, 1980.

[11]As reported in "Darts and Laurels," *Columbia Journalism Review,* September/October 1979, p. 27.

[12]Reported in "TV Host Admits Psychic Interview a Hoax," a news story composed of AP and UPI reports, *San Francisco Chronicle,* April 6, 1981, p. 20.

pacities of the several journalistic media permit. The bogus composite characters, the "reconstructed" misquotations, and the deceptive photograph were the exceptions rather than the rule.

WARNING INDICATORS

Some media critics and observers are willing to concede that the Jimmy story and the misquotation of the governor were probably isolated and aberrational. But they also contend that such incidents indicate the existence of a larger, more pervasive problem in journalistic writing.

That problem is the preoccupation of reporters, both print and broadcast, with getting drama and color into their copy, and the means used. They are tempted to infuse excitement into a story by tampering with quotations to make them more arresting and controversial than the actual utterance. Or they cast about in a situation for some person who can serve as the leading actor in the account, as a focal point for reader or viewer attention. Or they paint the lily by adding little touches to a story, even though they have no substantiation for the existence of those colorful details. Such practices carried to an extreme can lead to the invention of a Jimmy or the fabrication of quotes from the governor or another news figure.

These underlying practices in journalistic writing are far more widespread than the few notorious excesses that have come to public attention. Ben H. Bagdikian, a journalism professor at the University of California at Berkeley and a former *Washington Post* editor, said, "The doctoring of quotes and the invention of vivid details of scenes has gone too far with many people."[13]

In television news reporting this tendency shows in the pursuit of contentious quotes that can be juxtaposed with heated rejoinders to create a scene of controversy. It is evi-

---

[13]Quoted by Paul Blustein in "Some Journalists Fear Flashy Reporters Let Color Overwhelm Fact," *The Wall Street Journal* May 14, 1981, pp. 1, 16.

dent, too, in film or tape footage that lingers on the tear-streaked face of an accident victim's mother or that records picket-line skirmishes actually staged at the request of the camera crew.

Newspaper reporters trying to compete with television's action and drama hype their copy by investing it with dimensions that were not present in the news situation. Editors, Bagdikian charges, tend to "reward reporters who are stylistically distinctive, without looking at them closely enough to see that they're factually distinctive." This emphasis on style rather than substance can easily lead to departures from factual reporting. One newspaper writer turned in an arresting piece that depicted the thoughts of a criminal suspect awaiting trial. But when questioned, the writer admitted that the suspect had not been interviewed. "I knew in my gut" what the man was thinking, she said, since she had probed his background and talked about him with his friends and associates.

This approach reflects the school of "new journalism" (discussed further in Chapter 7) that grew up in the 1960s and 1970s. The new journalists were dissatisfied with what they considered the inaccuracy of the objectivity-oriented "old journalism." They pursued the "truth" about a news situation rather than settling for the facts. To get at that truth, they felt, it was necessary to provide minute detail, to penetrate the thought processes and motivations of news figures, and to borrow some of the fiction writer's techniques.

In gifted and responsible hands, the "new journalism" had something of its own to contribute to the news media. But, as in the case of interpretive reporting discussed in Chapter 2, the devices of "new journalism" may easily be abused by an inexperienced or over-zealous writer. Not everyone is equipped to divine the "truth" and report it without distortion. Perhaps *no one* is.

Chapter 6
News Media Ethics

Virtually every working day the men and women who gather, process, and package the news make choices that in one way or another test their sense of fair play and their perception of ethical values. The journalist often faces these choices as an individual, unsupported by the kinds of clear-cut guidelines and supervisory controls that point the way for persons in some other fields where ethical decisions are also a daily responsibility.

The judge, the doctor, the lawyer, and the minister all deal constantly with problems that have ethical implications. But there are codes of practice to guide them, and professional associations to police those codes. A lawyer who violates the ethics of the legal profession is accountable to the bar association and subject to disbarment; a doctor who oversteps the guidelines can expect to face similar admonitory or punitive action from the local medical society, and can lose the license to practice.

There are no equivalent policing agencies to make certain that the journalist adheres to the ethical standards of the field. The First Amendment effectively bars the establishment of any governmental watchdog agency to police the news media or license journalists. The various journalistic associations make no provision for the supervision or disciplining of members, and the First Amendment well might protect against such control.

To be sure, there are codes for journalists, lots of them. The Society of Professional Journalists (Sigma Delta Chi) has a code of ethics; the American Society of Newspaper Editors has a statement of principles; radio and television broadcasters have guidelines about what material should go on the air and how it should be presented; many specialized journalists' societies and numerous newspapers also have adopted formal codes of practice. All of the codes, however, are generalized; they deal little with the practical application of the principles; and they have no enforcement machinery.

This is not to say that the codes and the professional associations are meaningless. They do provide general guidelines and institutional reinforcement for those journalists who want to behave ethically, which is a useful contribution, but it is doubtful that the suasion applied by the codes and the trade organizations has brought very many willful backsliders around to the path of righteousness.

Some potential backsliders are presumably persuaded to stay on the straight and narrow by an influence on them before they begin their professional careers, the instruction in the schools and departments of journalism from which come many media practitioners. Most journalism education programs emphasize ethics, some in specific courses, others by integrating ethical guidelines into courses in reporting or editing. Individual educators and researchers also contribute by producing case studies and analyses that make the codes and guidelines meaningful in practical terms.

OMBUDSMEN AND MONITORS

There are other forms of encouragement to right conduct for journalists, particularly newspaper journalists. On some papers, as we noted earlier, there are ombudsmen to blow the whistle on questionable practices or corner-cutting.

The ombudsman concept works effectively—provided that certain conditions can be met. The ombudsman must be an experienced professional whose judgment will be respected by the staff, and there must be a significant degree of autonomy, preferably through a contract, so that the ombudsman's tenure will not be subject to the whim of management or of the staff. For it is certain that if the ombudsman does the job well, both management fur and staff tempers will be ruffled from time to time. Considering the built-in problems involved, it is not surprising that on only a handful of American newspapers has the experiment yet been tried (among them the *Washington Post* and the *Louisville Courier-Journal*).

Press councils are another attempt to provide a spur to ethical and responsible performance by both print and broadcast media. These are committees made up mostly of citizen volunteers not associated with the media. Their charge is to monitor the media output and receive and investigate complaints of misbehavior.

On the local level, the council concept has been tried in about a dozen communities, with middling success (e.g., Bend, Oregon, and Redwood City, California). The local councils usually served as consciousness-raising forums for the members of both the public and the paper's staff who appeared before them. Since the establishment of a local council has to have the cooperation of the community's publisher, the experiments have been undertaken only in communities already served by good journalism. To no one's surprise, the publishers who ought to be exposed to the oversight of a council never volunteered.

On the regional and national level, though, the council approach has been more promising. The media councils in Minnesota and Hawaii have been useful, not only in the consciousness-raising department, but also to give impetus toward better media performance.

The National News Council has also contributed. It receives complaints from individuals or groups whose interests have been injured or who want better media service, investigates the complaints, and then issues judgments or rulings. The rulings have at times been stern and pointed in their indictment of slipshod performance by a newspaper or network. Yet there is a structural weakness; the Council's punitive powers are limited to tongue-lashings. The judgment can be reached and handed down, but that's about the end of the matter. The errant newspaper or broadcaster can take note of the judgment and resolve to do better, or just ignore it, as the worst offenders usually do.

The Council's reports and rulings were published for several years in the *Columbia Journalism Review* and then in *The Quill,* both professional journals seen chiefly by those in the business, not by the general public. Occasionally a Council ruling will find its way into the main news flow (as was the case with the finding on the Pulitzer Prize feature writer who was judged careless and irresponsible). But a great many of the Council observations remain unseen, unheard.

So, since there are not many effective external influences, the reporters, editors, and newscasters—the gatekeepers—are left to make their ethical decisions as individuals responding to the historic traditions of the press and its responsibility to society.

By and large, their response is admirable. The majority of persons who have worked for a time in one or another journalistic role will testify that most of their coworkers take their obligations seriously. Though they are not monitored by the codes and agencies characteristic of other professions, they do indeed behave as professionals. They try their best to discover the facts and to relay them to their readers with as little distortion as possible. And they try to make ethical judgments in a spirit sensitive to the rights of individuals and with respect for the public duty of the press.

The cynical observer may find this hard to believe, citing the truism about the corrupting influence of power and pointing to the undeniable power held by the gatekeepers of the press. In the absence of formalized controls, why should journalists be immune to the temptation to abuse that power and forsake ethical standards? They are not, of course, immune. Some do wrongly use their positions, as we saw earlier, but the evidence is strong that most do not. One reason why they do not is suggested by a passage from Boris Pasternak's novel, *Dr. Zhivago:*

> If the beast who sleeps in man could be held down by threats—any kind of threats, whether of jail or of retribution after death—then the highest emblem of humanity would be the lion tamer in the circus with his whip, not the prophet who sacrificed himself. But don't you see, this is just the point—what has for centuries raised men above the beast is not the cudgel but an inward music, the irresistible power of unarmed truth, the powerful attraction of its example.

Most journalists would not put it so lyrically, but they would understand what Pasternak meant. Their response to the "inward music" shows in the decisions they make at nearly every turn in their day's routine. The decisions that pose problems of ethics for the journalist are so numerous and varied in character that it would be impractical to catalog all of them here. But anyone who hopes to understand how the media function should have at least some notion of the range and complexity of these problems, in order to be alert to the degree to which the local media attempt to perform within ethical boundaries.

ARE NAMES ALWAYS NEWS?

Most crime stories confront the reporter and editor with one category of ethical decisions: how to strike a balance between the need to inform the public about this important sector of community news, and the need to protect as fully as possible the rights of persons caught up in such news.

For example, should juveniles be identified when they are arrested on criminal charges? Is it more important to publish their names in order to alert the community at large, or would it be better to leave out the identification and avoid stigmatizing a youngster publicly and thus jeopardizing chances for rehabilitation? And what about identifying the victim in a crime story? Is it a necessary part of the news? Should there be one policy with respect to, say, a burglary story, and another one with respect to a rape arrest?

Arriving at a decision in such cases as these may not be difficult. Most editors and reporters adhere to a policy of withholding from publication the names of juveniles, particularly when first offenses are involved. Almost universally, too, they do not permit the publication of the name of a victim of rape. In both situations, the sensitivity of individuals weighs more heavily than the public's right to know. In the case of a burglary story, however, the decision will most often go the other way, on the ground that the identification of the home broken into is necessary to alert the neighbors and the community to a hazard.

But there are other situations in which the circumstances are more complex, and the identification of the paramount ethical values becomes much more difficult. Consider the following newspaper lead. The names and place references have been changed, but it otherwise appears just as it was originally published:

> RIVER CITY—A man whose career of lawbreaking was one of the most notorious in the state's history went free on parole Wednesday.
>
> John D. Doe, 41, shot a state policeman to death in 1947, led several prison break attempts here, set fire to the penitentiary flax plant and went over the wall in 1949.
>
> The FBI once called him a man of "wanton viciousness."
>
> But, said Warden Richard R. Roe Tuesday:
>
> "He has caused no difficulty at all in the six years I have been here."

Doe turned over a new leaf after failure of his last escape attempt some eight years ago. For a time he taught in the prison school. He has been an aide in recent years to the prison psychologist. The warden said: "He has made a good adjustment."

Doe, at the age of 16, began his criminal career with an armed robbery. Many crimes later, at 29, he gunned down a state policeman when the policeman halted him in a stolen car.

The account went on to detail the man's criminal record, and toward the end of the story noted that Doe was hoping to find a job and begin a new life.

Two different lines of argument can be developed about that news story.

A reader concerned about the concept of rehabilitation of criminals could work up a lively indignation about the damage done by the story to the released convict's chances of making a new life. What hope has Doe got of finding acceptance in society if, as he emerges from prison, all the lurid details of his criminal past are paraded once again to refresh the public's memory? How will he be viewed by a prospective employer if he arrives tagged as "one of the most notorious" lawbreakers in the state's history? How will he be welcomed by his new neighbors when he finds a home outside the walls? Isn't the likelihood great that he will, in desperation, eventually revert to his original pattern of criminal behavior, since it will be in that role that society pictures him?

Such a line of reasoning could be developed (and often is) about news stories reporting the release of criminals. But another, and also persuasive, argument can be put together.

BALANCING THE SCALES

Such stories as the one quoted, this second thesis runs, are not only defensible but necessary in the public interest. Unless the press tells us about the background of persons being released from prisons, how are we going to be alert to a breakdown in the parole system? Shouldn't we be kept informed of the functioning of that system so that we know what kinds of persons are being turned loose on society, perhaps prematurely? How else could we learn whether hardened criminals are buying their way out by exploiting a corrupt parole agency? After all, that sort of thing has happened, and not only once or twice.

So how does the editor make the decision? Should the paroled convict's right to a fresh start be put above the public's right to know how one important aspect of the machinery of justice is functioning? Or should the scales tip the other way? Is there any way to balance them precisely on center?

Now look at this same kind of ethical poser, but in a different and perhaps even more difficult context.

A prominent St. Louis businessman, Frank J. Prince, the chief stockholder in the Universal Match Corp., made a gift of $500,000 to Washington University in St. Louis. In grateful acknowledgment, the university made plans to name a building after Prince. The *St. Louis Post-Dispatch* set a reporter to work to get a background story on the university's benefactor. During the course of his investigation the reporter discovered that Prince, then 71, had during his early life served three prison terms, adding up to nearly ten years, after being convicted of forgery, grand larceny, and issuing bad checks. After he had served his time he had begun life anew and in the intervening years had made a success as a legitimate businessman.

The reporter and his editors then faced a decision: Should this part of Prince's life story be included in the paper's coverage, or should it be repressed? Was this something the readers of St. Louis had a right to know about a leading philanthropist of the community, or was it a chapter long past and properly forgotten?

The decision reached by the *Post-Dispatch* editors was reflected in the headlines that appeared over the story: FRANK J. PRINCE, UNIVERSAL MATCH OWNER, IS EX-CONVICT.

Time magazine, in its account of the episode, noted:

> The *Post-Dispatch* stories were factually accurate. Frank
> Prince did have a prison record. That record was known to

many if not all of his friends and business associates. It was
known to the Federal Bureau of Investigation, which had
nonetheless cleared Prince for defense contracts. It had even
been mentioned in Dun & Bradstreet. Indeed, among those
closest to Prince, two of the few who did not know of his record
were his wife and 24-year-old son.

But were the *Post-Dispatch* stories relevant as news? By the
paper's own accounting, Frank Prince had stayed in the clear
for the last 25 years.[1]

Others joined *Time* in criticizing the newspaper's handling of the matter. The *Post-Dispatch* editor responded
that: "I think the stories simply speak for themselves."

WHEN DOES PRIVATE BECOME PUBLIC?

A great many items in the flow of the news may involve deciding whether or not to include reference to something in
the past of a figure currently in the limelight. If a thrice-
divorced woman marries again, should the wedding story
mention her earlier alliances? Should a man who is now the
leader of a powerful labor union be revealed as one who,
twenty years earlier, had once held membership in the Communist Party? Or, to take a case that sounds too bizarre to
be true but actually did take place, should a man who had
made a successful career as the head of an extremist anti-
Semitic organization be "exposed" as one whose parents and
upbringing had been Jewish?

The *New York Times* published a story revealing that
a man named Daniel Burros, one of the leaders of the Ku
Klux Klan in New York and a spokesman for that organization's racist philosophy, was of Jewish extraction. Burros
had asked the reporter and his editor not to use the story
because Burros had concealed his background from his
Klan associates and contended that publication of the matter now would ruin him in his role as leader of the organization. When the story appeared despite his plea, Burros
shot himself to death.

[1] *Time*, February 22, 1960, p. 59.

Were the journalists who made the decision here at fault? Should they have acceded to the Klan leader's request? Probably the majority of society would support the action of the newspaper, since the organization involved is generally abhorred and its tenets rejected by most Americans. Still, in commenting on the case, the *Columbia Journalism Review* was troubled:

> How much of a man's past becomes fair game when his current activity becomes public? In this particular case, the line marking the edge of public life was blurred, for what the practitioners clearly thought were reasons of public interest. But blurring should not be taken to mean that no such line exists, or that it can be crossed at will.[2]

To ponder the complexities of the matter still further, consider how the issue might have looked had the circumstances been reversed. Suppose Burros had achieved leadership in a Jewish organization and in the process had passed himself off as a member of that faith, and suppose the newspaper had discovered that in fact he was not Jewish and had at one time been virulently anti-Semitic. What then should the paper have done? And how would the *Review* have analyzed the matter?

A few years later another very similar situation developed. Reporters for a Texas newspaper learned that a retired engineer had at one time been a Soviet spy and later an FBI double agent, and was still drawing a $5000 pension from Russia. The man acknowledged that the facts were correct, but urged that they not be used. He said he would kill himself if they were published. The story, the editors decided, was newsworthy and should run. As soon as it appeared, the engineer killed himself.

Editors in various parts of the country were polled, and most of those responding agreed with the Texas paper's decision. But some said that the man's doctor or others close to him should have been alerted to the situation so that they might be able to dissuade him from suicide.

[2]*Columbia Journalism Review,* Winter 1966, p. 3.

It is obviously not possible to lay down a convenient, precise formula for reaching decisions in such cases. An *ad hoc* balance must be struck, with the gatekeepers doing their best to respect both the rights of individuals and the right of the public to be accurately informed about matters that are justifiably the public's business.

A PRIZE FOR WHAT?

The use of pictures in the news media gives rise to numerous ethical problems for both photographers and editors. This is particularly the case with pictures of accidents or disasters. If human-interest content could be measured with some sort of Geiger counter, such pictures would run the needle off the scale. They contain elements of tragedy, heart-wrenching pathos, drama, and death—and whether such interest is becoming or not, all of us *do* have a deep and automatic interest in these elements.

A prize-winning entry in a national news photo contest one year constituted a classic of this genre. At one side of the picture was the body of a small boy who had drowned in a neighborhood swimming pool, and bending over him in vain was an ambulance attendant. The neighbor in whose pool the boy had drowned was seated in the background, hands clutched to her face in shock. Watching, his legs stiff and his head bent tensely, was the little boy's German shepherd. And at the far side of the picture were the victim's parents, clasped in each other's arms, the mother's face hidden, the father's twisted in terrible anguish.

The picture had enormous dramatic impact, and it is easy to see why the judges awarded it the prize, but such a picture poses some profound and complex questions for an editor to answer. By any measurement, the picture has great human-interest content and obvious news value. It also constitutes an invasion of the privacy of several persons in a searing moment they will never forget. Is the news value of the picture great enough to warrant intruding on such a moment, exploiting its ingredients for their effect upon the reader?

This is not a question to be answered easily. It requires—as do so many of the ethical problems that confront the journalist—some careful analysis.

The instinctive, humanitarian response would very likely be: Do not use it—do not fix that moment forever for the three stricken persons, do not traffic in their grief just to attract the reader's attention.

But the editor also has other considerations to weigh. Would the printing of the picture perhaps awaken some reader (or some dozens of readers) to the hazard posed to neighborhood children by his unfenced backyard pool? And would it thus perhaps result in the long run in preventive measures that might spare the lives of other toddlers and avoid a repetition of that tragic tableau in the photograph? Is the public interest better served by publication or suppression of the picture? Could a news story without the picture be counted on to have the same impact on readers who may not have realized their responsibilities as pool owners? Or would many overlook the news account if it were not accompanied by the picture?

A similar analytical evaluation goes on almost daily with one category of news pictures, those of auto accidents. Since the accident rate is high, such pictures are always available. How often should they be used? What considerations should dictate which ones should be used, and which tossed into the basket?

Safety experts are not in agreement about whether a photograph of twisted wreckage, with a body sprawled by the roadside, has a sobering, deterrent effect upon drivers who may see the picture. Some feel that such pictures do make readers and viewers more aware of the need to drive defensively and employ seat belts. Others contend that the death shots and the recitation of accident statistics on holiday weekends only make other drivers more nervous and possibly *more* likely to be involved in accidents themselves.

When editors do use such pictures, it is usually with the purpose of promoting greater care on the highway, rather than to exploit morbidity. Whether this use of accident pictures actually does result in a lowering of the highway accident rate is arguable, as has been pointed out, but the purpose is defensible.

Far less defensible is the practice of some photographers and editors who attempt to wring the utmost of pathos out of accident pictures. One metropolitan East Coast paper ran three multicolumn shots of the same accident. One of them showed the body of the small boy who had died in the accident being cradled in his mother's arms, while the shocked driver of the car stood in the background. It was a distant shot, borderline perhaps, but not indefensible under the wholesome warning theory.

But one of the other pictures used was a closeup of the mother's face as she looked up from her child's body. Her features were tortured, and tears ran down her cheeks. It was a powerful photograph, but its power was derived from the exploitation of the mother's grief. Ethical considerations had gone by the board when the decision to print that picture was reached.

"HAVE YOU NO HEART?"

It would seem logical to suppose that problems with pictures would arise more often in television than in the newspaper, for television coverage is more vivid and immediate than a still photograph. There have, indeed, been strenuous objections by viewers to some television footage. During the Vietnam war, for example, the television audience was shocked periodically by battlefront films, often depicting mangled bodies.

During a Viet Cong offensive against South Vietnam in 1968, one sequence that came in from an NBC film crew was particularly grisly. It showed a Viet Cong officer in civilian dress brought before the chief of the South Vietnam national police. The police general drew his pistol, aimed it from only a foot away from the prisoner, and pulled the trigger. The doomed man's face grimaced as the bullet hit, and then he toppled over, the camera following him as blood gushed from the body. When the film arrived in NBC's New York headquarters, the producer of the nightly news previewed it with anchor John Chancellor. Both men were shaken, and the decision was taken to edit the film, omitting the footage of the bleeding corpse. Still, what remained was enough to revolt many viewers.

There have been numerous other incidents that provoked negative audience reaction to some television stories of war, accidents, and tragedies, and also to the tactics of reporters and camera crews who pursue some harried newsmaker as though after a stag at bay. However, for several reasons newspapers feel the heat more often.

For one thing, as noted in Chapter 5, television cameras are not often on the scene when an accident or a bloody incident takes place (unlike the case in Vietnam in 1968). The film footage is likely to be of aftermath episodes—sheeted bodies being removed from the wreckage, or dazed survivors seated by the roadside. If television is present at a disaster scene, as at an auto racetrack when a car careens into another in a flaming crash, the views are likely to be distant ones rather than the closeups that viewers are most likely to find offensive.

Another factor also reduces the incidence of viewer objection to such television coverage. The television pictures flick by so rapidly that there is not time for the viewer's indignation to come to a boil. The tragic pictures are quickly succeeded by different, less disturbing subject matter. The newspaper photo, however, makes its impression over time and constitutes a semi-permanent record for the shocked reader to pore over. Finally, the newspaper's letters column provides a ready forum for reader objections; feedback to the broadcast media is less institutionalized. So newspapers are called on the carpet more often than television for using objectionable news photos. Consider a case:

A disturbed young man in New York climbed out on a building ledge and threatened to jump to his death. Office workers and police pleaded with him, but after a few minutes of indecision, he did. A newspaper photographer snapped a closeup shot of the falling youth, head down, his fists clenched before him as though anticipating the impact on the street below. The picture was distributed widely and used by many newspapers in various parts of the country, often on page one and in multicolumn size.

One West Coast paper that carried the photograph received numerous angry letters from readers. "Can it be," wrote one, "that you can splash a picture of a youth's agony and desperation all over the front page as if it were the weather?" Another asked: "Was the picture being used to inform or only to sell papers?" Some other comments: "If you are that desperate for a big story, why didn't you print a picture of the boy just as he hit the pavement? That would be even more shocking and more sensational." "The fact that any human feels compelled to take his own life is sobering and heart-wrenching enough without photographing the gruesome details. Have you no heart?"

Similarly outraged reactions were elicited when newspapers and newsmagazines ran a dramatic sequence of photographs of a baby-sitter and her charge falling from a collapsing fire escape in Boston: "Outrageous . . . atrocious front page. . . . If that's news, I'm cancelling . . . worst possible taste . . . insensitive and not a little perverted as well. . . . It is unfortunate that society's ills, suffering, and death are so profitable." The *Washington Post* received 70 calls on the pictures, the most the ombudsman could recall on a single story.

Yet virtually all editors were in agreement that the Boston pictures should be used. They were obviously newsworthy, and they might well serve to alert many building owners to the need to inspect their buildings' fire escapes to prevent other tragedies.

AN UNCERTAIN LINE

Drawing the line between pictures that belong in the news, because they add a significant dimension to coverage, and those that are exploitative is a difficult and wrenching obligation. Journalists must satisfy that obligation often, under deadline pressure, with perhaps only minutes to weigh all the considerations involved. Sometimes the line is not drawn as responsibly as it should have been, and not only indignant letter writers are bothered by the result. Kevin Starr, a columnist for the *San Francisco Chronicle and Examiner,* once took his professional colleagues to task over a rash of borderline pictures he had spotted in the news media over a short time span:

> Barbara Bush, the wife of the vice president, stumbles uncertainly on a step, and for a moment she falls to her knees. The camera catches this very distinguished, very kind woman while she is still on the ground—that look of surprise, shock even, on her face that all of us have when we fall. The picture goes over the wire and is run in thousands of newspapers.
>
> Humiliatingly defeated in his attempt at a second term, former President Jimmy Carter returns home to Plains, Ga. Not even the consolation of welcoming home the hostages as president would be his. A few days after his arrival at Plains, the former president goes out for his daily jog. Emerging around the corner of a hedge-lined path, he stumbles across a curb partly hidden by overgrown bushes. He falls to the ground. From somewhere in the distance tele-photographers catch the still-dazed former president half trying to rise from the ground with his arms, the same stunned look on his face that Mrs. Bush had. The photograph of the fallen Carter goes out on the wires and is published in thousands of papers.
>
> Alighting from an airplane, Nancy Reagan has her skirt blown up by a gust of wind. The camera catches it, and this incipiently voyeuristic photograph, filled with implicit sniggering, goes out on the wire and is published in thousands of newspapers.
>
> Pope John Paul II is presiding over the ordination of 15 priests at the Cathedral of Nagasaki, the most Christian of all Japanese cities. It is a solemn moment. Fifteen young Japanese men kneel before the bishop of Rome, the spiritual head of some 750 million Roman Catholics and allied rites. They are offering to the pontiff no less than their lives. . . . His Holiness is exhausted from nearly two weeks of incessant travel in the Philippines and Japan. For a split second during the solemn ceremony of prostration, the pope yawns into his folded hands. The camera clicks through its telephoto lens and the photo-

graph of the yawning pontiff before the young priests is published around the world, or at least the United States.

In each of these cases, the image selected for publication in
the newspaper was the image most allied to belittling ridicule.[3]

Presumably, the photographers who obtained those shots
and the editors who decided to publish them had concluded
that their newsworthiness outweighed the possibility that
they might give offense. As far as Starr was concerned, and
perhaps quite a few others as well, the conclusions had not
been the right ones.

"WHOSE BREAD I EAT, HIS SONG I SING"

Journalists also face difficult decisions in a quite different area
of journalistic ethics—conflict of interest.

The only cause that the journalist ought to be serving
is that of informing the public. Ties, associations, and obligations that might influence a reporter to further interests
other than those of the public ought to be avoided, but that
is much more easily said than done. Journalists are constantly
in contact with news sources in all walks of life. Common
courtesy calls for interaction of various kinds, some innocent,
some suspect. Distinguishing one from the other can be tax-
ing.

Let us look at one perennial trouble area, sports coverage. Sportswriters and broadcasters cover teams both at
home and on the road, both during the regular season and
during preseason training and exhibition games. They must
travel with the team, ride the same buses, fly in the same air-
planes, and stay at the same hotels. In the process they inevitably become closely identified with the fortunes and the
personnel of the teams they cover.

To what degree does such identification compromise the
journalists' ability to cover the teams objectively and impar-
tially? Suppose the sportswriter accepts the hospitality of the

---

[3]Kevin Starr, "Demeaning News Photos," *San Francisco Chronicle and Examiner,* March 15, 1981, p. 38.

team, sharing meals with the players? Suppose the team picks up the tab for the reporter's travel and lodging? How much has the reporter become beholden to the team? When internal disagreements arise on the squad, will the reporter help cover them up or will he report them fearlessly?

Such questions have been around for a long while, and they will stay. A survey of sports editors by the Associated Press Managing Editors Association in 1980 revealed that half of those responding allowed their reporters to accept favors from teams. Yet the ethical codes of the newspaper organizations generally prohibit gifts and favors from news sources as likely to cause conflict of interest problems.[4]

The issue of "freebies"—gifts, favors, or gratuities proffered to journalists by sources they are supposed to cover without bias—is not confined to the sports reporters and sportscasters. Editors go off on junkets paid for by foreign governments hoping for some favorable publicity (20 of them went on such a freebie excursion to Taiwan, all expenses paid, in 1979): Food editors are transported to luxury resorts to view a chicken-cooking contest sponsored by broiler producers who have hopes of free publicity: Travel writers are offered free air travel to distant vacation spots the promotors hope will later be mentioned favorably in the writers' columns.

When the movie "Superman II" was about to be released, the film's producer, Warner Brothers, flew a group of television reporters to Niagara Falls, put them up for several days in expensive accommodations, wined and dined them, and set up studio facilities so that each reporter could take home an individual taped interview with the star of the production, Christopher Reeve. The moviemakers counted on getting numerous free and localized "plugs" for their release, and if it is very likely that they were not disappointed.[5]

Some journalists lean over backward to avoid becoming

[4]Bob Fleischer, "Sports Freebies Remain Major Ethics Question," *APME News*, October 1980, p. 14.

[5]As reported by David J. Blum in "How Local Film Critics Meet the Man of Steel," *The Wall Street Journal*, June 5, 1981, p. 29.

enmeshed in even the most innocent-appearing conflict-of-interest situations. They decline membership on civic committees, insist on paying their own way when covering Rotary luncheons, and refuse passes to movies or plays that they are covering in the line of duty.

Others in the news media deride such a squeaky-clean approach as unrealistic and unnecessary. They feel that they can interact sociably with news sources without their integrity being tarnished, and they argue that no reasonable person would seriously believe that they could be corrupted for the price of a movie ticket or a highball and a hot dog in the stadium press box. They point out that journalists are uniquely qualified to serve on civic bodies and that they would be shirking their responsibilities as citizens if they used the conflict-of-interest excuse to avoid such service. They also contend that without the subsidies of sports writers on tour or travel writers on junkets to far-off resorts, the media would be unable to afford coverage of certain types of news wanted by their consumers.

But in the 1970s and 1980s the balance seems to have been tipping more and more toward the purist Caesar's-wife school where freebies and other conflict-of-interest hazards are concerned. An increasing number of newspapers and television stations insist that staff members, including publishers, avoid junkets of any kind ("If it's important enough to cover, it's important enough to pay for") and also steer clear of any situation that might lead the public to believe that the coverage and its emphasis have been bought. The trend seems likely to continue, for where the integrity of the news media is concerned, it simply is not possible to be "just a little bit pregnant."[6]

[6]For more discussion of media ethics, see John L. Hulteng's *Playing It Straight* (Chester, Conn.: Globe Pequot Press, 1981).

Chapter 7
Magazines of
General Interest

The word "magazine," from the French *magasin,* means "store." The place where explosives are kept aboard ship, the cartridge chamber of a gun, the flat metal container for Linotype matrices—these are magazines. The early magazines of journalism (*Gentleman's Magazine* in England in 1731 was probably the first publication to use the term in its title) were "stores" containing essays, stories, reviews, news, poems, and other items to delight and instruct the reader.

Editors refer to their magazines as "books," and it is true that magazines enjoy a close alliance with the book publishing industry. Some of the early quality magazines—like *Harper's Weekly* and *Harper's Magazine*—were by-products of book publishers. That influential and irreverent magazine of the 1920s, *American Mercury,* was published by the book publisher Alfred A. Knopf. Lately, a number of magazine publishers have gone into book publishing—Time-Life, for instance. Whether or not a magazine is owned by a book publisher or owns a book publishing firm, its stories or articles often end up in book form. Truman Capote's celebrated "nonfiction novel," *In Cold Blood,* appeared in installments in *The New Yorker* and was published later by Random House.

Magazines also have some qualities in common with newspapers. Like newspapers, magazines inform readers as well as guide and entertain them. Until the coming of television, in the more general magazines entertainment predominated. At one time the ratio of fiction to nonfiction was five to one. Now the reverse is true. Newspapers have competed with magazines by launching magazines of their own. Outstanding is the Sunday magazine section of the *New York Times,* which uses national and international news as a peg on which to hang its articles. Included in the Sunday editions of some newspapers are national syndicated magazine sections, like *Parade* and *Family Weekly.*

Sometimes, to gain readers, magazines resort to the same devices used by sensational newspapers of the kind we associate with William Randolph Hearst. *Life* for its February 1981 issue paid $8000 to an accused murderer of a prominent Washington, D.C., cardiologist to run pictures from a family album. That editorial decision resulted in a partial boycott in Washington.

Magazines differ from newspapers in that, ideally, almost everything in a single issue appeals to every reader. A typical issue may have only half a dozen stories and articles; if just one of them is beyond his interest, the reader is likely to feel cheated. A newspaper, with its hundreds of items daily, can run any number of them for the benefit of only a few readers.

The student of magazine journalism quickly sees real differences in magazines, even those that on the surface seem to serve the same audience. A magazine reflects the interests and biases of its editors. A magazine develops a personality, a style that sets it apart from others in its field. There is such a thing as a typical *Reader's Digest* article title or a *New Yorker* story ending. *Mad* magazine in some of its features and the *National Lampoon* with its parody issues have been at their best satirizing the affectations of various magazines. *New York* magazine based one of its back-of-the-book contests on the tendency of magazines to go with predictable titles. A tongue-in-cheek title or cover blurb offered by Louis B. Raffel for *Town and Country* was "Keeping Fit Without Fatigue—Exercises the Servants Can Do for You." For *Philadelphia Magazine* Marilyn Crystal submitted "Two Things to Do After 9:00 P.M." Albert G. Miller suggested for *Reader's Digest* "Thumb-Sucking Can Cost You Your Job."

It is easy enough to capture the essence of some magazines with a single descriptive phrase or sentence. Other magazines are too complicated—or at least they think they are—to fit any easy description. James M. Lawrence, editor and publisher of Canada's *Harrowsmith,* a back-to-the-soil magazine with a keen eye on the environment, said that "Upon publication of our first issue, I was asked to describe *Harrowsmith* in six words or less and couldn't do it. [Now, four years later,] I still can't and it still seems a good thing."[1] The magazine liked its flexibility.

Although with their tabloid formats they may look like newspapers, the *National Enquirer* and its imitators belong in the magazine category. The *Enquirer* has a large circulation, 5.2 million, but the magazine is mostly fluff and sensation. Its preoccupation with celebrities and their alleged improper conduct has lately resulted in a number of libel suits. Carol Burnett won a big judgment for the publication's sloppy reporting.

It is impossible to count all the magazines published. "In America, it appears, if three or more people get together their first act is to form a committee and their second is to launch a

---

[1]"Editorial," *Harrowsmith,* September 1979, p. 4.

publication; generally it is a magazine," observes Prof. Roland E. Wolseley of Syracuse University.[2] No subject is too esoteric. Calvin Trillin, tongue in cheek, in a review in *Life* claimed he was coeditor of *Beautiful Spot, a Magazine of Parking.* If by "magazines" we mean bound publications (distinguishing them from newspapers) of eight or more pages issued on a regular basis (weekly, biweekly, monthly, bimonthly, or quarterly), an estimate of 20,000 in this country alone seems reasonable. No one directory—not even N. W. Ayer & Son's *Directory of Newspapers and Periodicals*—lists them all, no one trade organization represents them all.

One way to consider magazines is to separate them into *general circulation* and *specialized* categories. Under *specialized* go the professional and trade journals (like the *Journal of the American Medical Association* and *Iron Age*), which largely contain news, advice, and reports of research; the company magazines (like *Ford Times* and *Caterpillar World*) designed to do a public relations job either to employees or outsiders, or both; the struggling literary quarterlies; the journals of opinion; magazines for hobbyists—the list is endless.

The smaller magazines force the bigger magazines to upgrade content. A few of the company magazines, for instance, are more brilliantly edited, more handsomely produced than most of the slicks.

General circulation magazines (or "slicks") are few in number compared to specialized magazines but high in total circulation. They go out on a subscription basis, but, unlike specialized magazines, they also sell on newsstands. Such sales are important, because advertisers feel that people who buy single copies of a magazine are more responsive, at least to advertising, than people who get the magazine delivered to them. One promotional campaign pointed out to media buyers in advertising agencies that the reader of *Family Circle* had to go out of her way to get the magazine. The impli-

In the United States and in other countries with a high literacy
rate, newsstands offer a wide selection of magazines for sale.
Some magazines depend solely, and some mainly, on newsstand
sales to survive. Such magazines give a lot of attention to their
covers, designed to intrigue readers.   (*Source:* © Gloaguen/
VIVA 1982, Woodfin Camp.)

cation was that while she was out, she bought, and having
bought the magazine, she would read it when she got home.

Note the distinction between *circulation* and *readership. Circulation* figures are clearly measurable—the number of copies sold either through subscription or on the newsstand. The figures are watched over by the Audit Bureau of
Circulations, an organization set up by advertisers, agencies,
and the media to keep circulation claims honest. Magazines
futher try to measure, though these figures are less reliable,
the *readership,* which presumably is always higher. A copy
gets passed along in a family or to friends and neighbors.
Two, three, or more persons read each copy.

IMPACT OF MAGAZINES

It was a magazine, *New West* (now *California*), that first exposed the Peoples Temple cult of San Francisco. The article started out as a newspaper feature, but the paper's city editor decided not to run it, so reporter Marshall Kilduff teamed with *New West* staffer Phil Tracy to do the magazine piece. About the time of the article's publication, possibly because of it, the Rev. Jim Jones moved to Guyana where, late in 1978, the sect came to its tragic end.

While it is impossible to measure precisely the impact of magazines on our society, it seems reasonable to conclude that the impact, at least on the middle classes, has been substantial. Looking back on magazine development, in his *Magazines in the Twentieth Century* Theodore Peterson of the University of Illinois concludes that, as an editorial medium, magazines were "inclined to perpetuate the ideological status quo."[3] As an advertising medium, they "played a significant part in raising the material standard of living in the twentieth century."[4] Major magazines gave readers pretty much what they wanted, Peterson observes, skirting controversial issues so as not to offend either readers or advertisers. They left experimentation to the little magazines, who had less to lose.

The big magazines were, in Peterson's phrasing, "highly imitative." When a subject caught on, all the magazines came forward with their versions. They had an almost naive faith in the advances of science. They preached the line that, using the appropriate techniques, *anybody* can do *anything*. The women's magazines provided the illusion that complete fulfillment was guaranteed for those who are married.

Yet some of these magazines operated some of the time in the vanguard of public opinion. The big, national magazines led the way toward social reforms shortly after the turn

---

[3]Theodore Peterson, *Magazines in the Twentieth Century*, 2nd ed. (Urbana: University of Illinois Press, 1964), p. 445.
[4]Ibid., pp. 442, 443.

of the century. The "muckrakers," as they were called, pressed for honest government, better regulation of industry, safer food processing, and other measures. Peterson draws up a list of seven contributions made by magazines:[5]

1. Magazines in the twentieth century were responsible "in some measure" for social and political reforms.
2. They put issues and events into perspective, adding a dimension not offered by the newspapers.
3. They fostered "a sense of national community." They created a bond among peoples. For instance, they made the techniques of southern cooking nationally known; they helped spread the idea of ranch-type houses from the West eastward.
4. They provided low-cost entertainment, from stories in the pulp magazines to stories in quality magazines by important and thoughtful writers.
5. They offered instruction in the art of daily living; how to raise children, decorate the home, and so on.
6. They provided education in our cultural heritage. They explored the past through historical articles and biography. They helped us appreciate art.
7. Magazines brought variety to the lives of readers. Each magazine sought out its own audience and tried to serve it with special interest articles. "The typical magazine was not edited for just 'everybody'." This gave readers innumerable choices at the newsstand.

MAGAZINES AND THE "NEW JOURNALISM"

The "new journalism" probably got its start with Tom Wolfe in the mid 1960s, when, writing for the Sunday magazine of the *New York Herald Tribune,* he developed his with-it style, peppered with exclamation marks and made-up words. He delighted in taking on sacred cows, including *The New Yorker* and its respected editor William Shawn, which attack brought cries of "foul" from the literary establishment. One

[5]Ibid., pp. 448–451.

of his most memorable pieces was *Radical Chic,* a book-length look at white "limousine liberals" who got their kicks identifying with Black Panthers. Wolfe later ridiculed art critics in *The Painted Word* and still later investigated the astronauts in *The Right Stuff.* His *From Bauhaus to Our House* took on the architecture Establishment.

Much of Wolfe's work has been first-rate and all of it readable, allowing for some stylistic excesses. Looking over his work, a *Time* writer in 1979 pronounced it a "jazzy mix of facts and fictional technique. . . . It is still called the New Journalism, although the form is as old as the Beatles. . . . Like the Beatles, Wolfe has had a revolutionary impact on his field. His imitators have spread like dandelion fluff, and his work still stirs furious debate."[6]

A number of magazines have been associated with the "new journalism," *Esquire, New York,* and the *Village Voice* among them. *Esquire*'s "new journalism" days spread through the 1960s, when many considered it one of America's most interesting publications. *New York* was an outgrowth of the *Herald Tribune*'s Sunday magazine, relaunched when the paper itself died. The *Village Voice,* founded as a leftist newspaper in 1955, was originally a publication that gave its writers plenty of latitude to roam all around a subject, provided the writers were committed to a cause. Later the *Village Voice* grew more conservative.

Like newspapers, magazines have from time to time been plagued by dishonest reporting. Despite the great contributions it made, the "new journalism" brought on some of the problem by applying fictional techniques to the writing of nonfiction. Which characters in the article were "composite characters"? What anecdotes were invented rather than merely told? It was often hard to tell. Some writers without a background in the objectivity that journalism schools teach were not burdened by any desire to stick with the facts. "Truth" became more important, even if it had to be invented.

[6]R. Z. Sheppard, "Skywriting with Gus and Deke," *Time,* September 24, 1979, p. 81.

When a 1981 Pulitzer Prize was returned because the *Washington Post* story that won it was false, that caused all the media, magazines included, to reexamine existing practices. Someone at *Cosmopolitan* discovered that printed instructions to freelance writers invited the invention of authority for citation purposes. When brands were mentioned in articles, they had to be brands of *Cosmopolitan* advertisers only, and those advertisers were not to be criticized in articles. These rules were eliminated in 1981.[7]

THE CHANGING MAGAZINE

Magazines find it necessary to change with the times. *Rolling Stone,* for instance, the magazine that from 1967 gave itself over almost entirely to rock 'n' roll music, squeezed such coverage into the back of the book in 1981 to become "a more general-interest journal appealing to older readers and corporate advertisers," Philip Nobile noted in *New York.* The magazine at that time went to slicker paper and a more sedate look. Nobile said that *Rolling Stone* in the 1970s was one of "the smartest magazines in the country. It was to the seventies what *Esquire* had been to the sixties." But with the fading of the record industry and rock 'n' roll in the late 1970s, *Rolling Stone* faded too. Hence the new emphasis. Politics and movies became more important to the editors.

Boy's Life has also changed with the times. The oversize pages have reduced themselves to *Time* magazine size. That saves money. Big color pictures appear on pages that used to feature smaller black-and-white ones. That gets attention. Articles are shorter. "We used to publish articles that ran up to thirty-five hundred words. Now, though, if we go over fifteen hundred words, . . . [readers] won't stay with it," editor Robert E. Hood told *Esquire* writer Bob Greene.[8] *Boy's Life* started in 1911 and has survived where other boy's magazines failed because its subscriptions have been sold largely through Boy Scouts of America. Subscription rates for this

---

[7]" 'Cosmo' Style Sheet Is Out of Style," *New York,* June 8, 1981, p. 10.
[8]Bob Greene, "Boy at His Best," *Esquire,* June 1981, p. 16.

magazine must carry most of the load because advertisers are not much interested in young boys, who do not buy as much as young girls or young adults.

Sometimes magazines die, then come back again with a different editorial slant or with new owners who think they know what went wrong earlier. *Life, Look,* and *The Saturday Evening Post* all came back. *Look* gave up after a few issues.

THE BUSINESS SIDE OF MAGAZINE PUBLISHING

The business side of magazine publishing involves the solicitation and processing of advertising, the acquisition and maintenance of subscribers, the distribution of the publication, and, of course, its production, including its printing. "Magazine publishers generally recognize four, and not two, certainties in life: Death, taxes and increases in paper and postage costs," observes Michael Levy, publisher of *Texas Monthly.*

To get new subscribers, magazines often use inserts and direct-mail pieces and put ads in their own and other publications. When time to resubscribe comes along, magazines send a series of direct-mail pieces, each more urgent than the previous one. In their advertising it is necessary to appeal to people with interests that coincide with the magazine and its advertising. *Psychology Today* has done it with a full-page ad, in magazines like *Time,* that asks: "Do You Close the Bathroom Door Even When You're the Only One Home?" There follow 29 questions demanding "Yes" or "No" answers, questions like "When stopping to talk to someone on the street, do you remove your sunglasses?" and "Is the fruit you take the one about to go bad?" The more times you answer Yes to the questions, says the ad, the more likely you are to like *Psychology Today,* "a magazine that's as fascinating to read as the palm of your hand."

Successful magazines tend to launch additional publications because then they can offer package deals to advertisers. They can also buy paper at more attractive rates, and they can make more use of editorial staffs whose work can cross magazine lines. One successful magazine leads to another, and perhaps then to a book publishing concern and a book club. In recent years, the launching of specialized newsletters to take advantage of mailing lists has become popular.

Some magazines cut publishing costs by becoming arms of nonprofit educational foundations. *National Geographic, Smithsonian Magazine, Ms.,* and *Natural History* operate in this way, which carries tax and mailing-rate advantages for the magazines. Other magazines, like Ralph Ginzburg's *American Business* and *Moneysworth,* are little more than come-ons to build mailing lists for use by mail-order businesses. *The Wall Street Journal* reported that in 1979 each of the 220,000 subscribers to *American Business* received an average of 110 pieces of direct-mail advertising. "We're essentially in the mailing-list business," admitted Ginzburg, who charges very little for his magazines. "It's the list business that bails out the whole company."[9]

MAGAZINES AND MADISON AVENUE

Magazines in the United States date from Andrew Bradford's *American Magazine* (it lasted three months) and Benjamin Franklin's *General Magazine* (it lasted a little longer, six months), both started in January 1741. Not many of the early ones survived. The impetus for magazines came in the next century with the development of high-speed presses and, more important, a rapid, long-haul transportation system to provide nationwide marketing of brand-name products. The Congress, to encourage dissemination of knowledge, gave magazines an added boost when it passed on March 3, 1879, the act that set up cheap second-class rates for periodicals.

Advertising agencies refer to general circulation maga-

[9]Jeffrey H. Birnbaum, "After Eros . . . ," *The Wall Street Journal,* March 18, 1980, p. 16.

zines as *consumer publications* because of their singular importance as vehicles through which makers of popular products can reach consumers and potential consumers with appeals to buy. Such magazines exist, it is fair to say, *primarily* because they are excellent advertising media. Without revenue from advertising, these publications, with their high production costs, would have to price themselves right out of business. What subscriber would be willing to pay $100 or more for a subscription to, say, *Newsweek?*

Advertising agencies, then, through their decision as to which ones will deliver the most responsive audiences to their clients, largely decide which magazines survive and which die. To name some of the expendables: *Country Gentleman, Pathfinder, Household, Liberty, Coronet, Collier's, American Magazine, Woman's Home Companion, American Boy, Show, Show Business Illustrated, The Reporter, Look,* and the original *Saturday Evening Post* and *Life.* Recent magazines to die include *New Times, Next, Panorama, Quest, Viva,* and *Photoplay,* and the list continues.

Advertising agencies also determine how big a particular issue shall be. To make a profit, a general circulation magazine should be about two-thirds advertising. Anything less than one-half is dangerous. Just before Christmas, issues are fat because advertisers want in on the consumer buying spree. Immediately after Christmas and in mid-summer the issues are thin; it really does not pay to publish then, and some magazines double up on issues.

To better serve the advertisers, magazines in recent years have gone in for *regional* and *demographic* editions. Now it is possible for an advertiser to buy space in only copies that go to certain parts of the country—to advertise *regionally.* It is also possible in some magazines to advertise only to certain *classes* or *professions.* This means an advertiser of a specialized product can pay a lower rate and reach only persons who clearly are interested in the product. In most cases, it is only the advertising that is different in regional or demographic editions, but a few of the magazines also change editorial content.

Magazines offer advertisers a further service, split runs, by which it is possible to run two different ads in a single issue to determine (by counting coupon returns or through some other procedure) which ad is the more effective. Magazines also offer advertisers certain merchandising services, such as "seals of approval," reprints of ads in attractive poster or brochure form, and dial-a-number information on where advertised merchandise can be purchased.

Magazines, through the Magazine Publishers Association and other organizations, promote what they consider their superiority as an advertising medium. They cannot offer the huge audience of television, magazines admit, but they can offer more specialized audiences, and they can offer better printing quality than newspapers.

Research sponsored by the Magazine Publishers Association shows that magazine advertising draws more favorable reaction from consumers than television advertising does. One study shows a 25 percent difference. The same study shows that negative reaction to advertising averages 2.5 percent higher in television.[10]

A typical magazine gets half its revenue from circulation, half from advertising. A few magazines get almost all their revenues from circulation. Opinion magazines like *National Review, New Republic,* and *The Progressive* get little if any help from advertising. As a result they limp along in the red for most of their lives, helped occasionally by financial angels.

Not that the opinion magazines do not want advertising. They would accept it—most of it—if it came in. But opinion magazines strike many advertisers as poor media in which to place advertising. The magazines are controversial, their readers are not particularly product oriented, they have small circulations, and they are hard to keep track of. Advertisers can spend their money more efficiently elsewhere with less bookkeeping.

---

[10]"Consumers Like Magazine Ads 25% Better Than TV Ads," *Folio,* October 1979, p. 25.

Some of the smaller magazines band together to offer their combined circulations to advertising. For instance, *The New Republic, National Review, Foreign Affairs, World Press Review, Commentary, The New York Review of Books, Technology Review,* and *Columbia Journalism Review* belong to an organization called the Leadership Network, with a total circulation of 600,000. "We feel it is pretty hard to find a so-called opinion leader who doesn't read at least one of the magazines," says an editor at *CJR.* Advertisers buying space in at least half the magazines in the Network get a discount.

Alumni magazines at Brown, Columbia, Cornell, Dartmouth, Harvard (the *Business School Bulletin* there), Pennsylvania, Princeton, and Yale have a similar organization claiming a 1979 combined circulation of 420,000. The advertiser gets "top-flight demographics and remarkable cost-per-thousand efficiency." (The cost-per-thousand rate is based on the amount it takes to reach one thousand readers with one black-and-white page of advertising. Using this yardstick, advertisers and their agencies can compare costs of a low-circulation publication with those of a high-circulation one. Is the high-circulation publication worth the difference? Of course, cost-per-thousand measures only price, not audience responsiveness.)

UNDERSTANDING THE EDITORIAL PROCESS

Magazines carefully plan their issues three to six months or longer in advance, conjuring up ideas for articles, assigning them to staffers or regular contributors. But they still rely on ideas and unsolicited articles from freelancers.

Who are the freelancers? They are newspaper reporters who moonlight, college professors who publish lest they perish, novelists between books, housewives who write as a hobby or to supplement the family income, students in college magazine-article-writing courses, retired persons with time on their hands—all kinds of people. A few, but very few, freelance full time; they are the professionals. The Magazine

Publishers Association estimates the number in this latter category at just a few hundred.

Smaller magazines, especially, rely heavily on freelancers. A freelancer introduces an idea, usually, with a "query" to the editor; if the editor thinks the idea has merit for his magazine, he encourages the writer to go ahead with it. But the writer works "on speculation"; the editor is not obligated to buy the final product. If the article is accepted, the writer gets anywhere from a penny or two up to a dollar or more per word, depending on the magazine and the number of times the writer has sold to that magazine. The average article for one of the slicks brings the writer $2000 or $3000, and for a small magazine perhaps not more than $50 or $100. The rates have stayed pretty much the same during the past 10 years. Pay goes to the author when the article is accepted. At one time, most authors were paid only "on publication," which could be months later, or maybe not at all if the editor in the meantime lost interest in the article. Keeping freelance writers informed on changing market conditions and advising them on techniques are several trade magazines, the most important of which are *Writer's Digest* and *The Writer,* both monthlies.

Sometimes the writer is a public-relations person affiliated with a company that stands to benefit from the publication of the article, but this does not necessarily bother the magazine. It pays the writer as it would any freelancer. The magazine realizes that *every* article tends to help certain people or companies and hurt others, no matter by whom it is written; the test is, is the article of interest to the reader? Magazines, and newspapers, too, used to edit out any product or company mention, arguing that such mention was really advertising. Now editors generally take a more liberal position; if a character in the story types on an Olivetti, *let* him. "Olivetti" says more than "typewriter." If the criminal escapes in "a black Mustang," let him; "a black car" is not nearly so descriptive.

Like newspaper reporters, magazine writers get much of their information through interviewing. What prompts an interviewee to give time away, maybe valuable time, to someone writing a magazine article? Vanity is part of the answer. A desire to serve is another part. And so is the prospect of affecting people's attitudes. The person being interviewed may have an axe to grind, which means that writers must accept some of what they hear with a degree of skepticism.

Where the story or article is to appear may make a difference, as far as the interviewee is concerned. Jerry Falwell, the founder of Moral Majority, criticized Jimmy Carter for granting an interview to a writer for *Playboy* (it was the interview in which Carter admitted he had felt lust for women other than his wife). When *Penthouse,* another men's magazine, ran an interview with Falwell, the angry minister sought unsuccessfully to ban distribution of the magazine (March 1981) because the interview, he said, had been fraudulently obtained. Falwell said one of the authors involved said he was doing a book for Doubleday. The other author, Falwell understood, was doing a piece for a London newspaper. "I have never given interviews to smut magazines, nor do I practice swimming in cesspools," AP quoted Falwell as saying.

From the reader's standpoint, one of the most disturbing practices in magazine-article writing today is the putting of quotations into the mouths of the interviewees. It came out during one of the libel cases against *The Saturday Evening Post* during its "sophisticated muckraking" days in the early 1960s that one writer simply *made up* quotations because, as he explained, they were quotes that were typical of what the subject might have said. The practice has grown as magazines encourage writers to appropriate fictional techniques for nonfiction pieces. Quotes in newspaper stories are often inaccurate too, but through sloppy reporting, not usually by design.

Many magazines employ full-time fact-checkers who underline each fact in an accepted manuscript and check it with a source. Whether the manuscript is from the staff or a freelancer makes no difference. *Newsweek,* a staff-written magazine, employs 38 checkers. *Mother Jones,* not nearly so well financed, employs one. Sometimes ordinary copyreaders double as fact-checkers. Fact-checkers help magazines avoid libel suits. They also help develop the magazines as publications not given to making errors. Perhaps *The New Yorker*'s dogged checking department, the first in the industry, has been the most successful. Even the fiction in that magazine undergoes a check.[11]

Some magazines expect authors to turn in their notes, tapes, and other research effects with their articles. Some, before accepting an article for publication, obtain a warranty from the writer stating that certain legal conditions are met. The magazine does not want to be sued, so it asks the writer to guarantee that the piece is original, that the author is the sole creator of it, that it has not been previously published, and that it is not libelous.

Magazine editors and freelancers sometimes clash over editorial changes made in manuscripts. Only the author's name goes over the article, but the editor may insert words or phrases not belonging to the writer, who may end up disagreeing with what the article says. Some magazines submit any revisions to the original writer for approval, and the writer may also see galley or page proofs.

Some magazines insist on owning all rights to an article when they buy one. That means that the magazine can republish the article later or put it into a book or resell it without consulting with or paying more money to the writer. Many writers, therefore, sell only first-publication rights to their articles, which means they can resell their articles to other noncompeting markets. A single article can sell a half-dozen times. Such selling can make freelance writing profitable. Moreover, a writer doing research for an article looks for other angles and milks the original idea for several different articles on the same subject.

The editorial department where all dealings with writers go on is one of five main departments of a magazine. The

[11]Pamela Ridder, "There Are TK Fact-Checkers in the U.S.," *Columbia Journalism Review*, November/December 1980, p. 62.

EVERYONE KNOWS that drinking and driving don't mix. And it's common knowledge that alcohol is an ingredient in at least half of fatal car crashes. These simple facts lead to a simple, time-honored rule: If you drink, don't drive; if you drive, don't drink.

But many of us make the choice to break that rule, especially during holiday seasons. And once we do, the consequences are no longer simple or straightforward.

There is, for example, no distinct line between drunkenness and sobriety. Far more fatalities are caused by moderate "social" drinkers than by chronic alcoholics.

Nor is there any foolproof method for determining how much alcohol is too much for any given driver. The effects of alcohol depend upon how much you drink (quantity and strength), how much you weigh, the type and quantity of food you have in your stomach, what kind of mood you're in, and the length of time you wait before getting behind the wheel of your car.

By plotting these factors on a graph, it is possible to determine whether or not you are illegally under the influence of alcohol.

DRINKER'S CHOICE

While these calculations may help you avoid arrest, they won't guarantee a safe trip home.

Once alcohol is in your system, only one thing will remove it — time. Contrary to popular belief, black coffee, fresh air or a cold shower cannot sober you up. The liver dissipates alcohol through oxidation, a process which occurs at a fairly constant rate and cannot be artificially stimulated. According to the National Safety Council, the body needs at least one hour to burn off an average drink.

Thus, if you want to drive as safely as possible, you have only two options. Either don't drink at all, or drink, then wait. The choice is yours.

Standard Oil Company of California prepared this "house ad" for the back cover of its company magazine for employees. The artist was Mas Miyamoto.   (*Source:* The *Standard Oiler,* Standard Oil Company of California.)

others are advertising, circulation, production, and administration. On a large magazine, according to the Magazine Publishers Association, about 8 percent of the budget goes to the editorial department, and on a small magazine, about 17 percent.

Many magazines operate with only a few people. A staff made up of only a half dozen would not be unusual. A newsmagazine staff may employ hundreds. *Boy's Life,* with a circulation of about 1.5 million, employs a staff of 23.

Job titles and responsibilities vary greatly on magazines, but on the editorial side of many, two people stand out, the

Two styles of art greatly influenced magazine design as they be-
came more visually oriented after the turn of the century, art
nouveau, left, and art deco. Art nouveau, as in this example from
The Studio magazine of England, was flowery and decorative.
Art deco was geometric and decorative. This example is from
Original Art Deco Designs by William Rowe (New York: Dover
Publications, 1973), a source of copyright-free illustrations for
publications and advertisements.

editor and the art director. The role of the art director has
only recently taken on great importance. The art director
("design director" would be a better term) decides on what
kind of art to use and puts it together with textual matter
and display type (type used for titles, headings, etc.), striving
for beauty and impact and at the same time keeping things
readable. The bigger magazines have a number of lesser editors who are in charge of special sections. *Ms.* has an unusual
arrangement, at least according to the masthead. There are
no chief editors, just listings of people under such headings
as "Editing," "Editorial Research," "Design," and "Copy and
Production." Very democratic, but some would argue that
that is no way to run a magazine.

Unlike newspapers, most magazines do not have their
own printing facilities, although many these days are doing
their typesetting "in house," and the pasteup of the magazine's pages is often done at the editorial offices. The pages
then go outside to a printer, sometimes to one in a far-away
city.

THE BIG ONES

When the original *Saturday Evening Post* announced in 1968 that it was cutting its 6.8 million circulation by more than half, readers not familiar with the economics of journalism shook their heads in disbelief. Why would a magazine want to do it? Was it not a magazine's main function to build a huge circulation so it could charge high rates to advertisers? What about the circulation wars of the 1950s, when magazines, competing with television for mass audiences, cajoled, begged, twisted arms, and made sweet deals to gain more and more subscribers, when their circulations went up from three to five to eight million and beyond?

The truth was that the *Post* had been unable to match the circulations of *Life* and *Look* (each with about eight million). Nor were advertisers willing to go with an also-ran when for just a few dollars more they could buy space in the bigger books. The *Post* had to move in some other direction.

What the *Post* action really showed was that the magazine world had undergone a rather dramatic change. The age of specialization had caught up with it. There had always been specialized magazines, of course (the trade journals, religious magazines, science magazines, literary quarterlies, etc.), but now even *general circulation* magazines were operating in narrower fields, digging deep rather than wide. They were appealing to readers with similar, intense interests. Readers wanted such treatment. More important, advertisers demanded it.

The *Post,* after decades of domination over middle-class America, could not, in the mid twentieth century, adjust to a new society.[12] It revolutionized itself, both in content and format, in the early 1960s, but the change only alienated a hard-core, old-line following without convincing advertisers and younger readers that the magazine mattered. So now the *Post* was dropping all pretenses of serv-

---

[12]*The Saturday Evening Post* claimed Benjamin Franklin as its founder, but magazine historian Frank Luther Mott showed the claim was farfetched.

ing everybody and was directing itself to a select group of "with it" readers. "Our circulation is at an all-time low," bragged the magazine in one of its ads to advertising agencies. "Why? Because *The Saturday Evening Post* has made a publishing decision based squarely on marketing considerations. By reducing circulation, *The Saturday Evening Post* now delivers the better part of 3,000,000 customer-families precisely in the A and B markets where advertisers account for the bulk of their sales."

Essentially it bought off rural and small-town subscribers by switching them to other magazines, giving them refunds, or not inviting them to resubscribe. It was not the first time a magazine had voluntarily given up readers. *Farm Journal* earlier had pruned its nonfarm subscribers because implement manufacturers and others felt they were wasting their money advertising to them. *True Confessions* and *Motion Picture* eliminated all regular subscribers to go strictly to newsstand circulation. But, because it was such an important American institution for so many years, the *Post* move stirred the country. In one of his columns Art Buchwald dealt with an imaginary family whose subscription was cancelled. "If this gets out we'll be ruined," cried the man of the house, a lawyer. "They seemed like such nice people," one of the neighbors remarked later. The bank refused the man a loan; the gasoline company failed to renew his credit card; clients deserted him. His child came home from school with the tale: "They said my father was a *Saturday Evening Post* deadbeat." The family at last moved to another town and resubscribed under a different name, but the father lived in fear he would one day be found out. Observed Buchwald: "When you're dropped by the *Saturday Evening Post,* you have no choice but to live a lie for the rest of your life."

But the *Post*'s attempt to change from a mass to a class magazine came too late, and with its February 8, 1969 issue the magazine gave up. "The *Post*'s frenzy of rejuvenation was really a dance of death," observed *Time.* Stewart Alsop, who had left the *Post* when he saw it dying, observed in a column in *Newsweek:* "It was television that killed the *Post,* though television had a good many willing little helpers, in and out of the Curtis Publishing Co."[13]

Its remaining circulation went over mostly to *Life*, which then surged ahead of *Look*, but *Life* was having problems of its own. It died later. So did *Look*. All three magazines tried to make comebacks, but only the *Post* and *Life* succeeded, and they are not quite the magazines they used to be.

One magazine that survived the changes brought about by television is *Reader's Digest*. DeWitt Wallace, who died in 1981 at age 91, and Lila Bell Acheson, his wife, founded the magazine in 1922 in a Greenwich Village basement, using $5000 in borrowed money. A year later he moved the magazine to Pleasantville, a New York suburb with a name suitable to the magazine's content. The *Digest* grew rapidly, inspiring many imitators, but few lasted long enough to give the *Digest* any serious competition. At the time of Wallace's death, *Reader's Digest* enjoyed a circulation of 30.5 million in a total of 163 countries and was published in 16 languages. Its circulation in the United States came to 17.9 million, not far behind *Parade* and *TV Guide*, both weeklies. The *Digest* comes out monthly.

It was not until 1955 that the *Digest* began accepting advertising, after a survey of readers asking whether they preferred seeing advertising or paying higher subscription rates. At first there were no liquor or cigarette ads, but gradually the magazine relaxed its rules on liquor ads. It is not likely ever to carry cigarette ads because it has been persistent in telling of the harm cigarettes do.

DeWitt Wallace's original idea was to take articles from other magazines, boil them down, and present them—about 30 each issue—in a simple, convenient format. Gradually, as some magazines began withholding reprint rights and Wal-

[13]For insiders' looks at the last days of *The Saturday Evening Post* see Otto Friedrich's *Decline and Fall* (New York: Harper & Row, 1970); Matthew J. Culligan's *The Curtis-Culligan Story* (New York: Crown, 1970); and Martin S. Ackerman's *The Curtis Affair* (Los Angeles: Nash Publishing, 1970). See also the novel by Clay Blair, Jr., *The Board Room* (New York: Dutton 1969).

DeWitt Wallace, with his wife Lila Bell Acheson, founded *Reader's Digest* in 1922 after several established publishers rejected the idea of a digest magazine. He played an important role in running the popular magazine until his retirement in 1973. *(Source:* Fabian Bachrach. Courtesy *The Reader's Digest.)*

lace found too few articles coinciding with his own rather conservative ideals, he began developing articles on his own, "planting" them in other publications, and then picking them up for reprinting. Then the magazine started running originals along with the reprints. The magazine does not now fit fully the "digest" designation. As one of the nation's most attractive if hard-to-crack markets for freelance writers, the *Digest* is swamped with contributions.

One of the best-known articles ever published anywhere was a *Digest* original that Wallace assigned to J. C. Furnas in 1935: "—And Sudden Death," with its vivid descriptions of mangled bodies and twisted automobiles, made a strong plea for safe driving. Reprints went out everywhere. Probably no other magazine article had been so widely promoted.

In updated versions, the article continues to appear from
time to time in other publications.

In *Little Wonder,* an amusing and disrespectful book
about the *Digest,* John Bainbridge cited three reasons for the
success of the magazine:

1. The articles are simple. Any high school student can under-
    stand them.
2. They are dogmatic. Bainbridge, in 1948, when he wrote
    the book, suggested the dogma was becoming more pro-
    nounced. He cited someone as saying the *Digest* was suf-
    fering from "hardening of the articles."
3. The articles are optimistic. *Through science and hard
    work, we can solve any problem* is a recurring theme.

David Ogilvy, the advertising man, has praised the *Digest* for its ability "to present complicated subjects in a way
that engages the reader." He calls the magazine a crusader.
"They [the editors] crusade against cigarettes, which kill people. They crusade against billboards, which make the world
hideous. They crusade against boxing, which turns men into
vegetables. They crusade against pornography. They crusade
for integration, for inter-faith movement, for the Public De-
fender system, for human freedom in all its forms."

He adds: "Some highbrows may look down their noses
at the *Digest,* charging it with superficiality and over-
simplification. There is a modicum of justice in this charge;
you can learn more about the Congo if you read about it in
Foreign Affairs Quarterly. But have you time?"

The popularity of the magazine does not extend to intellectuals who, able to side with the magazine on some of these
crusades, nevertheless distrust it, partly because they prefer
all articles in their original form but mainly because they detect a bias against, among other things, government programs to solve social and economic problems. And of course
they do not accept Ogilvy's contention that complicated issues can be explained, successfully, in simple terms. But
praise for the magazine from time to time comes from unexpected sources. Susan Sontag, an intellectual and a writer

with solid liberal credentials, told a gathering in 1982 that "a steady reader of the *Reader's Digest* [over the years] would have gotten a better sense of 'the reality of Communism' than a steady reader of, yes, *The Nation.*"[14]

In late 1981 *Reader's Digest,* after much planning and testing, launched *Families,* a magazine that, as one executive put it, took off from where *Parents* magazine stops. The new magazine was for a slightly younger audience than *Reader's Digest* appeals to. Around the *Digest* offices, as the magazine evolved and before it took its name, people referred to it as *Breeder's Digest.* Families lasted only a few months.

One of the most widely circulated magazines in the United States—up to 20 million copies a week—is devoted to another medium, television. The magazine is *TV Guide,* and much of what it contains is also carried in local newspaper listings. The magazine started in 1953, when television was new. John J. O'Connor, television/radio critic for the *New York Times,* sees the magazine as one containing, in addition to its program listings, "generous servings of trivia sprinkled sporadically with crumbs of substance."[15] But the magazine has not acted merely as a promoter of TV. It has also acted from time to time as a critic of mundane programming. In recent years, especially, it has published thought-provoking pieces by known writers. Some of its articles have appeared in book collections.

It has been estimated that nearly a third of the households in the United States use *TV Guide.* One of its virtues is its compactness. The listings vary from edition to edition, of course, but the articles that wrap around the listings stay the same for a given issue. For a full-color ad on one of *TV Guide*'s small pages, a company—if it wants exposure in all 94 editions—pays more than $61,000. Ad revenues are higher than for any other magazine.

[14]Quoted by D. Keith Mano in "The Strange Agony of Susan Sontag," *National Review,* April 16, 1982, p. 439.
[15]John J. O'Connor, "Sprinkle with Crumbs and Serve," *Columbia Journalism Review,* November/December 1978, p. 55.

In 1979, the magazine with the biggest U.S. circulation was *Parade,* the weekly syndicated Sunday newspaper supplement. It had a circulation of 21.8 million if the circulation of all its newspaper clients is counted.

One of the real magazine success stories of the 1970s involved *People,* which made "personality journalism" popular. By 1979 *People,* a weekly, found itself in fifth place among magazines in the number of advertising pages it carried. Its 2.3 million circulation pushed it past *Sports Illustrated.*

Where most big new magazines take five years or more to operate at a profit, *People* was doing it in a year and a half. *Us* and various imitators came out, a couple of popular TV shows took a "people" approach, and other magazines stepped up their gossip content and ran more personality sketches. Like most of the newer magazines, *People* directed itself to readers in their twenties and early thirties, because in our society they are the willing-to-spend people most advertisers want to reach.

THE NEWSMAGAZINES

With the idea that in their day-to-day operations newspapers were not able to put the news into proper perspective and that they were too much wedded to the idea of objectivity, Henry Luce and Briton Hadden in 1923 brought out the first issue of *Time,* the weekly newsmagazine. The first issues carried mostly rewritings from the *New York Times* and the wire services, but a saucy if too-cute style freshened the material. Wolcott Gibbs ridiculed *Time* style later in a *New Yorker* piece: "Backward ran sentences until reeled the mind"; and, because its writers could no longer use the style with a straight face, *Time* gave it up. Still, the magazine remained lively and fact-filled.

Dwight Macdonald felt that the magazine had an "obsession with factual trivia." "A huge and expensive research department produces a weekly warehouseful of certified, pasteurized, 100 percent double-checked Facts," he said, "and everything is accurate about any given article except its main points." He added: "As smoking gives us something to do with our hands when we aren't using them, *Time* gives us something to do with our minds when we aren't thinking."

In recent years, *Time* has made moves to respond to charges raised by critics like Dwight Macdonald. It launched

Henry Luce was perhaps the most important magazine innovator of this century. With Briton Hadden, he founded *Time* in 1923. Later he founded *Fortune, Life,* and *Sports Illustrated.* (*Source:* Alfred Eisenstadt, *Life* Magazine, © Time Inc.)

its weekly "Time Essay," a well-researched and well-reasoned discussion of current problems. And where it used to crowd 200 different stories in a single issue, it now runs half as many, but runs them in greater depth.

Some people feel that the magazine's back-of-the-book section is better than the front. In special departments there *Time* is less anxious to impose its point of view on readers. Professional people whose fields are covered consider the departments too popular, too simplistic, but the average reader finds them informative.

One of the most successful promotional ideas for any magazine has been *Time*'s "Man of the Year" cover. To watch the build-up for this in the letters column at the close of each year is to watch public relations in its finest hour. How so many people could give so much credence to so trivial an event—what a magazine will put on its first cover of the year—is a mystery perhaps even to *Time* itself. Someone has likened *Time*'s handling of the process to a person contemplating his own navel.

Time easily dominated the newsmagazine scene until the 1960s, when *Newsweek* revitalized itself to become "the hot book," appealing more to younger readers. Advertisers liked the lively editorial base it provided. More than *Time*, *Newsweek* covered the social changes of the time, becoming, in the process, a bit trendy. *Newsweek* never quite reached *Time*'s circulation, and in the late 1970s *Time* adopted a new, modern dress and seemed to grow stronger.

The third newsmagazine, *U.S. News & World Report*, capitalizes on its plainness with an advertising campaign directed to both readers and advertisers. The campaign boasts of a no-nonsense approach to the news.

All three newsmagazines have moved away from the anonymous writing that had characterized them in the past. The magazines run signed pieces giving credit, often, to both writers and researchers. *Newsweek* features a number of regular columnists. Often the magazines show the same people or events on their covers, understandable when you consider the desire of magazine people to keep up with the times, and the attitudes of news people about what deserves the best display. David Shaw, writing in the *Los Angeles Times* in 1980, noted that in 1973, during the Watergate scandals, *Time* and *Newsweek* had basically the same covers 23 times, an average of once every other week.

QUALITY MAGAZINES

Much material of quality appears on the pages of the big slicks. With all their resources, they offer readers some of the best-researched, best-illustrated, most worthwhile, most brilliantly written articles on both historical and contemporary subjects available anywhere. This section puts certain other magazines under the "quality" heading only because their articles are more consistently significant. At the least, the "quality" magazines appeal to a generally better educated audience.

We start with one that is unique, *The New Yorker*, not edited, as they say, for the old lady in Dubuque. Patterned in some respects after the British *Punch* and started in 1925 by Harold Ross as a magazine for The City, *The New Yorker*, after a few years of uncertainty, rose to become one of the most successful magazine properties of all time. And yet, it has purposely held its circulation at about a half million, 16 times less than that of any of the big ones.

For all its affluence, *The New Yorker* has always been a socially conscious publication, and without being stuffy. This is the magazine that regularly gave us such writers as James Thurber, E. B. White, and Robert Benchley. It was one of the first magazines to devote a whole issue to a single subject: John Hersey's article on Hiroshima.

Journalism professors go to the reporting in *The New Yorker* for examples of the art of interviewing at its finest. They like the hard-to-find combination of accuracy and a casual style. English teachers point to the stories, although perhaps not as often now as formerly, as models to go by. The "profiles" have greatly influenced all magazines in their handling of personality sketches. There is a relaxed quality about them. Writers interview enemies of the subject as well as his friends, and sometimes a writer doesn't interview the subject at all.

The look of the magazine is remarkably subdued. Editorial matter seems to be wrapped around the ads as a means of separating them from each other. Any graphic beauty in the book comes from the full-color ads. This is one reason advertisers are comfortable in *The New Yorker*. They fight no visual competition.

Nor does the magazine have any sacred cows. It ridicules anyone, anything—including its own advertising. Readers seem to particularly enjoy the cartoons and the back-of-the-book fillers such as "Most Fascinating News Story of the Week," "Words of One Syllable Dept.," and "Our Own Business Directory."[16]

The magazine recently has become more militant, with a leftist slant. Some of the front matter sounds like something out of *The Nation* or *The New Republic*. Some of the world's most honored writers appear on its pages, and the articles and stories they write often appear later as best-selling or at least favorably reviewed books. Editor William Shawn claims to edit the magazine "for ourselves" rather than to guess what the readers would want, which gives it a personality and integrity it would not have otherwise. "But in editing it for ourselves," Shawn says, "we have the profoundest respect for the reader. We don't think of him being a different kind of creature [from ourselves]."[17]

Unlike other magazines, *The New Yorker* gives full authority to the editor, not to editorial committees. That makes it more tightly run than other magazines. Still, writers who contribute or who work as staff members enjoy considerable

---

[16]The three biographies of Harold Ross tell much about what gave the magazine its unique character: Dale Kramer, *Ross and The New Yorker* (Garden City, N.Y.: Doubleday, 1951); James Thurber, *The Years With Ross* (Boston; Little, Brown, 1959); and Jane Grant, *Ross, The New Yorker and Me* (New York: William Morrow, 1968).

[17]Jane Perlez, "William Shawn: A Man for All Seasons," *Washington Journalism Review*, September/October 1979, p. 67.

Harold Ross founded *The New Yorker* in 1925 and served as its editor until his death in 1951. Although a high school dropout, Ross produced a highly successful and sophisticated magazine celebrated for its literary quality, solid journalism, and humor. *(Source: The New Yorker.)*

freedom in expressing themselves. It is their facts—and their usage of the language—that must stand up to close scrutiny. *The New Yorker* sets a standard for other magazines in its checking procedures. Its reputation for infallibility faltered briefly in the late 1970s when a quote charged that a famous restaurant served turbot that was frozen (it was not true) and a review was shown to be partly plagiarized.

It is by no means merely a city magazine. About 80 percent of the circulation of the magazine is outside New York City. Unlike other slick magazines loved by advertisers, it publishes but one edition.

Two other magazines easily belong in the "quality" category. *Harper's* and *The Atlantic,* similar in content and fairly even in circulation, are allied in the sale of advertising space, but are independent otherwise. Westbrook Pegler used to call them "Doubledome" and "Deepthink."

Harper and Brothers, the book publishing concern, launched a monthly magazine in 1850 to keep its presses busy when they were not being used for printing books and to serve as an advertising medium to sell them. It would be correct to say that *Harper's Magazine* was in its beginnings a house organ (company magazine). *Harper's Weekly,* the illustrated journal featuring the work of Thomas Nast, among others, was launched seven years later. The monthly publication devoted itself primarily to the work of English authors, as did the parent company, and in those early years the magazine was primarily literary. Only in our century did it change its emphasis to nonfiction.

While *Harper's* is based in New York, *The Atlantic* (founded in 1857) is a Boston magazine, and the New England influence, once marked, is still felt. Also more journalistic now than literary, it remains more concerned with literature and the arts than *Harper's,* which tends somewhat to emphasize the social sciences. Neither magazine is afraid of controversy. *The Atlantic* is the magazine that created a stir in late 1981 with an article carrying quotes from David Stockman, head of the Office of Management and Budget, that greatly embarrassed the Reagan administration.

In an ad selling itself to potential readers, *Harper's* describes itself as *"not* the magazine you think it is." It is "neither Liberal nor Conservative, left nor right, Democrat nor Republican. The magazine is a forum for writers with intelligent and authoritative opinions, whatever position they take." The ad said that *Harper's* differs from *The Atlantic* with its "belle-lettres" approach, from *Saturday Review* with its "short takes," and from *Esquire* with its "advice for the young man about town."

Founded in 1924 as the *Saturday Review of Literature, Saturday Review* for many years served only as a book-review medium, then branched out to include articles and columns on cultural, social, political, and even scientific matters. Norman Cousins served twice as its editor, taking over a second time in 1973 after a couple of promoters ran it into bankruptcy with their trendy approach. It went through several ownerships and editorships before suspending publication in 1982. There were hopes that someone would come along to revive it.

MAGAZINES BY SEX

Society of late has played down the differences between the sexes, but certain magazines are still edited to appeal only to women or only to men.

The first newspapers and some of the first magazines automatically excluded women. Everything was written from the man's point of view. The women could not vote, anyway; there was no need to keep them informed or to mold their opinions. Gradually, separate sections evolved in which women found advice on such topics as how to run the home better. In the mid 1800s came their first important magazine: *Godey's Lady's Book,* which, after half a century of eminence, gave way to the *Ladies' Home Journal.* Late in the 1950s, when circulation battles among women's magazines reached a fever pitch, the *Journal* fell behind *McCall's.*

The upsurge of *McCall's* was remarkable. Way behind in the circulation race, in the mid 1950s it had adopted the idea of "Togetherness," attempting to serve the entire family. But this theme, merrily punctured by columnists and cartoonists, soon withered, and a new editor, Herbert Mayes, in 1958 turned the magazine completely around. It took on a new sophistication, both in content and format. Soon it was number one among women's magazines. Like *Ladies' Home Journal,* it broadened its interests to include politics and social problems.

Not that the women's magazines completely gave up their alliance with trivia. More than other media, they lent dignity to the astrology craze of the late 1960s, treating "as established fact the notion that stars and planets influence people's lives." A *Ladies' Home Journal* article provided, in its words, "a completely original way for you to discover your secret self, and the influence of stars on your life."[18] Several of the women's magazines ran regular horoscopes.

In *The Lady Persuaders* (1960) Helen Woodward documented a case against the women's magazines that they relied rather shamelessly on veiled but sensationalized sex— "sex with a false face," she called it—in the frightening late 1940s (television was coming on the scene) and the frantic 1950s, with such titles (from the *Ladies' Home Journal*) as these: "Chastity and Syphilis," "I Love My Husband's Best Friend" (doesn't that belong in *True Confessions?*), and "I'm Tempted to Have an Affair." She credits *Good Housekeeping* and the grocery-store–circulated women's magazines (*Family Circle* and *Woman's Day*) with staying above the battle.

Women's magazines returned to an emphasis on sex at the end of the 1960s, as what magazine did not? As one writer put it:

> Even the most casual study of women's magazines—from *Seventeen* at one end of the age scale to *Ladies' Home Journal* at the other—reveals an almost frantic attempt on the part of editors to get with the sexual revolution, the new permissiveness,

[18]Mervin Block, "Flapdoodle Writ Large: Astrology in Magazines," *Columbia Journalism Review,* Summer, 1969, pp. 51–54.

call it what you will, that manifests itself these days in advertising, motion pictures, television, and best-selling novels with sex and perversion as the themes.[19]

Perhaps the best illustration of this trend is Helen Gurley Brown's *Cosmopolitan,* a magazine which almost wholly gave itself over to sex—for the single girl.

As the women's magazines flourished and as the general audience magazines began devoting more of their space to women, it was inevitable that magazines edited especially for men would appear. In this category we can place the nude-picture magazines and the adventure magazines at one end and *Esquire* at the other.

Started during the Depression years as a fashion magazine with literary pretensions, *Esquire* slipped into something flimsy to titillate World War II servicemen, but in the early 1950s it decided, in the words of Publisher Arnold Gingrich, "to buck the juvenile, high schoolish direction we had been following." At first the magazine lost readers, but it also gained back some of its blue-chip advertisers. In the 1960s and early 1970s *Esquire* ranked among the best magazines in the world for innovation and quality writing, and, with many women readers, it more properly fit the *quality* than the *men's* category.

"One of the beauties of the magazine," Gingrich said, "is its diversity of style. I adhere to an old adage with a personal alteration: 'He who edits least, edits best.' " This made for a magazine of some inconsistency, but it also attracted important writers who did not like their work tampered with and who were willing to write for *Esquire* at rates that were considerably below what they got from other magazines.

The covers were always intriguing, and, like so much of the content, boldly irreverent. The article titles differed from those of any other magazine. The editors followed no rules in writing those titles, and space did not bother them. Take

[19]Peter T. Chew, "Women's Magazines Dig New Ground," *The National Observer,* June 23, 1969, p. 1.

this one for an article critical of newspapers (*Esquire* often ran articles on the mass media): "The American Newspaper Is Neither Record, Mirror, Journal, Ledger, Bulletin, Telegram, Examiner, Register, Chronicle, Gazette, Observer, Monitor, Transcript Nor Herald of the Day's Events. It's Just Bad News." In a lead article about *Esquire, The Wall Street Journal* in 1968 remarked: "Sometimes, the articles are as good as the titles." The *Journal* expressed admiration of *Esquire* because the magazine was "ideologically uncommitted" and therefore "freer than most magazines to support unpopular people and causes and to knock the unknockables."

Like other magazines, *Esquire* had its mundane service features on fashion, travel, food, but these, along with the reviews, were much better than most. Its gimmick features struck some readers as sophomoric, like the "Establishment Charts" showing who's in and who's out. And there was that feature, "The 100 Best People in the World." But perhaps *Esquire* had its tongue in its cheek.

Lately *Esquire* has faced tough times and undergone ownership changes.

Some people consider *Playboy* in a class with the earlier *Esquire.* It runs some excellent articles and some fiction by well-known writers, and some of its Q. and A. interviews are notable. While it is true that *Playboy* has improved since its peeping-Tom start in 1953 as the idea of Hugh Hefner, who still owns it, it remains basically a well-designed "skin" magazine.

The name of the magazine alone is enough to keep it penned in its hedonism. Further, how can one give serious consideration to a magazine that runs ads for its own products like the one that urges "Smoke the Pipe That Hef Smokes" or that runs a feature like "The Playboy Adviser"? Sample question: "I was in Philadelphia on business, and I found myself strongly attracted to a girl I met at a cocktail party. I would like to know if it's acceptable to write her and ask for a date." *Playboy* assured the reader it would be all right. Another feature, "The Playboy Forum," prolonged for years a tedious series on "The Playboy Philosophy," which, judging from the response, many otherwise thoughtful people took seriously. Kyle Haselden, late editor of the liberal *Christian Century* felt that *Playboy* was "more obscene and more threatening to authentic morality than is much of what we call pornography . . . because . . . [it] preaches a fundamentally dishonest doctrine of sex, of womanhood, and of the highest good of life."[20] He quoted Ralph A. Cannon as saying that *Playboy* "panders to juvenile fascination with sexual trivia while calling itself sophisticated." Mike Royko, the columnist, questions Hugh Hefner's claim that he and his magazine are responsible for the sexual revolution in America. "It wasn't his magazine and his incomprehensible philosophical babbling that changed [America's attitudes]," Royko wrote in a 1978 column. "It was something known as 'the pill'."

Playboy lived through hard times in the 1970s, when it turned more raunchy to meet the competition that had sprung up and when drug use and an inner-circle suicide rocked the staff. The aggressive *Penthouse* proved to be especially strong competitor. With the fuss created by a girl-with-popcorn cover in November 1975 *Playboy* did a turnaround to become more generally acceptable. *Advertising Age* in 1982 observed that *Playboy* had gone "from smut to smarts." Hefner's daughter Christine has played a major role in running the magazine recently.

Playboy has enjoyed its share of headlines, as when in a long interview it quoted Jimmy Carter as saying that he had, in his heart, lusted after women and when, later, it had Edward Koch making disparaging remarks about rural and suburban living. When the Koch remarks were published, the embarrassed New York mayor, who could not deny making them, was making a run at the governorship and needed votes from outside New York City. He had some explaining to do.

The economy of the early 1980s made things difficult for

[20]Kyle Haselden, *Morality and the Mass Media* (Nashville, Tenn.: Broadman Press, 1968), p. 106.

all magazines, but the Big Seven among women's magazines and "shelter" magazines—*Ladies' Home Journal, McCall's, Good Housekeeping, Redbook, Family Circle, Woman's Day,* and *Better Homes and Gardens*—seemed especially hard hit. Advertising fell off for all but *Good Housekeeping.* Interest in these magazines waned, apparently, because they continued to serve women in the traditional mold. Some called the magazines old-fashioned. The fashion-oriented women's magazines—*Vogue, Glamour,* and *Mademoiselle*—seemed to be in better shape. With their racier articles, they had moved in the direction of *Cosmopolitan.*[21] The wave of the future appeared to involve magazines more interested in the liberated woman. *Ms.* started the trend in the early 1970s. *Self* and *New Woman,* relatively new, also set out to appeal more to working and professional women than to housewives. *Savvy,* with its contemporary look and feel, aimed for professional and executive women.

[21]Philip Nobile, "Worry Lines at the Women's Magazines," *New York,* May 18, 1981, pp. 19–20.

Chapter 8
Magazines
That Specialize

It is hard to imagine an American interest group, organized or not, that does not have its own magazine, or several of its own magazines. Take military magazines. There are hundreds of them. To name only two, *Army Reserve* goes to 585,000 subscribers bimonthly, and *Ladycom* goes to 400,000 military wives. All the veteran's organizations have magazines, too.

Musicians can turn to such magazines as *International Musician, Music Journal, Virtuoso, Accent, The Instrumentalist,* and *Music Educators Journal.* Narrowing the field down, piano teachers can turn to *Clavier,* piano players to

Contemporary Keyboard, guitar players to *Guitar Player,* drummers to *Modern Drummer.*

America's renewed interest in health and fitness has given new life to magazines like *Let's Live, Life & Health,* and *Prevention,* and encouraged the launching of several new ones. *American Health,* to get in on the health and fitness boom, made its debut in 1982. One of its competitors was *Health,* which had earlier incorporated *Today's Health* and *Family Health.*

A few magazines are beginning to devote themselves to the older crowd, which has been referred to as "the fastest growing generation." About time, too—advertisers have discovered that not only is the average age of Americans rising each year, but also the spendable income at advanced ages is worth tapping.

The biweekly *Advocate,* to name another specialized publication, calls itself "America's leading gay newsmagazine." In its promotion, the magazine claims that homosexuals are "the most affluent of any minority," hence good prospects for advertisers.[1]

Henry Fairlie, writing in the *Washington Post* from his British perspective, sees American newsstands as reflecting "the tastes of a population who as individuals have only the very narrowest interests and concerns." The rise of narrow-interest magazines, he points out, coincides with the rise of "single-interest" politics in which people vote for candidates almost solely on the basis of how they stand on a given issue. For instance, a gun lover might vote against a candidate who is "wrong" on gun registration even though that candidate is "right" on all other issues.

The general-interest magazines that survive, like *People,* run only short articles, realizing that most readers these days do not have the attention spans of yesterday. Largely gone are the 4000-word and longer articles that the old *Saturday Evening Post* and other magazines used to run. A few lesser-

[1]"Gays: A Major Force in the Marketplace," *Business Week,* September 3, 1979, pp. 118, 120.

known magazines hang on, however, to provide a place for the longer, more thoughtful articles that used to occupy a bigger place in American journalism.

OPINION MAGAZINES

At the end of the Civil War an Irish journalist, E. L. Godkin, in America to write about the South and slavery, founded *The Nation,* an independent weekly for intellectuals. An early issue said the magazine intended to "bring to the discussion of political and social questions a really critical spirit, and to wage war upon the vices of violence, exaggeration, and misrepresentation by which so much of the political writing of this day is marred."[2] In 1881 it merged with the *New York Evening Post.* It became an independent magazine again in 1918, a time when political activists and reformers were launching a number of opinion magazines.

The slicks had discovered at the turn of the century that they could increase their circulations by investigating and reporting corruption in government and business. The magazines, called "muckrakers" by Theodore Roosevelt, who was something of a "muckraker" himself, brought some reform and changed the lives of a few industrialists. But within a few years, fattened on their swollen circulations and increased advertising linage, they moved to safer ground, leaving a void that a number of new magazines moved in to fill. We know these as *opinion magazines. The Nation* was their prototype.

Not that opinion magazines have any corner on opinion in journalism. The editorial page is the heart of most newspapers, general circulation magazines have always offered some opinion to their readers, and some magazines run editorial pages. *Reader's Digest* and the women's magazines are filled with opinion. But readers do not buy slick magazines for the opinions they carry; they buy them to relax with.

[2]Quoted by Theodore Peterson in *Magazines in the Twentieth Century,* 2nd ed. (Urbana: University of Illinois Press, 1964), p. 419.

Readers buy opinion magazines so they can agonize over national and world problems. They buy them to reinforce their already rather firmly held convictions.

Opinion magazines lead a precarious existence. One that died was *The Masses,* which has been described as "one of the most remarkable ventures in the history of American journalism."[3] Combining art with radical editorials and articles, it claimed to be a magazine for the working man, but it was far too literary for that. Starkly realistic drawings, displayed on its oversize pages, influenced art in other magazines. Irving Howe remembers the magazine for both its "gaiety" and "innocence." Its antidraft stand brought its editors to court, and though they were not convicted, the magazine died in 1918, to be succeeded by the *Liberator,* which became a Communist Party organ in the 1920s. *The New Masses* succeeded the *Liberator,* and it preached a Stalinist line in the 1930s.[4]

The *American Mercury,* a magazine started by George Jean Nathan and H. L. Mencken in the 1920s, similarly attacked middle-class values, but it had less faith in the common people to solve their problems. Condescending, irascible, and highly readable, the magazine became a sort of bible on campuses. In 1926 Walter Lippmann called Mencken "the most powerful personal influence on this whole generation of educated people." The *Mercury*'s skepticism turned to reaction in the 1930s, and the magazine lost its following among intellectuals.

From the standpoint of circulation, *The Reporter,* founded in 1949, was the most successful of all the opinion magazines. A biweekly, it sold well and was slick enough to find space on many newsstands. (Other opinion magazines circulate almost entirely by mail.) *The Reporter* was a liberal but strongly anticommunist biweekly. Max Ascoli, its found-

---

[3]William L. O'Neill, ed., *Echoes of Revolt: The Masses,* 1911–1917 (Chicago: Quadrangle Books, 1966), p. 17.
[4]See Joseph North, ed., *New Masses: An Anthology of the Rebel Thirties* (New York: International Publishers, 1969).

er-editor, strove to make it "objective but not impartial." His was a magazine widely admired for its reporting in depth. One of the early issues, on the "China lobby," created a sensation in Washington. Later issues took too hawkish a line on the Vietnam War to satisfy many of its liberal readers.

While other liberal magazines in the 1960s moved further to the left, *The Reporter* maintained a more traditional liberal stance, siding with President Lyndon Johnson when it was no longer popular among liberals to do so. The magazine lost increasing sums of money, and Ascoli appeared to lose interest in running it, so with the June 13, 1968, issue he killed it, even though it had a circulation of 210,000, more than any of the other opinion magazines. *Newsweek* quoted him as saying he might have kept the magazine alive if Johnson had remained in the presidential race.

The slickest yet shrillest of the opinion magazines was *Ramparts,* originally published in San Francisco, later published in Berkeley. It started in 1964 as an intellectual Catholic quarterly, but, said founder Edward Keating, "There weren't as many independent Catholic intellectuals as I had thought."[5] It went secular, became a monthly, and moved further to the left. "There is nothing in American journalism quite like *Ramparts,*" a *National Observer* writer said in 1967.

One of the editors, Warren Hinckle III, once pointed out that the magazine tended to be kinder to the right wing than to the liberal center. "The right wing will at least debate the issues even though their solutions may be simplistic and primitive. But the liberals won't even talk about them."

It made its biggest impact when it uncovered CIA activities in universities and youth organizations in early 1967. The story was so hot it couldn't wait, and so *Ramparts* took out full-page ads in the *New York Times* and the *Washington Post* to tell it.

---

[5]Keating and the editors fought over money matters. The board of directors in 1967 fired Keating as publisher after he had pumped $860,000 into the magazine.

Its editors maintained they did not define their audience and then go out after it, as the slicks do; they edited the magazine for themselves. Partly through the promotional efforts of the late Howard Gossage, the magazine was able to build its circulation up to nearly a quarter of a million copies, but it spent wildly and soon died.

Hinckle left *Ramparts* in 1970 to launch a new magazine in New York, *Scanlan's,* which, after a big splash, found an unenthusiastic reception even among leftists who would be expected to applaud it. Peter Steinfels in *Commonweal* called it "an average blend of New Journalism and underground-press styles." It was a magazine with a sense of humor. In one of its promotion ads it announced it would charge readers for printing letters to the editor, since such letters are "a form of the Vanity Press." The rate was 25 cents per word. "Letters which we find particularly dumb or boring will cost $1.00 per word, and they will only be put into type after the writer's check clears the bank."

Of those opinion magazines that survive, most were founded in this century, several after World War II. All live from issue to issue, their rather high subscription rates barely, if that, taking care of their costs. A small amount of advertising, mostly from book publishers, helps some; family fortunes and donations from believers help more. Subscribers are often asked to kick in some additional money to keep their magazine alive. For instance, William Buckley, editor of *National Review,* once wrote to subscribers asking for donations "because a special emergency has arisen. . . . We define a special emergency as one that interrupts our regular emergency."[6]

The typical lineup of features in an opinion magazine includes editorials, letters to the editor, articles, reviews of books, movies, and plays, and a few ads. The typical issue contains 32 pages. Some editors like to mask the thinness of their issues by numbering pages consecutively from the first issue to the last issue of the year.

[6]William F. Buckley, Jr., letter to subscribers, February 26, 1964.

Much of the content originates outside of the staff. The editors write the editorials, but professors, mostly in the social sciences, write many of the articles. Moonlighting journalists write their share. They find here that they can be more outspoken, certainly more subjective, than in their newspaper pieces.

Forward-looking as they are in editorial policy, opinion magazines seem to operate under nineteenth-century ideas of format and design. Martin Fox in *Print* has observed they have "the visual appeal of a flight insurance policy." In the 1960s, though, despite their cheap paper and cost-saving printing procedures, a few put on more attractive dress. One of the most attractive is *The New Leader,* whose design was set by the late Herb Lubalin.

Opinion magazines differ from general circulation magazines in the nature—but not necessarily in the subject matter—of their articles. Where general circulation magazine articles are concrete and anecdotal, opinion magazine articles are philosophical and abstract. In contrast to general circulation magazines, opinion magazines tend to be intense and moralistic. For some readers they are dull and pedantic. They discuss politics, social sciences, and, to a lesser extent, the humanities. In some respects, *Harper's, The Atlantic, The New Yorker, Esquire,* and similar publications belong with the opinion magazines. But their larger circulations, slicker appearance, and stronger dependence on advertising revenue and newsstand sales put them more properly in the "general circulation magazine" category. Besides, they are not so single-minded.

In some respects, quarterly journals like *Partisan Review* belong with opinion magazines. But they are much more devoted to the humanities than are the opinion magazines. Almost none of the opinion magazines run short stories; few run poetry.

Most of the opinion magazines exist with circulations under 100,000, some with circulations under 20,000. A small daily newspaper does as well, and its circulation is concentrated in one area.

Then why are the magazines influential?

The answer is: because the reader of an opinion maga-zine typically is an educator, editor, legislator, or member of the clergy passing along what's read to much larger audi-ences.

Robert Sherrill, Washington correspondent for *The Na-tion*, sees the influence of opinion magazines as "probably far less on the younger generation than it is on that thing called 'mass media,' which watches the opinion magazines closely and imitates them and draws coverage from them in approaching touchy topics. . . . Partly because of the example of opinion magazines, the old stuffy monthlies, *Harper's* and *Atlantic*, are no longer stuffy."[7]

What an opinion magazine publishes often makes news. A newsmagazine, network, or wire service, sensing the arti-cle has important implications or that a quotation from it is controversial, may give it additional exposure, crediting the source and elaborating upon the article.

Many of the articles in opinion magazines get additional circulation as reprints. Others appear in anthologies. Some go on to become full-length books, their authors having merely tried out their ideas in the opinion magazines, which have always been in the vanguard. Carey McWilliams, late editor of *The Nation*, suggested that the opinion journals function as media for "trial balloon" ideas. "When we print it, and the sky doesn't fall, . . . [the mass media] may do some-thing with the same thing."[8]

Professor John H. Schacht of the University of Illinois College of Communications cites a number of articles in opinion magazines that influenced political and social affairs in the United States. But the influence of the opinion maga-zines is more cumulative than sudden. Issue after issue, the publication chips away at a single social evil, issue after issue

[7]Robert Sherrill, "Weeklies and Weaklies," *The Antioch Review*, Spring 1969, p. 42.
[8]Quoted by John H. Schacht, *The Journals of Opinion and Reportage: An Assessment* (New York: Magazine Publishers Association, 1966), p. 61.

it propounds a point of view. Schacht in his assessment entertains the "probability" that "in the long run the journals [of opinion] do exert an influence on public affairs in the United States."[9]

Schacht observes that it is no coincidence that "American social and economic development, foreign relations, even 'life and manners,' have developed during this century along lines held for the most part initially and for the most part consistently by the liberal segment of these journals."[10] He concludes, "No medium of comparable audience has exerted as great an influence for change."[11]

MAGAZINES ON THE LEFT

In the late 1960s, general circulation magazines became more and more willing to engage in controversy, and most of them—even the Luce publications—moved somewhat to the left. This presented the liberal and leftist opinion magazines with a problem. Their area of coverage was being preempted. Some held fast, trying to exist without the visual excitement of the slicks. Others moved further to the left, where to some extent the underground press was already operating. Neither course proved entirely satisfactory. Some observers thought the opinion magazines were losing their earlier influence.

The Reagan administration in the 1980s gave *The Nation* and similar magazines a target they could again attack with enthusiasm. The spread between ordinary magazines and liberal publications again became noticeable.

Like other opinion magazines, *The Nation* has devoted full issues to exposing what it considers abuses in the military, FBI, CIA, and other groups. Such exposés often end up in book form.

Any magazine that takes strong stands on controversial

[9]Ibid., p. 39.
[10]Ibid., p. 78.
[11]Ibid., p. 79.

matters is bound to have its inter-office squabbles,[12] and *The Nation* has had its share, especially during the 1940s, when the magazine seemed to some staffers too sympathetic to Russia.

While *The Nation* is edited in New York, *The New Republic,* a weekly much like it, is edited in Washington, D.C. It has always been a little more sympathetic than *The Nation* to the Establishment. Still it is strongly liberal. Lately it has been gaining space on newsstands, where opinion magazines are not usually welcome—they don't sell well enough.

The New Republic, born shortly before World War I, built a staff out of some of America's most brilliant journalists and thinkers. Walter Lippmann was an early editor. Henry Wallace was editor in the 1940s, prior to his resignation to run for the presidency in 1948. When it early jumped on the John Kennedy bandwagon before the 1960 election, it became a sort of house organ for the "New Frontier."

At its 50th anniversary dinner in 1964, Walter Lippmann said: ". . . if the original editors were reading *The New Republic* today . . . they would regard it as the fulfillment of their hopes. For what they hoped for was a journal of unopinionated opinion—one that would be informed, disinterested, compassionate and brave."[13]

One of its best writers was the late John Osborne, an expert on Richard Nixon. The fact that Osborne sometimes sympathized with the President prompted *Newsweek* to say that Osborne "sometimes appears to be the house conservative." *The Nixon Watch* (New York: Liveright, 1970) is a collection of his writings. (Richard L. Strout, who does the TRB column, is also widely admired.)

The Progressive, started by Sen. R. M. LaFollette, Sr., in Wisconsin in 1909, represents a midwestern brand of liberalism. Robert Sherrill calls it "a kind of literate, left-wing *Read-*

---

[12]Read Wilfrid Sheed's novel, *Office Politics* (New York: Farrar, Straus and Giroux, 1966).
[13]"1914–1964: Remarks on the Occasion of this Journal's 50th Year," *The New Republic,* March 21, 1964, p. 14.

er's Digest." One of its frequent contributors was Milton Mayer, a writer whose subtleties of style delighted the thoughtful reader. Mayer wrote hundreds of articles for *The Progressive* and hundreds more for other magazines.[14]

Occasionally *The Progressive* will put out a special issue, all the articles dealing with aspects of a single theme, as in "The Crisis of Survival" issue for April, 1970. Or the magazine will consist of one long, well-developed, book-length manuscript. In June 1969 it devoted an issue to "The Power of the Pentagon," which got more notice than any issue since April, 1954, when the magazine examined Sen. Joseph McCarthy. Because of requests for extra copies, the Pentagon issue went to three printings within the month, even though the first printing was for twice the usual number. The Viking Press later brought the issue out in book form.

As a monthly, *The Progressive* cannot keep on top of the news as well as the other opinion journals, and hence operates under a handicap.

Another important opinion magazine is *The New Leader,* started in 1923 as a socialist tabloid. It became a biweekly magazine in 1950. By that time it had severed its ties with the Socialist Party. Some feel it is closer to the center than *The New Republic* or *The Nation.* It claims to have been the first magazine to publish Martin Luther King's "Letter from Birmingham City Jail," which powerfully indicted the complacency of white moderates.

A publication called *Mother Jones,* sensing a sameness among magazines in the 1970s and into the 1980s, advertised itself as "The only magazine left for you." The *Boston Globe* saw it as a "radical new departure." Given to exposés and left-wing politics, the magazine, published monthly in San Francisco, took off early against the Ford Pinto, the CIA, the military, nuclear energy, shopping malls, Bell Telephone, and other units of the Establishment. Why *Mother Jones?* Mary Harris "Mother" Jones (1830–1930) was something of

[14]See Milton Mayer's *What Can a Man Do?* (Chicago: University of Chicago Press, 1964.)

a heroine to the magazine's founders, who read about her
starting up unions, launching strikes, campaigning for prison
reform, and referring to herself as her hundredth birthday
approached as "a hell raiser."

MAGAZINES ON THE RIGHT

By far the most influential conservative opinion magazine
is the *National Review,* founded in 1955 by William F.
Buckley, Jr. A biweekly published in New York, it goes to
nearly 100,000 subscribers and newsstand buyers. It has a
bigger newsstand sale than most opinion magazines. It also
carries more advertising than other opinion magazines,
probably because some company owners believe in its point
of view and are willing to support the magazine whether or
not the advertising increases sales enough to justify the expenditure.

It uses slick paper stock, original art, and full color on
the cover. You'll find a better writing style here than elsewhere, primarily because so much of it is done by Buckley
himself, one of the great stylists in journalism. One must be
pretty well informed to keep up with him. Probably no other
magazine editor is so widely known. He has even made the
cover of *Time.* He writes best-selling spy novels.

Opinionated and articulate, William Buckley is both
writer and public performer. Unlike most True Believers, he
has not lost his sense of humor. Once he ran for Mayor of New
York. When asked what he would do if he won, he said, "I'd
demand a recount." When he sent Norman Mailer a copy of
one of his books, he wrote "Hi!" after Mailer's name in the
index. A letter writer to *Time* called him "a mental muscle-
beacher who can't resist rippling his grey matter to dazzle
bystanders."

One gets the impression that Buckley does not mean always for his readers to take him literally. He resorts to cleverness sometimes at the expense of understanding. In defense
of extremism, he once said, "When a liberal Catholic lies
dying, does he receive moderate unction?" He called Fr.

James Groppi, a militant priest from Milwaukee, a "man of gosh."

Once a reader of the *National Review*, Roger Cole of Bethesda, Md., wrote the editor to explain why he would not renew his subscription. After a page and a half of single-spaced arguments against the magazine, he added: "In any case, this letter is becoming too long. It has already taken enough time that it has occurred to me that despite the faults I find, there are aspects of *National Review* I appreciate and cannot obtain a substitute elsewhere—so I'm enclosing both the comments and a check for renewal."

The *National Review* is not above mixing levity with serious prose. Readers have to be on their toes reading the magazine. Announcing the death of Mr. Ed, "the talking horse," *NR* (March 30, 1979) said he was "the star of a television show in the 1960s that ran for five years, and later served three terms in Congress." In another short item in that issue, the magazine, having some fun with government agency names (and misfortunes), stated, "The Federal Equal Employment Opportunity Commission Has Been—oops, the title's over—has been found guilty of illegal discrimination against one of its own employees. . . ."

In 1982 *National Review* offered a "modest prize" to the first reader who could find a "substantial newspaper or TV report" about any proposed cut in federal social spending that didn't dwell on "poor, aged, crippled, blind, minority, starving, homeless victims"; and the magazine said it would double the prize if the report even hinted "at the plight of taxpayers."

One of the most outspoken of the conservative journals is *The American Spectator,* published in Bloomington, Ind., far away from the communications capitals. *Time* has said that the opinions of its editor, R. Emmett Tyrrell, Jr., "are couched in some of the liveliest prose since the passing of H. L. Mencken." The magazine's own advertising speaks of a form of journalism that "stirs the blood and engages the mind." That the magazine does not always take itself seriously, either, can be seen in its masthead, which used to proclaim that it "was founded in 1924 by George Nathan and Truman Newberry over a cheap domestic ale in McSorley's Old Ale House." In 1967 it changed its name to *The Alternative: An American Spectator.* But in 1977 "the word 'alternative' had acquired such an esoteric fragrance that in order to discourage unsolicited manuscripts from florists, beauticians, and other creative types . . . [the magazine] reverted to . . . [its] original name."

Other magazines that would be classified as conservative are *Human Events,* a weekly tabloid rather far to the right, and *Conservative Digest,* a militant monthly.

In the past in the United States, intellectuals have congregated mostly in the liberals' camp. Liberal philosophy still appeals to intellectuals, but there is some movement away from the camp. Peter Steinfels deals with this in *The Neoconservatives* (New York: Simon and Schuster, 1979). Neoconservatives include people who identified once with liberal causes but who became disillusioned with what they saw as liberal excesses, especially during the 1960s. Two opinion magazines that best express the neoconservative line are *The Public Interest,* a quarterly edited by Irving Kristol and Nathan Glazer, and *Commentary,* a monthly edited by Norman Podhoretz.

LITTLE MAGAZINES

Little magazines differ from opinion magazines in that they come out less frequently—usually quarterly—and carry literary material rather than political polemics. They also come in a book rather than a magazine size, hence they are "little." They are "little," too, of course, because of their anemic circulations. In their struggle to stay alive they sometimes pay contributors—poets, essayists, and short-story writers—in copies of the magazine rather than in money. When they deal with political matters on their pages, they are likely to see things from the left.

Some of our popular writers—like Ernest Hemingway, William Faulkner, and Joseph Heller—appeared first in the little magazines. Book publishers scan the magazines looking for novelists with promise. These publications, of which there are some 1500, no longer carry the prestige they once carried. *Time* says they now "print anything and wind up sounding the same."[15] But for writers with experimental styles and avant garde ideas, little magazines may represent the only avenue of publication. Many of them are affiliated with universities. The word "Review" is often part of the magazines' names. So is "Quarterly."

HUMOR MAGAZINES

It would be hard to prove that today's college students do not have the sense of humor their predecessors had, but it is a fact that today's students are not publishing magazines like those that used to send their parents into spasms of uncontrollable laughter. College humor magazines are now largely defunct. Perhaps they were never as good as undergraduates thought they were. "Gawd, These Jokes Were Painful!" Robert Russell mused in an article in *Esquire.*[16]

The first of the college humor magazines was *The Harvard Lampoon* (1876), which seemed willing then to settle for what Russell calls "the faint smile." The *Lampoon* has put out annual issues parodying other publications. One on *Playboy* had a center spread with a girl tanned only where a bikini would be worn; the rest of her body was untanned. Other magazines appeared in emulation of the *Lampoon,* and in 1923 an off-campus publication, *College Humor,* made its debut to reprint the best from these magazines. It died several times, was revived again, and finally gave up for good in 1943.

After World War II the campus magazines themselves found the going rough. The vets, back from the war, thought them silly. The whole campus scene was changing, and few of the magazines survived.

[15]"Notable," *Time,* March 12, 1979, p. 93.
[16]December, 1968, pp. 164–169.

The success of the *Lampoon* inspired some Democrats in 1877 to launch the wildly funny *Puck,* which passed harsh judgment on Republicans. *Life* (not to be confused with the latter-day magazine of the same name) came along six years later to make people laugh, and by this time the newspapers began running humor columns as regular features.

Humor, some of it with a social conscience, appeared in all the media, but as a full diet in magazine format, it never really caught on. New humor magazines popped up periodically, like *Ballyhoo,* but they never stayed around for more than a few years. Only a few hold forth today. One is *Mad.* Its success has been remarkable, its contribution to opinion formation largely overlooked by those who should be interested.

Mad started in 1952, the brainchild of Bill Gaines, whose father started the comic book industry in the 1930s. Carrying no advertising, it is, as a theologian has observed, a magazine with an old-fashioned morality.[17] Designed for the 10 to 20 age-group, it systematically satirizes parental hypocrisy, far-left and far-right political thinking, smoking, and especially the press. For the young, it is probably the most effective critic of the press we have.

Who can forget its takeoffs on the *Reader's Digest,* on the *Chicago Tribune-New York News* Syndicate brand of comic strips, and on the whole field of advertising? With its parodies on current advertisements, it gives readers a healthy skepticism about advertising's claims.

J. M. Flagler in *Look* remembered fondly one of *Mad's* versions of the typical kids' program. The announcer says, "Let's have some music, Mr. Piano . . . don't bump into Mr. Camera." A kid in the audience says: "I just threw up on Mr. Floor." In one issue *Mad* took off on gun magazines. A cover for *Passionate Gun Love* features these articles: " 'I Cleaned an Unloaded Gun—and Lived!' The Story of a Once-in-a-Lifetime Miracle"; "A Heart-Warming Memoir: 'The Most

[17]See Vernard Eller, *The Mad Morality: Or the Ten Commandments Revisited* (Nashville, Tenn.: Abingdon Press, 1970).

Unforgettable Duck I Ever Slaughtered' "; and "106 Exciting Ways to Make Love to Your Gun."

Mad believes in humor first, philosophy second. The politics of the staff and contributors range from far left to far right. Its pages have been collected into innumerable paperback books. In 1969 World Publishing Co. brought out *The Ridiculously Expensive Mad* ($9.95).

Another important humor magazine, for an older audience, is *The National Lampoon,* started by some former editors of *The Harvard Lampoon.* One of its best parodies was a complete Sunday newspaper, the *Dacron Republican-Democrat,* that carried under its nameplate the slogan, "One of America's Newspapers." The *Republican-Democrat* showed that Midwestern newspapers were preoccupied with the local angle in news coverage. A front page story almost ignored the destruction of Japan by a volcano. A larger story concentrated on two local women traveling in the Orient who were thought to be missing. One of the headlines elsewhere over an investigative piece (the year was 1978) was, "Negroes, the Problem that Won't Go Away." To Margaret Engel, writing in *Nieman Reports,* the paper was "a better textbook than any I had in journalism school."[18] Another successful *National Lampoon* parody was the 1964 high school yearbook.

RELIGIOUS MAGAZINES

"Religious magazines" is not a precise term because the category includes publications of widely varying beliefs. Included are Christian magazines and magazines representing other faiths. Among the Christian magazines are Protestant and Catholic publications. Even "Protestant magazines" is not narrow enough, for Protestant magazines differ greatly. So do Catholic magazines. At one end of the Protestant magazines, for instance, you have evangelical magazines like

[18]Margaret Engel, "A Publisher's Bible of Deadly Sins," *Nieman Reports,* Winter 1978, p. 49.

Christian Life, Eternity, Moody Monthly, Christian Herald,
and *Christianity Today.* At the other you have magazines
like *The Christian Century* and *A.D.* with liberal philosophies. Of course, people who read the evangelical magazines
carefully see strongly held doctrinal differences even there.

Some religious magazines seem more interested in political and social matters than in religious matters. Many are
independent of organized churches or denominations.

As an example of narrow specialization among religious
magazines, consider *Solo,* a magazine published in Tulsa for
Christian singles, telling them about activities around the
country for single adults and advising them on building
"healthy, wholesome, lasting relationships."

SCIENCE MAGAZINES

A science major getting his second master's degree—this one
in journalism at the University of Oregon—conducted an informal study of science magazines in 1981 and concluded,
not surprisingly, that *Scientific American,* which he called
"the granddaddy of all general-interest science magazines,"
". . . provides a standard of technical excellence against
which to measure all others." He added: "For the most part,
however, its long, scientist-written articles are tedious going
for the layman." Yet 700,000 subscribe to it or buy it each
month.

The student, Tom Hager, made some other observations:

Science Digest, he found, is "a fat, slick, colorful pot-
pourri of science articles written for the layman." *Science 81*
is "a very polished magazine for the well-educated layman
interested in the variety and beauty of science." *Omni,* a
general science magazine from the publishers of *Penthouse,*
is "a glossy mixture of science fact and science fantasy—such
a mix that it's often hard to tell which is which." *New Scientist* is "a twice-monthly British science magazine that falls
in tone somewhere between *Nature,* Britain's premier general science journal for scientists (highly technical for the

most part, but somewhat involved with ethical and economic questions in science), and general news magazines." *The Sciences,* published by the New York Academy of Sciences, is "a provocative, authoritative—but readable—monthly for scientists interested in the common ground between science and the humanities." *Discover,* published by Time/Life, is a "major entrant in the science-for-the-layman magazine field" in "an exceptionally pleasing package. . . ."[19] Hager now writes for some of these magazines.

The surge in interest in science magazines in America is accompanied by a surge of interest in Europe, where many new science magazines have appeared. One of the biggest is *PM,* started in Germany in 1978. Its circulation in 1981 was 350,000.[20]

MEDICAL MAGAZINES

The medical field is crowded with all kinds of professional journals and an increasing number of magazines for laymen concerned about good health and nutrition.

The *New England Journal of Medicine,* a weekly with a circulation of about 200,000, is the world's most widely read professional medical publication. It gets some 3,500 contributions a year from doctors and others who write on medical topics, and it publishes about 12 percent of what it gets. All that is published goes through heavy editing, and no writer is paid. Writers like appearing in the *Journal* for the prestige it brings and the influence it has.

Often a specialized magazine like the *Journal* exerts an influence far beyond its primary audience. What was to become the first chapter of Norman Cousins' best-selling *Anatomy of an Illness* appeared originally in the *Journal.* The *Journal* often finds its articles quoted on the front pages of the nation's newspapers. One of its widely quoted articles in

[19]Interview with Tom Hager, June 5, 1981.
[20]Anika Michalowska, "The Science of Reader Interest," *Advertising Age,* October 19, 1981, p. S-67.

1980 showed that nonsmokers exposed to smokers' fumes do suffer detectable lung damage. "What turns up in the *Journal* one week is likely to influence policy at your local hospital or clinic the next."[21]

SPORTS AND OUTDOORS MAGAZINES

The running craze and the growing interest in leisure-time activities have given impetus to sports and outdoor magazines. Some of these are general, but most narrow in on single activities. For instance, there are mountaineering magazines, and then there is a *literary* mountaineering magazine, *Mountain Gazette,* published in Denver. In addition to several general runners' magazines, there is a specialized one, *Women's Track.*

One of the most impressive of the outdoor magazines—it is also the oldest—is *Sports Afield,* a publication that is as interested in conservation as in hunting and fishing. *Outdoor Life* serves a similar, if less wealthy, audience, as does *Field & Stream.*

Sports Illustrated, the major spectator sports magazine published by Time Inc., faced some new competition in 1980 with *Newsweek*'s launching of *Inside Sports. Inside Sports* considers itself a feature magazine not much interested in reporting the results of games. It dwells on major spectator sports only, whereas *Sports Illustrated* gets over into some esoteric areas. *Inside Sports* also puts different covers on regional editions.

The Sporting News, one of the oldest magazines in the country, started out as a baseball-oriented publication. It now calls itself "*The* publication of record for all major sports." Sports magazine editors are convinced that sports coverage on TV helps rather than hurts sports magazines. People like to read about what they watch. But *Sports Illustrated*'s best-selling issue each year is not the one given over to the World

[21]Joseph P. Kahn, "My Magazine, the Doctor," *Esquire,* November 1980, p. 57.

Series or the opening of the football season, but the annual bathing suits issue published during the winter, warming readers "with sunny scenery as well as suntanned beauty." *Inside Sports* now publishes a similar issue.[22]

Women sports enthusiasts in the 1970s saw the launching of several magazines of interest to them. Regional sports magazines also began to appear.

BUSINESS MAGAZINES

The Big Four among business magazines are *Business Week, Fortune, Forbes,* and *Nation's Business. Business Week,* the most profitable, deals largely with business news. It has a relatively young, on-the-way-up audience. A thick weekly, it carries more pages of advertising each year than any other magazine, business or general. *Fortune,* a lavish biweekly, uses a literary approach to appeal mostly to upper-level business people. *Forbes* is an aggressive, even feisty publication that refers to itself as "the capitalist tool." *Nation's Business,* published by the U.S. Chamber of Commerce, tells business people how they can react to what is going on in Washington. *Dun's Business Month* and *Inc.* also serve the needs of business people.

All of these publications compete to some extent with a daily newspaper, the prestigious *Wall Street Journal,* and its sister publication, *Barron's,* a weekly. *Money* is a popular magazine more for consumers and small investors than for business people. Recently a number of city and regional business publications have started up. The Association of Area Business Publications (AABP) reported 54 such publications in 1981, and that number was expected to grow rapidly.

TRADE JOURNALS

Magazines serving a cross section of people in a business, industry, trade, or profession are called "trade journals," "busi-

---

[22]John Peter, "The Leading Edge," *Folio,* June 1981, p. 56.

ness publications," or "professional journals," none of the terms fully describing the nature of all the publications in the category. Unlike company magazines (see below), which are published for public relations reasons, trade journals (or whatever you choose to call them) are published to make a profit for the publisher. They carry a wealth of ads. In fact, some trade journals are read mostly for their ads. They are considered to be "horizontal" publications because they spread across all companies in a particular industry. (A company magazine, dealing with a single company, would be considered a "vertical" magazine.)

Several trade magazines serve the people who run grocery stores, for instance. *Progressive Grocer,* a monthly, is the oldest. *Supermarket News,* a weekly, has the largest full-time staff: more than 20 people. Among other grocery trade journals are *Supermarket Business, Grocer's Spotlight, Convenience Store Merchandiser,* and *Convenience Store News.*

Trade journals go out to readers mainly by subscription. Few sell at the newsstands. Many trade journals are "controlled circulation" publications, going out free to qualified persons. Some of the magazines maintain subscriptions lists in the hundreds of thousands, but the average circulation for a trade journal stands at 50,000. Some trade publications take a newspaper rather than a magazine format.

The American Business Press (ABP) is an organization that serves 115 publishing companies putting out some 600 trade magazines and newspapers. Itself a publisher, ABP issues 13 monthly newsletters and occasional booklets and folders about and for the industry.

Among the biggest companies publishing trade magazines and newspapers are McGraw-Hill, Cahners Publishing Co., American Broadcasting Companies, Fairchild Publications, and Penton/IPC.

COMPANY MAGAZINES

"Company magazines" is another term that does not adequately cover a field in journalism, a field alive with all kinds of publications published by profit and nonprofit organizations mostly for public relations reasons. Once they were known as "house organs," but people in the business do not like the term. Some editors call what they publish "organizational publications." Ordinarily the publications do not attempt to make money for the publisher, and few carry advertising. They range from the most elaborate of publications, handsome and useful, even in a general sense, to the most modest of publications using inexpensive printing and paper stock.

Some companies publish several magazines and newspapers. Each plant in the company may have its own weekly or monthly newspaper, while a slick-paper magazine may go out to all employees every month, every other month, or quarterly. A separate publication may go to management people, and another one to retired employees. In addition, a slick magazine of general interest may go to thought leaders, media people, politicians. Still another magazine may go out to dealers. Then once a year the company may issue an annual report, or a couple of them, one for stockholders and one for employees. With all these regular publications added to the occasional publications (employee handbooks, recruitment booklets, product folders, etc.) the company becomes a major publisher with a staff of several journalists and designers, all working to improve and maintain good public relations. American Telephone & Telegraph Co. alone puts out 250 company publications, including 120 newspapers. The other publications include magazines, newsletters, and single-sheet bulletins.

As a public relations tool, a company magazine tends to ignore controversy and unpleasantness. An early 1979 issue of Pacific Southwest Airline's *California Magazine* that summarized 1978's major news stories failed to mention a PSA disaster at San Diego in which 144 persons were killed. "We don't normally include articles about hijackings, problems of the airline industry or crashes," the publisher of the magazine explained. Nor would anyone expect a public relations publication to cover such things.

JOHN DEERE

TRACKS

AUG./SEPT. 1981 · JOHN DEERE DUBUQUE WORKS/JOHN DEERE DAVENPORT WORKS

JUMPING OUT OF PLANES AND OTHER SUMMERTIME FUN
DEERE DIGS ITS WAY TO THE TOP IN A RIP-ROARIN' "HODEO!"
SUCCESSFUL PEOPLE ARE GOOD LISTENERS—ARE YOU A GOOD LISTENER?

A big company like John Deere publishes several publications for employees, company officials, and even outsiders. *Tracks,* an 8½-by-11-inch magazine, comes out bimonthly for employees at its Dubuque and Davenport, Iowa, plants. Although this arresting cover photograph superbly illustrates the lead article, it mostly shows farmland, for which John Deere machinery is made. (Cover photograph of *Tracks* by Gary Olsen, editor of *Tracks.)*

It is impossible to count all the company publications in America, but John N. Bailey, executive director of the International Association of Business Communicators, in 1978 estimated that the total circulation of these publications comes to 200 million, more than three times the circulation of U.S. newspapers. Of course, most company publications come out less frequently than daily. Monthly or bimonthly frequencies are more common. Some come out quarterly. These figures do not include annual reports, which companies issue to stockholders and employees, but they do include publications issued by nonprofit organizations as well as businesses.

The typical company publication contains news and features about the company and employees along with advice on safety and other matters. As public relations tools, company publications cannot be expected to criticize management. A few companies, however, do allow criticism and even exposés. Atlantic Richfield's *ArcoSpark* once published charges against the company made by a politician running for office; Upjohn Company's *Intercom* ran an article about the moral dilemma it faced doing business with South Africa; American Airlines' *Flagship News* ran an item about illegal contributions paid by company officers to President Nixon's 1972 reelection campaign.[23]

IN-FLIGHT MAGAZINES

Partially filling the void left by the disappearing general-circulation magazines are the free in-flight magazines offered by the airlines to keep travelers occupied. Where once the magazines were thin and bland, they now are fat and colorful, with coverage that ranges from expected travel pieces to less expected articles on politics, the law, and even social problems.

East/West Network, Inc., publishes a number of them under contract to several airlines, including United and Pa-

[23]Stephen Grover, "Most Firms' House Organs Emphasize Employee News and Avoid Controversy," *The Wall Street Journal,* November 7, 1978, p. 12.

cific Southwest Airlines. The man heading this publishing empire is Jeffrey S. Butler, who got his start as a public relations director for PSA. His work there convinced him that the industry was ready for some upgraded in-flight magazines. Webb Co., St. Paul, is another publisher of in-flight magazines. Among its clients are TWA and Northwest. Ziff-Davis Publishing Co. publishes in-flight magazines, too. Among its clients is Pan Am. Several airlines, American and National among them, publish their own magazines.

But whether the magazine originates in a publishing office like East/West or in the office of the sponsoring airline, it has all the markings of a publication put out solely by the airline. It is, then, a "company magazine" issued for an external audience. As for most magazines, advertising pays for much of the cost, and freelancers contribute many of the articles. These characteristics make in-flight magazines different from most company magazines.

CITY AND REGIONAL MAGAZINES

The big news in magazine publishing at the beginning of the 1980s was the growth in city and regional magazines, and city magazines began to specialize further. A number of cities saw the birth of *business* city magazines. Some cities and states could boast of their own home and garden magazines.

The general-interest city magazines covered what the daily newspapers largely ignored—how better to enjoy, and survive, the city. Other city and state magazines specialized in in-depth reporting. Among the best of these is *Texas Monthly,* founded at Austin in 1973. With its intelligent approach, *Texas Monthly* enjoys something of a national following. Texas, like many states, has a number of city and regional magazines, including *D, Houston City, San Antonio Monthly,* and *Corpus Christi Magazine.*

One of the largest and most successful city magazines for a time was *Chicago,* which by 1979 was regularly running 250 pages or more per monthly issue. One of the oldest is *Philadelphia,* established in 1910; it has earned a reputation for its hard-hitting investigative pieces. The first of the modern city magazines was *San Diego,* founded by Ed Self in 1948.

New York remains the best-known of the city magazines (*The New Yorker* is a national magazine, not a city magazine), partly because of the strong role it played in developing the "new journalism" and partly because of its large circulation outside New York City. Established in 1968, it inspired a sister publication on the West Coast, *New West,* launched in 1976 and now owned by *Texas Monthly.* Because it is mostly about California, not the entire West, it changed its name to *California* in 1981.

The magazines were numerous enough to form a City and Regional Magazine Association in 1978. Watching this success of the city magazines, a number of newspapers retaliated with "lifestyle" sections and consumer-oriented stories. There is some evidence that the introduction of a local independent magazine in a city causes the daily newspaper to improve.

Of course, the new publication in the city means additional competition for the advertiser's dollar. To lure advertisers away from newspapers, city magazines point to a longer life per issue, better paper and hence better printing for ads, and an audience bent on spending.

ETHNIC MAGAZINES

A few years ago only a few magazines specifically served the black market. Two were *Ebony,* patterned after *Life* magazine, and *Jet.* The 1980s saw many smaller, more specialized magazines serving that audience.

Black Enterprise, for instance, which deals with the business world from a black perspective, is one important specialized magazine in this field. *Black Family,* a quarterly, deals with home and family. *Black Collegian* is interested in careers for black college graduates. *Essence* is a classy magazine for black professional women. *Dawn Magazine* is a Sunday supplement going out to a number of black newspapers.

In addition to magazines for blacks, there are magazines for Hispanics and other ethnic groups.

NEWSLETTERS

Newsletters carry specialization in magazine publishing one step further. A newsletter is a no-nonsense publication, usually without visual frills, put out generally in an 8½-by-11-inch format, often using a typeface that looks as though it came right out of a typewriter. It usually comes out weekly, and subscribers pay a heavy price, up to $500 yearly, for its timely, practical information. Since they already own mailing lists that can be tapped, many magazines launch newsletters as part of their expansion activities.

Many newsletters, however, grow up independently of magazines. Newsletters not only inform, they editorialize, and many of them forecast. Readers feel they are in the know, and early. One of the earliest and most successful was published by W. M. Kiplinger, who wrote as though for a single reader. The idea was to make readers feel that they were getting regular typed letters from an authority. Among other things, Kiplinger advised the small-business person on money matters. His newsletter led to the launching of a magazine, *Changing Times.* McGraw-Hill, publisher of books and trade magazines, in 1980 was publishing 22 newsletters.

As with magazines, the test of a successful newsletter lies in its renewals. If fewer than 50 percent of subscribers renew at the end of a year, the newsletter is in trouble.[24]

A popular and much quoted newsletter of the 1970s and 1980s, in "the days of lines and hoses," as someone called the period, has been the *Lundberg Letter,* reporting on the gasoline industry and gasoline supplies to those interested enough in the service to pay $400 a year for it.

Some magazines use the newsletter gimmick of publishing a page or two of last-minute news items and forecasts on

[24]Robert Luce, "Should You Also Publish a Newsletter?" *Folio,* June 1980, p. 67.

tinted paper inside regular issues, making readers feel that they are getting two publications for the price of one. To save costs, a number of company magazines come out in a newsletter format.

THE UNDERGROUND PRESS

Serving youth as no other publications could, or would, in the 1960s and early 1970s were several hundred units of what came to be known as the "underground press." Although they took mostly a newspaper format, they performed more of a magazine than a newspaper function and so will be discussed here.

The phenomenon of publications existing for the sole purpose of chipping away at established institutions was nothing new in America, of course, but the proliferation of them, the tone of their diatribes—that *was* new.

What made them possible was the sullen mood of a rather sizable body of activists and revolutionaries, the tolerance of the courts, and the availability of an inexpensive printing process, offset lithography, with its ability to utilize crude pasteups and cheap, cold-type composition. Anyone with a commitment and a few dollars collected from sympathizers could enter the field. Art Kunkin, publisher of the Los Angeles *Free Press,* largest of the papers, with a staff of more than 40, started his publication in the mid 1960s with an investment of $15. By 1970 it was grossing about $700,000 a year.

One of the best known of the underground papers, the *Berkeley Barb,* in 1969, just five years after its founding, enjoyed a circulation of 86,000 and a yearly profit of about $130,000. But that was the year staff members, irritated about their low pay and the penny-pinching ways of owner-founder Max Scherr, rebelled. Scherr let it be known his paper was up for sale. Staff members considered buying Scherr out, but then decided to establish a rival underground paper, the *Tribe.*

From a design standpoint, a few of these publications

were remarkably creative, but most resorted to what a writer in *Communications Arts* called "seasick graphics." From a writing standpoint, they are lively and provocative, but "taken in large doses, very, very boring."[25]

The underground Los Angeles *Oracle* justified the underground press this way:

> Almost without exception, most established newspapers and magazines . . . tend to reflect the prejudices of their sponsors; they are short-sighted, slow-moving, usually defensive of the status quo. The underground press is more concerned with conveying truth than earning money. . . . It fulfills the need for independent information about the turbulent currents of our rapidly changing way of life.[26]

But *Esquire* observed: "Despite its refreshing vitality, the underground press is too noisy. This is not to denigrate its objectives or its considerable achievements; rather, because its methods are so deliberately crude—full of illiteracies and self-righteousness, and devoid of wit—a dispassionate reader is tempted to turn off."[27]

Their main targets were the military, the straight press, the police, and narcotics agents. A measure of their impact was felt in 1969 when the Los Angeles *Free Press* published a stolen list of names, addresses, and telephone numbers of narcotics agents in California and, in effect, invited readers to harass them. Many of the papers promoted the legalization and use of marijuana. They were never objective, but argued that true objectivity is a myth, anyway. To them, news was a four-letter word.

Eventually they became anything but "underground." The newspapers were hawked from the street corners of major cities and university towns and were available even at newsstands. Much of their circulation came from tittering

---

[25]See David Sanford, "The Seedier Media," *The New Republic,* December 2, 1967, pp. 7, 8.
[26]Quoted by John Gruen, "The Ear-Splitting Underground Press," *Vogue,* February 15, 1968, p. 44.
[27]"Editor's Notes," *Esquire,* October 1969, p. 12.

businessmen attending conventions and office workers on their lunch hours buying papers out of curiosity, especially to read the "want ads" in which deviate attempted to make connection with deviate.

Although part of this was put-on, it was inevitable that publications would arise to devote themselves fully to the one enduring attraction of the underground press, its blatant pornography. So then came the new underground sex papers: *Pleasure, Kiss, Screw, Rat,* and *The New York Review of Sex.*

The two publications said to have started it all were *The Realist,* a magazine founded by Paul Krassner in 1958, and *The Village Voice,* the weekly Greenwich Village paper that first appeared in 1955.

Krassner had previously worked with *Mad.* Calling his new magazine "the fire hydrant of the underdog," Krassner filled it with outrageous interviews, articles, and literary miscellany, sprinkled with obscenities, but with an offsetting lift of humor. By 1968, he had built his more-or-less monthly publication, edited from incredibly poorly ordered offices, to a circulation of 100,000, more than most of the serious opinion magazines.

Krassner once stated his philosophy: "Existence has no meaning, and I love every minute of it."[28] *Life* called him the dean of the underground press. Krassner's magazine was clearly above the level of the papers started in the shadow of *The Realist.*

The Village Voice stood well to the left of regular New York newspapers and paid particular attention to the arts. It introduced the work of Jules Feiffer, among others. By 1963, the paper was operating in the black. Once in the vanguard, the *Voice* now finds itself written off by some as hopelessly square. A writer in *Evergreen Review* called it a "middle-age matron in [a] miniskirt."[29]

Publications that start out on the fringes often become

---

[28]"Easygoing Advocate of the Outrageous," *Life,* October 4, 1968, p. 46.
[29]J. Kirk Sale, "The Village Voice (You've Come a Long Way, Baby, But You Got Stuck There)," *Evergreen Review,* December 1969, p. 25.

more respectable as they pick up circulation. Two of the papers, the *East Village Other* and *Rat,* hired the capitalistic Dun & Bradstreet Collection Division to hound nonpaying subscribers, a writer in *Playboy* reported, and according to a writer in *Esquire,* employees at the Los Angeles *Free Press* started punching a time clock.

In 1966 five papers, including the *Free Press,* banded together to form the Underground Press Syndicate to exchange cartoons and other features and to solicit advertising. Then in 1968 came another underground press agency: Liberation News Service, selling news stories, reviews, and essays. Editors of underground newspapers found themselves in demand as panelists at journalism conventions, and there, with obvious delight, they castigated their more conservative colleagues.

The underground press clearly had some influence on the straight press. For example, the *Detroit News,* frankly imitating the format and to some extent the content of underground newspapers, in 1969 launched "The Other Section," an every-Thursday part of the regular paper that attempted to bridge the gap between young and old. Among other features were articles critical of the Establishment press.

The art and graphics of the underground press inspired both advertising and publications designers. Its angry, scatological prose furthered the "new journalism" found in some of our magazines. One observer concluded that youthful readers, when they graduated to the straight press, would not be content with the dullness there.[30]

THE ALTERNATIVE PRESS

Standing to the right of the underground press but to the left of the Establishment press are a few publications press schol-

---

[30]Jack A. Nelson, "The Underground Press," *Freedom of Information Center Report No. 116,* School of Journalism, University of Missouri, Columbia, August 1969. See also Robert J. Glessing, *The Underground Press in America,* (Bloomington, Ind.: Indiana University Press, 1970).

ars now refer to as the "alternative press," militant papers that buck the journalistic tide and do it responsibly. Alternative papers move away from objectivity and even traditional values and look for surprises. For instance, *Valley Advocate* of Springfield, Mass., in launching a weekly feature to be written by readers, said that the only requirement was "that the pieces be well-written and stylistically or politically venturesome."

Some alternative papers serve a hippie-like audience, others an audience of young professionals. *New Times* of Phoenix, Arizona, calls itself a "News and Arts Journal." *The Weekly*, a classy tabloid in Seattle, calls itself a newsmagazine. It puts Seattle affairs in an interpretive setting, and offers advice on where to eat and where to go for entertainment or culture. The covers, looking like magazine covers, feature large photographs or portraits. One cover carried this large-type blurb, "75 Bars: Sizing Up Seattle's Watering Holes—from Adriatica to the Unique Grill."

Some of the papers are circulated free, relying solely on advertising to foot the bills. *Reader*, a hefty tabloid, is "Chicago's Free Weekly." *City Paper*, a weekly in Baltimore, carries "FREE, FREE, FREE, FREE" over the top of the nameplate. In 1982 it was circulating from stands in 400 stores, restaurants, and clubs in the greater metropolitan area.

Pacific Sun, Mill Valley, Calif., is a handsome, savvy tabloid dealing with the concerns of young, affluent, and adventurous residents of Marin County. The want ads confirm the fact that the area offers many counseling, health, and recreational services. One ad implores: "Let my gifted hands massage you. Better yet, ask me to be with you in any activity you choose."

Most of the alternative papers like to keep an eye on the regular newspapers in their areas. When the *San Francisco Chronicle* in 1982 reprinted a critique of itself that appeared originally in the *Columbia Journalism Review*, it left out a sentence: "The Chronicle [say critics] traffics in sex and sensationalism." The *San Francisco Bay Guardian* on its pages pointed out the omission.

One of the earliest of the alternative papers was *The Real Paper* of Boston, a weekly. In 1980 it went through redesign and moved to shorter and lighter features, but it died a year later. Another Boston alternative paper is *The Phoenix*, called by *Willamette Week* (itself an alternative paper) "Perhaps the country's most lucrative alternative weekly." *Willamette Week* says *The Phoenix* "has never jettisoned its hard-nosed news and its analytical approach in favor of lighter material. In *The Real Paper's* rush to be 'modern' and 'lively,' it forgot what instigated the alternative press in the first place—the need for news more reliable and more informative than the local mainstream press."[31]

Most of the alternative papers are tabloids, and they often publish special sections to bring in the advertisers. In 1978, the papers formed their own organization, which in 1982 became the Association of Alternative Newsweeklies.

GETTING THE MOST FROM MAGAZINES

Pity the writer for the confession magazines. The articles there do not get by-lines. One good reason is that a few professional writers turn out most of the pieces. Confession magazine editors thus cannot assign by-lines. Even readers with only confession-magazine mentality would get suspicious after a while if they saw the same name issue after issue. A person could not have *that* many love tangles.

The confession writer is not alone. Even the writer of more worthwhile pieces for more significant magazines, including specialized magazines, remains largely anonymous. Who looks at the by-lines on magazine articles? Who can name even a half dozen writers of magazine articles?

Yet, a serious reader should note the author's name before reading any article and should know something about the writer. In most magazines the information is in a footnote near the article's beginning or on a separate page near the front of the magazine, as in "Backstage with *Esquire.*" As one

[31]"The Real Story," *Willamette Week*, June 29–July 6, 1981, p. 8.

becomes familiar with an author's work one can better judge the stated facts and evaluate the opinions.

When one sees a double by-line, with a big name accompanied by an "as told to" or "with" followed by another name, one should realize that the owner of the big name had little to do with the actual writing of the article. In fact, articles with single by-lines by prominent political and entertainment figures are in all likelihood "ghost-written." Rare are the Steve Allens and Woody Allens who can write as well as perform.

A researcher taking information from magazines should make a distinction between *magazine* comment and *writer* comment. There is a difference. If the material appears in the magazine unsigned—without a by-line—it can be attributed, correctly, to the magazine itself. If it is signed, it should be attributed to the writer, giving secondary credit to the magazine in which the work appears.

A specific magazine article can be found by consulting one of the various indexes available in any library. Some indexes cover technical, trade, and other specialized magazines, others cover more popular magazines. The index most often consulted is *Readers' Guide to Periodical Literature,* published at frequent intervals during the year by the H. W. Wilson Company, New York. *Readers' Guide* lists, by both author and subject matter, articles appearing in selected magazines. From time to time librarians vote on which magazines to include. For a magazine, making *Readers' Guide* is a little like an athlete's making All-American.

Chapter 9
The Book World

"I've given up reading books," said Oscar Levant. "I find it takes my mind off myself." Someone else said, "Why should I buy a book? I already have one." But there are enough people buying them and reading them these days to keep some 5,000 publishers in America producing about 40,000 different titles a year, if we count new titles as well as new editions of existing works. True, most do not sell more than 400 or 500 copies, but some go into sales of hundreds of thousands.

When sales of a given book are brisk enough, the publisher orders it back on the press for a new *printing*. A book may go through several printings. If after a few years a new audience develops for the book, and if some of the material in the book is outdated, the publisher asks the author to revise the book; then the publisher brings it out in a new *edition.* (That is what happened to *The Fourth Estate.*) When an edition of a book is sold out, if the publisher decides not to bring out a new printing or edition, the book is no longer "in print." But often buyers wanting an out-of-print book can find it through one of the many dealers in second-hand books.

The Library of Congress, Washington, D.C., houses the biggest collection of books and booklets in the country: 18 million of them. These in addition to all the newspapers and magazines, tapes, records, etc., make up a total of 76 million items.

In world history, books antedate printing itself. The first books were "published" by scribes, making word-for-word copies of original manuscripts. The printing press, and especially movable type, revolutionized book publishing. Still, it took centuries before publishers really brought out books for the masses.

In the North American colonies, the first press, set up at Cambridge, produced its first piece of printing in 1639, a book of psalms that preceded by half a century the first newspaper. With the coming of each new medium—first the newspaper, then the magazine, then radio, finally TV—the book industry thought its days were about done, but by reassessing its audience and broadening its base, it has managed to survive.

In his *Book Publishing in America* (New York: McGraw-Hill, 1966) Charles A. Madison divides the history of the industry into four eras: from the colonies' beginnings to 1865—emergence of book publishing from local ventures to nationwide enterprise; 1865–1900—the parallel growth of genteel publishers and "gilded age" merchandisers; 1900–1945—the commercialization of book publishing with its hospitality to "men of literary discernment as well as to gross bookmongers"; 1945–present—postwar concentration on textbooks, paperbacks, mergers, and public financing, with "the persistence of publishing as a cultural activity."

CATEGORIES OF BOOKS

Publishers divide books into two broad categories: (1) textbooks and reference books and (2) trade books. The first category includes all books published specifically for classroom use plus books meant to be reference sources, like dictionaries and encyclopedias. The second category includes all other books, fiction as well as nonfiction.

Increasingly, professors are adopting trade books, especially paperbacks, as textbooks, so the two categories become blurred, but publishers continue to regard them separately because their marketing programs differ. For one thing, trade books generally have a shorter sales life than text and reference books.

Publishers find textbooks rather consistent if unspectacular moneymakers. They find trade books much more exciting, and frustrating. A few trade books make unbelievable profits. Most fail. The trade books that really take off are almost always works of nonfiction, controversial or inspirational or practical or gossipy. A few novels do almost as well, but most do miserably.

Not many publishers produce novels, but many people feel that the novel is the book publishing industry's highest form. A novel can carry great truth without being burdened by excessive facts, although many novels require a great deal of research by their authors. A novel often requires more creative effort than a piece of nonfiction requires, but because novel writing looks easy to aspiring writers, many attempt it, and some of this dross gets published to appear on shelves alongside the enduring novels.

Nonfiction books represent a much bigger part of the trade book category because they are more obviously useful. Self-help books predominate, works that promise greater happiness, more success, better health, easier times, clearer instruction. Cookbooks are especially popular with publishers because they do not quickly go out of date. In 1978, for instance, 400 new titles or editions of cookbooks came out.

The distinction between fiction and nonfiction grows dimmer these days. Because fiction does not sell as well as nonfiction, some novelists have turned to writing nonfiction books, bringing to them fictional techniques not so well understood by journalists who write nonfiction. Conversely, some writers with real-life stories to tell have written novels rather than nonfiction books, with real persons disguised, sometimes thinly, as fictional characters, which has not prevented real persons from suing for libel when the stories were too sordid. Some publishers question the ethics of blurring fact and fiction.

Even when publishing nonfiction books, publishers do little checking of facts. The book is the author's, a publisher feels, and the author knows more about the subject than the publisher does. In textbook publishing, though, publishers are more particular. The author may be more of an expert than the writer of ordinary nonfiction, but a textbook is subject to adoption by other experts, so what the book says must be carefully scrutinized. A textbook cannot afford to be controversial, any more than it can be inaccurate; thus the author's manuscript usually goes out to several other professors for review before it is set in type.

TEXTBOOKS

Some firms publish only trade books, some only textbooks, some both. A firm publishing both may separate the departments so completely that they operate as though they were different firms. Textbooks, now such a substantial portion of publishing, were not always a part of the educational process. They came about, especially in America, as a result of a shortage of teachers. European educators took to textbooks in the 1800s in what was known as "the American system."

One of the most successful textbooks to be published in this country was David Saville Muzzey's *An American History*, which, in its several editions, lasted 60 years in the schools. It was first published in 1911. Like most textbooks in those years, *An American History* celebrated all the old virtues, including patriotism. Muzzey's book was written with style. A more recent example of a successful textbook is Paul A. Samuelson's *Economics,* which, first published in 1948, had sold close to 3 million copies by 1979.

Like trade books, textbooks are advertised, but not to the people who buy them. They are advertised, instead, to professors, teachers, and school boards likely to adopt them. The advertising usually takes the form of direct-mail folders. The books themselves aid in the advertising. Several hundred or, in some cases, several thousand sample copies go out free to professors who might adopt the book for their classes. A professor may get as many as 50 different books a year to consider.

Textbook publishers, more than other publishers, face pressures from various organized groups. In the 1970s, because of pressures from women and minority groups, the books published gave more prominence to people in nontraditional roles. Publishers often set up quotas to make sure that various groups were fully represented in photographs; some publishers even have a quota for handicapped persons.

Other critics of textbooks fail to see improvement.[1] Traditional values and solid learning are missing, these critics argue. If the 1970s were the decade of criticism from liberals, the 1980s began as a decade of criticism from conservatives.

The publishers of textbooks for high schools and elementary schools, especially, find the business frustrating. Selection committees in various states approve books to be used in the schools. To pass the screening of these committees, the books themselves are written by committees. The middle ground the books take results in blandness and indecisiveness.

Because a greater percentage of college students these days have weaker academic backgrounds than their predecessors had, textbook publishers have made their products more attractive and less demanding, downgrading the vocabulary, upping the type size, bringing in more art and color. "The books have everything except pop-outs, and I

[1]"The Textbook Debate," *Newsweek,* December 17, 1979, p. 102.

imagine they're coming," said Leonard Freedman, who teaches political science at UCLA.[2]

At the college level, sales representatives or travelers, who are often called "editors" to give them more prestige, call on professors to acquaint them with available books.

THE BOOK PUBLISHERS

Hugh Kenner, writing in *Harper's* (June 1979), points out that book publishers observe but two seasons—spring, which "culminates in vacations and novels," and fall, which brings on Christmas and "thirty-dollar books you buy for somebody else." It is true that publishers try to concentrate their releases at times of the year when people are most likely to buy. In the textbook field, most books are issued just after the first of the year, in time to get a full year's ride on the year of copyright and in time, too, for professors to make decisions for fall classes.

In the past, the major book publishers have augmented their profit-making books with a few artistic or culturally enriching volumes, but with the takeover of so many book publishers by hard-nose financiers and conglomerates in the 1970s, books that from the start had no chance of making money have mostly vanished. And book publishers have turned more and more to hard-sell techniques, striving for as much media exposure as possible. Their authors, for instance, appear more regularly on television and radio talk shows.

Book publishing has tied in to other media as well. It has always had close ties to magazine publishing; many book publishing concerns are, in fact, outgrowths of magazines. *Time* and *Life, Newsweek, Playboy, Rolling Stone, Advertising Age, Art Direction, Writer's Digest, The Writer* have all gone into book publishing. It works the other way around, too. *Harper's* is an outgrowth of Harper & Bros., the predecessor of Harper & Row.

[2]Quoted by William Trombley, "College Text 'Dumbing' Aids Sales," *Los Angeles Times*, January 10, 1982, p. 1.

Time-Life Books has enjoyed enormous success, partly because it is able to use its mailing lists of magazine subscribers. This publisher sells its books on a subscription basis, just as it sells its magazines. Barbara Demick, writing in *The New Republic*, reported that Time-Life Books is the United States' fourth largest publisher.[3]

Closely allied with some of the major book publishers are *imprint publishers*, small entrepreneurs who came on the scene with the personal touch as regular publishers became corporate giants. Imprint houses are often one-person operations, editors who have their own string of writers they give a lot of attention to. They attach themselves to big houses, who take care of distribution. For instance, in 1978, *The World According to Garp*, a widely publicized novel by John Irving, was published by an imprint publisher, Henry Robbins, who had an affiliation with Dutton. An imprint publisher is not likely to have a staff any bigger than two or three persons and an annual output of no more than 10 to 20 books. Yet, some of the biggest sellers of the season are imprint books, proving the judgment of the imprint editor who finds them.

One of the earliest of the imprint publishers was the husband and wife team of Kurt and Helen Wolff, who, beginning in the early 1960s, arranged for English translations of European works for Harcourt Brace Jovanovich. Another early imprint publisher, Seymour Lawrence, working with Delacorte, brought out *Slaughterhouse-Five*, giving national recognition to Kurt Vonnegut.[4]

Some small *independent publishers* tie in with major houses, too, but just to take advantage of the big publishers' sales forces. For instance, Sierra Club Books, San Francisco, uses Charles Scribner's Sons, New York, to distribute the dozen or so books it publishes each year.

[3]Barbara Demick, "The Post-Industrial Bookshelf," *The New Republic*, August 18, 1979, p. 21.
[4]Scott Haller, "The Discreet Charm of the Ego Logo," *New York*, December 4, 1978, p. 113.

As in the advertising business, employees, picking up enough know-how, sometime leave their firm to form another. The new one starts off small, publishing one or two books the first year, maybe, then grows to a point where *it* becomes a training ground for a new publisher. David A. Broehn, for instance, started his Sterling Publishing Company that way in 1949. Sterling remains small by industry standards, publishing about 60 titles a year, most of them "how-to" books. In 1957 Sterling acquired the American hardcover rights to *The Guinness Book of World Records,* and today it and its spinoffs account for 40 percent of Sterling's sales.[5]

New York remains the headquarters city for most book publishers, but Boston, Chicago, and other cities have publishers, too. Los Angeles, although an important market for books, has only a few small publishers because "investment capital there is tied up more in electronic than in linear industries."[6] A few publishers locate in small towns or medium-size cities where they publish regional or specialized books. Grand Rapids, Michigan, for instance, boasts of four religious publishers, all with an evangelical bent—Kregel Publications, Baker Book House, William B. Eerdmans Publishing Co., and the Zondervan Corporation. Zondervan likes to talk about its religious best sellers by big-name people. It has established a chain of religious book stores in shopping malls. Eerdmans is the most cerebral of the four, with books by C. S. Lewis, Dorothy Sayers, Helmut Thielicke, and Jacques Ellul on its list.[7]

America's largest publisher is the U.S. Government Printing Office, Washington, D.C. Established in 1895 to meet librarians' needs for systematic distribution of government-sponsored publications, the GPO now acts as publisher and bookseller for all government agencies, with "editorial

[5]Phil Mintz, "David A. Boehm," *Publishers Weekly,* August 6, 1979, p.8.
[6]Patricia Holt, "The View from the West," *Publishers Weekly,* December 25, 1978, p. 31.
[7]LeRoy Koopman, "The Netherlands Quartet," *Publishers Weekly,* September 26, 1980, pp. 63, 64.

offices" scattered throughout the federal government. Its most popular publication is *Infant Care*, first published in 1914 and still selling briskly.

GPO publications are sometimes reset and repackaged by private publishers and sold at fancy prices. Private publishers can do this because what the government publishes cannot, and should not, be copyrighted.

People associated with the book publishing industry predicted that the 1980s would see a big growth in numbers of small, independent publishers. Large publishers would concentrate on fewer, bigger sellers, leaving marginal books to the hundreds of small publishers. In many cases, smaller publishers set their own type on inexpensive in-house machines.[8] The big publishers usually contract for such services. Some of them even contract for editing and copyediting services. Large or small, almost every book publisher buys the printing from outside.

Some small book publishers put out a single book and stick with it for years. It may be the publisher's only book. John B. Cassidy learned to juggle in his hours off from teaching at Stanford and published, through his Klutz Enterprises, Palo Alto, *Juggling for the Complete Klutz,* a paperback with three bean bags attached to each copy. Sales were slow until major distributors took over, and by 1981 (the book was published in 1977) 200,000 copies had sold.[9]

Some books come out in several versions, each by a different publisher. The Bible is one such book, but the many versions still have not satisfied everyone. In the 1980s a group affiliated with the National Council of Churches was working on a "nonsexist" version. The *Reader's Digest* had already begun work on a *condensed* version, cutting away at the 800,000 words of the Revised Standard Version, excising half the Old Testament and a quarter of the New. It was

[8]See "Predictions: The Publishing Community," *Publishers Weekly,* December 24, 1979, pp. 24, 25.
[9]Ray Walters, "Paperback Talk," *The New York Times Book Review,* June 14, 1981, p. 36.

not the first shortened version of the Bible, but unlike the others, the *Reader's Digest* version was not an "abridgement," in which whole blocks were cut, but a condensation for which the *Digest* people did their cutting line by line.

The book industry estimates that 60 percent of the nation's book readers are women. This partially explains the wealth of women's-issues books now on the market and the resolution of the industry to eliminate "sexism" from manuscripts accepted for publication. McGraw-Hill led the way with a directive to all its writers, but the admonitions applied only to nonfiction. Novelists were still free to indulge themselves. Today even the most conservative book publishers as much as possible shy away from the generic "he" and other words and phrases some readers find might offensive or not inclusive enough.

UNIVERSITY PRESSES

Many universities have gone into book publishing, but their books are meant for small, elite audiences. The books are seldom published to make money. N. R. Kleinfield, a *New York Times* reporter, calls university presses "those staid processors of scholarship that boast big theories and drowsy sales." They are that, mostly, but a few venture into fields served by ordinary trade book publishers. At least one, Iowa State University Press, publishes textbooks. The Bison series of books published by the University of Nebraska compete with other paperbacks on grocery and drugstore book racks. Some university presses even produce calendars.

One of the most promotion minded is Harvard University Press, which issues important books in the humanities, history, biological sciences, psychology, economics, and business. This publisher sends some of its authors out on tour.

PAPERBACK PUBLISHERS

The paperback "revolution," starting with Pocket Books in 1939, was not so much a revolution as a renaissance. Paperback books, known then as "dime novels," had been popular in the nineteenth century and died out only because the publishers killed each other off in price wars.

In making their comeback, paperbacks at first offered readers only reprints and low-quality original material. Gradually the paperback publishers improved their offerings. Eventually, major publishers themselves got into the paperback business. Today, hardbound books and paperbacks complement each other. Sometimes a publisher brings out hardbound and paperback editions of a given book simultaneously. Often one house publishes the hardbound book, and another house the paperback version.

The book industry divides paperbacks into two classes— mass-market paperbacks, the cheaper books one finds in grocery and drug stores as well as in bookstores; and trade paperbacks, the more expensive and better-made books that, except for the soft covers, resemble hardbound books in printing quality, paper, binding, and size. Trade paperbacks sell mostly in bookstores. Mass-market and trade paperbacks account for half the dollar volume of bookselling.

The mass-market paperback industry consists of some 14 large houses and a number of smaller ones. Bantam Books, the publisher with a rooster as its symbol, rules the roost, putting out the equivalent of a book a day.[10] Some paperback publishers specialize. Harlequin Books and the more recent Silhouette Books (a subsidiary of Simon & Schuster) produce sweet romances for women readers.

Returns of unsold books are the bane of the industry. For some books the rate of return stands at 50 percent. To get credit for unsold paperbacks, the booksellers do not return the complete books, just the covers. The insides are shredded or otherwise destroyed. Where once paperbacks sold for 25¢ each, they now sell for several dollars a copy. People seldom walk out of stores with several books anymore. A single purchase may turn out to be enough of a commitment.

[10]N. R. Kleinfield, "The Problems at Bantam Books," *The New York Times Book Review,* May 4, 1980, p. 7.

To many publishers of paperbacks, the backlist becomes the real foundation for profits. When a book continues to sell well for a couple of years, it becomes part of the backlist. When sales tail off, the book dies. A steady seller on a backlist may be promoted as heavily as a freshly published book.

"INSTANT BOOKS"

Books enjoy a reputation as long-lasting units in the communications picture, the result of careful writing, meticulous editing, and quality packaging. As much as a full year goes by before a book manuscript evolves as a real book, and the manuscript in many cases has taken years to write. However, books, especially paperback books, can be almost instantly produced, too, and they may be no more worthy of permanence than a daily newspaper.

Small publishers as well as large publishers are able, when necessary, to publish "instant books." When Bob Dylan shocked the Woodstock generation in early November 1979 with news of his conversion to born-again Christianity, immediately And Books, South Bend, Indiana, and Entwhistle Books, Glen Ellen, California, worked out details for Paul Williams's *Dylan—What Happened?* so that the 128-page book was written and published within one month.

One of the most instant of the instant books was *The Suicide Cult,* among the flood of books covering the Jim Jones sect in Guyana after the massacre in late 1978. Four days went into writing, two weeks into publishing. Marshall Kilduff and Ron Javers, *San Francisco Chronicle* reporters, aided by other reporters, wrote the book and Bantam published it. In fact, Bantam originated the idea and hired the writers. The book was typeset in Tennessee and printed in Chicago.

A publisher has to be sure of the potential of such books, because when it publishes an instant book it pays high production costs plus air freight charges and puts up with disruptions in its regular publishing program while all staff members concentrate on the one book that has to get through.

WHAT THE IMPRINT TELLS

Before deciding to give time to a work of nonfiction, the wise reader finds out something about the author's qualifications. Perhaps the reader knows the author through his earlier works. Perhaps the dust jacket biography convinces the reader that the author is an authority on his subject.

To a lesser extent, the publisher's imprint says something about the book. Generally speaking, well-known houses like Harper & Row, Random House, McGraw-Hill, Doubleday, and Little, Brown put out a more reliable, or at least a better edited, product than the smaller houses. Quality, even among the big houses, varies considerably. Random House in late 1969 put its Vintage imprint on *The Woodstock Nation: A Talk-Rock Album.* It took five days to write. Author Abbie Hoffman reported: "Lying on the floor in an office of the publisher, I'm flying high on adrenalin, excitement, no sleep, rock music and pot. Using what I can find lying around, I write out every word by hand."[11]

The big houses have catholic tastes. We expect books of popular appeal from them, so we are surprised when a house like Viking Press announces, as it did in 1966, the publication of *European and American Snuff Boxes: 1730–1830* (on sale then for a mere $30).

Certainly the top editors of major publishing firms would not agree with the theses of all the books they publish. It would be hard to imagine anyone at Houghton Mifflin, for instance, applauding what Hitler said in *Mein Kampf,* yet the firm published that book in the 1930s because it felt, rightly, that it should have the attention of American readers.

Occasionally a big house will bring out a book of high literary or social significance that appeals only to a limited audience, knowing full well the book will lose money. The house does this to add to its prestige. Perhaps it will succeed in getting librarians, at least, to notice other books on its list.

[11]"Random House Rushes 'The Woodstock Nation,'" *Publishers Weekly,* September 29, 1969, p. 46.

On the other hand, to add to its profits for the year, it may bring out a book of confession-magazine quality, but, to protect its image, the publisher slaps a subsidiary imprint on this book.

It is easier to come to a decision about the worth of a book when the imprint is that of a smaller house, one that produces fewer, say, than 50 books a year. These houses tend to specialize. Their product is predictable.

Some small imprints have become rather familiar. Who did not know the specialty of Grove Press a few years back? A cartoonist showed a nude at a switchboard. She was saying into the receiver, "Grove Press." This was the firm whose premises were taken over temporarily in April 1970 by the women's liberation movement with its demands related to "crimes against women." The movement's leaders charged that the firm had "earned millions off the basic theme of humiliating, degrading, and dehumanizing women through sadomasochistic literature, pornographic films, and oppressive and exploitive practices against its own female employees."[12] But Grove Press, which first came into prominence with the publication of the unexpurgated version of *Lady Chatterley's Lover* and later the books of Henry Miller, is now much more than a publisher of scatological works. It published *Games People Play* and Malcolm X's *Autobiography*. Some of its works in sociology are notable and are widely adopted as textbooks in colleges. It is the house that in 1981 brought out in paperback John Kennedy Toole's widely acclaimed novel, *A Confederacy of Dunces*.

Lesser known to the ordinary reader are imprints belonging to Franklin Watts, which specializes in juveniles; Watson-Guptill Publications, in art books; R. R. Bowker Co., in books about books; Arlington House, in books that take conservative political stands; Wm. C. Brown Co., in textbooks; Stackpole Books, in books about guns and the outdoors; Charles E. Tuttle Co., in books about Japan. The list goes on.

[12]"Grove Fires Union Activists; Women's Lib Seizes Offices," *Publishers Weekly,* April 20, 1970, p. 38.

The 1960s saw the beginnings of a number of lively, small houses that found it possible to publish books without the usual staff and facilities. One of these was Chelsea House, so named because its founders lived at the Chelsea Hotel (the firm eventually moved to its own quarters). The hotel switchboard operator used to answer the phone, "Chelsea," and callers naturally assumed she was an employee of the publisher.

Chelsea specialized in publishing works in the public domain. It was the first to bring out a reprint of an old Sears, Roebuck catalogue. Other Chelsea books included a collection of inaugural addresses of the Presidents and a collection of State of the Union addresses. These do not make very good reading, but they represent the kind of books libraries cannot resist buying.

PUBLISHING PROCEDURES

The book publisher is esssentially an intermediary between the writer and the audience. Presumably, the publisher knows book audiences better than the author does, and has the facilities to reach them.

A publisher does not, usually, do its own printing, but hires that out. If it publishes 500 or 600 titles a year, obviously it uses many different printers. It may use more than one printer to produce a single book—one for the illustrations, another for the text, another for the dust jacket.

In most cases it is the author who comes up with the book idea and sells it to the publisher, but sometimes the publisher conceives of a book, then hunts for an author to do it. *The Guns of August* was suggested to the author by the publisher. Some houses have been known to survey the market *first* to see whether a book will sell, then assign it to an author.

The specialized nature of the book publishing industry has prompted the setting up of a number of summer courses and institutes for potential editors across the country. Among them are the Publishing Procedures Course at Radcliffe College, the Denver Publishing Institute, the Sarah Lawrence

Publishing Laboratory, the Rice University Program, the Summer Workshop in Book Publishing at New York University, the Stanford Publishing Course, and the Careers in Publishing Course at Eckerd College, St. Petersburg, Florida. *Publishers Weekly* in 1979 estimated that the courses that year prepared 450 students for book publishing careers.

There is a lot to learn. Book publishing involves manuscript acquisition, editing and copyediting, proofreading, designing, production, handling permissions, exploring possibilities for further use of the manuscript, promotion and advertising, and distribution.

DESIGN AND PRODUCTION

So far as sales are concerned, the design of a book can be almost as important as what a book says. The effects of design start with the jacket or cover, which works like a poster for books in the stores. Often an advertising designer rather than the book's designer does the jacket because the jacket is, really, an advertisement, designed to stop the browser or passerby and do a selling job.

The design of a book starts with a decision about format—the size and feel of the book. A picture book, for instance, may require large pages and slick paper. Some books call for unusual formats. *Quit,* a book offering advice on giving up smoking, came out in a format the same size as a cigarette package.

With the basic format decided, the designer chooses a typeface, taking into consideration, among other factors, the primary market for the book. Picking the right type, seeing that it is spaced correctly, and arranging it with proper margins on the page is perhaps the book designer's most important function. Some publishers are so interested in their typography that they run colophons at the backs of their books to spell out details. Of course, the designer is also concerned about placement of the art.

The production (or manufacturing) department handles the logistics of book production. It works closely with the printer and compositor and makes decisions about paper stock, typesetting, reproduction of illustrations, methods of printing and binding, routing and coordination of proof, schedules, and final delivery. "You [sometimes] get paper from one part of the world, typesetting from Korea or Hong Kong, separations from Switzerland, printing from Japan and binding from somewhere else," Digby Diehl observed when he was editor-in-chief at Harry N. Abrams, New York, a specialist in art books.

Are books permanent? Not anymore. Since 1850, books have been printed on machine-made paper that comes largely from wood pulp. The acid content of such paper causes it to deteriorate faster than that made by hand from cotton and linen rags, the paper used for earlier books. The cheaper papers have functional life spans of only about 25 years. To keep costs down further, publishers have resorted to glued rather than sewn bindings for some of their books and cheaper materials for the covers. As a result, libraries all over the world face a crisis as their collections self-destruct (to use a *U.S. News & World Report* term). The Library of Congress estimated in 1979 that 6 million of its 18 million volumes were in "an advanced stage of deterioration."[13]

The Committee on Production Guidelines for Book Longevity has asked publishers to use acid-free paper for important books and to run a statement under the copyright notice concerning the longevity of the paper used. Books printed on acidic paper need special handling and storage by librarians if they are to survive for longer than 25 years. Some books now are being microfilmed, not only to preserve them after the original paper deteriorates, but also to save shelf space.

INDEXING

If a book is nonfiction, it probably needs an index. An index differs from a table of contents in that it lists, alphabetically, all the names, places, concepts, and things in the book that

---

[13]"America's Self-Destructing Libraries," *U.S. News & World Report*, February 12, 1979, p. 42.

might conceivably interest a user. A table of contents, which does not include much more than a listing of chapter titles, appears in the front of the book. The index appears in the back.

Often the author does the indexing, but there are professional indexers, too, organized since 1968 into the American Society of Indexers. Naturally, they think indexing is too specialized to be left to authors. On the other hand, nobody knows the book better than the author, who may choose to do the index to save the several hundreds of dollars it would cost (sometimes out of royalties) to turn the job over to an outsider.

Indexing takes place at the page-proof stage. At that time the indexer reads each word and jots down on separate sheets of paper key words and phrases along with page numbers. These slips are alphabetized and coordinated later. A typical index takes about two weeks to complete, and computers, even if available, are not of much help.[14]

GIVING BOOKS THEIR TITLES

The author provides the title, but often the publisher comes up with something different that will increase sales. When Kathleen Winsor wrote her first and highly successful novel back in the early 1940s, she wanted *Wings of the Morning.* The publisher chose *Forever Amber,* "Amber" being the name of the heroine who had many lovers and, unusual for the times, suffered no consequences.

Ideally, the title should be both intriguing and descriptive. S. J. Reichman's *Great Big Beautiful Doll* was a book giving health and beauty advice to women who are size 14 or larger. Raymond A. Moody, Jr.'s *Reflection on Life After Life* was about people who were pronounced dead or who were close to death and who lived to tell of their experiences.

A new book title often repeats an earlier one, usually out

[14]Alice Edmunds, "For the Professional Indexer a Book Needs That Listing in the Back," *Publishers Weekly,* August 14, 1978, pp. 31, 32.

of coincidence. Book titles cannot be copyrighted, so no one bothers to sue, but similar titles can cause mixups in book ordering. A publisher can avoid title duplication by consulting *Books in Print* and *Forthcoming Books* to see what has already been used.[15]

THE AUTHORS OF BOOKS

Nearly everyone who writes for publication—every reporter, freelance magazine writer, advertising copywriter, public relations person—wants to write a book. So do unpublished people like aunts who look back on pleasant childhoods, uncles who tell tall stories, students who travel to Europe, cooks who remember their mothers' recipes. These people dream of putting what they know into book form, but mostly they procrastinate, which may be a good thing. Chances are remote that their books would interest publishers.

People who succeed in writing books and seeing them published are highly organized and deeply motivated, not easily put off by skeptical publishers. Even with publication, though, authors by and large earn little for their efforts. A study conducted by Columbia University's Center for Social Sciences and released in 1981 showed that the average book author makes less than $5,000 a year. The top 10 percent of the 2239 authors who responded to the study made $45,000 or more. About half of the authors held other jobs to supplement their income. The study also showed that book authors' incomes fluctuated greatly from year to year.

Publishers take at least six weeks to decide on a submitted manuscript. Nine times out of ten the decision is "Sorry." When a manuscript is accepted, the publisher sends the author a contract setting forth the terms of acceptance. On nonfiction books a publisher may offer a contract

[15]Vinson Brown, "Duplicating Titles," *Publishers Weekly,* December 3, 1979, p. 7.

after seeing only an outline and a few sample chapters. In such cases, the publisher agrees to give the author an "advance," a sum of money ranging from a few hundred dollars to several thousand dollars. The publisher deducts the advance from the first royalties due the author after the book begins to sell.

The standard royalty arrangement gives an author 10 percent of a book's selling price on the first 5000 copies, 12½ percent on the next 5000, and 15 percent on copies beyond 10,000. When a book is successful enough to go into a second or third printing, costs of printing and paper by then have increased along with the royalty rate, yet the book's price to buyers may remain the same. Publishers sometimes become victims of their own promotional efforts. In the 1980s a number of authors, especially novelists, were accepting lower royalties in cooperation with their publishers to keep book costs down.

At the turn of the century some writers began employing agents to place their manuscripts and to dicker with publishers over royalties. Naturally, publishers preferred to deal directly with their authors. They found agents a little hardheaded when it came to money. Cass Canfield of Harper & Row tells the story of a London publisher who asked one of his writers, A. G. Gardiner, how he was coming with his life of Christ. Gardiner said the first part was in the hands of his agent. The publisher looked hurt. "To think, Mr. Gardiner, that you should have dealt with an agent, particularly in a case involving the life of Our Saviour, is really more than I can bear."[16] Today nearly every serious freelance writer has an agent. Publishers now prefer to work with agents for one reason—agents weed out incompetent writers. Writers find it as hard to get good agents to represent them as it is to sell their manuscripts directly to publishers.

Rejection continues to plague authors, even those who

[16]Cass Canfield, *The Publishing Experience* (Philadelphia: University of Pennsylvania Press, 1968), p. 58.

have already had books published. Writers of first novels are almost always turned down. To prove that first novels do not get much of a hearing, Chuck Ross, a Los Angeles freelancer, in 1975 picked out the National Book Award winner of 1969 (*Steps,* by Jerzy Kosinski), typed it, and sent it out to 14 publishers, including Random House, who had published it; all rejected it. Comments from editors included "The drawback to the manuscript, as it stands, is that it doesn't add up to a satisfactory whole" and "While your prose style is very lucid, the content of the book didn't inspire the level of enthusiasm. . . ."17

All books, even novels, involve a certain amount of research, and that includes interviewing. Some writers think they can write "off the tops of their heads." They seldom succeed in impressing publishers. The research for a book can be extensive and take years to accomplish. David Halberstam (who got an advance of $300,000 from publisher Alfred A. Knopf) took five years to complete research on *The Powers That Be* (1979), a book that examines CBS, Time, Inc., the *Washington Post,* and the *Los Angeles Times* (but not the *New York Times* because so much had already been written about that paper). *Newsweek* reported that Halberstam conducted interviews with 700 persons, some of the interviews taking up to a half-dozen return visits. Halberstam likes to start his interviews with lesser people, moving to more important people later. That way, he can cite earlier findings and perhaps elicit forthright responses. The big people will know he has the goods on them. "You talk in a way that rekindles their memories, and they realize you know, you understand. Often you get information by giving information."18

Interviewing is not the only form of research engaged in by book writers. They also work from secondary sources, materials already published. Here they run into some restrictions, for published materials are usually copyrighted.

The federal law on copyright, applicable to all the

17"Polish Joke," *Time,* February 1979, pp. 95, 96.
18"Reporting the Reporters," *Newsweek,* April 30, 1978, p. 91.

media, prevents anyone from plagiarizing the work of another, selling it, and thus depriving the original author of the revenue the work might otherwise earn. The law does not keep an author from taking *part* of what someone else has written, however, and republishing it, but the original author should be credited, and only a limited portion of the original work may be used. The copyright on a piece of published writing lasts for the lifetime of the author of the piece, plus fifty years.

How much can an author safely take from another without violating the copyright law? The law does not say specifically. Generally speaking, an author can take a paragraph or two and feel safe from a violation-of-copyright suit. The new author willing to quote *indirectly* from the original source, or to rephrase the information, can take as much as desired. After all, it is the *way* of telling something that can be copyrighted; information and ideas are in the public domain and cannot be copyrighted.

To be on the safe side, most writers, if they borrow more than a few lines and quote them directly, write first to the original writer or publisher and obtain permission to do so. Permission is usually readily granted. Sometimes a fee is requested.

GHOSTWRITERS

The person whose name appears on the book's title page is not necessarily the person who wrote the book. David Shaw quotes one book editor as saying, ". . . you would be amazed how many [books] might never get published if someone other than the person whose name appears on the cover didn't provide an awful lot of help with the actual writing."[19] The help may come from the editor, someone the editor hires, or someone the writer lines up. A book manuscript may have to be completely rewritten to make it readable.

[19]David Shaw, "Ghostwriting: Who Really Wrote Your Favorite Book?" *San Francisco Chronicle*, March 27, 1979, p. 17.

Sometimes the person who helps another person write a book gets part of the credit, but in many cases the helper remains anonymous; such a writer is a "ghostwriter."

Ghostwriters are most common in nonfiction books, including books written by celebrities. A few novels are ghostwritten, too; perhaps a well-known novelist is old or ill or is facing writer's block, and both the novelist and the publisher want to continue to profit from the novelist's fame, or it happens that the "name" writer has the idea and works out the plot and farms out the actual writing. As in all human endeavors, factory methods and specialization can set in.

What kind of money does a ghostwriter make? Plenty, when collaborating with a celebrity. Sometimes the deal is for 50 percent of what the book makes. In other cases the ghostwriter charges a flat fee.

THE "VANITY PRESS"

No wonder some writers turn to subsidy publishers, the "vanity press," as it is known in the industry. Not willing to accept the "Sorry" verdicts of agents and regular book publishers, they respond to advertising in the writers' magazines, and a few other magazines, where several subsidy publishers each month hint at easy money and quick fame. Perhaps these writers know better, but the urge to get into print is too strong. They send their manuscripts in and, sure enough, they get encouraging letters in return. "This manuscript is indicative of your talent." That kind of a line, honest enough when you consider it, could send writers scurrying to the bank, and soon they could have books to their credit, but each at a cost of several thousand dollars. For under a subsidy publisher's contract, the writer has to pay the costs of publication. The book does not sell, because often it is an abomination to begin with, and the publisher's facilities to promote and distribute it usually are limited.

Most "vanity press" authors come from the ranks of the elderly and the poorly educated, but others among the writers are well educated. Some of the presses advertise in opinion magazines and academic journals.

The head of Exposition Press, Ed Uhlan, is surprisingly frank about his operations in *The Rogue of Publishers' Row,* a book the firm circulates to prospective authors. Despite the admissions, the clients keep coming. Once the Federal Trade Commission conducted some hearings into subsidy publish-

Like other subsidy publishers, Vantage Press goes after writers with ads placed in various magazines and newspapers, this one in *Pennsylvania Gazette,* an alumni magazine. A subsidy publisher offers book writers who have been turned down by regular publishers a chance to be published, but the writers must pay for the privilege.

ing, and Uhlan's firm suffered—or so it thought—from the publicity. But with the papers carrying full accounts of the hearings, in came an old gentleman who said: "I saw your ad [!] in the paper this morning. I didn't understand all that part about that there FTC, but I read enough to know you're the fellow I want to publish my book. It's about my mother's childhood in Idaho."[20]

Major publishers get into subsidy publishing, too, when they agree to publish histories of companies who in turn agree to buy a given number of copies. Passing out copies of a company history bearing a famous publisher's imprint helps a company build its image. If some of the books sell in the bookstores, so much the better. *Eyes and Tomorrow* about Procter and Gamble (Ferguson/Doubleday) and *From Three Cents a Week* about the Prudential Insurance Company (Prentice-Hall) are examples of company histories.

Some company-instigated books work more to sell the products than to build images. Roy Benjamin specializes in producing books like this for companies and placing them with publishers. His firm produced *Creative Cooking with Foil* for Reynolds Aluminum, for instance, and got Grosset & Dunlap to distribute it.[21]

Some of the "who's who" books are vanity books in that they sell mainly to the persons listed. Even the most prestigious and useful "who's who," *Who's Who in America,* relies to some extent on sales to biographees.

SELF-PUBLISHING

Some people confuse subsidy publishing with self-publishing. There is a big difference. Self-publishing pushes the author into all aspects of publishing, including working directly with the printing, distribution, and promotion. The author pays

[20]Told by Eleanor Morehead in "How to Pay for Writing," *Esquire,* February 1961, p. 96.
[21]N. R. Kleinfield, "The Business of Vanity and Vice Versa," *The New York Times Book Review,* March 28, 1982, p. 26.

for everything and hopes that enough copies will be sold to cover costs and make a profit. People who publish themselves need a business sense as well as a background in journalism, especially in production for printing. Some self-publishers do their own typesetting. A self-publisher comes up with a name for the firm and probably rents a post office box to receive orders, for part of the sales will probably come from mail orders.

Robert J. Koenig of Giddings, Texas, tried the self-publishing approach with some success after his novel was rejected by nine publishers. "I haven't found anything a publisher can do that I can't, and it takes them much longer to do it," he says.[22]

Peter James Spielmann, another self-publisher, compares the setting up of one's own house to a Mickey Rooney/Judy Garland movie, in which someone says, "Hey! We'll write, direct and produce it ourselves, just us kids!", then makes all kinds of mistakes from amateurism. Spielmann and a colleague, Aaron Zelman, became publishers when their exposé of the insurance industry, *The Life Insurance Conspiracy,* appeared to be too hot for regular publishers to handle. They paid $1200 to a printer in 1976 to produce 1000 copies of their 100-page book, but they had to arrange for typesetting themselves and they had to paste up the pages, a project that took the amateurs one week. The book sold out and reprints with other printers followed, and eventually, with 9000 copies in print, Simon & Schuster, the big New York publisher, took over the book.[23]

What should be the charge for a self-published book? The author/publisher must put the price at *at least* twice what it cost to put the book out. If a bookstore picks off the usual 40 percent, that leaves only 10 percent, what a commercial publisher might award in author's royalties, but there is no commercial publisher doing all the promoting

[22]In a letter to the editor of *Writer's Digest,* June 1980, p. 4.
[23]Peter James Spielmann, "Tale of the Bull and the Bear," *Writer's Digest,* June 1980, pp. 58, 64.

and distributing. A more realistic price for the book would be triple its printing cost.

To promote the book, the self-publisher must send press releases to local media and review copies of the book to media interested in the subject. The author would also be outgoing enough to offer to appear on talk shows, and the publisher would suggest to editors that the author is a promising subject for feature stories. Self-publishing is not for the reticent.

THE VICISSITUDES OF BOOK PUBLISHING

All publishing, and book publishing especially, is a gamble. Cass Canfield of Harper & Row estimated that "The element of chance in trade publishing is less than in poker and about the same as in baseball."[24]

Sometimes an author fails to get his manuscript in on time, and the publisher has to revamp the schedule and announce a new publication date to the trade. Or a manuscript, when it does come in, fails to live up to expectations, and the publisher must write off a sum of money already invested in the project. And sometimes a natural—a book with all the ingredients of a big seller, one beautifully written, carefully edited, and fully promoted—falls flat.

What makes a book sell? Nobody really knows, but the subject matter of the book, the way it is advertised, and the way it is promoted are all important.

1. *The subject.* Sometimes the subject alone will do the job. In the distant past, books about Lincoln did well, as did books about doctors, and dogs, causing one observer to suggest the ideal book title: *Lincoln's Doctor's Dog.* More recently, anything about the Kennedys did well. In the 1980s books on fitness became popular, and for a time several big sellers involved cats. In early 1982 four different "Garfield"

---

[24]Cass Canfield, *The Publishing Experience* (Philadelphia: University of Pennsylvania Press, 1968), p. 45.

collections made the "Paperback Best Sellers" list of *The New York Times Review of Books.*

Books like other media often appear as spinoffs of earlier successful ventures. Sometimes a book appears as an answer to another. Cat lovers offended by the collection of *101 Things to Do with a Dead Cat* cartoons could console themselves in 1981 with *Cat's Revenge: More Than 101 Uses for Dead People* and later a *Cat's Revenge II.*

With the introduction of Rubik's cube, at least a half-dozen different books appeared in stores to tell people how to solve the puzzle.

Book publishers like to get in on trends, and early. When they see changes coming, they rush into print with books that capitalize on them. Increased interest in and tolerance of homosexuals, for instance, resulted in many new titles. Some publishers published nothing but books for homosexuals. Others, like St. Martin's Press, made homosexual books a strong part of their total output. A speaker at an American Booksellers Association convention in Chicago in 1980 estimated that the country has 22 million homosexuals, and that they are mostly adults with more "discretionary spending money" than "straight" adults have, making them good prospects for booksellers; one estimate puts their book buying at nine times that of "straights."[25]

When a book becomes successful, a number of others rush to the market to take advantage of a newly discovered audience. Sometimes success breeds parody. Books on running sold well for awhile; thus Lew Grossberger and Vic Ziegel pretended to find a new audience with their spoof, *The Non-Runners Handbook* (New York: Macmillan, 1978). Non-runners spend an estimated $665 billion on products totally unrelated to running, the authors pointed out. One of the chapters was entitled "How to Avoid the Boston Marathon," another was "Distinguished Non-Runners of History." In a review of *The Non-Runner's Book* (New York: Collier, 1978),

[25]"Marketing Gay Books," *Publishers Weekly,* July 4, 1980, p. 61.

John Leo in *Time* reported that "Non-running is America's most popular form of recreation. Nearly 200 million engage in the sport each day, and many are said to devote entire weekends to remaining stationary."[26]

Derek Evans and Dave Fulwiler ridiculed the "who's who" books in their *Who's Nobody in America,* being compiled in San Diego in the late 1970s. Calling themselves "utility infielders of life," they hoped to line up 25,000 persons for listings. Application forms carried a space for "schools dropped out of." Evans and Fulwiler carefully screened the applicants to make sure no somebodies got into the book.

Book writers keep looking for gimmicks. One prolific book writer came up with an idea that keeps him on lists of the good—if not the best—sellers. He places himself in unfamiliar spots or professions and records his reactions and experiences. "Participating journalism," he calls it. He is George Plimpton, who got his start on *The Harvard Lampoon* when editors talked him into running in the Boston Marathon. He was, he says, "prudent enough to enter it about two blocks from the finish."[27] Among the Plimpton books are *Paper Lion* and *Mad Ducks and Bears.*

One sure-fire way to write a big-selling book, as the 1970s showed us, is for a person to gain notoriety and then give "my side of the story." Whether the author is the hero or the villain does not seem to make any difference—consider all the books that grew out of Watergate. Another way is to attach oneself to a celebrity and then, after the celebrity is deceased and defenseless, recite the sordid details of the life lived beyond the public eye. Even the spouses and adopted children of the stars can get in on the act.

2. *Advertising.* Occasionally a book does much better than the publisher expects. These are the "sleepers." *Games People Play* was one. So was *The Peter Principle.* When a

---

[26]John Leo, "Running Gag," *Time,* November 6, 1978, p. 118.
[27]George Plimpton, "Paper Lecturer," *Pennsylvania Gazette,* December 1978, p. 14.

book like *Games People Play* catches on, its publisher, even at that late date, goes into an extensive advertising campaign to capitalize on the book's rising tide.

Books present a unique selling problem. Each new one requires its own well-thought-out marketing program, and some publishers produce as many as two a day. The publisher, for instance, cannot very well use as a theme in an advertising campaign, "Buy a new book today." The advertising must play up the special appeal of each new book.

By other companies' standards, book publishers' advertising budgets are low, no more than a couple of thousand dollars per book, usually, but a promotion-minded publisher will spend up to $100,000 to get a book noticed, if it is judged to justify the investment.

Book publishers use all the media of advertising, of course, but a favorite is direct-mail advertising, because so much of the business, perhaps 25 percent, comes from mail order sales. People buy books by mail because book stores are not always nearby, because they still get a kick out of opening packages that come in the mail, and sometimes because they may be embarrassed about the nature of the books they buy.

Publishers of specialized books find that they can reach their selective audience easier by mail, by renting a mailing list, than by any other way. A book publisher who specializes in mail order sales can operate with a very small staff and on a very small budget.

Someone ought to conduct a study to find what percentage of books purchased are actually *read* by the purchaser. Publishers are aware that book buyers are not necessarily book readers. Books do have value as shelf fillers and status symbols. A whole range of overpriced "coffee table" books comes out before Christmas each year to catch people when they are in a buying mood.

3. *Promotion.* One way Stein & Day promoted *The Arrangement* by Elia Kazan was to offer free copies to every head of a household in Mount Pleasant, Iowa. It was a stunt

to capitalize on an announcement by the library board there that the book was "too obscene to have in our library." The board had returned the book to the publisher. In a press release, the publisher said it was making the offer "so that citizens can decide themselves whether Mr. Kazan's book is 'obscene' as their library alleges, or whether the Library Board is practicing censorship inconsistent with American traditions." This got the book considerable additional nationwide attention.

One of the most highly publicized books of modern times was William Manchester's *The Death of a President,* published by Harper & Row. The book got mixed reviews—some said it was beautifully written and significant, some found inaccuracies in it and quarreled with the author for doing it as an "authorized" book subject to review by the Kennedys. Mrs. John Kennedy, because of some passages she considered embarrassing, insisted that revisions be made prior to publication. Manchester balked. *Look* magazine became involved because it was serializing the book. (Someone at the time suggested the magazine be renamed *The Manchester Guardian.*) The fight that resulted was so widely publicized that another author, John Corry, wrote a book just about that, *The Manchester Affair* (New York: Putnam, 1967). There was some speculation in the book publishers' trade press that in this case the publicity resulting from the fight was too intense, for sales of the book itself were actually less than expected. Reading the book apparently would have been an anticlimax.

In recent years the book publishing industry has involved itself in "media tie-ins," as when a paperback book evolves from a movie. A novel is sometimes developed with the hope—maybe a promise or even an agreement—that it will evolve into a movie, or if not a movie, into a script for television. The person who writes the book often is not the person who writes the movie or television script. A Hollywood publishing firm, in the late 1970s, combined movies with books in "Fotonovels," which were collections of photographs taken directly from movie film along with much of the dialogue. One of these, *Grease,* sold to one million buyers in the United States and two million in other countries.

If a book is to achieve the status of a best seller, its author must be willing to appear on television talk shows and be something of an entertainer or a controversial figure. Just the mention of a book on, say, the *Today Show* can set it off. Because there are financial ties between some publishers and networks and movie studios, certain books have a better chance of successful media exploitation than others that may be more deserving.

A publisher can put flashy covers on them, stack them in prominent displays, buy space to sell them in magazines, get reviewers to say nice things about them or at least notice them, send their authors around the country to appear on talk shows—but nothing sells books as effectively as word-of-mouth advertising, and that activity cannot very well be controlled. The long-term success of most books, after all, depends upon their quality and usefulness.

"BEST SELLERS"

The sports world is plagued with its All-American lists, the book world with its "best sellers."

What is a "best seller"? Well, it's almost anything one wants to make of it. In the past any book selling more than 20,000, 30,000, or 40,000 copies was considered a "best seller," but the industry now generally puts the minimum figure at 100,000 for hardbound books and 1 million for paperbacks.

Whose list should we believe? Few of them are scientifically compiled. Someone calls around to selected bookstores and asks, "What's selling?" and the bookseller looks around and guesses. Maybe there is a display up front of an overpriced book the store wants to get rid of. Well, it *could* be a best seller.

An eager publisher, knowing which stores the *New York Times Book Review* calls to compile its list, could hire people to make a run on a given book at those stores. Once a book gets included on one of the "best seller" lists, it gets the attention it needs and it becomes, quite literally, a "best seller," whatever it was before it made the list.

Of course, some of the books that make this list are junk books, there because they pander to mass tastes. To counter this, some newspapers and magazines with book review sections run not "best seller" lists but lists they call "Among the Best Sellers." Then the media can be a little choosy. Other publications run a supplemental list of books that *should* be on the "best seller" list, like "Recommended Books" or "New and Recommended."

The all-time best selling book is the Bible. In 1979, for instance, total sales of Bibles in 273 languages came to 15 million. The Bible "comes with a longer than lifetime guarantee," says an ad for The Laymen's National Bible Committee, Inc., "and it's the only book in the world that gives the reader the highest royalties." For some 60 years after it was published in 1887, the closest rival to the Bible in America was Charles Sheldon's *In His Steps,* a religious novel with estimated total sales of eight million.

REMAINDERS

Although publishers, for most of their books, order initial press runs of no more than a few thousand, their press runs may still be too high. Not all copies sell. Even a book that goes into additional printings and sells well for a while eventually reaches the point when further efforts to sell it do not pay off. For most books, two years is long enough. Unsold books lie there in the publisher's warehouse, no one having ordered them. Some have been returned by stores. Something has to be done with those remaining copies.

The publisher declares the book "out of print" and "remainders" the leftover copies. This involves selling copies at a sacrifice to houses that specialize in marketing books at bargain prices. Some books in their new "remainder" state find their way back to book stores, where they are used in sales promotions. Only hardbound books and quality paperbacks are remaindered. Cheap mass market paperbacks are destroyed.

The person buying a remainder may get a book that is a few years old but, unlike some book club editions, it is the book in its original state and at a fraction of its original cost.

BOOK CLUBS

In 1926 the book-club idea took hold with the Book-of-the-Month Club and the Literary Guild. Booksellers wrung their hands at first, but they found that the clubs not only did not cut into retail sales of books, but actually made book buyers out of people who previously did not buy them.

Book clubs (there are scores of them now) usually decide on a book before it is published, while it is in a galley-proof stage (before the type has been arranged in pages). Some clubs publish their own editions, smaller in page size than the original editions and often with cheaper paper and binding, but, as their advertising suggests, "not a single word is cut." Sometimes the book club rents the printing plates from the original publisher.

Book clubs must advertise extensively to replace members who drop out after the first year. About half do leave after the first year, but some come back later.

Book-club profit revolves around people's laziness and disorder. The club asks members to go out of their way to fill out cards saying "No" to the current selections; if they fail to do that, they have ordered the books. When the books come, people find it too much trouble to rewrap them and send them back.

Book publishers work very closely with the book clubs. Some publishers own their own book clubs, in fact, or even several of them.

BOOKS AND THE CENSORS

Of all the media of communication, books have been freest of censorship. The reason is clear: books are read primarily by an educated elite, the group least likely to sit still for censorship. Still, censorship is never more than an ideology away. It can come from any quarter, not just the right wing, which ordinarily gets the blame.

Recently so innocuous a work as *Mary Poppins* felt the wrath of the "protectors." This time librarians themselves took the book off the shelves—in San Francisco. The book was found to insult members of minority groups for its unenlightened language. A committee had concluded that the book, written fifty years ago, takes "the English view of the white man's burden . . . that is naturally offensive to minorities." Oregon's *Eugene Register-Guard,* in an editorial, said that if librarians continue in their "purification binge" they might end up getting rid of "Shakespeare's 'The Merchant of Venice,' on the grounds that it is anti-Semitic, virtually all of Mark Twain's works, on grounds that they are racist, the United States Constitution, on grounds that it is proslavery, and the Bible, on grounds that it is sexist."[28] The *Guard* made the point in its editorial that a library should contain both "good" and "bad" books and that literature of the past should be read to understand the past better.

In 1982 one school, caving in to charges of racism, took Mark Twain's *Adventures of Huckleberry Finn* off a required reading list. It was an irony Twain would have appreciated, for the book actually satirized racism. And its critics failed to view it as a product of its time.

Even *Snow White and the Seven Dwarfs* is not safe. When a fashionable school in Chicago put on the play in 1979 the faculty members in charge changed the name to *Princess in the Woods* to avoid offending anyone who might have felt that the White was, vaguely, "racist." Bob Greene, columnist for Field News Service, reported that a few years earlier feminist groups had complained that the play was "sexist" because it had Snow White waiting dutifully on seven male dwarfs.

A school board banned *Making It with Mademoiselle* be-

[28]"A Spoonful of Censorship," *Eugene Register-Guard,* November 12, 1980, p. 10A.

cause of the book's provocative title, but cancelled the ban later when it found that the book was only about dressmaking with dress patterns.

That private persons other than buyers can affect the fortunes of book publishers can be illustrated by the activities of Norma and Mel Gabler of Longview, Texas. "The Gablers have . . . inspired attacks on textbooks by a host of community groups and thousands of parents throughout the U.S.," observes *Time*. [29] The Gablers, incorporated as Educational Research Analysts with a staff of six, look for moral and patriotic lapses in textbooks and call these lapses to the attention of those who adopt textbooks, especially in Texas, where orders are large and centralized. *Time* says that "Texas education officials swear by the Gablers" because they reflect what parents want, but publishers and other educators, of course, are less than enthusiastic.

WHAT BOOKS CAN ACCOMPLISH

Book writers can profoundly affect the course of events. Consider the case of Ralph Nader. When as a student at Harvard Law School he drove across country and witnessed several accidents, he saw how easily the cars had crumbled at impact and began to ask questions. He found that in a lawsuit growing out of an accident, the driver, not the car manufacturer, carried the burden of proof. It seemed to this young man that the design of the car and the way it responded should be considered, too.

As he probed further, he discovered that the public was generally apathetic, the car makers not very cooperative. He began writing, first magazine articles, then a book, *Unsafe at Any Speed*. One Chevrolet model, the Corvair, literally bowed out as a result of the author's revelations. His book brought about an admission from the car makers that they should indeed share some of the blame for accidents. Congress got interested, new laws were passed, and highway

[29]"Was Robin Just a Hood?" *Time*, December 31, 1979, p. 76.

safety, at least insofar as car design is involved, was somewhat improved. Now even after cars are sold they are called back by manufacturers to correct defects. All because Ralph Nader wrote a book, it could be argued.

One knew Nader had arrived when the cartoonists and the magazines took off on his book (which earned him $60,000). A *New Yorker* cartoon showed a sports car that had crashed through a fence, its driver defending himself to the police. "I was waiting for *Unsafe at Any Speed* to come out in paperback." *Grump* ran an "exposé" on furniture manufacturers and called it *"Unsafe at Any Sitting."* The article called for padded head rests on rocking chairs to prevent "chair lash" when rocking. In late 1969 *Time* put Nader on its cover.

Nor was this the first time a book-writing journalist had affected a nation.[30] Rachel Carson did it with *Silent Spring*. Jessica Mitford did it with *The American Way of Death*. Years earlier, Upton Sinclair did it with *The Jungle,* a book that brought about the 1906 Meat Inspection Act.

Although it was a novel, Joseph Heller's *Catch 22,* published in 1961, is said to have helped bring on the antiwar sentiment that developed in the 1960s. Betty Friedan is said to have started the women's movement with the 1963 publication of *The Feminine Mystique,* a nonfiction work.

BOOKS ARE ONLY HUMAN

It is easy to point to books that revamped our thinking and changed and enriched us, but just as books have the capacity to do great things, they also have the capacity to cause great mischief and unrelieved boredom. One can find shoddy writing, questionable logic, and misinformation in books just as in all the other media.

Some book publishers pander to bad taste. One of these

[30]See Robert B. Downs, *Books That Changed America* (New York: Macmillan, 1970).

Norman Mailer autographs copies of his 1979 book, *The Executioner's Song*, a novelistic treatment of the 1977 execution of convicted murderer Gary Gilmore. Mailer, who has won both the Pulitzer Prize and the National Book Award, has written both fiction and nonfiction. His nonfiction often stirs controversy, and the flamboyant Mailer himself is a newsmaker. (*Source:* Heitner, Taurus.)

was Bernard Geis and Associates, which gave us what one observer called "snickering sex." B.G. and A. came up with an intriguing idea, to publish novels with heroes based on real people. Readers could not miss the identities, which were off just enough to keep the publisher from getting into libel suits. *The Carpetbaggers*, for instance, was not about Howard Hughes. *The King* was not about Ronald Reagan and Frank Sinatra. *The Exhibitionist* was not about Jane Fonda. *The Voyeur* was not about Hugh Hefner.

As a protest against the novels of Jacqueline Susann and Harold Robbins (Geis authors), 25 writers for *Newsday*, a Long Island, New York, newspaper, wrote chapters for a potboiler called *Naked Came the Stranger* (Lyle Stuart, New York, 1969), and saw it rise to the best-seller lists. It was the idea of Mike McGrady, columnist on the newspaper, who outlined the plot and assigned the chapters. He told his writers, "Good writing will be blue-pencilled into oblivion, and there will be an unremitting emphasis on sex." None of the writers knew what the others were doing. McGrady did some editing in fitting chapters together and chose the name Penelope Ashe as the "author" of the book. Within a few days after publication it had sold 25,000 copies, and a paperback contract and movie rights had been negotiated. After the hoax was revealed sales went much higher. One of the writers, John Cummings, who spent four and a half hours on his chapter, said the book is "just a collection of clichés and sexual aberrations."[31]

An extreme in self-help books materialized in Great Britain in 1980 with the promised publication of *A Guide to Self-Deliverance*, 10,000 words on how to end your life. It was to be published by Exit, an organization of people who feel they may one day want to turn to suicide. One had to be a member for three months to be eligible to buy the book. Reaction to the news of the publication of the book was so intense that the publishers cancelled plans for publication—a law against helping people commit suicide was a factor, too. The book was scheduled for later publication in Scotland, where no such law was in force.

One way for an author to make a book impressive is to make it long. A thick book does not cost a lot more to market

---

[31]Mike McGrady wrote a book on the hoax, *Stranger than Naked, or How to Write Dirty Books for Fun and Profit: A Manual* (New York: Peter H. Wyden, 1970).

than a thin one, but the publisher can charge a lot more for it, and its bigness alone says to some book buyers that a lot of thought—and probably a lot of research—went into it. Moreover, the thick book makes its readers feel good about having waded through it. They feel they have accomplished something.

Unfortunately, a book is often thick because no one edited it, insisted that each phrase count, and took out the author's padding. Some critics felt that Halberstam's book, for instance, needed editing to cut the number of pages.

It can take longer to write a short book than a long book. "The way in which a writer can best conceal that he has little to say is not, as the innocent might conjecture, to write a short book . . . , but to use every artifice to make the book spill on to the seven-hundredth page. Our minds grow so clogged by the words that we cease to ask if they contain any substance or meaning or significance," observes British journalist Henry Fairlie.[32]

Authors further conceal the fact that they have little to say by resorting to vagueness. Critic Bryan Griffin thinks that many writers use vague terms because they have nothing to say. "Perhaps . . . [the writer] believes . . . that the only legitimate function of the contemporary writer of fiction is to dress up old truths in fuzzy new robes—to smudge the picture a little, to pretend that deliberate ambiguity is subtlety, or even originality."[33] Vagueness also comes from a writer's fear of offending not only the book's readers but also the people and organizations entering into the story. The possibilities of a libel suit prove to be an inhibiting factor, too. Vagueness also comes from a writer's inability to state things clearly. For some writers, clarity is even more elusive than style and flair.

In the area of book advertising one sees much to criticize. Some readers have been hard-pressed to find much similarity between a book and the dust-jacket description of it,

[32]Henry Fairlie, "The Pen is Not the Sword," *Harper's*, June 1979, p. 81.
[33]Bryan Griffin, "Literary Hype," *The Atlantic*, June 1979, p. 49.

not to mention what paperback publishers can do with their covers. How exactly does the nude on the cover relate to the story inside? Art Buchwald has shown that an enterprising publisher could even do a job on *Snow White and the Seven Dwarfs*. Buchwald's blurb reads: "The story of a ravishing blonde virgin who was held captive by seven deformed men, all with different lusts." And on *Alice in Wonderland*: "A young girl's search for happiness in a weird, depraved world of animal desires. Can she ever return to a normal, happy life after falling so far?"

Nowhere is creativity more in evidence than on the flaps or the back panels of book jackets where authors' accomplishments are recorded. Only job resumes can make more of routine roles. To cite one example, the jacket for *Jackie Oh!*, published by Lyle Stuart, said that author Kitty Kelley had been "press secretary" to Senator Eugene McCarthy (D. Minn.) for four years. Well, it turned out she simply helped distribute press releases. "All a misunderstanding," *New York* quoted the publisher as saying.[34]

WHY READ REVIEWS?

"Nature, when she invented, manufactured, and patented her authors, contrived to make critics out of the chips that were left over," said Oliver Wendell Holmes. Nevertheless, every author must face the critics. Critics can make the difference as to whether or not a book sells. Nothing pleases an author more than to find expressions like "must reading" and "a long-needed book" in a review. The review does not have to be admiring. Just getting the book *noticed* by reviewers is enough to spur sales. And the promotion department of a book publisher can find *something* in even the most scathing review, pull it out of context, and play it up in the ads. "The book is both original and interesting, but the parts that are original are not interesting and the parts that are inter-

[34]Neal Travis, "Kitty Oh! Press Secretary's Tale," *New York*, December 4, 1978, p. 8.

esting are not original," a review might read. The publisher in his advertising could then quote only this from the review: "original and interesting." Here is one of Dorothy Parker's typical dismissals of a book: "This is not a novel to be tossed aside lightly. It should be thrown with great force." What prevents the book promoter from using just the first sentence?

To get a book reviewed is no simple matter. Every publisher would like every one of its books noticed in *The New York Times Book Review*, *The New York Review of Books*, *Library Journal*, *Publishers Weekly*, *Choice*, and other major book review media as well as magazines like *Time*, but only a few make the grade. A book's chances are best in the specialized magazines—an art book might be noticed in an art magazine, a sports book in a sports magazine, a religious book in a religious magazine. Every magazine running book reviews is flooded with requests. *Harper's* gets as many as 400 books a month, all clamoring for attention, the publishers hoping for published notice at the time the book is first displayed in the stores.

Another problem concerns assigning the book for review. Should it go to a person who has written a similar book, who knows a lot about the subject but who might be wary of the competition, or should it go to someone more removed? Should the book go to a friend of the author's, who might be too kind, or to an enemy, who might be unfairly critical?

In his article in *The Atlantic* Bryan Griffin complains, "There isn't much to read these days, and when something even semiliterate comes along, a kind of panic sets in."[35] By "panic," Griffin means excessive praise by reviewers, some of the praise taken from the book's jacket. "A major literary event" is one common phrase. "Probably the best espionage novel ever written" is how a UPI writer sized up Graham Greene's *The Human Factor*. How does a writer for a wire service know that? Griffin observes that such a re-

[35]Bryan Griffin, op. cit., p. 46.

viewer would like you to think that he "reads an awful lot of spy stories and that he is pretty much the final word on these things."[36]

Some favorite reviewer's clichés, guaranteed to mark one as a paid-up member of the fraternity, if one wants to write reviews, are these:

1. "At last . . ."
2. "Once every decade a book comes along that . . ."
3. "A good read."
4. ". . . sensitive . . ."
5. ". . . moving . . ."
6. ". . . profound . . ."

With readers' standards lowered—with the attitude so much around that anything created is good—today's reviewers seem more given to praise than criticism, especially if the work is by a name writer. If the work has some kind of a gimmick, like an absence of punctuation, so much the better, apparently. "It is the quality of the personal vision, not the degree of its eccentricity, that determines the ultimate worth of any written work," Griffin cautions.[37]

So what is in a review for the reader? Why should people read book reviews?

1. *For news about books.* Obviously, the reader cannot possibly see each of the new books issued every year. Turning to the reviews, the reader can take note at least of the books deemed important by book-review editors and expect to find descriptions there less biased than jacket copy, because reviewers, theoretically, are not trying to sell books.

Theoretically; unfortunately, there is a lot of back-scratching among reviewers, some of whom write books themselves. Their attitude seems to be: You say nice things about my book and I'll say nice things about yours. Furthermore, reviewers tend to write to impress their colleagues rather than to serve the reader.

[36]Ibid., p. 45.
[37]Ibid., p. 56.

2. *For evaluation of books.* The reader thinking about buying a book will want to know something about it first. Will it be worth the money? Should the reader put a reserve notice in for it at the library? A reviewer can help with the decision.

But some reviews sound as if the reviewer did not even read the book, much less study it. Perhaps the reviewer made notes from information on the jacket, taking literally Sydney Smith's remark: "I never read a book before reviewing it. It prejudices one so!"

The reader has a right to expect to be told *why* a critic likes or dislikes a book. Barbara George, responding to Granville Hicks's review of *In Cold Blood* in the *Saturday Review,* said in a letter to the editor that she didn't like Hicks's final sentence, "I will point out, however, that although this is a very, very good book, *Crime and Punishment* is a great one." Barbara George wanted to know why Hicks felt this way. "He indicates in his closing sentence that he has judged the book by some higher standards and found it wanting. I will point out, however, that, until Mr. Hicks will tell us what these standards are, he will remain a very, very good critic, but not a great one."

The review reader should pay particular attention to the reviewer's credentials. A person who is an expert in the field covered by the book can better evaluate the book than some peripatetic reviewer who wants to be a kingmaker. If possible, the reader should read more than one review of a given book. Intelligent reviewers with good intentions can differ wildly.

However, the reader should not read reviews *instead* of reading the book. A review is, after all, second hand. If the review interests the reader, chances are the subject in its original state of discussion will be even more interesting.

3. *For tangential benefits.* Some reviewers are not content to stay with the book under discussion. They use the book as an excuse for writing an essay. Reviewers in *The New York Review of Books* are guilty of this. While this practice may annoy the books' writers and publishers, it may well re-

ward the reader. Some of these "book reviews" can stand by themselves in the information they impart and the ideas they bring out.

If nothing else, the review reader learns something about the fine art of putting someone down. "The covers of this book are too far apart."—Ambrose Bierce. "Mr. Henry James writes fiction as if it were a painful duty."—Oscar Wilde. "A redeeming feature of the work is that no talent was wasted in the writing of it."—*The New Yorker*.

FOR THAT MATTER, WHY READ BOOKS?

In no other medium does an author have so much room to maneuver as in a book, room to explain all the subtle turns of the subject, room to cite and identify all sources, room to list other books on the same subject, and, in the back of his book, room for an index to all the information in the book, making it easy for the reader later to find exactly what is wanted. All this gives a book its unique value to readers.

Putting a piece of writing into a book does not in itself make it any worthier than writing found in less permanent form. As was pointed out earlier, quality varies in book publishing just as it varies in newspaper and magazine publishing. When readers sharpen their critical faculties, they will conclude that a majority of the books published, quite apart from the fact that they deal with areas the reader is not interested in, are not worth their time. Too many publishers think H. L. Mencken was not kidding when he said that no one ever went broke underestimating the intelligence of the American public. Charles A. Madison observes: "Good books have always been the exception rather than the rule."[38]

Time magazine and other observers have described one group of books—those put together with scissors or tape recorder to cash in on a ready market—as "nonbooks." Ghost-written autobiographies, "as told to" books, books of photo-

---

[38]Charles A. Madison, *Book Publishing in America* (New York: McGraw-Hill, 1966), p. 403.

EX LIBRIS

HON MARY FRANCES
HARRIET BORTHWICK

Book lovers, especially in the past, pasted personal labels, called
bookplates, in the fronts of all their books to identify the owner
and maybe insure their safe return if the books were borrowed.
Just as there are many book collectors, there are many collectors
of bookplates. This one was designed by R. Anning Bell in 1895.

graphs with cute captions, some inspirational books (like the completely serious book, *The Power of Prayer on Plants*), and many self-help books (like *The Secrets of Long Life*)[39] would certainly fall into the nonbook category.

Yet when all of this has been said, the fact remains that the minority of genuinely good books among any year's crop of titles represents the peak of achievement in journalism and the arts.

The format of the book offers writers their best chance to utilize their creative skills fully and to explore their topics in searching depth. Moreover, of all the various forms of journalism and writing, the book involves the most relaxed set of publication deadlines and thus affords the opportunity for the kind of careful editing and polishing that may not be possible in most magazine and newspaper writing. When a piece of writing of book length is good, it is very, very good indeed.

As the educational level of Americans rises and their leisure time increases, the book continues to thrive, despite competition from other media. More visually oriented media have their newly won place, of course, but they cannot do the whole job of communication.

Perhaps writer David Dempsey has the best response for those who, like the late Marshall McLuhan, preach the demise of the book: "Has anyone ever said, 'How well I remember the slide transparency that changed my life'?"[40]

[39]This book, by Dr. George Gallup and Evan Hill, published by Bernard Geis and Associates, got this reception from *Time:* "Longevity statistics that a newspaper could summarize in half a column, padded to book length by some extraordinarily foolish anecdotes and a questionnaire in which the reader can test his chances of living long enough to see publishing get even worse."

[40]David Dempsey, "Humanist Wedges to Learning," *Saturday Review,* July 12, 1969, p. 28.

Chapter 10
Not by Words Alone

So far, this book has concerned itself mainly with words and their effects on readers. This chapter will deal with nonverbal aspects of the news and opinion media, specifically: art.

Like so many terms in journalism, "art" defies a clear-cut definition. In a narrow sense, it means drawings, paintings, cartoons, maps, and charts. Recent usage has broadened its meaning to include photographs. In an even broader sense, "art" means the overall look of the pages—the design of the type and the way it fits with the pictures.

The first publications to come from printing presses when they were perfected in fifteenth-century Germany consisted of words alone. Any embellishments were put there by hand after the printing was done. Prior to Gutenberg's experiments in type cutting and type casting, some pictures had been printed, of course, but they had first been carved out of blocks of wood. They were necessarily crude. It was several centuries beyond Gutenberg before intricate drawings and paintings could be reproduced in full fidelity.

It was the middle of the nineteenth century before the camera was perfected. In 1872, in France, the principle of photography was applied to the reproduction of artwork,— illustrations and decorations—and photoengraving was born. By the turn of the century, reproduced pictures— photographs, drawings, and paintings—were commonplace in newspapers and magazines around the world.

ART DIRECTION

A reader following a story down a column on the newspaper's front page and onto another page inside does not notice what a typographer or a student in a class in typography would see, that the story is set, say, in 9-pt. Corona on a 9½-pt. slug, or that its headline is set in Bodoni Bold.[1] If the newspaper decides to experiment with ragged-right columns or to change its headlines from Bodoni Bold to a sans serif face like Helvetica, the reader may be vaguely aware of the change and a bit uncomfortable about it because it's different and not fully compatible with usual reading habits. But in a few days the reader will be perfectly at home with the new format, paying full attention again to what stories say rather than how they look on the page.

Yet, a publication must attend to the matter of which typeface or typefaces to use, and how to arrange stories and other elements on a page. Type houses offer editors several thousand different typefaces, and each face comes with its own personality. Each face conveys its own mood; some typefaces, because of their design, suggest urgency, others

[1] Printers use "points" (abbreviated "pt.") to measure type height. Seventy-two points equal one inch.

A crude woodcut from the nineteenth century. At one time all illustrations for newspapers had to be done in this medium. The white areas were created by carving away the surface, leaving the design in mirror image. The block surface was inked and pressed against the paper to print the design.

elegance, others power, others dignity. How stories and headlines and pictures are arranged on a page can also have a psychological effect on the reader, an effect quite apart from what the stories themselves say.

Most publications help establish a personality for themselves by setting all stories in a single typeface and confining headlines to two or three typefaces at the most. Furthermore, they establish a basic format so that each issue has some resemblance to previous issues.

Magazines, some as long ago as in the early 1930s, have added art directors to their staffs to supervise the selection of typefaces, the design of the publication, and the assignment and use of artwork and photography. Newspapers— bound by tradition and facing deadlines that make difficult any serious attention to the subtleties of typography and design—were slow to employ art directors. Some papers still leave to their various editors the responsibility for making up the pages and working with the staff artists and photographers.

HOW PICTURES ARE REPRODUCED

It is one thing to turn out a good print in a darkroom working from a photographer's negative, but another thing to reproduce the print in a publication. It is one thing to sit down at a drawing board and make a sketch in pen and ink, yet quite a different thing to reproduce it.

To reproduce either a photograph or a drawing, a publication must see that someone takes a picture of the art and uses the negative to make an exposure on a sensitized piece of metal. The piece of metal, after it is further treated, becomes a printing plate.

The reproduction of a photograph is a little more complicated than the reproduction of a drawing. A photograph has varying tones of gray. The printer's ink is black, pure black, yet it must create the *illusion* of grays. This is done by putting a screen (a piece of glass with crosshatched lines) between the lens and the film when the negative is made. The light reflected by the picture goes through the screen and breaks down into a dot pattern. The plate made from this negative is called a *halftone.*

The dots are easily seen by looking closely at a photograph in a newspaper. As the eye moves back from the photograph, the dots blur into gray areas, dark gray where the dots are big and close together, light gray where they are small and farther apart.

Color photographs require the same screening, but to reproduce them a platemaker must make several plates. A color photograph requires several superimposed printings, one for each primary color and, for better printing jobs, an extra plate for black.

Most newspapers and magazines these days are printed by offset lithography, a process that has made the reproduction of artwork less costly than in the days of letterpress printing. But, whether the printing process is offset or letterpress or even rotogravure (a process suited to long press runs), art must go through the steps described above to find its way onto the printed page.

STOCK ART

When woodcuts were all a newspaper could use to illustrate a story, readers could expect to see a picture in one issue that

When a photograph is reproduced as if it were a black and white drawing, avoiding the use of a screen in photographing it for a plate, the resulting image is harsh and strong, without middle tones, which have "dropped out." The photograph ends up looking like a line drawing. The effect can be striking, as it is here. *Soil and Water Conservation News* used this art, showing ripples of wind-blown soil encroaching on abandoned farm machinery, for one of its covers. The original photograph was by Gene Alexander.

was the same as in an issue some weeks before. Suppose a fire broke out in a downtown building, but there wasn't enough time to make a new drawing and cut it out of wood. One fire looks pretty much like another, the editor reasoned, so why not use a picture of an earlier fire?

Publications still use "stock" art, as ready-made artwork is called. Photo houses and art studios can provide by mail inexpensive "canned" illustrations for use by budget-conscious editors or advertising executives. The art is slick but predictable; it is, of course, more decorative than topical. If the publication wants more elaborate art, it can buy already printed covers featuring full-color photography. When these arrive, the publication—usually a company magazine of some kind—prints its own name across the top of the picture and wraps the covers around sections printed locally.

PHOTOGRAPHS VERSUS ARTWORK

Generally speaking, editors prefer photographs for nonfiction (news stories and magazine articles), drawings and paintings for fiction. But, as photographers have moved from literal recordings of what they see to experimental and creative photography, the distinction between the two kinds of art has diminished.

To the chagrin of illustrators, photography, because it is faster and, in most cases, cheaper, has overtaken artwork as the chief source for art in journalism, in magazines as well as newspapers. But the reader can still expect to see artwork used under these conditions:

1. When the item to be shown is not in season. The editor wants to show snow, for example, but none is on the ground.
2. When conditions for taking pictures are not ideal. There is not enough light.
3. When the editor wants an exaggerated realism. It is true that certain lenses can elongate or condense or otherwise distort, but a drawing or painting can still do the job more dramatically.

4. When the editor cannot get a model's release. Under certain circumstances in journalism—and always when advertising is involved—the subject enjoys a right of privacy. A model who is willing to be pictured must sign a statement to that effect, and often one does so for a fee. An illustrator can create his own person, who cannot object to being used.

5. When the editor wants the person in a picture to look like no one in particular, to be a composite character.

6. When the editor wants a flat, decorative, or cartoony look.

If it is not immediately possible to tell how the picture was produced, whether through photography or through art techniques, look for a signature. If the work is signed, it most likely is a painting or drawing. Photographs usually carry credit lines set in type outside the picture.

SYMBOLISM

Pictures can be realistic or abstract. As communicators move from the realistic to the abstract, they make sure their audiences are ready for the move. For, generally speaking, it takes a better educated, or at least a better indoctrinated, audience to understand abstraction.

The two journalists most devoted to abstraction are the editorial cartoonist and the advertising person. The editorial cartoonist takes familiar objects or legendary figures and makes them stand in for real people or events, creating a situation or a scene and asking the reader to pretend that real people are playing the roles. The advertising person creates an abstraction by using symbols to represent products, services, ideas, or the companies themselves. The symbols are *trademarks*. The best trademarks are simplified renditions of objects easily recognized and clearly appropriate to the company—such as CBS Television's eye—or they can be stylized art pieces that have to be invented and shown again and again before the reader ever associates them with the sponsor. An example is the bow-tie-like symbol Chevrolet uses.

Symbols are interesting because they mean different things to different groups of people. This is what makes their use such a challenge to the journalist. Adding one more point to a five-pointed star, for instance, makes it stand for something entirely different. Take the case of the umbrella. In the 1920s, thanks to the persistent efforts of an editorial cartoonist, Rollin Kirby, it came to represent Prohibition. Kirby showed Prohibition as an old, skinny, crotchety man, dressed in black, and always carrying an umbrella. Then, in the 1930s, the English Prime Minister, Neville Chamberlain, made a deal with Hitler for "Peace in our time." Because he had been photographed carrying an umbrella, the umbrella, at least in the hands of cartoonists, became associated with appeasement. In the 1960s an insurance company, not much worried about any earlier association with the symbol, adopted it as its trademark. To the readers of this company's advertising, the umbrella stands for "protection."

In the prolife/prochoice controversy of the early 1980s, the antiabortion forces used a red rose, a symbol for life and love; those who would allow abortion held up a wire coathanger, which stood for tools used where abortions were performed illegally.

OPTICAL ILLUSIONS

Everyone is familiar with graphic experiments in which the eye is tricked into accepting one line as being longer than another or one ball as being bigger than another. The lines are really the same length and the balls are really the same size; they just *look* different. You can "elongate" a line by adding supplemental lines that "pull" the eye out from the edges of the original line. You can make one ball look larger than another by surrounding the one with smaller balls and surrounding the other with larger balls. By *comparison,* one ball looks bigger than the other.

You can take two squares, fill one with vertical lines and the other with horizontal lines, and one will look like a vertical rectangle and the other like a horizontal rectangle. The eye gets into the habit of moving in one direction, and it keeps moving.

Architects realize the eye is tricked by perspective and foreshortening, and so, in their designs, they *build in* error in order to make truth possible. Typesetters do the same thing. Spacing between letters, if perfectly consistent, results in an uneven appearance. Certain letters then, because of their shape, must be moved closer together; certain other letters must be moved farther apart.

Both photographic and drawing-board art are subject to optical illusions, intentional or accidental. Pictures are not always what they seem to be.

THE FICKLE LINE

One of James Thurber's classic gags has a father and son looking at a photo album, the mother sitting in another part

Thomas Hood's "A Lady of Our Village" illustration is an optical illusion. A first quick glance, or a glance from a distance, suggests a curly-haired person with an open mouth. A second glance reveals a village church framed by two trees and two birds. The illustrator wants both reactions. Editorial cartoonists often use optical illusions to make their political points.
(*Source:* From *Humor, Wit and Fantasy*, Hart Picture Archives, Hart Publishing Company, New York, 1976.)

of the room, just listening. "That's an old beau of your mother's. He didn't get to first base." The gag is meaningless except for the expression on the mother's face. Were it an ordinary smile, the gag would not work. Were it a frown, it would not work either. Thurber used a cartoonist's favorite trick of combining a slight smile with a frown, an expression difficult for a real person to work up. In a cartoon, where such an expression is possible, the effect is instantaneous—the look is evil incarnate. You just *know,* if the father and son do not, that the man pictured in the album certainly did get to first base or at least came close enough to make it a tough call for the umpire.

There is a less celebrated cartoon showing a little boy crying, standing next to a middle-aged man at the beach. The man is saying: "But I tell you, I don't have your miserable beach ball!" Again, if the man were ordinary looking, the gag would not come off. But the cartoonist has given him a pot belly about the size of a beach ball, and that small, curved line makes all the difference.

In each case, just the slightest twist in drawing is everything. A couple of tiny diagonal lines in Thurber's case, a half-moon line in the other.

ART AND STATISTICS

Nowhere in journalism is the placement of a line more crucial than in the making of a chart or graph. Charts and graphs have the feel of authenticity because they are, after all, based on statistics.

Cite statistics in support of an argument, and readers do not—cannot—argue back. "Unquestionably, for the moment, numbers are king," observed *Time* in an essay on "The Science & Snares of Statistics." "But perhaps the time has come for society to be less numerically conscious and therefore less willing to be ruled by statistics." Benjamin Disraeli said: "There are three kinds of lies: lies, damned lies, and statistics." A given set of statistics can "prove" almost anything. What, for instance, does the Chamber of

Commerce claim, "Our average temperature is 70 degrees," really mean? That on most days 70 is how hot it is in that town? Or that half the time the temperature is over 100 and half the time the temperature is barely over freezing?

And how can readers be sure that, as reported, 40 percent of the population feels one way about a given issue and 60 percent feels another? Has the pollster provided evidence that his sample was truly representative? Was a large enough group reached? Did the pollster include all types in his sample: rich and poor, young and old, professional men and workers, men and women, swingers and squares, blacks and whites?

In his delightful *How to Lie with Statistics,* Darrell Huff criticizes the use of statistics not only in their raw form but also in their more dramatic form, graphs. He shows readers that in line graphs, bar charts, and pie charts, it is possible to create any impression the chartmaker wants to create, regardless of the statistics involved.

In a line graph, where the upward trend is not convincing enough, all the chartmaker needs to do is to press the two outside verticals in toward the center, keeping his unit scale the same. (In a line graph, the sequence of time runs along the bottom, the number of units up the side.) The more compressed the extremities, the steeper the angle of rise.

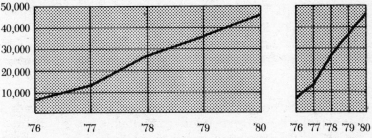

Which growth record is the more impressive, the one represented by the graph at the left, or the one by the graph at the right?

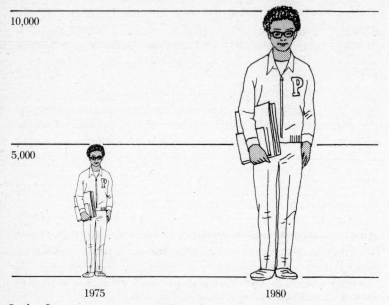

10,000

5,000

1975   1980

Is the figure representing 1980 only twice as big as the figure representing 1975?

In a bar graph, the most common lie occurs when the chartmaker changes the ordinary bar graph to a picture graph. An example: to show growth in enrollment, the chartmaker makes a drawing of a student (you can tell it's a student by the no-nonsense expression on the face, the glasses, and the books he's carrying) that represents 5,000 for the year 1975. Right next to that the chartmaker makes a similar drawing, this time twice as high. It represents 10,000 for the year 1980. But is the second drawing really only double the first? Of course not. Any person twice as tall as another person is also considerably wider and considerably bigger around. If the figures are drawn at all realistically, the second figure is *much more* than double the first figure. The effect, if not a lie, is certainly misleading.

An error almost as common in the making of bar charts is to cut out part of the center sections of bars when there

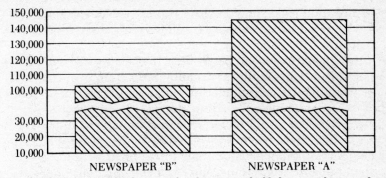

Does Newspaper "B" have only about one-half the circulation of Newspaper "A"? Look again.

is not enough space to run them in their entirety. Both—or all—bars in the chart are affected. But, obviously, proportions as well as size are changed when the same-size section is taken out of a short bar and also out of a long one. The intent may be only to show that one bar is taller than the other, but the relative sizes are also changed.

THE PHOTOGRAPHER AS JOURNALIST

Photographers play an increasingly important role in the dissemination of news and opinion. On newspapers, news-oriented magazines, and trade journals, photographers are full-time employees going out on a story just as a reporter does. On many publications, photographers are combination people, writing stories and taking pictures, too. For general circulation magazines and advertising agencies photographers take pictures, usually, on assignment as free-lancers.

Like writers on the staff, photographers subject their work to editing, not always with good humor. Photographers almost to a person object to word-oriented persons having the final say on visual matters. Photographers usually submit a generous supply of contact prints from which editors, or art directors, make selections. Out of scores of prints submitted, only two or three may be picked. The photographer then supplies carefully printed enlargements, "glossies," for reshooting by the platemaker.

Writers need not be there when a news event takes place; they can gather information later from eye witnesses or from participants. Sometimes photographers can operate in the same way, re-creating the event for picture-taking purposes. But accident and tragedy cannot be re-created, and when these occur a publication cannot show them unless a photographer happened to be on the scene or got there soon afterwards. In many cases, an amateur photographer, or one not ordinarily associated with the publication, steps forward. A Dallas dress manufacturer, who happened to have a movie camera focused on President John F. Kennedy when he was shot, sold his 8 mm color film to *Life* for $50,000.

The photograph became a powerful social force during the Depression years of the 1930s when photographers brought out, more vividly than writers could, the plight of the dispossessed and the unemployed. Many of today's photographers are less interested in simply recording what they see than in creating works of art or influencing people to courses of action.

FROM LEFT TO RIGHT

Photographs in journalism sometimes tell a complete story. The photograph of Hitler dancing for joy after one of his victories in World War II did not need words to explain it. The photograph in the late 1960s of the South Vietnamese national police chief shooting a prisoner at close range was shocking enough by itself. So was the picture in 1970 of the girl on her knees beside a mortally wounded student at Kent State University.

Most photographs, however, need a few words to place them in context; especially, people pictured need to be identified. Newspaper people often call the words that go with photographs "cutlines," because the photographs are printed from "cuts" or plates; magazine editors call them "captions."

Cutlines often do not add enough to an understanding of the photograph to make them worthwhile. The photograph shows an army general pointing to a map, and the cutlines begin: "General A. B. Blank points to a map of . . ." Obviously. Perhaps the trouble with cutline writing in many cases is that the photograph is not worth running to begin with, and certainly not worth writing about. The clichés of journalistic writing show up in cutlines, too. A Northwest newspaper once showed a body wrapped in a blanket, tied, lying in a wooded area. The cutlines read: "This body of an unidentified woman wrapped in gray blanket and sheet, bound with rope, was discovered Friday just off Evergreen highway six miles east of Washougal. Foul play is suspected." Foul play is *suspected?*

DO PHOTOGRAPHS LIE?

Readers put more credence in a news story than in a magazine short story. They are more willing to believe a biography than a novel. After all, facts are facts. But do the facts add up to the truth? Is it not possible for a piece of fiction to tell more about a person and human problems than a literal report, accurate as it may be?

Photographs as used in journalism are a little like news stories—apparently literal, accurate, factual. Readers believe them. After all, a precision instrument was used to produce the picture. What the film recorded was exactly what was going on in front of the camera.

Or was it?

Russell Wiggins, the former *Washington Post* editor, considered this question in an address to journalism students at the University of North Dakota. "It has been said that the camera does not lie. But the camera does lie. It is a notorious, compulsive, unashamed and mischievous liar. . . . Readers . . . have difficulty in understanding that the camera is a congenital liar, condemned to prevarication by the mechanical limitations of a contrivance that could only tell the whole truth if it were equipped with lenses as all-encompassing as the very eye of God."

Editor & Publisher, the trade journal for newspaper people, after reporting the talk, asked for reaction from photographers and found that, to nobody's surprise, they were outraged. "Wiggins reflects the current non-think of the journalism profession," a teacher-photographer fired back. Another photographer complained that Wiggins "impugns the motives, honesty, and integrity of every photographer." Someone else questioned how an editor "can say a camera lies when it is a machine with no brains." "An honest picture can be made dishonest by the direction of some editor, by his cropping, by what he has written or failed to write in the picture caption," countered another. "Many of the so-called camera lies that Wiggins referred to were not camera lies but interpretations made by the viewer," said another.[2]

It was not the first time the camera had come under attack. "The camera . . . is . . . the great lie of our time," wrote Malcolm Muggeridge, trying to suggest that caricature was more believable than photography.

> As is ever the case with deceit, the camera's deceitfulness varies in direct ratio with its plausibility; because it has the reputation of not being able to lie, it lies the more effectively. In this sense, "good" photographs are more harmful than bad ones, and the greater the photographer the greater is liable to be the lie projected.[3]

It is easy to understand photographers' response to this kind of criticism when you consider the rough time photographers have had establishing their place with the media, especially with newspapers. Columnist Heywood Broun

[2]Don Maley, "Photojournalists Blur Charge: Camera, a Machine, Isn't a Liar," *Editor & Publisher,* March 29, 1969, p. 11.
[3]Introduction to David Levine, *The Man from M.A.L.I.C.E.* (New York, Dutton, 1966), pp. 5, 6.

Two ways of showing a statue at the entrance to a small city.
One might illustrate a story on urban blight, the other a Cham-
ber of Commerce brochure about the city. Which is "true"?
(Photos by Stan Bettis.)

once wrote: "Some of my best friends are newspaper photographers. . . . And yet I feel that when one or two are gathered together for professional reasons you have a nuisance, and that a dozen or more constitute a plague." Nor have photographers enjoyed the same rights reporters enjoy. Since the days of explosive flash powder, judges have kept photographers out of courtrooms, and do so now in spite of the fact that pictures can be taken in natural light with inconspicuous 35 mm cameras.

To circumvent this, newspapers and television stations and networks have sent sketch artists to cover important trials. But in the James Earl Ray trial in 1969, Judge W. Preston Battle even drew the line there—no sketch pads. "It would be disconcerting to the participants to know they're being sketched," he said. That did not bother one artist, Howard Brodie, who said, "It's better to draw by memory—you're really forced to observe." In 1956 Colorado became the first state officially to allow cameras in the courtroom. For many years it stood alone, but in the 1970s a number of other states followed Colorado's example.[4]

While some of the attacks on the camera do seem overdrawn, it is clear that, whoever is at fault—the camera, the photographer, or the editor—photographs do sometimes give readers a wrong impression. They may make a factual statement that is valid at the time the photograph was taken, but the fact as pictured may be completely out of context. A familiar example of this is the photograph of the man holding up his freshly caught fish; if he holds it out toward the camera, it will, of course, look considerably larger than it really is. Foreshortening puts the fish out of context, setting up a false scale by which the viewer measures size.

Photographs can lie at three different stages:

[4]Frank Wm. White traces the growth of courtroom photography in *Cameras in the Courtroom: A U.S. Survey,* Journalism Monographs, Association for Education in Journalism, School of Journalism, University of Kentucky, Lexington, April 1979.

1. *When they're taken.* Photographers can use special lenses to distort distances between items in a picture, creating an unnatural scale. They can use filters to exaggerate cloud formation and make a scene more beautiful than it really is. They can take the picture from an unnatural angle to make the subject appear to be bigger or smaller than it really is. They can take the picture at just the right time to make a person look stupid or profound, depending on the photographer's or newspaper's bias. The timing may be unintentional, but the photograph's use is not. Stopped with mouth open in the middle of a word, any speaker can be made to look ridiculous.

Once during the 1952 presidential campaign, a photographer, shooting from a low vantage point, got a picture of Adlai Stevenson, the Democratic candidate for president, sitting on a chair with his legs crossed. The focus was on the sole of his shoe, which happened to have a hole in it. The photograph was widely printed, to the delight of the Democratic Party, actually, because it at last gave their candidate, brilliant but a little too much the intellectual, the common touch: as happens to any man, his shoes had worn down and he needed to have them resoled. Stevenson's supporters thought enough of the shot to use a shoe sole with a hole as a lapel pin in the 1956 race, when Stevenson ran again. It was a fetching device but probably not a very accurate symbol for that solvent statesman.

2. *When they're adjusted.* Much can be done in the darkroom to change the mood of a print as it is being made from a negative. The light source can be stepped up in one part of the print, held back in another. To change a print more spectacularly, a retouch artist can paint over it, by hand or with an airbrush, and make it say something quite different from what the photographer intended.

For instance, a public relations organization representing the lumber industry has a photo it wants to use in a booklet on fire prevention. It is a dramatic shot, but a logger in the foreground is smoking a cigarette (cigarettes are a major cause of forest fires) and he is not wearing a hard hat (companies like to point to their safety measures in woods operations). Ideally, the cigarette should disappear and a hard hat should appear. No problem. A retoucher can airbrush out the cigarette and paint a hat on the logger.

Retouching can be done on the negatives as well as the prints. And certain changes in the photograph can even be made by the platemaker. It is a simple matter to make a man face left when in the original photograph he may be facing right. It takes a one-word instruction to the plate-maker—"flop."

It is also possible to take two or more prints and combine them or to make a single print from two negatives.

Finally, it is possible to edit a photograph by "cropping" it, cutting away a part that is not wanted. Sometimes the editor does this to improve the composition. Sometimes he does it to change the shape of a photograph so it will fit the space that has been provided for it. It is possible, too, to crop a photograph to get rid of an undesirable element, thus changing the meaning of the photograph.

3. *When they're used.* An editor can control what photographs say through his selection of which ones to run and where and how to run them. An editor who happens not to like Reagan has two stock photographs of the man; one focuses on wrinkles, the other shows the face from a good angle and in a flattering light. Which photograph represents the truth?

When it appeared that John F. Kennedy would be the presidential nominee of the Democratic Party in 1960, *Human Events,* a right-wing publication, stepped up its campaign to make Barry Goldwater the Republican nominee. It devoted one of its front pages to a comparison of the two men. The editor had to select photographs from among many that were available. The one he chose of Kennedy showed him sitting in a rocking chair. The one he chose of Goldwater showed him smiling broadly, in uniform, waving from the cockpit of a plane. Was this an accurate comparison of the two potential candidates?

Sometimes it is a question not of which photograph to

run but whether the editor should run the one photograph that is available. Should an editor run a photograph taken for one occasion to illustrate a story about a later occasion? The subject is smiling broadly, and yet the story deals with tragedy. Is the photograph, then, true?

Nowhere do pictures have a better chance of lying than in television. The photographer can edit, and therefore distort, at the moment the picture is taken, and, of course, a great deal of editing goes on afterward. There is little editing for Meet the Press–type programs, more for newscasts, a great deal for programs like "60 Minutes."[5] Some people who have been hurt by television editing demand live interviews. They will not sit for filming or taping. "Still, it is clear that filmed, taped, or live, the televised image is never more accurate or precise than the cameraman, editor, or reporter allows it to be," a *Saturday Review* writer observes.[6]

THE CARTOONIST

In the early 1940s, when America was involved in an all-out war, Peter Arno did a cartoon for *The New Yorker* showing a military plane crashing into the earth, probably just after taking off on a test run. Angry and disturbed, high officers and maintenance men are seen rushing over to where the plane has crashed. An ambulance speeds over, too. Walking away from it all, looking a little foolish, carrying his plans, is the little man who obviously had designed the plane. He says, "Well, back to the old drawing board." Arno's cartoon is one of the classics among gag cartoons; his gag line, because it expresses so beautifully the inability of people to react fully to life's tragedies, has passed into general usage. Another one of Arno's gag lines made *Bartlett's*.

Arno himself (he died in 1969) was probably the

[5]Peter Funt, "Television News: Seeing Isn't Believing," *Saturday Review*, November 1980, p. 30.
[6]Ibid., p. 32.

world's best-known gag cartoonist, a specialist within a speciality. He and people like him serve as the clowns of journalism, but they also do more. With their barbs and contortions, through both under- and overstatement, they chip away at our pretensions. Cartoonists instruct and influence even while they entertain.

"The thing to remember in cartooning is that there are no rules—ever," says George Booth, *The New Yorker* cartoonist who specializes in decrepit interiors, people, and cats and dogs. "If there are rules, you violate them when you feel it is necessary. I do have one guideline: I've discovered that reality, all by itself, is funny, and you can't top it. I know better than to try to make my cartoons compete with real life."[7]

Cartoonists tend to pick a social level, perhaps one they are associated with, and concentrate their humor there. Jules Feiffer identified with upward-bound liberals with anxieties, and when he started his strips in the late 1950s, they were the people who became his leading men and women. They were, he said later, "Americans who hadn't yet been recognized in any official way. . . . Even though they were being used as material, they responded because there was something flattering in this sudden attention."[8]

No matter how unflattering a cartoon may be, the person depicted often writes to the cartoonist for the original. This is especially true of politicians responding to editorial cartoons. Their walls are likely to be decorated with a number of framed originals. Organized groups and members of professions seem to have less of a sense of humor. Sometimes a libel suit results. A cartoonist does not even have to name or show a person to bring on a suit. AP reported in 1980 that an irate lawyer in Brazil sued a newspaper for running an *Andy Capp* comic strip by Reg Smythe that was "disrespectful of lawyers in general, ridiculing the plaintiff and his colleagues who struggle for the brilliance of their

[7]Margaret Staats and Sarah Staats, "Seven Masters of Visual Wit," *Quest/79*, June 1979, pp. 22, 23.
[8]Ibid., p. 28.

work." The episode in question showed Andy and his wife Flo being asked for a $30 fee before sitting down in a lawyer's office. The couple spins around and leaves, with Andy saying, "For that kind of money we don't visit, we move in."

What a cartoonist can get away with is not always clear. When Robert Bierman in the British Columbia *Victoria Times* drew a public figure gleefully pulling wings from flies in 1979, he and his paper were sued for libel successfully. The judge ruled that the public figure, who was in charge of "human resources" for the province, was made to look like "a person of cruel and sadistic nature who enjoys inflicting suffering on helpless people." William Black, a law professor at the University of British Columbia, saw a danger in the ruling. It meant, he said, that "it's okay to attack a politician on his public policies but not personally. How do you differentiate between the two when your criticism uses symbolism, satire and hyperbole?"[9]

Like other artists, cartoonists get calls from editors or art directors to illustrate stories, articles, and books. Sometimes they get assignments to illustrate advertisements. A few cartoonists both write and illustrate books of humor or children's books. But when people think of cartoons, they think of three distinct forms: gag cartoons, the special province of the magazines; comic strips, the province of newspapers; or editorial and political cartoons, also the province of newspapers.

We start here with the gag cartoon, the newest of the cartoon forms. We move then to comic strips. We end the chapter with a discussion of editorial cartoons.

GAG CARTOONS

To the real cartoon connoisseur, gag cartoons represent the ultimate in the cartoon art. A gag cartoon is to be savored, not just looked at and read. The subtleties of the art are

[9]Leonard Zehr, "Tribunal in Canada Draws a Line Around Political Cartoons," *The Wall Street Journal*, January 19, 1979, p. 3.

considerable. The whole point revolves around a single line printed underneath the cartoon, and everything within the drawing must substantiate that point. The cast of characters remains small in a gag cartoon, the setting simple. The cartoonist makes clear at once, without benefit of balloon, just who within the drawing is doing the talking.

Sometimes the gag gets across to the reader without a single word below. The gag is in pantomime.

Gag cartoonists come onto their gags in a number of ways. Sometimes they dream up a scene and then try to think of a gag line to fit. Sometimes they start with the line and then try to imagine a scene that will make it funny. Most gag cartoonists also buy ideas from outside sources. They pay the writer 25 percent of what the cartoon earns and keep 75 percent for themselves. Only the cartoonist signs the cartoon.

It has been said that the novelist has only a few basic plots to work with. Similarly, the gag cartoonist has only a few basic ideas. The setting, the props, the characters change, the words in the gag lines vary, but the ideas stay the same. Gag cartoon ideas generally involve a cliché, an understatement, a bit of exaggeration, a letdown, some ingenuity on the part of one of the characters, evidence of stupidity, a character in the wrong setting, a character playing out a part to the point of absurdity, a ridiculous situation, or simply a slice of life.

Unique among cartoonists, gag cartoonists have no particular axes to grind, no real people to put down, but they do make general statements about the human condition. Gag cartoonists are never happier than when, in the words of critic Stephen Becker, they are "jabbing away . . . at our shams and illusions, in the end touching upon some social truths."[10]

Gag cartoonists produce a completely new work each time, not a continuation of an established work, as the comic-strip artist does, but they work often with a set group

[10]Stephen Becker, *Comic Art in America* (New York: Simon and Schuster, 1959), p. 127.

of character types. Charles Addams likes to play around with explorers, archeologists, monsters, ghouls, and the Addams family that lives in a haunted house. The Addams family started in *The New Yorker,* where Addams does most of his work, and for a time it served as the basis for a television show.[11]

Like other artists and entertainers, a gag cartoonist can suddenly turn hot, capturing public fancy that for years had been elusive. George Booth, who was mentioned earlier, falls into this category. Booth does not need expensive tools for his cartoons, just a Bic pen for the lines, a felt-tip pen for solid-black fill-ins, and the cheap ledger paper on which he draws.[12] His unique style and off-the-wall humor has only recently earned its large following. For years he could sell only to the trade journals and lesser magazines, but now Booth has about all the advertising and greeting card assignments he can handle in addition to his gag-cartoon commitments.

Every cartoonist's first choice of markets is *The New Yorker,* which pays from $400 to $600 a cartoon. No other magazine matches *The New Yorker* as a gag-cartoon showcase. *Playboy* and the women's magazines are on the next level.

COMIC STRIPS

A child of the William Randolph Hearst–Joseph Pulitzer circulation battles of the 1890s, comic strips quickly became the most popular diversion in the mass media. Other media came along—the movies and the electronic media—to offer entertainment in an even more palatable form, and for a time interest in the strips waned except among the very young and the poorly educated. Still, that audience was big enough in itself to keep strip syndication profitable.

[11]Margaret Staats and Sarah Staats, "Seven Masters of Visual Wit," *Quest/ 79,* June 1979, p. 24.
[12]William Mathewson, "Humble Humorist," *The Wall Street Journal,* April 11, 1980, p. 1.

When in the 1950s the syndicates began circulating strips that were truly comic again, to replace or supplement the adventure strips, interest stepped up, and not just among people who moved their lips when they read. Today the audience for this fare includes the young and the poorly educated, as always, but also the more sophisticated reader.

Still, comic strips today have nowhere near the single-minded following they enjoyed in the early part of the century. Gone are the days when a cartoonist like Chic Young could offer $50 for a name for Blondie's new baby and get 400,000 entries, as once he did. It is hard to imagine it today, but once, when New York newspapers were on strike, the mayor himself took to the air to read the comic strips aloud for the benefit of the city's deprived youngsters.

America's first "comic strip," *The Yellow Kid,* introduced before the turn of the century, was really more a panel than a full-fledged strip. Distinguished mainly by the extra press run of yellow to color in the Kid's cloak, the feature proved such a circulation builder that its creator, Richard Outcault, was lured back and forth between New York's *World* and *Journal* by successive increases in salary, finally settling with the *Journal.* The *World* hired another artist to continue its version of *The Yellow Kid.* Not only did both papers scramble for novelty in cartoons; both laced their news stories with sensation, causing an editor of a third paper to lump all of that kind of journalism together as "yellow," a term still useful today.

The early strips, originally drawn for adults, concerned themselves with the communities of "foreigners" making up America's Eastern Seaboard cities. These people were the strips' chief readers. If they were not insulted by the humor in *Bringing Up Father* and *Happy Hooligan* (for the Irish), *The Katzenjammer Kids* (for Germans), *Alphonse and Gaston* (for the French), *Abie the Agent* (for Jews), and *Black Berries* (for blacks), they should have been.

Another kind of strip, dealing with the emerging middle class and concentrating on the family, took its place alongside the racial strips. The first was *The Gumps* (1917), a rather ordinary strip that nevertheless had a big following. Another was *Gasoline Alley,* the first strip to allow its characters to mature, marry, and have babies to grow up and serve as new characters for later episodes. Both of these, and several others, were the brainchildren of Captain Joseph Medill Patterson, founder of the *New York Daily News.*

Chester Gould introduced real violence to comic strips when he launched *Dick Tracy* in 1931. "I was disturbed by the fact that the Prohibition gangsters in Chicago and other cities were repeatedly beating the rap," he remembered late in life. "I thought it would be a good idea to have someone just shoot these fellows down. When they were caught red-handed, why bother with a trial and all that baloney?"[13]

The advent of *Dick Tracy* spelled the virtual end of "comic" strips; most of them by the 1930s had turned into adventure strips. One that remained genuinely "comic" was George Herriman's *Krazy Kat,* perhaps the only strip in those days (1916–1944) that appealed to intellectuals.[14] But when Herriman died his strip died with him. His humor was too subtle, his drawing style too individualistic to be continued under anyone else's direction.

By the end of World War II, the strips were in disarray. The adventure in them could hardly match the real life adventure of the war, television came along to compete, and

---

[13]Daniel Greene, "The Titans of the Funnies," *The National Observer,* September 12, 1966, p. 24.

[14]In an unsigned review of George Herriman's *Krazy Kat* (edited by Woody Gelman, Joseph Greene, and Rex Chessman and published by Grosset & Dunlap, New York, 1969), *The New Yorker* for March 14, 1970 (p. 156) said, *"Krazy Kat* is visibly the ancestor of much of our best comic art: Ignatz Mouse hurling his bricks at Krazy clearly becomes Lucy endlessly betraying Charlie Brown in 'Peanuts,' and there are clams with legs that anticipate 'B.C.,' a creation-by-drawing that obviously inspired Crockett Johnson's 'Harold and the Purple Crayon,' and a world of animal characters that must have influenced 'Pogo.' It may even be that Coconino County was the forebear of Faulkner's Yoknapatawpha County, and that *all* our arts derive from Herriman's fertile genius."

people did not seem much in the mood for the strips' original fare, slapstick humor. It was in this setting that Walt Kelly came up with *Pogo,* which some considered the successor to *Krazy Kat.*

And just in time. Sex and violence had infiltrated the adventure strips, and parents, preachers, and educators mounted campaigns against publishers. Especially outspoken was psychiatrist Frederic Wertham with his alarmist book, *Seduction of the Innocent.* The comic book industry drew up a code and editors at the syndicates did a little more policing. But what saved comic strips was the new wave of humor and good fun represented by *Pogo* and then *Peanuts, Beetle Bailey, Miss Peach, B.C.,* and *The Wizard of Id.*

One can understand the strips' continued appeal to nonintellectuals; what is more noteworthy is the interest in the strips among intellectuals. Some may be slumming, some may regard the strips as high camp, but some obviously have a real affection for them. The late Al Capp can be forgiven his hyperbole for saying: "Comic strips are the best art being produced in America today. I judge them by the same standards I apply to Daumier or Michelangelo. And by those standards comic strip art is damned good." It was the comic strip that inspired a whole new movement in the fine arts, Pop Art.

Let a given strip catch on too well with the masses, however, and let its creator cash in on its popularity, then disillusion sets in. In the words of critic Richard Schickel, the artist's discoverers are

> no longer compelled to clip his cartoons and pin them up on the office bulletin board, quote them at parties, and discuss their hidden depths with fellow cultists. . . . Too many people have come to have a vested interest in taking the whole business [of popular culture] entirely too seriously. In the process we are beginning to forget that, whatever the excellent and amusing qualities sometimes achieved by the popular artist, such qualities are always incidental to his basic function, which is to make money. Very simply, the popular artist must

be "sold out" from the beginning. His glory lies in the fact that he occasionally rises above his origins.[15]

The strips do not originate with the newspapers that run them but rather with feature syndicates. With many editors sharing in the expense, each gets big-name art at a fraction of what it would cost to buy it directly from the artist in its original form. *Editor & Publisher 1981 Syndicate Directory* lists more than 350 syndicates in the United States and Canada, ranging from giant King Features to one-person operations. Together, these syndicates offer daily and weekly newspaper editors more than 200 different cartoon panels, about 260 daily comic strips and 155 Sunday strips, and nearly 90 editorial cartoon features, plus hundreds of columns on astrology, books, bridge, business, fashion, food, health, politics, religion, science, sports, travel, and women's interests.

The typical cartoonist draws each strip about six weeks in advance of publication. He need not, probably does not, live in New York, where his syndicate is headquartered; rather, he mails his strips in, usually in sets of six or seven to cover a full week's series. The syndicate takes care of making the plates and circulating the mats to subscribing newspapers, who pay for the feature on the basis of their circulations. A small daily gets a strip at a cost considerably less than what a big paper pays. The syndicate offers the feature to the newspaper on an exclusive basis; that is, it agrees to withhold the feature from any other newspaper in the paper's circulation area. This explains why most successful comic strips have imitators, circulated by competing on even their own syndicates, to service papers that have been denied the original.

Of the net income from the strips, the syndicate usually takes half, the cartoonists the other half. A few cartoonists have tried to beat the system by syndicating their own

[15]Richard Schickel, "Smaller Peanuts, Bigger Shells," *Book Week*, December 27, 1964, p. 9.

stuff, but without the syndicate's resources behind them and without the sales staff, they soon learn that half of a lot of money is more than all of almost nothing.

The syndicates these days busy themselves looking for new features to offer newspapers to build readership among young adults, where newspapers are weakest. The television generation has not made newspaper reading a habit as earlier generations did. United Feature Syndicate in 1979 offered for the first time *Drabble,* a daily and Sunday comic strip about Norman Drabble, a 20-year-old student. It started off with 100 papers. Kevin Fagan created it, and, at 22, became the nation's youngest syndicated cartoonist. Other strips designed to appeal more to young readers than the middle-aged or older are Cathy Guisewite's *Cathy,* Pete Hansen's *Lolly,* and, of course, Garry Trudeau's *Doonesbury.* One of the biggest recent successes was a strip based on a television series, *Dallas.*

Taking on a new strip is easy enough for a newspaper, provided it can find space for it, but dropping a strip after it has run for a few years *does* present problems. The comic-strip industry likes to record cases, and there are many of them, where switchboards light up with angry calls and editors are flooded with stern letters, some of the letters threatening subscription cancellations. The problem is serious enough that John B. Mauro, director of research for Media General Inc., Richmond, Virginia, wrote an article for *Presstime* telling editors "How to Drop Comics Without Dropping Readers."[16] His advice was to measure first the number of readers *and also* the intensity of the readership of the strips. The intensity factor was something editors had been overlooking.

The comics are a strong enough draw that some Sunday newspapers wrap themselves in a full-color comics section instead of a front news section. Some advertisers find the Sunday comics section a good medium, mostly because there is little ad clutter there. Other advertisers sign up fa-

[16]December 1979, pp. 30, 31.

mous comics characters to help sell their products, paying a fee that is split between the syndicate owning the feature and the artist drawing it.

Over the years comic strips, when they have strayed into politics, have stirred the wrath of editors, most of whom like the strips to stick to entertainment, leaving the stating of opinion to editorial writers. In the 1930s, for instance, *Little Orphan Annie,* by Harold Gray, preached against aspects of Franklin D. Roosevelt's New Deal, causing an occasional Democratic editor to delete a sequence. *Pogo* also occasionally found itself dropped for a day or two when its creator, Walt Kelly, became too political or when he touched a sore spot. Lately editors have become sensitive to "women's issues." Mort Walker's *Beetle Bailey,* despite its wide following, produces angry reactions from some editors and some readers. Miss Buxley's portrayal turns out to be offensive. A sensitized editor of the Minneapolis *Tribune* in 1981, for instance, withdrew one "sexist" strip that had Miss Buxley say, "I'm just not all here, today." "If there was any more of her here," said the General, watching her walk out the door in her short skirt, "I don't think I could take it."

Doonesbury was a strip that often stirred controversy. Because of its political themes, some editors ran it on the op-ed page or somewhere other than on the comics page. The strip won a Pulitzer Prize—for *editorial* cartooning. Occasionally the strip wandered far enough into controversy to find itself removed from a newspaper. When its creator, Garry Trudeau, showed Gov. Edmund G. Brown Jr. as having ties to organized crime, a number of papers dropped the strip temporarily because, they said, the satire was libelous and certainly unsubstantiated.

Al Capp, who created *Li'l Abner,* another strip marked by controversy, was one of America's best satirists. His early strip ridiculed conservatives and the Establishment, his later strips went out after hippies and leftists, so Capp succeeded in making enemies all along the political spectrum. He killed off his strip a couple of years before his death in

1979. It was the kind of strip nobody else could do. "A humorist has one duty—to be funny," AP once quoted him as saying. "Some are funny about kids, some about dogs, some about mothers. I chose fraud. Whatever was fraudulent, I attacked."

When everyone else praised rebellious youth, Capp attacked them where they lived—on college campuses. One student asked why he would speak at the colleges, where he was so despised. "For the $3,000 fee," Capp answered, "and I wouldn't spend an hour with a bunch like you for a nickle less."

Most successful comic-strip artists hire assistants to ink in the strips or to do the lettering, and many hire writers. Not Charles Schulz, creator of *Peanuts.* Although many of his other projects are turned over to hired artists, the strip is all Schulz's. It all started in 1950, after the young St. Paul cartoonist, not long released from the army, approached United Feature Syndicate with his cute-kids idea. He previously had sold a few gag cartoons to *Saturday Evening Post* and had worked as an instructor for a correspondence school of art.

Peanuts now goes out to 2000 newspapers in 60 countries with an estimated daily readership of 100 million. It is translated into 20 languages. In the period 1965–1980 the strip's characters appeared in 28 television network specials, 4 motion pictures, and 2 musicals. Charlie Brown's "Good Grief!" has become something of a classic exclamation, and Linus's security blanket is one of the world's important symbols. Although books have been written analyzing the theology and psychology of *Peanuts,* Schulz does not consciously work a message into his strip as Trudeau did, at least not now. "I'm less and less of a preacher," he says. "I have no axes to grind; I'm not the sort of person for giving advice." Still, "It's difficult to be funny without making some sort of comment on human conditions."[17]

[17]Blake Green, "Good Grief—Charlie Brown is 29," *San Francisco Chronicle,* May 18, 1979, p. 26.

Nothing among the other strips comes close to *Peanuts* in world-wide popularity, but four others have crossed the 1000 mark in numbers of newspaper subscribers—*Blondie, Beetle Bailey, Garfield,* and *Hagar the Horrible.*

EDITORIAL CARTOONS

The final form to be discussed here is the editorial cartoon. Since it developed as a modern art form—it goes back to the days of Honoré Daumier in early nineteenth-century France—the editorial cartoon has taken one of two tacks; either it has expressed an opinion—vividly, dogmatically, even crudely—or it has solidified some event in the news, presumably making it clearer for the reader. The latter tack, the more recent, grew out of America's penchant for objectivity in news reporting. With this clarifying kind of cartoon, a cartoonist can stay uncommitted. Little thinking is needed.

Clearly, the trenchant editorial cartoon, the editorial cartoon in its original form, is much more memorable. Furthermore, to be remembered, the cartoon of opinion must criticize, not praise. The British cartoonist David Low observed in his autobiography:

> On the face of it one would not say the attitude of political caricaturists was one of admiration or even goodwill. The traditional terms of their expression are perhaps better adapted to censure than to praise. Admiration is for the poets. A satirist perverted to hero-worship becomes pathetic and sickening. His approval can best be expressed by leaving its object alone.[18]

Possibly Don Hesse, editorial cartoonist of the *St. Louis Globe-Democrat,* gave the best description of editorial cartooning in the title of an article he wrote for the *Quill,* "The Ungentlemanly Art." Stephen Hess and Milton Ka-

[18]David Low, *Low's Autobiography* (New York: Simon & Schuster, 1957), p. 204.

plan picked it up, acknowledging its source, and used it as
the title of their admirable history of American political
cartoons.[19]

Editorial cartoonists in most cases work directly for a
newspaper, although, if they are good enough and if other
papers and magazines begin to reprint their stuff, they, like
comic strip artists, can be syndicated. Papers with circulations of more than 100,000 generally employ their own editorial cartoonists, while papers with smaller circulations get
their editorial cartoons from a syndicate. Among the big-
city dailies, only the *New York Times* gets by without its
own editorial cartoonist (the *Times* doesn't run comic strips,
either), but it does sometimes reprint the work of cartoonists on other papers.

Many big-city newspapers allow on their editorial
pages the work of syndicated columnists whose points of
view may be antithetical to their own, but editors want
their own editorial cartoonists to preach the same dogma
they preach, probably because they feel readers identify
the local editorial cartoon with the staff-written editorials.
Occasionally, an editorial cartoonist disagrees with his
paper's editorial stand, with its endorsement of political
candidates, for instance; in that case, the cartoonist picks
some other subject or maybe, as the *Washington Post*'s
Herblock has done, takes a vacation during the campaign.

On a typical newspaper the staff editorial cartoonist, if
there is one, sits in on daily conferences with editorial writers to learn what editorials are to be written and what
stands are to be taken. Then the cartoonist roughs out some
cartoon ideas, lets the editor of the editorial page pick out
the one that shows the most promise, and produces a finished drawing. On some papers the cartoonist works more
independently.

Editors and editorial writers seldom supply the cartoon
idea itself. "It's been my experience," said Karl Hubenthal,
then editorial cartoonist for the *Los Angeles Herald Examiner,* "that editors are much too literal-minded to be good

[19]New York: Macmillan, 1968.

idea sources. When one suggests 10,000 Chinese crossing the Viet Nam border, he actually means draw 10,000 Chinamen all marching. It doesn't occur to him that one big figure would tell the same story and be more effective doing it."[20] And be a lot easier to draw.

What editors sometimes forget is that the editorial cartoon is a figure of speech in graphic form. It does not make its point directly; instead it resorts to analogy.

Assume, for example, that the cartoonist wants to show that the oil interests are not acting in the best interests of the country. He cannot very conveniently draw them "not acting in the best interests." How could he? So he puts a fat man in an oculist's office, sits him down right in front of an eye chart, and labels him "Oil Interests." The first line on the eye chart is a big dollar sign. Oil Interests is looking at that and smiling. The second line, almost as big, is "U.S. Welfare." A worried Uncle Sam points to it and asks Oil Interests, "Can you see the second line at all?" (A Herblock cartoon.)

Editorial cartoonists use labels to make their analogies and captions outside the cartoon to hammer home the point. They seldom use balloons inside the drawing anymore. The caption can be either (1) the cartoonist's comment about the cartoon, further explaining it, often unnecessarily, or (2) a bit of conversation coming from one of the characters in the cartoon, in which case quotation marks are added. The conversation caption is more popular these days and is evidence of the effect of gag cartoons on editorial cartoons.

Sometimes the idea is so natural and appropriate it needs no explanation. The cartoonist doesn't bother with labels or caption. Bill Mauldin's famous obit cartoon on the assassination of President Kennedy serves as an example. It simply showed the Lincoln Memorial's statue of Lincoln, another martyred president, with his head bowed.

As an aid to quick communication, the editorial car-

[20]Karl Hubenthal, "Editorial Cartoons: The Role They Play in a Modern Paper," *California Publisher,* September 1965, p. 23.

toonist has developed a varied array of symbols, and every newspaper reader by this time understands them. The most familiar is the gangly, bewhiskered character called Uncle Sam, by now so outdated that some cartoonists no longer use him. Scholars think Uncle Sam is the original Samuel Wilson (nicknamed Uncle Sam) of Troy, New York, who, during the War of 1812, furnished beef and other supplies to the government. About as familiar are the elephant and donkey, symbols of the Republican and Democratic parties either invented or resurrected by Thomas Nast.

Caricature, of course, is another important tool of the editorial cartoonist, and it is another term in journalism likely to give the student trouble. Originally, it was the word for what we today call the "editorial cartoon." Librarians still file books dealing with cartooning under the heading "caricature." To most cartoonists, however, "caricature" is only a drawing that shows a figure and face so exaggerated that it makes the subject hideous, yet at once recognizable. Before the days of photojournalism and television, a cartoonist found it necessary to put a label on each figure telling who he was, even though the caricature was right on target. Now, provided the cartoonist is good enough, no labels are necessary; everybody has seen photographs of the person caricatured and recognizes him. Generally speaking, the more amateurish the editorial cartoonist, the more labels used.

Even when the idea is sound and the labels clear, some readers are likely to miss the point. LeRoy M. Carl, a journalism professor at Temple University, some years ago found in a survey of readers in three northeastern cities that a substantial majority read entirely different meanings into cartoons from what the cartoonists intended. One cartoon showed "Jim Crow" blackbirds flying north. More persons thought it meant "northern migration of Negroes" than thought it meant "increased northern bigotry." Commented Professor Carl: "The assumption has been made by many that editorial cartoons are easy to understand—easier than the written word. Some of the cartoonists . . . have in-

Harold Montiel demonstrates the caricaturist's art with this drawing of W. C. Fields. It is essentially a vertical tube with a little detail along the way. Horizontal divisions mark the hat-band, brim, collar, and tie. The bulbous nose filled in with pen crosshatching, to suggest redness coming from heavy drinking, provides some tone to contrast with the black. (*Source:* From *Humor, Wit and Fantasy,* Hart Picture Archives, Hart Publishing Company, New York, 1976.)

dicated a complete unawareness of the communications barriers between them and their public."[21]

Some people remember cartooning as a vital force in American life. Editorial cartoons like those of Thomas Nast and Homer Davenport could bring robber barons to their knees and change the fortunes of political administrations.

[21]Leroy M. Carl, "Editorial Cartoons Fail to Reach Many Readers," *Journalism Quarterly,* Autumn 1968, p. 535.

They *said* something, those cartoons, at least those that survived to be reprinted in the history books. "But," says Karl Hubenthal, "look at their daily output over the years and you will be absolutely astonished at the stacks of puerile pap they [early editorial cartoonists] ground out . . . every one of them. There is a greater percentage of really good cartoonists working in this country today and a lesser percentage of trite cartoons being produced than at any time in the history of journalism."[22]

Time in 1980 noted a resurgence of interest in editorial cartoons as the times became more confused and the politicians more vulnerable. "Like any predatory species, editorial cartoonists multiply in proportion to their quarry: incompetence, folly and hypocrisy." The magazine put the number of practicing editorial cartoonists at 170, an increase of about 60 over the past decade. "Their wit has grown sharper and more personal."[23]

In some respects, despite their new militancy and even meanness, editorial cartoonists are not as free to say what they wish, to draw as they want, as in the past. Organized pressure groups make editors, if not cartoonists, nervous. Paul Szep, a Pulitzer-prize winner, drawing for the *Boston Globe* and other papers, in 1980 showed a group of blacks, looking agitated and determined while they march down a staircase. One of the blacks turns to write on a building: "CARTER IS A DOUBLE CROSSIN' CHEAP HONKY." One black is saying, "We'll simply switch to Reagan. He'll give us all the social programs we want." It was a jab at the Congressional Black Caucus, and Rep. Louis Stokes (D.) of Cleveland was furious. "You have members of the Black Caucus being portrayed and depicted in a stereotyped fashion—the accentuated lips, the kinky hair." Stokes also didn't like the word "Honky" on the building. "None of us [members of the Black Caucus] speak like that."

Szep labeled the reaction to his cartoon "politically ju-

[22]Karl Hubenthal, op. cit., p. 29.
[23]"The Finer Art of Politics," *Time*, October 13, 1980, p. 74.

venile." He asked, "Are they immune to criticism? Actually, the cartoon was not criticism. It was a cartoon of a particular incident. I don't know why they should take exception to it." Like most cartoonists, Szep feels that blacks should get the same irreverent treatment whites get. Such treatment often involves the use of stereotypes.

Pulitzer-prize winner Pat Oliphant, perhaps the most widely syndicated of the editorial cartoonists, sets off waves of protest from various groups for his vicious caricatures. His fat, obnoxious ERA advocate, for instance, never fails to outrage feminists. Oliphant shrugs off charges that his work is often in poor taste. "You have to decide 'good taste' for yourself, and you're always going to offend somebody." Oliphant often, but not always, leans to the left in political controversy. Actually, he trusts no politician. "With political figures, I think there's no such thing as a good one, and I go on from there."[24]

The little penguin in the corner is Oliphant's way of working in one more jibe, something a little stronger than what the cartoonist can say in the main drawing. That little corner episode is so small editors tend to overlook it. Up large, the comment there conceivably could result in editorial cutting.

Oliphant, who is much imitated, is one of the first editorial cartoonists to use Grafix Duo-Shade on a regular basis. This is a drawing paper with a built-in pattern brought out by the brushing on of chemical solutions. He has recently returned to pure ink drawing. Oliphant uses a reducing glass (the opposite of a magnifying glass) from time to time while working on his cartoons. "Looking through this has the same effect as standing back. You can see if the perspective is screwed up." His work is careful enough to merit that kind of attention.

One of the hottest editorial cartoonists is Jeff MacNelly, who quit the business in late 1981 to concentrate on his

---

[24]James Stevenson, "Endless Possibilities," *The New Yorker,* December 31, 1980, p. 46.

comic strip *Shoe* and other projects but who came back early in 1982 because he missed the editorial forum. Unlike most of the other big-name editorial cartoonists, MacNelly is more conservative than liberal, although neither side is safe from his attacks, and he is more likely to go for a laugh than to try to change the world.

If the editorial cartoon is not as effective as it was at the turn of the century, it may be because its setting has changed. Then little else competed for the reader's attention, no radio squawked, no television glared. Films were in their infancy. Magazines did not dazzle the reader with their pictorial excellence. In those days, the cartoonist could afford to clutter the drawing with many labels, much shading, many asides. The cartoonist, covering a lot of ground, knew that readers would study the drawing and talk about it over their morning coffee.

Today the editorial cartoonist must make the point quickly, almost as a billboard does a selling job on the passing motorist. The reader cannot be bothered with more than a quick glance.[25]

---

[25]Recent book-length assessments of the cartoon world include Randall P. Harrison, *The Cartoon: Communication to the Quick* (Beverly Hills: Sage Publications, 1981); Roy Paul Nelson, *Cartooning* (Chicago: Contemporary Books, 1975); and *Comic Art and Caricature* (Contemporary Books, 1978). All three carry extensive bibliographies. Concentrating on caricature and satire are William Feaver's *Masters of Caricature* (New York: Knopf, 1981) and Steven Heller's *Man Bites Man* (New York: A & W Publishers, 1981).

Chapter 11
The Message
in Popular Music

A measure of the importance of popular music to people and the devotion they hold for performers could be seen in the nation's reaction to the murder of John Lennon in 1980. Fans gathered outside his New York apartment for days, and groups met in mourning all over the world. The death of a beloved political leader would not have caused such a stir. The entire Beatles story was retold in the newsmagazines and other publications. Television ran clips of Beatles performances and reran interviews with Lennon. Radio played Beatles records, and the records sold briskly again. *The New Yorker,* not a magazine given to hero worship, es-

The Beatles perform for a TV broadcast. An English rock group, the Beatles profoundly influenced rock and popular music, as well as manners, both in England and America in the 1960s. Their concerts became scenes of mob adulation, and their records sold by the millions. They wrote much of what they played and sang, and their lyrics ranged from the playful to the critical. (*Source:* Syndication International, Photo Trends.)

pecially worship of an entertainment figure, ran a moving "Talk of the Town" item on Lennon. The magazine spoke of his "great gifts as a composer, poet, and performer." He was, said the magazine, "truly a man of the spirit." He "did not lecture us but, rather, spoke to us quietly, and in ways that we all understood."[1]

People not caught up in rock 'n' roll in the 1960s were amazed at all the fuss. Meg Greenfield in her column in *Newsweek* said, "I can't remember a time when I felt so left out as I did when John Lennon was killed and a kind of generational outpouring of grief engulfed us all. I was as-

[1]"Notes and Comment," *The New Yorker,* December 22, 1980, p. 25.

tonished. . . . Speaking . . . as . . . one whose main connection with '60s music was to threaten to call the police if the people next door didn't turn it down, it was a revelation—and a poignant one—to me to read all those accounts of how this music had sung to, awakened, even transformed young lives in America. The bond of these people has persisted into their early middle age."[2] *Newsweek*'s Jack Kroll, recalling the Beatles, said that "Good music is instant evolution; it changes your breathing, the way you focus your eyes at the world; it shifts the rhythm of your thinking, hoping, fearing. It dances your mind into places where its ordinary processes, however subtle, would never take you."[3]

Popular music can change society by promoting offbeat lifestyles and by bringing groups together to give them identity. These effects of popular music on society are cumulative.[4] Therefore, it is not surprising that political and religious leaders have from time to time looked upon music as an evil influence, or that they have dictated how it should be used. Hitler, who liked Wagner, banned jazz and swing as "depraved." Nikita Khrushchev in Russia said, "We stand for melodious music with content, music that stirs people and gives rise to strong feelings, and we are against cacophony." In 1979 Ayatollah Khomeini banned music on Iran radio stations, saying music "stupefies persons listening to it and makes their brains inactive and frivolous."[5]

Prof. Charles R. Townsend of the West Texas State University history faculty, observes that "The United States has not only been a melting pot for the races and nationalities

[2]Meg Greenfield, "Thinking About John Lennon," *Newsweek,* December 29, 1980, p. 68.

[3]Jack Kroll, "Strawberry Fields Forever," *Newsweek,* December 22, 1980, p. 42.

[4]Some of the ideas in this chapter come from Bill Lingle, assistant professor of journalism at Linfield College, McMinnville, Oregon. Lingle is a student of popular music and an occasional film critic.

[5]Quoted in an AP story, July 26, 1979.

of the world, it has also been a melting pot for the world's music. American music has been as varied and pluralistic, as sad and tragic, as boisterous and bungling, as happy and exciting, as creative and inventive as the people who gave it birth." Townsend cites the music of Bob Wills, a band leader who invented Western Swing, as representative of the pluralism of American music. Wills, who was white, brought together "the fiddle [which he played well himself] and string music of whites and the blues and jazz of blacks."[6]

The study of popular music is a study of its many variations. In this century one of its most durable and influential forms is jazz.

JAZZ

Jazz started at the turn of the century, but it really created a stir in the 1920s, a period often called, "the jazz age." Ministers preached against the music. In 1922 the Illinois Vigilance Association claimed to trace "the fall of 1000 girls" to "jazz music," Nat Hentoff reports.[7] Since the 1920s jazz has gone through near-dormant periods, then revived. In the late 1940s it broke away for a time from popular music, of which it had become a part, to become "bebop" and take on other exotic forms less pleasurable to the general listener but more complex, more exciting to musicians. In the late 1970s it was back again as a vigorous part of popular music; a "jazz explosion," as Hentoff calls it, had indeed occurred.

Many music buffs argue that jazz is more interesting than other forms of music, including rock 'n' roll. One can go back and listen to the same jazz song, the same record, many times, yet it still holds surprises. One of the early jazz

[6]Charles R. Townsend, "Bob Wills and American Music," notes for "Bob Wills and His Texas Playboys: In Concert" record album sleeve, Capitol Records, Inc., 1976.
[7]In a feature written for Independent News Alliance in 1980.

greats, Bix Beiderbecke, found it impossible to play a song the same way twice. "That's one of the things I like about jazz. . . . I don't know what's going to happen next."[8]

Jazz is a singularly American phenomenon that has greatly influenced music throughout the world. It was an outgrowth of Negro spirituals and blues, songs sung by field workers in the South. Its brilliance lies in its improvisation. Forms of jazz include Dixieland, ragtime, swing, and bebop. Cities like New Orleans, Chicago, Kansas City, and New York have put their special stamp on the music.

Among the greats in jazz are "Jelly Roll" Morton, said to be the first to give form to the music, Louis Armstrong, and Duke Ellington. "Morton was not, of course, the first musician to be influenced by the streams of sound that swirled through his native New Orleans," Chris Albertson has written. "But he *was* the first to combine them all—French, Spanish, English and Italian melodies, hymns and slave chants, blues and ragtime—into an ordered system that had rules and principles (many of them first enunciated by Morton) and that still left room for individual inspiration."[9]

Jazz never had the impact that rock had because it did not have television to promote it, nor did it have millions of young people around with lots of money to spend on records.

ROCK 'N' ROLL

Jazz, at least at the beginning, had been largely the preserve of blacks. Rock 'n' roll, which came onto the scene in the 1950s, was a white variation but with plenty of black participation. It drew not only from jazz but also from country music (then called "hillbilly music") and later from folk music. Rock 'n' roll combined with folk music became just

[8]Loc. cit.
[9]Chris Albertson, *Giants of Jazz: Jelly Roll Morton* (Alexandria, Va.: Time-Life Records, 1979), p. 3.

plain rock. Folk music, a real story-telling form, had made guitar players out of many young people in the 1960s, so it was natural that guitars would play a big part in the development of rock music.

In 1969, 400,000 lovers of rock music gathered at a dairy farm at Bethel, New York, for a wild three-day Woodstock Music and Art Fair, where three people died. There have been many rock festivals since then, but none to get the press coverage that Woodstock got.

Rock fans do not suffer lightly the cancellation of a concert. When it was announced at a concert in Toronto in 1980 that Alice Cooper would not appear because he was ill, fans threw bottles at police, smashed stage equipment, and fought among themselves. Fourteen people were injured, 35 arrested. Also, patience to get into a concert can wear thin. Before a concert of The Who in Cincinnati in late 1979, 11 persons died in a stampede for seats.

For those caught up in rock 'n' roll in the 1960s, music was more than entertainment. It expressed anger and frustration and preached rebellion and self-indulgence. If older listeners could not understand the message or recoiled at it, so much the better, as far as the musicians and fans were concerned. Music helped segregate the generations.

Drugs became an important part of the music scene. Several important stars died of overdoses, Jimi Hendrix and Janis Joplin among them. Not that drugs and alcohol were new to musicians. Jazz and country artists years earlier had turned to these diversions, many paying for their excesses by dying young.

In the 1970s rock music became mellower, the message became less important. Preferences of its listeners broadened to include jazz, country and western, and other sounds. Activism among rock stars was not dead, however. The Tom Robinson Band of England carried on the tradition in the late 1970s. Among the band's releases in 1978 were "Better Decide Which Side You're On" and "Glad To Be Gay." Leader Tom Robinson often asks his fans to sing along with him at concerts. *Newsweek* quotes him as saying rock 'n' roll should be "nasty, crude, rebellious people's music." He continues: "If there's one thing we learned from the '60s, it's that rock 'n' roll cannot change the world. But music has the power to break down barriers."[10]

At the beginning of the 1970s, Ralph Gleason said, "Music gives us the community that politicians have never given us. . . . Music in this age has become not only the entertainment, but the religion, the educational system and the community, a network of electricity linking people together by invisible chains of sound. The message of rock has fundamentally altered their values in the way they look at the world and that is going to effect society inevitably."[11]

Cummings G. Walker said, "Rock is one of the few continuous themes which has defined and held the generation together. From Elvis' first million-seller and the hundreds of white imitations of black music in the early '50s—through the Beatles Revolution in 1964—and all that has followed this, this generation has listened to rock music, danced to it, marched to it and even rioted to it. Rock music has been a primary force in shaping and articulating their ideas and life-style."[12]

By the late 1970s, rock had broadened its appeal. "As American popular entertainment, it has become a dominant, over-the-counter force, a rival of television and movies as a shaper of the country's shared myths, symbols and experiences, not to mention one of its primary leisure time outlets," one observer noted.[13]

A new movement, short-lived, that entered the scene in the late 1970s was "punk rock"—white, urban, political, and crude. "Punk rock" came from an Englishman, John Simon

[10] Quoted by Barbara Graustark, *Newsweek,* July 30, 1979, p. 72.

[11] Quoted by Joseph Haas, "Rolling Stone: Where It's at in the New Rock Culture," *Chicago Daily News,* June 6–7, 1970, p. 5.

[12] Cummings G. Walker, "A Report on the Rolling Stone," *Communication Arts* 11, no. 3 (1969), p. 45.

[13] Wayne Robins, " '70s Rock Features 'Hyphens'," *The Oregonian,* Portland, November 2, 1979 (*Los Angeles Times-Washington Post* Service), p. D1.

Ritchie, who adopted the name Sid Vicious. An interesting aspect of "punk" was its alignment with the graphic arts; many of the performers had art backgrounds, and visual elements, especially in dress, were important. "American children had to read about it in *People* or *Vogue* in order to know what to wear or how to act," Tom Wolfe says. He adds that while the 1960s gave us the "pseudoevent," in which something took place primarily to be covered by the press, the 1970s gave us "knockoff pseud," "forms of life that existed *nowhere* but in the press but were then acted out by people who believed they were real."[14]

The "new wave" music of the early 1980s was a cleaned-up version of "punk." A writer in *Parade* saw "new wave" music as experimental but with "no-frills lyrics—often expressing dissatisfaction or disillusion with modern life."[15] Prominent among the "new wave" groups were the Talking Heads, Blondie, and The Knack.

THE BEATLES

Ed Sullivan, the ex-newsman who ran a popular Sunday night variety show on television from 1948 to 1971, helped launch the careers of many performers. Elvis Presley's career "exploded after Sullivan gave him an unprecedented three-time spot on his show—albeit only from the waist up," Geoffrey Stokes observes in *Rolling Stone.* Sullivan did the same thing for the Beatles, who were already popular in England.

The Beatles' manager, Brian Epstein, also worked hard to give his group exposure in the print media, including articles in *The New York Times Magazine* and *The New Yorker.* All kinds of public relations tricks and gimmicks were used to build up Beatlemania upon the group's first visit to America in the early 1960s. The Beatles got the good press they

[14]Tom Wolfe, "Tom Wolfe's Seventies," *Esquire,* December 1979, p. 37.
[15]Andy Edelstein, "Rock Rolls into New Wave," *Parade,* February 24, 1980, p. 23.

did because they handled reporters' questions with wit. Among the many consequences of that visit was the turning of young people, and older people later, to long-hair styles.

The Beatles helped create an audience in America for rock music, and they succeeded in appealing to "teenyboppers" as well as to more sophisticated audiences with what Jack Kroll of *Newsweek* was to call "great songs. If they are pop, then clearly pop is capable of greatness in expressing the gathering pathos of mass society."[16]

The Beatles's following dwindled somewhat in the late 1960s as they grew tired and became controversial. John Lennon earned criticism, especially in the South, with his comparison of Beatle fame with Christianity. "Christianity will go. It will vanish and shrink. . . . We're more popular than Jesus Christ right now." Geoffrey Stokes commented: "The sort of folks who had always known the Beatles were Commies were delighted to be appalled by this confirmation that they were atheists as well."[17] Some radio stations, at least for a time, banned Beatle records.

DISCO MUSIC

Tom Wolfe observes that since World War II, the styles in music, dance, and dress have been set by "marginal or outcast groups." He points out that poor whites and blacks created rock music, and male homosexuals, he says, created disco, a bland "seamless music" little concerned with messages, but much concerned with flashing lights and heavy beats. Appealing mostly to the very young, but broadening its base to take in the hotel dancing crowd, disco in its rather short stay encountered all kinds of criticism. Eve Zibart, writing for the *Washington Post* Service in 1979, complained that disco music was more "sexist" than rock 'n' roll music

[16]Jack Kroll, "Strawberry Fields Forever," *Newsweek,* December 22, 1980, p. 42.
[17]Geoffrey Stokes, "The Beatles: Some Years in the Life," *Rolling Stone,* December 25, 1980–January 8, 1981, pp. 107–125. This was an excerpt from his book, *The Beatles* (New York: Times Books, 1980).

of the 1960s. In the summer of 1979 women singers had the five top singles, and each of the songs, including Anita Ward's "Ring My Bell," were suggestive or cute. Four were written by men. Zibart contrasted the late 1970s with the early part of the decade when popular songs said "I Am a Woman" and "You're So Vain." Gay Talese, working on his book on sexual attitudes, thought the trend was there because "Men like to hear a woman's voice saying what men want the women to be saying."[18]

Gerald Nachman, the humor columnist, was not willing to write off disco in 1979, but he was not very enthusiastic about it, either. "The problem with disco is, they don't cater to minority groups, such as regular people," he wrote. "If discos plan to attract the great masses of Middle America, they'll have to bring us along slowly, perhaps at disco halfway houses that play Rod Stewart at quarter speed. It's too big a step to go directly from Jo Stafford to Sister Sledge."[19]

Disco and rock people did not get along. In Chicago in 1979, hundreds of people rioted at Comiskey Park after an antidisco demonstration between games in a doubleheader baseball match. Patrons of disco and rock 'n' roll nightclubs also clashed that summer.

COUNTRY MUSIC

Question: What city hosts more recording sessions than any other?
Answer: Nashville, home of country and western music, called hillbilly music in its less ambitious, less accepted days. Nashville, which calls itself Music City USA, is also the home of "Grand Ole Opry," the show every country and western performer dreams of making.

[18]Quoted by Eve Zibart, "Sexism Lives in Disco Beat," *Milwaukee Journal,* July 9, 1979, p. 1.
[19]Gerald Nachman, "Sleazing It with Disco," *San Francisco Chronicle,* June 4, 1979, p. 44.

It all started in 1925 with the "WSM Barn Dance," which, after several years, became "Grand Ole Opry," the most listened-to radio program of its time. People traveled from all over the country to get into the auditorium to watch the performers in person. A few years ago the "Opry" moved from the old Ryman Auditorium to a new home, Opryland USA, a park with rides, museums, and all kinds of music, not just country music.

What drew people to country music was not only the simple tunes and strong beat but also the words that somehow rang true. Most songs celebrated love gone wrong and hard times. It was usually possible to draw a moral from the words. Lately the lyrics, like lyrics in other songs, have been less preachy, even suggestive and sometimes explicit.

Prof. Raymond Rodgers of North Carolina State University, who has been studying country music, thinks its appeal lies mostly in the lyrics. "You don't find people singing along with Kiss," he says. "You sing along with Merle Haggard. The lyrics are narrative; they make some kind of a moral point." But with all the mergings going on in music, all the crossovers, Rogers finds it hard to single out country music songs. He has to accept how the charts categorize them. If the charts say country, they're country. He says he feels like the judge who could not define obscenity but knew it when he saw it. "Well, I know country music when I hear it."[20] Many fans can accept Kris Kristofferson's definition of the form: "If it sounds like country, man, that's what it is. It's a country song."[21]

Perhaps no one country music performer was more popular than singer Hank Williams, who during his short life wrote hundreds of songs, sung by pop as well as country singers. His son, Hank Williams, Jr., carries on the family tradition, but with a more contemporary sound.

[20]Bruce Douglas, "Country Lyrics . . . , "*Eugene* (Oreg.) *Register-Guard,* January 31, 1980, p. 3D.
[21]Dennis John Lewis, "Morning Glory: Radio's Prime Time," *Washington Journalism Review,* September–October 1979, p. 51.

One of country music's big stars in the 1970s was Merle Haggard, whose music appealed largely to working-class people. His "Okie from Muskogee" (1969) spelled out some values quite different from those of the San Francisco hippies the song criticized. Haggard enjoys the luxury of writing about his own life, which has its lows, including some time spent in prison. He is unique in insisting that the instrumentalists in his band, who are well respected in the industry, share the limelight with him. His voice is flexible and gritty but, as they say, "sincere." Nat Hentoff, in an appreciative essay in *The Village Voice,* wrote, "There's nobody in country music, and few anywhere else, who can sing as tender as Haggard."[22]

Loretta Lynn rivaled Haggard with best-selling records in the 1970s. Her twangy popularity was great enough to put her autobiography, *Coal Miner's Daughter,* on the best selling lists and into a popular movie that, surprisingly, impressed the critics.

RELIGIOUS MUSIC

Music plays an important role in worship services, setting the stage for the sermon, in some cases, or putting parishioners into a proper mood. For evangelical Christians, music does even more. Singer/Piano-Player/Evangelist Jimmy Swaggart, whose record sales by 1980 topped 8 million, reminds us of the fervor of Pentecostal services, with hand clapping and arm waving that lead, in some cases, to speaking in tongues. What altar call has not been accompanied by congregational singing of songs like "Just As I Am" and "Softly and Tenderly"? ". . . show me a church that worships God in great exclamation of joyful song, and I'll show you a church on fire for God," Swaggart says.[23] (His cousin Jerry Lee Lewis has been popular among country-western and rock 'n' roll

[22]Nat Hentoff, "White Line Fever," *The Village Voice,* July 1, 1980, p. 8.
[23]Jimmy Swaggart, "Contemporary Music," *The Evangelist,* July 1980, p. 2.

audiences. Another cousin, Mickey Gilley, is a country-western star).

SONG WRITING

In the 1940s, up-front singers like Frank Sinatra became more important than the bands they sang with. The big bands became little more than providers of background music. Earlier Bing Crosby, with his relaxed style that came to be called "crooning," had revolutionized the singing of popular songs. Fred Astaire was another 1930s singer who, without much of a voice and with few gimmicks, kept the people humming and the sheet-music stores busy.

In those days the lyrics were all-important, and superb ones were written by Cole Porter, Ira Gershwin, and Irving Berlin, to name only three. Paul Simon, more recently, after breaking up his act with Art Garfunkel, wrote some of the most popular songs of the 1970s.

Some songs bring words and music together in just the right concentration to win lasting favor with a large body of listeners. Mary Jo Kaplan, who sings in piano bars, says that in her line of work you need to know but ten songs: "Feelings," "Send in the Clowns," "My Way," "What I Did for Love," "More," "The Way We Were," "You Light Up My Life," "I Left My Heart in San Francisco," "Misty," and "As Time Goes By."

A large percentage of country and western and rock stars write their own words and music. Some cannot read music. They simply pick out the tunes on their guitars until the tunes are right. (An advantage of writing both words and tunes is keeping all the royalties.) A few performers start out as song writers and decide that they can sing as well, or as badly, as the next person. Willie Nelson wrote a lot of big country songs before he developed a reputation as a singer.

Some of the writers get hung up on "messages." Frank Zappa, for instance, uses deliberately crude passages to push for free speech. In one of his songs, a man pleads for an incestuous relationship with his daughter. You get the impression that some writers set out deliberately to antagonize older, conservative listeners. Even country music these days delights in titillating audiences. "Oh, Darlin', how I'd love to lay you down," admits Conway Twitty in one of his songs. Lorretta Lynn in one of hers pays tribute to the pill. Barbara Mandrell purrs that "You Can Eat Crackers in My Bed Anytime."

What popular songs say has been much praised, but what merit they have comes mostly from sentiment, not artistry. Reading the bald lyrics without benefit of the tune or beat can be a disappointment to word purists. The writers of country songs, particularly, settle for only *almost* appropriate words. Never mind if the rhyming is not even close. One line ends with "mind," another with "wine," and nobody, apparently, cares much.

Like other writings, the lyrics to songs often tell stories or make political or social points. Sometimes they appear senseless, but people in the know can read beyond them. "Don't step on my blue suede shoes," for instance, means "give me some breathing space." "They don't write songs like that anymore" is a statement difficult to defend, but it is easy to see, at least, that the lyrics of the earlier songs were more polished.

THE CHANGING MUSIC SCENE

Rock music continued to absorb strains from other popular music sources to help it stay alive. A number of rock groups picked up on the country sound. Kenny Rogers moved from rock to country and became a big star after his "Lucille" in 1976. Dolly Parton moved from country to pop and managed to hold onto most of her country fans while gaining a lot of new ones, but she could have gone on indefinitely as merely a country star. Country music listeners are remarkably loyal. Ernest Tubb, who first gained national attention in the 1940s, kept his following into the 1980s.

Rock music fans tend to be more fickle. Singers and performers there enjoy their day in the sun, then fade away. One of the most durable rock groups turned out to be the Rolling Stones, whose members were able to adapt to rapidly changing tastes.

Another group that held up was The Who, known for its fever, if not excesses. The Who made its first American appearance in 1965. Jay Cocks in *Time* recently observed, "No other band has ever matched its sound, a particular combination of sonic onslaught and melodic delicacy that is like chamber music in the middle of a commando raid."[24] In their early days, members of this group used to smash up their instruments after each concert. This was to reflect the group's "unwitting honesty."

The Grateful Dead also survived. "The audience we have now is not the audience of the 60s," Jerry Garcia of the Grateful Dead told the Associated Press in 1979. "Also, we changed style. There's no real limit in music. You can always find something fresh to do."

One of the most surprising changes came to Bob Dylan, described by *Newsweek* as "rock's adenoidal poet of protest." In 1979 he came out with a widely different kind of album, *Slow Train Coming.* Dylan, with a Jewish background, had become a born-again Christian. His concerts that year proved a disappointment to some of his followers, who wanted him to sing the "Lay, Lady, Lay" songs he wrote earlier.

RECORDS

The rock 'n' roll music of the 1950s spread largely through 45-rpm records and, of course, the radio stations that played them. Rock music of the 1960s spread through long-playing records. By then recording studios' sound techniques had improved greatly, and instruments had become electrified. Music and the ability to reproduce it with high fidelity became a preoccupation of many Americans. Expensive equip-

[24]"Rock's Outer Limits," *Time,* December 17, 1979, p. 86.

ment was commonplace in homes, apartments, and college dorms, and people felt the need constantly to upgrade their equipment with each new development.

Thomas A. Edison and an assistant built the first recording machine in 1877. Then several others began experimenting with machines, and a legal battle over patents developed. The first commercial recordings, on cylinders, came from Edison's company in 1889. Earlier, in 1887, Emile Berliner had patented a Gramophone that made use of discs rather than cylinders. Unlike cylinders, the discs could be mass produced. They could be more easily stored, too. By the end of the 1800s, several companies had entered the sound-recording business to compete vigorously with each other.

Eldridge Johnson founded the Victor Talking Machine Company in 1901 and brought some stability to the business. Johnson's company and the Columbia Phonograph Company became the industry giants during the first part of the twentieth century. Important performers who had looked upon recordings as playthings began to see their possibilities and aligned themselves with recording companies. One of the most successful was Enrico Caruso, the celebrated Italian opera tenor with the brilliant voice.

The early recordings were scratchy and lacking in fidelity, but they soon became a popular new medium. Not all sounds could be recorded. Some musical instruments were not even considered recordable. To make a recording, the performer had to stand in front of a big horn and shout.

Radio came along in the early 1920s to threaten the recording industry. The early programs on radio, including the music, were live, and radio offered better sound than recordings could offer. The techniques of recording were improved, and soon radio began playing records rather than relying on live performers and bands. By then the Great Depression of the 1930s was upon the country, and record sales fell sharply.

The jukebox, which played records in restaurants and other establishments, helped rescue the recording industry.

Then World War II created shortages, and not enough records could be manufactured to meet the growing demand. Another blow came from the American Federation of Musicians, which, in 1942, forbade its members to cut records because of the competition they were giving to live performances. It took a year for the AFM and the record companies to come to an agreement that would resume the making of records by AFM members. Records bought during that period had people humming in the background to replace the orchestra that usually accompanied a singer.

After World War II, the advent of tape recording brought greater sound fidelity to the business. People with tape recording equipment began buying tapes rather than discs. Still, discs remain an important product in the industry. They started out as thick, brittle products to be played at 78 revolutions per minute. In 1948 Columbia introduced the long-playing record, which was thinner, practically unbreakable, and had microgrooves capable of holding several cuts per side instead of the traditional single cut, and it played at a slower 33⅓ rpm. RCA Victor fought back with its small 45s with the large center holes, and sold 45-rpm record players at a loss to accommodate the records. Because customers were confused about what to buy, the industry settled for 33⅓s for albums and 45s for singles. By 1955 the old 78s were dead.

New, smaller recording companies began competing with the giants, and records began to be sold in drug and grocery stores as well as record and department stores, often at discount prices. Gone were the days of listening to a record at the store before buying it. Records also were boosted by radio. With the coming of television after World War II, radio suffered a setback, then forged ahead again as a news-talk-music medium, and records became an important part of the package. Today, of course, exposure on radio is what sells many records, especially singles.

The recording industry, supervised largely by the young and appealing mainly to that group, soars and sinks as tastes change, and tastes change rapidly. A performer or group, helped along by media blitzes, can pick up a large following fast, but that audience becomes bored quickly, too.

The industry records more than music. All kinds of talking records are also available, including old radio programs and comedy routines. Some of these become enormously popular for a short time, then die, the artists who make them quickly forgotten. (How often can one listen to the same routine?)

What happens to some of these people? Vaughn Meader in 1962 recorded *The First Family,* a comedy album satirizing the Kennedys in the White House. Up until then, it was the biggest selling album ever issued. When the President was assassinated, Meader, the mimic, dropped from sight. In the late 1970s, he was back as "Johnny Sunday," "a cross between Johnny Paycheck and the Ancient Mariner, with a touch of Walter Huston in *The Treasure of Sierra Madre,*" as one writer described him. He had "baleful eyes, midriff bulge, and unruly beard. . . ." He sang "peculiar songs about religion. . . . I thought about Johnny Cash on acid."[25]

About 1500 record companies, some operating under more than one name, release about 4000 LPs and 6000 45s a year. Most of these records, like most books issued by publishers, lose money. The challenge is to find the right group, the right song, the right sound to create a best-seller. An LP that sells 500,000 copies or a 45 that sells 1 million brings the artist a gold record award, a mark of prestige in the industry. Royalties to recording artists run from 10 to 15 percent, about the percentage book authors get. A few artists, probably with a gold record or two, command as much as 20 percent.

By 1980, the record industry made a recovery as unnecessary promotional costs were eliminated and artists like Barbra Streisand and Bruce Springsteen put out records that appealed to large audiences; but the industry continued to

[25]Carol Flake, "Vaughn Meader Resurrected," *New York,* July 2, 1979, p. 7.

worry about the growing trend of home recording off of radio broadcasts. Record companies urged radio stations to avoid playing LPs without commercial interruptions. Economist Alan Greenspan estimates that home-taping of music cost the American record industry more than $1 billion in retail sales in 1981. About two-fifths of home taping was done in lieu of record purchases, he said. He argued for a royalty on blank tapes and recording devices to help offset the losses.[26]

The Recording Industry Association of America estimated that in 1980, 84 percent of records falling into the popular music category failed to break even. On the other hand, a successful LP record can gross $40 million, as much as a successful motion picture. The record may cost a mere $300,000 to produce, compared with the $10 million it would cost to produce the motion picture.[27]

By 1982 music buffs were getting used to digital recording, a still-evolving process vastly different from analog recording in that instead of recording directly the vibrations of sound waves, it picks up sound and transfers it to a computer, which translates the waves into a series of numbers. The computer stores these numbers as binary words. When the recording is played, the computer retranslates the numbers and re-creates the sound waves.

[26]Cynthia Kirk, "Home Taping a Costly Loss," *Variety,* April 15, 1982, p. 1.
[27]Stephen Grover, "Hot Selling Albums . . . ," *The Wall Street Journal,* December 24, 1980, p. 24.

Chapter 12
The Hollywood Version

Thomas A. Edison produced one of the first motion pictures when he recorded the inauguration of William McKinley following the election of 1896. Others began experimenting with short takes of dances, prize fights, parades, and other events, and soon "nickelodeons" opened in most cities. Citizens for a nickle could enjoy the novelty of going to a darkened theater and watching an hour-long series of short films. *Harper's Weekly* in 1907 noted that nickelodeons were spreading "as thickly as saloons."[1] A few saloons installed screens and projectors of their own, just as bars installed tele-

[1] Erik Barnouw, *Mass Communication* (New York: Holt, Rinehart & Winston, 1956), p. 17.

vision sets years later when television threatened to keep people home.

One of the earliest films with a plot was *The Great Train Robbery,* a seven-minute-long film produced in 1903 by one of Edison's assistants. Integrated sound did not come until the mid-1920s; *The Jazz Singer* in 1927 featured for the first time dialogue that could be heard while the picture was being shown. Color came in the mid-1930s.

After several decades of escapism, the pictures playing in theaters after World War II increasingly explored social issues. They dealt frankly, sometimes shockingly, with racism, anti-Semitism, drug addiction, juvenile delinquency, and mental illness, among other problems.

The 1960s saw the blending of reality with fiction in some films. In *Medium Cool,* for instance, actual scenes of the riots that took place in Chicago during the 1968 Democratic Convention became an integral part of the story. A crew filmed *The Rain People* against a real-life background in a trip across the country.

From 1967, the time of *The Graduate,* films dwelt on purity-of-youth themes. In both the notable movies like *Easy Rider* and their third-rate imitators, the heroes were always free spirits. This was nothing new—the main characters in the cowboy and gangster movies were free spirits, too. What was new, as Craig Karpel pointed out in *Esquire*, was the relationship between the subject and the customer. They were one and the same. "Imagine if there had been lines of cowboys stretching around blocks waiting to pay $3 to see *The Virginian,* gangsters to see *Scarface."*

In recent years many movies have gone after special audiences, like those interested in martial arts or black culture or rock music or horror or making out as teenagers. Today's movies continue to appeal mostly to the young, and the people who make them are themselves young.

Foreign-made movies have their followings and earn praise often from the critics, but America continues to be the biggest exporter of movies. When times are bad, the movie industry in America seems to pick up. The escape value of movies can hardly be overestimated.

In the beginning, a multitude of voices rang out across the wires and rumbled: "Locations!" ***A***nd out of the darkness sprang forth a land filled with cities great and small. Farms and forests. River towns. Southern settings. Urban lights. Industrial sites. Shores and harbors. All heavenly. ***A***nd so the producers saw Illinois and said that it was good. ***T***hen the voices sought casting directors. And talent begotten in the images and likenesses of the script. ***A***nd lo, casting was fruitful. And extras multiplied. ***Y***et the voices coveted crews of great strength. State of the art equipment. Post-Production. And were fearful of the cost. ***B***ut Illinois calmed the voices. And the producers read the bottom line and saw that it was good. Very good. ***C***aterers and hotel rooms were found. And the voices made a joyful noise. ***S***till they desired a covenant with those most high. And it came to pass that city and state officials were perfect angels. ***T***he sea of red tape parted. ***A***nd the producers looked upon all that had gone before them in Illinois, gave thanks and said: "***L***et there be Lights! Camera! Action!" ***Word has it that Illinois is a divine place to shoot. Contact Lucy Salenger, Managing Director, Illinois Film Office. Department of Commerce and Community Affairs. 310 South Michigan Avenue, Chicago, Illinois 60604. (312)793-3600.*** **Illinois**

She'll make a believer out of you.

Like a number of states, Illinois has a film office that runs promotional ads like the above to attract movie makers to its area. (*Source: The Hollywood Reporter.*)

THE BUSINESS OF MOVIE MAKING

At first, motion pictures were made anywhere in the country and especially in New York, the financial capital, but in the winter New York was cold, sometimes even snowbound. So after 1910 the industry began its move to Southern California. The little town of Hollywood, with a good hotel and climate to allow year-round outdoor shooting, turned out to be the center of everything for the movie industry. Hollywood was within easy distance of all kinds of scenery, good backdrops for all kinds of films, especially westerns.

Labor was cheaper in the West, too. There were plenty of people—transplanted Midwesterners, mostly—who crowded the studio gates trying to sign on as extras for crowd scenes. "Everybody had an excitement about the whole thing that I've never seen since," said writer Adela Rogers St. John. "None of us knew what this picture business had come to; the greatest form of art and entertainment the world has ever known was put together there for a while."[2]

Today Hollywood no longer completely dominates the industry. New York has regained some of its popularity as a place to make films, and moviemakers have moved back from in-studio to on-location shootings.

Lloyd Shearer, writing in *Parade,* refers to movie making these days as "a dog-eat-dog business. . . ." Part of the problem, he believes, lies with the movies' tie to television, a medium that moviemakers once avoided as a threat. Before a movie goes into production now, the producer may negotiate a sale to a television network and make other commitments for it, including its showing on cable television, its distribution overseas, and its conversion to video-cassette tapes. Shearer quotes *New Yorker* critic Pauline Kael as saying, "The studios no longer make movies to attract and please

---

[2]Quoted by Kevin Brownlow, "Why Hollywood?" *Esquire,* October 1979, p. 91.

moviegoers. They make movies in such a way as to get as much as possible from the prearranged and anticipated deals."[3]

Television has affected movie making by encouraging the production of films that, like situation comedies or car-chase dramas, require little of viewers. Viewers are used to talking and indulging themselves with food and drink in front of their television sets; they do as much in movie theaters these days. Movies like *Serial,* William Wolf argues in *New York,* use "heavy-handed delivery, pat situations, and . . . glib, upbeat ending[s]" and differ from television fare only in their offering "four- and ten-letter words." Wolf further charges that movies, taking a note from television, are shallow and contrived, and that their production seems rushed.[4]

Made-for-television movies put more emphasis on close-ups, because of the small screens on which they are shown, and the sets for movie making are kept simple compared to what they were when movies were made only for large-screen showings.

The tie between the movies and *all* the other media is more pronounced these days. A television series becomes a full-length movie for theater showing (*Star Trek,* for instance), and vice versa (*The Odd Couple).* Many books become movies, and sometimes successful movies based on original scripts become books. Movie sound tracks become LPs, songs become singles, and both are loudly and repeatedly promoted to the limit. The captains of the communications industry understandably look for further ways to cash in on their products. Even if all these movie spin-offs make little money, they help enormously in selling the parent movies to the public.

An AP dispatch in 1980 said that 186 new films were released, 37 of them earning more than $10 million each. Members of the Motion Picture Association of America spent

[3]Lloyd Shearer, "Academy Award Picks: The Best of a Lean Year," *Parade,* March 29, 1981, p. 4.
[4]William Wolf, "What Television Is Doing to the Movies—and to Moviegoers," *New York,* June 16, 1980, p. 59.

an average of $8.4 million on each movie they made. A year later *Time* said that the average movie took $10 million to make and $6 million to publicize. Because costs got out of hand, MGM in 1981 put a limit of $15 million on each of its productions and was attempting to keep each picture from going over the industry average of $10 million.

A highly successful movie is likely to inspire a sequel, and the sequel may inspire another sequel. Furthermore, a successful movie is likely to inspire imitations from other makers. Some movies, with all their sidelines, become fully-developed industries. *Superman: The Film* and *Superman II,* for instance, spurred 200 licenses for more than 1200 products, including sweatshirts, pillowcases, watches, and even bars of soap shaped like a telephone booth.

Each year in the spring the industry builds interest in movies with its Academy Awards telecast. *Time* calls it "a spectacle that combines the solemnity of graduation day at West Point with the giddy naiveté of a greasers' sock hop."[5] Just getting nominated gives a movie added attention. Professor Lauren Kessler of the University of Oregon, who is also a film critic, notes the buildup after the first of the year—the full-page ads in *Variety,* the *Time* and *Newsweek* covers, the columns in newspapers and magazines, the "Tonight Show" appearances. "Then . . . one of the most cunningly orchestrated media events in America climaxes as millions of Americans—many of whom haven't been in a movie theatre for years—tune into that orgy of self-congratulation and corporate backpatting. . . ."[6]

ATTENDANCE TRENDS

Between the coming of television in the late 1940s and the beginning of experimental filmmaking in the 1960s, the feature-film industry appeared to be dying. Theaters by the hundreds closed their doors. One theater got a call one night

[5]"The New Hollywood: Dead or Alive?" *Time,* March 30, 1981, p. 66.
[6]Lauren Kessler, "Hollywood Heaven: Time for Oscar," *Willamette Valley Observer,* March 26, 1981, p. 8.

asking what time the feature started, and the cashier answered, "What time can you get here?" Only the drive-ins seemed solvent, and for reasons probably independent of the motion pictures they showed. The cartoonist Robt. Day in *The New Yorker* showed a lot of cars at a drive-in with the picture on the screen upside down. One projectionist was saying to the other, "O.K., pay me. Ten minutes and nobody's said a word."

The Graduate and *Tom Jones,* among others, brought young people back into the theaters in the 1960s, and movies continued their appeal in the 1970s. Going back to a given movie became a badge of respect for some moviegoers. *Star Wars,* especially, had a see-it-many-times appeal for a large number of viewers. *The New Yorker* reported that one 22-year-old devotee went 137 times to see *Harold and Maude,* a somewhat eccentric story of a love affair between a young boy and an old woman. It is both sophisticated and sentimental, which may be a part of why it still has a following. Movie buffs argue that too much is missed in a movie the first time through, that it takes a second viewing and more to appreciate a movie's subtleties. Some movies, no doubt, are kept complicated enough to lure audiences back.

Movie going in general, however, is not as popular as it used to be. There was speculation in 1981 that many of the 17,600 movie theaters then operating would have to close. High ticket prices, deteriorated interiors, the growth of pay television offering very much the same fare, and the quality and quantity of the stories all contribute to the problem. Fear of crime in city streets at night keeps people home, too. But then, as in the summer of 1982, a movie like *E. T.* comes along, and theaters all over the country begin to fill again.

THE PEOPLE IN CHARGE

The two most important people in movie making, not counting the stars, are the producer and the director. In some periods of film history, the producer is the most important person to a film's success; in other periods, the director is the most important. The producer puts the package together, in most cases making major decisions about money and executive personnel. Past this stage, some producers stay in the background, while others involve themselves in day-to-day decisions. Producers also find the scripts and pick the directors. The director is the person who interprets the script and works with the actors and actresses to convey the story through film. The director also watches over technical matters, including photography.

The producer covers the business side of the film; the director covers the creative side. Some producers also direct their films. Sometimes directors produce their films. In a few cases, a principal actor in the film acts as director or even as producer. Sometimes one person tries to do it all. Orson Welles, at age 25, was producer, director, coauthor, and star of *Citizen Kane,* a 1941 movie, based loosely on the life of publisher William Randolph Hearst, that some put among the greatest films ever made. Commenting on Welles' arrogant self-assurance, his coauthor, Herman Mankiewicz, said of him one day on the set, "There, but for the grace of God, goes God."[7]

Among American film producers, the late David O. Selznick stands out for the artistry of his films. His most celebrated motion picture was *Gone with the Wind.* He also produced *Rebecca* and *Duel in the Sun,* among others. It was Selznick who brought Alfred Hitchcock over from England as a director.

Another important producer was John Ford, who gave us *Grapes of Wrath, How Green Was My Valley,* and *Stagecoach.* Howard Hawks was another great American producer. He directed pictures he produced, and, oddly, gave greater emphasis in the picture credits to his directing role than to his producing role.

It was D. W. Griffith who invented most of the film techniques that producers and directors use to this day.[8] In 1915

[7]Edward Sorel, "Citizen Kane," *Esquire,* October 1980, p. 128.
[8]How the directors got their special effects in some 400 movies is outlined in Harold Schechter's and David Everitt's *Film Tricks* (Harlin Quist, 1981).

"Citizen Kane," based loosely on the life and career of newspaper publisher William Randolph Hearst, is considered by some movie buffs and critics as one of the best movies—if not the best movie—made in America. This scene involves actors Everett Sloane, Orson Welles, and Joseph Cotten. Welles co-authored, produced, and directed. The movie won an Academy Award. (*Source:* Culver.)

Griffith gave America *The Birth of a Nation,* a remarkable film in spite of its glamorizing the Ku Klux Klan. The offensive nature of the film's subject matter today causes disruptions at theaters where it is shown as a milestone of film making. A Spokane, Washington, film festival in 1981 had to cancel the showing of *The Birth of a Nation* when a pressure group intervened.

One of the director's main concerns is how to end the picture. Great thought must go into the ending. In many cases, a couple of endings are made and test audiences help the director decide which works best. "Movies with two endings, or no endings, or three endings, or appended endings, are as much a part of Hollywood history as Schwab's Drugstore or Hedda's hats," reports *Time.*[9]

Sometimes the director cannot decide how to end the film until the last of the shooting. *Time* said that Ingrid Bergman, while acting in *Casablanca,* complained that she did not know how to respond to Humphrey Bogart and Paul Henreid because she did not know which of the two she would end up with.

In motion pictures made in Europe in the late 1950s, directors like Ingmar Bergman, rather than actors or actresses, became the stars, and reviews of the pictures often dwelt on directors. The European pictures were less rigid than those made in America. In the 1970s directors of American pictures became more important than before. Some of the more serious moviegoers chose movies by directors' names as much as anything else, and those names sometimes went up on the marquees.

Some of the new directors, young and idealistic and, perhaps, overly concerned with the art of their productions, became hard to work with, like the actors and actresses of an earlier period. "Never mind the expense," they seemed to say to the financiers in their assiduous hunt for "authenticity." As a result, motion pictures became enormously expensive to produce. One 1980 picture that suffered from directorial self-indulgence was *Heaven's Gate,* with Michael Cimino in charge. It is estimated that as much as $45 million was spent putting it together; yet the critical response was so bad that after opening night it was cancelled, prints were recalled, advertising stopped, and the director began a complete revamping to salvage it. The reissue fared no better. There were grumblings in the motion picture industry that decisions would go back to the board rooms from which financing comes.[10]

The late Alfred Hitchcock, nearly everybody's favorite

[9]"Playing the End Game," *Time,* July 30, 1979, p. 84. Hedda Hopper, referred to here, was a famous movie gossip columnist.
[10]" 'Heaven' Turns Into Hell," *Newsweek,* December 1, 1980, p. 87.

"Apparently, my over two hundred screen credits didn't mean a damn thing."

Source: Drawing by Dana Fradon; © 1982 The New Yorker Magazine, Inc.

film director, was much more than a master of suspense. His films went deeper than that. As a director he was concerned with the ambiguities of existence. His films showed that civilization is but a thin veneer on nature and human behavior. Among his best films were *Vertigo, Psycho,* and *The Birds.* In effect, Hitchcock wrote as well as directed his films. He worked very closely with his writers, revising as the film was in progress. As a director, Hitchcock capitalized on our fears, especially our fear of being falsely accused. He liked to let the viewer in on a secret early in his films and to keep the secret from the film's hero.

Time called him the only director to have his name appear *above* the titles of his films. He was more of a draw to filmgoers than the actors and actresses he used. Viewers of Hitchcock films liked to watch for his brief appearance in each one, a custom he started in Great Britain, where he made low-budget films and had to cut down on actor's costs. That appearance continued to be an integrated part of the film, "not just a gimmick," Bill Lingle, a film buff and a journalism professor, points out.

Critics have said that Hitchcock put technique above content and that he did not address serious issues. Upon his death in 1980, critics reassessed his contributions, and the verdict seemed to be that Hitchcock contributed more to our understanding than was previously thought. His themes included the decline of moral order and the intrusion of evil and disorder on society's institutions. One of his most memorable films, *The Birds* (1963), showed a part of the natural world (a region above San Francisco) out of the control of humans, who are besieged by ordinary birds that have become determined killers. The group of people most affected by the birds manage to escape. In one ending, rejected in the editing process, the people come onto the Golden Gate Bridge to find it covered with perched birds, ready for another attack.

Hitchcock was not above lending his talents to television. While other producers and directors derided the new medium, Hitchcock saw its possibilities. Television shows had to be shorter, but Hitchcock saw this as no real problem. "The art of the moving picture . . . is the art of cutting," he said. *Alfred Hitchcock Presents,* a half-hour series of offbeat mystery shows, started on CBS in 1955 and lasted until 1965. The opening always showed him, portly, in a side view, moving to the left of the screen to step into a caricature drawn with just a few lines. He introduced each program with droll observations. Crime often went unpunished in these shows, but Hitchcock assured viewers, not very convincingly, that the criminal eventually would be caught.

A number of editorial cartoonists found Hitchcock's

death in 1980 worth recording (not many people, certainly not many entertainers, rate "obit" cartoons), and they recorded it with macabre scenes showing Hitchcock acting as his own pallbearer or lifting the lid of his coffin. There was that kind of humor in some of his films. His approach to motion-picture making was often tongue-in-cheek. Ingrid Bergman, who starred in his *Notorious,* said, "Hitch is a gentleman farmer who raises gooseflesh."

THE BIG STUDIOS

The colorful, eccentric, domineering men who originally ran the major studios have been replaced by young, efficient, business-minded persons who have managed to keep the studios alive partly because of expansion into other activities. MGM makes more money, probably, from its hotels and gambling interests than from its movies. Paramount became part of Gulf and Western. Other major studios are 20th Century–Fox, Warner Bros., Columbia, and Universal. Where once the major studios ignored television, they now produce much of what goes into that medium. The majors also went into the record business.

Although many motion pictures these days come from the independents, the major studios "represent the permanent fabric of the . . . industry," says Dennis Stanfill, chairman of the board at 20th Century–Fox. "We provide a network of power which keeps the industry going. We've got pictures shooting all the time, providing employment in every category. . . . Studios have the staying power to see movies through the adversity of overruns, production problems, foreign exchange, financing and distribution. We've survived the good times and bad and have learned how to cope."[11]

Students of the film are able to characterize movies by the people and studios who make them. In the 1930s, Warner Bros. films tended to have a New Deal social consciousness.

[11]UPI dispatch, "Non-Movie Makers Making the Movies," *Eugene Register-Guard,* November 8, 1979, p. 13D.

MGM films struck some critics as more bland. (MGM produced many of the musicals of the late 1940s and early 1950s.) RKO musicals during the Depression years of the 1930s were supposed to lift our spirits.

THE STAR SYSTEM

Actors today do not have the following or the longevity of actors in the past. It has been said many times that the star system is dead. People go to the movies now more for the stories than for who is playing the lead.

Among the great male actors in American films are, beyond question, James Stewart, Humphrey Bogart, Cary Grant, and Gary Cooper. They dominated their films. Some were cast in predictable roles. Others, like James Stewart, were more versatile. Among great female stars, Ingrid Bergman ranks high for her depth, believability, and freshly scrubbed beauty. She was lucky, or smart, enough to appear in great films. Bette Davis, less versatile than Bergman, was a great actress who appeared mostly in mediocre films. Part of Greta Garbo's lasting intrigue comes from her remaining aloof. People still remember her arresting acting and finely chiseled beauty. The late critic Kenneth Tynan put it this way: "What, when drunk, one sees in other women, one sees in Garbo sober."

It did not occur to people that, aside from their well-developed egos, stars were ordinary people with ordinary needs. The media built them up to a point where they seemed to be superhuman, and some found they could not live up to their billings. Under the old star system, no actor or actress met the press head on. Always a press agent intervened. Stories were invented, speeches were ghost-written. "Everyone in Hollywood 'wrote' or 'spoke' with the same stilted correctness and exaggerated tact, as if they had all learned English from condolence cards."[12]

[12]Mark Crispin Miller, "The Lives of the Stars," *The New Republic,* September 15, 1979, p. 31.

THE MESSAGE

Actors and actresses sometimes use their fame to promote causes or speak out for politicians they identify with. In addition to her participation at public rallies, Jane Fonda chooses to appear in films with messages she supports. *Coming Home,* one film she starred in, explored the personal tragedy of war; *China Syndrome* dramatized danger in nuclear reactors; *The Electric Horseman* dealt with commercial exploitation; *Nine to Five* explored office sexism. Even without such open dedication, it is almost impossible to make a movie without doing some preaching. For instance, *Ordinary People,* released in the early 1980s, relentlessly made the points that people should be frank with each other and that they should love each other.

Movies like *Victor/Victoria, Personal Best, Making Love,* and *Partners* in the 1980s attempted to change moviegoers' opinions about homosexuality. *Absence of Malice,* a movie of the early 1980s, questioned the ethics of newspapering. *The Border,* a movie released at about the same time, criticized the handling of Mexican immigrants.

Missing dealt with an assassination in Chile. Interestingly, critic John Simon, who, because of his conservative leanings might be expected to damn the film, thought it "should be seen." Stanley Kauffmann on the other hand, writing in the liberal *New Republic,* said of the picture that it was "a perfect Hollywood liberal picture, playing to a gallery of trained seals and to another gallery of the gullible, for the happiest kind of Hollywood profit—big returns plus big ego-satisfactions. . . ."[13]

Sometimes the message gets out of hand, as it did, at least for some critics, in *The Women's Room,* a made-for-television movie aired by ABC in the summer of 1980. William Hickey, television critic for the *Cleveland Plain Dealer,* called it

[13]Quoted by George F. Will, " 'Missing' Is Missing the Truth," *Eugene Register-Guard,* March 16, 1982, p. 15A.

"clumsily scripted, suspiciously motivated" and "heavy handed." He objected to the constant parade of men as villains or losers. "Only one male in the entire three hours passes human muster, and even he is a borderline case. . . ." A central theme of the movie, as he saw it, was that "A real woman gets out there in the working world and lets someone else take care of her children so she can do something important." Hickey reports that at a private screening for television critics, most of the reaction, from liberals as well as conservatives, was unfavorable, not so much for the message itself as for the lack of balance.[14] Similar complaints have been directed at movies that depict women as brainless sex objects.

Sally Helgesen, writing in *Harper's*, sees the movies of the 1970s as having created a new image for males through men who were timid, self-obsessed, petty, even hysterical. She blames some of this on the appearance in the early 1950s of Marlon Brando as hero; he with the thick, sluggish tongue—vulnerable, defensive, confused. Montgomery Clift and James Dean carried on the tradition. "Few successful actors since the late 1950s have escaped the influence of this trio."[15]

William Wolf complains in *New York* that while movies are realistic on the surface, with plenty of swearing, lots of attention to the details of killing, and close focusing on sex scenes, "when it comes to more challenging realism—portraying the deeper truths about people, relationships, and life on our planet—movies still tend to be shallow, shifty, and sugarcoated." He points out that *Kramer vs. Kramer* really needed a tougher ending, but that the movie took the easy way out by giving the child to the "extremely likeable" Dustin Hoffman, and *Ordinary People* failed to

[14]William Hickey, "Critics-Remick Love Affair Ends," *Cleveland Plain Dealer*, September 11, 1980, p. 10C.
[15]Sally Helgesen, "The Man in the Movies," *Harper's*, October 1980, p. 80.

explore the complicated nature of the woman played by Mary Tyler Moore. "Giving the mother her due would have made the film more complex, increased the demands on viewers—and ruffled the dramatic tidiness of the ending."[16]

Wolf's models for realism come from post–World War II Italian "masterpieces" like *Open City* and *Bicycle Thieves.* He does not mean to imply that all films have to be realistic. "There is no reason to sneer at good films made for escapist entertainment; the letdown comes when a film pretends to be deeper than it is."[17]

THE MOVIES' INFLUENCE

In the words of Professor Bill Lingle, movies have been "infinitely influential" in America and probably the rest of the world. Moving into the movie age was more traumatic for society than moving from the movie age to the television age. Before movies came along only the upper classes had any contact with the visual arts, for instance. They visited museums and galleries. Movies brought visual experience to common people. We are all more visually aware as a result, but at some cost. We are reading less now. We have moved back to more primitive reactions, getting away from the abstract. Movie watching is less an intellectual exercise than is book reading.

In recent years, as audiences become jaded by movies of great violence, later movies become preoccupied with even bloodier and more senseless violence. Examining the movies of what he calls the "brutalist" directors—Walter Hill, Paul Shrader, Martin Scorsese, and Brian De Palma—Robert F. Moss asks in *New York*, ". . . aren't we justified in being alarmed by audiences who can be manipulated into howling for blood? Surely the purpose of art, whether it's cre-

[16]William Wolf, "Ducking the Tough Ones," *New York*, June 22, 1981, p. 51.
[17]Ibid., p. 52.

ated for the few or the many, should be to make us more human, not less."[18]

One performer carries an attitude up or down to one level, a later performer carries it to a level beyond that. Mae West helped bring sex into the open in the movies in her days, even ridiculing it, but sexual explicitness and nudity in movies in the 1960s and 1970s struck her as going too far.

The movies have always exercised great influence on fashion. Because so many movies were made in Hollywood, California designers who designed clothes for the stars put the California look in strong competition with the East Coast look. A star would wear a unique outfit in a movie, and soon the outfit or others like it would be in the stores everywhere. The movies have also played a big role in determining how women and men would wear their hair.

That nearly everyone in the movies drove convertibles probably contributed to the popularity of such cars. Hollywood preferred convertibles, of course, because it was easy to photograph people inside. When film and photographic techniques made it possible, the through-the-windshield shot became the fashion, and convertibles lost their starring roles and, it seems, their purchasing public.

The movies have been credited with killing off the hat industry—few men wore them in the movies, largely because the settings were often in warm southern California—and with helping people make other decisions about what to wear or not to wear. When Clark Gable took off his shirt in *It Happened One Night,* moviegoers saw that he had no undershirt on and sales of undershirts plummeted.

It was a movie in 1980, *Urban Cowboy,* that made high fashion out of western wear and that put rocking, twisting mechanized saddles, "mechanical bulls," into bars and clubs across the country. People vied with one another to see how long they could stay in the saddle. As its setting, the movie used the nightclub of Mickey Gilley, where the first mecha-

[18]Robert F. Moss, "The Brutalists: Making Movies Mean and Ugly," *New York,* October 1980, p. 18.

nized saddle (or one of the first) was located. All across the country, discos changed to country and western bars.

With their depiction of glamour and conspicuous consumption, movies made the have-nots, including third-world peoples, dissatisfied with their lot. Movies also painted distorted pictures of contemporary life in America and of American frontier times, the settings of many movies. People reaching the western part of the country were sometimes surprised to find streets paved and people civilized.

THE STATE OF THE ART

That people wait in long lines to see some movies does not mean, necessarily, that the movies are good or even that audiences really like them. The lines could mean that those movies are merely the best, or most entertaining, of the ones currently being shown.

Frank Capra, one of Hollywood's important producers and directors, considers the present "artistic status" of movies as "very low." One reason is that, with simpler and smaller equipment available, movies can be easier and less expensive to make. "What happens is that young financiers collect money, make pictures they think the kids will like, and the public winds up with junk films, just like junk foods."[19]

Pauline Kael, writing in *The New Yorker*, sees a good reason for bad movies: "Rotten pictures are making money." Movies are planned from the start for sales possibilities to television and overseas distributors, they use predictable themes, and what goes into them these days is not much more than what goes into ordinary television shows.[20]

Stanley Kauffmann, *The New Republic* movie critic, looking at moviemaking in 1980, offered additional reasons for the "drab time." One is money. A movie must gross from

[19]Frank Capra, "The Great Days of Hollywood Are Over," *U.S. News & World Report*, August 25, 1980, p. 66.
[20]Pauline Kael, "The Current Cinema," *The New Yorker*, June 23, 1980, p. 85.

$30 million to $40 million at the box office, he said, just to break even. Another reason is "intrinsic artistic problems." In a reaction to the "personal films" of the late 1960s and the 1970s, many of which lost money, moviemakers today are afraid to innovate and are sticking to "proven stuff." Still another reason is "impulse." There is none. Instead ". . . everyone seems to be scurrying for a gimmick, a hot topic, or a best seller to adapt." A final reason for the poor times in movie making is "lack of nourishment." "This century hasn't done much to foster a nourishing tradition for our playwrights. Despite all the conferences and college courses, that tradition is yet to thrive."[21]

THE CRITICS

Critics working for newspapers, syndicates, magazines, and television help people decide which movies they will see, which ones they will avoid. People who make the films read the reviews carefully, looking for excerpts they can play up in their advertising. Not that critics mean for their opinions to work their way into advertising, but they cannot very well keep themselves from being quoted. It is easy enough for an advertiser to pick one favorable comment out of a generally unfavorable review, use it, and thus embarrass a critic. Movie advertising is replete with out-of-context quotations.

Some critics know a lot about movie technology. Their reviews are more complete, perhaps more useful, than reviews written by critics who pay attention only to story line and acting. Some reviews turn out to be more than mere guides. They are also beautifully written. A critic can be an essayist. One of the best known of the essayists is *New Yorker* critic Pauline Kael, whose reviews have been republished as books. Critics have their own critics. For instance, some say that Kael is too chummy with some producers, too narrow

[21]Stanley Kauffmann, "Domestic Troubles," *The New Republic*, Nov. 22, 1980, pp. 24, 25.

in her interests, that she dismisses some films because she does not like the genre.

Kael was the victim of a spirited attack by Renata Adler, a fellow *New Yorker* writer, in *The New York Review of Books* in 1980. Adler said that Kael's work was "worthless," containing "nothing certainly of intelligence or sensibility." Adler was criticizing one of Kael's collections of reviews: *When The Lights Go Out.*

Some movie critics are almost impossible to please. John Simon of *National Review* finds fault in most of what he sees. Other critics act as though they are turning out press releases for the films they see. It makes a difference, of course, where the reviews appear. Critics for narrow-interest publications judge movies on the basis of how well they cover those narrow interests.

MOVIE CENSORSHIP AND RATINGS

The open eroticism of the movies in the 1920s, and the reported excesses of the actors themselves, resulted in censorship by state and local agencies and self-censorship by the industry. Censorship tended to single out the movies because the movies were considered an art form, certainly not a journalistic medium protected by the First Amendment. They were merely entertainment, and for the uneducated. Films as art came later.

The start of the breakup of movie censorship came in 1952 with the U.S. Supreme Court ruling in *The Miracle* case that movies were included in First Amendment guarantees. The State of New York (to name one state) censored films from 1921 until 1965, when another U.S. Supreme Court decision ruled that the state's film regulation law was unconstitutional. In the New York system, both the film itself and the script were reviewed, and often bits had to be removed before the movie could be shown. Anything tending to "corrupt morals" or "incite to crime" had to go. About 7 percent of the movies shown in the state were censored.

The industry's own production code caused changes or dictated settings in many movies. In 1934, for instance, a blanket had to be hung up between Clark Gable and Claudette Colbert, who had to spend the night in the same room. In the 1950s and 1960s the industry, prodded by an invasion of foreign films, greatly liberalized its code. In 1968 the industry abandoned its code altogether, setting up instead a set of ratings to help patrons decide what level of sex and violence they and their children could tolerate. One trouble with the current industry-sponsored G–PG–R–X rating system is that "X" lumps porno films and some really serious films together, and a "G" rating is almost a kiss of death with its Goody-Two-Shoes image. *Little Miss Marker* got a little last-minute profanity from its producer for no other reason than to move it from a G to a PG rating.[22] *Midnight Cowboy*, an X-rated movie, caused some embarrassment when it won an Academy Award.

With changes in society and within the Roman Catholic Church, the Catholic Film Office, formerly the Legion of Decency, closed its doors in 1980 after decades of rating films for their objectionable content. The Office worked closely with the industry's self-censoring bodies, often causing changes in movies so that they would not be condemned by the Office.

NEWSREELS

Although the motion-picture medium became primarily a storyteller rather than a news-disseminator, a minor industry grew up to make and distribute what came to be known as "newsreels." Unfortunately, these films were universally bland and trivial, concentrating on ship launchings (the bottle never seemed to break), bathing-beauty contests, fashion shows, sports events, and animals acting up in the zoo.

[22]William Wolf, "X-ing Out the Ratings," *New York,* September 15, 1980, p. 44.

With the coming of television after World War II, both national and local newscasters utilized newsreel techniques, but the newsreel as a separate entity all but died. A few companies continued to produce them until the late 1960s, but theater audiences considered them as nothing more than popcorn breaks between features.

DOCUMENTARIES

In 1935 *Time* magazine brought the newsreel and the feature-film idea together in a series of short films called *The March of Time*. This series, which played for several years in major theaters, differed from the ordinary newsreel in that its producers, not satisfied with spot-news coverage alone, *reenacted* events, using in some cases the original participants, in other cases paid actors. It treated events that up until then had been considered controversial. The series also had a point of view. It was to the newsreel what *Time* magazine itself was to the newspaper.

Going a step beyond *The March of Time,* a number of organizations began using films as instruments of propaganda. The New Deal philosophy of Franklin Roosevelt came through clearly in a government-sponsored film, *The Plow That Broke the Plains,* and later in *The River.* When World War II broke out, this government, as well as all others caught up in the fighting, turned to motion pictures to ready their citizens and soldiers. Thus, documentaries were born.

The Academy of Motion Picture Arts and Sciences has defined documentaries as films "dealing with significant historical, social, scientific or economic subjects, either photographed in actual occurrence or re-enacted, and where the emphasis is more on factual content than on entertainment. . . ."[23] Because the fictional techniques of the feature film are incorporated into documentaries, facts give way to something a little broader: truth, or truth as the film maker sees it.

---

[23]Quoted by A. William Bluem in *The Documentary in American Television* (New York: Hastings House, 1965), p. 33.

The documentary owes much to the feature film and much to the newsreel; it borrowed its techniques from both. It owes more to television, because, as A. William Bleum points out, television gave it its financing and its mass audience.

The two people who did the most to make the documentary part of American television were Edward R. Murrow and his colleague Fred Friendly. Murrow had been the most listened-to voice of World War II, broadcasting from both Britain and America. Unlike most radio personalities, Murrow, with his rich voice and deep concern, was able to make the switch easily to television. *See It Now,* the documentary program he and Friendly did for CBS beginning in the mid-1950s, for the first time in the new medium examined important, controversial issues and took stands. One of the programs took a hard look at the then greatly feared Sen. Joseph McCarthy, who saw Communists everywhere in government, or said he did. Using skillfully edited film clips of the senator in action and providing appropriate comment, Murrow contributed substantially to the senator's eventual downfall.

The modern-day equivalent is CBS's "60 Minutes," a hard-hitting, controversial program ranking among the top 10 shows on television. Seventy people work on it. A favorite technique of Mike Wallace and others on the program is to get an interviewee relaxed, then come in with some damaging evidence and a blunt question. The interviewer holds an advantage over the interviewee because the interviewer is used to the camera, and is asking the questions. Some say the show engages in overkill and one-sided editing. "Whatever its shortcomings, no other regularly scheduled network program aspires to nearly so much as '60 Minutes'—or achieves it quite so often."[24] One of the program's victims in 1980 fought back. Illinois Power Company, Decatur, did not like how it was treated and so issued its own documentary, *60 Minutes/Our Reply.* Its fast pace mimicked "60 Minutes";

[24]Harry Stein, "How '60 Minutes' Makes News," *The New York Times Magazine,* May 6, 1979, p. 90.

it reproduced the segments in question and stopped them where necessary to correct what the company believed to be misstatements.[25]

Independently produced documentaries are more likely to show on Public Broadcast Service than on any of the networks. Networks prefer producing their own documentaries. Mike and Sonja Gilligan found this out with their *Christina's World,* the story of the crawling-toward-the-house young woman in Andrew Wyeth's famous painting. After four years of trying to sell it to the networks, the Gilligans went to PBS. The documentary, with Julie Harris doing the narrating, won Emmy awards for outstanding documentary, editing, cinematography, and writing and direction.

Documentaries have always had their critics. Even the famous Murrow show on McCarthy came under some attack, and not only from right-wingers. Some liberals thought that this use of television threatened anyone with controversial ideas who, lacking the charisma of a public performer, could not fight back. So much depends upon the integrity of the people making the documentaries. In addition to all the other chances for exercising biases, documentary makers can edit film to change the sequence of events. One of the most artful deceptions in film editing came with *Operation Abolition,* a documentary produced by putting various unrelated film clips together to "prove" that opposition to San Francisco hearings of the House Committee on Un-American Activities, as it was then named, was directed by Communists.

Documentary makers can put their special imprint on what they report by using tricks of lighting, camera angle, focus, musical background. The way one scene changes to the other—abruptly or through "dissolves"—makes a difference, too. So does the narration that accompanies the film.

One of the most important of the documentary makers is Frederick Wiseman, who has covered such subjects as wel-

[25]Kenneth K. Goldstein, "Turning the Tables on '60 Minutes,' " *Columbia Journalism Review,* May/June 1980, pp. 7, 9.

fare, the schools, and law and order simply by focusing the camera on groups for long periods, avoiding any narration. The people shown do their own talking, apparently unconscious of the filming. *Model,* shown on public broadcasting channels in 1981, examined the empty and hectic world of high fashion.

Just as some magazine and book writers have mixed fiction with their nonfiction, some documentaries have mixed fact with drama and show business, turning themselves into a new form called "docu-dramas," which do not distinguish clearly between real happenings and writers' fantasies.[26] This is not to say that the average documentary is any less reliable than the average story or article appearing in print. Yet, like words, pictures—moving or still, with or without sound—do not always dwell on the truth. A person can use film to mislead viewers, whether intentionally or accidentally. Wise viewers use their critical facilities in looking at documentaries just as they do in reading columns of type.

[26]"Do TV 'Docu-Dramas' Distort History?" *U.S. News & World Report,* May 21, 1979, p. 51.

Chapter 13
Where Madison Avenue
Meets Main Street

Wolcott Gibbs in *The New Yorker* wrote it off as "a remark-ably silly book," but *The Hucksters,* Frederic Wakeman's 1946 novel exposing big-time advertising, provided the im-petus for a number of novels in which ad people played lead roles. A selection of the Book-of-the-Month Club, *The Huck-sters,* later became a movie starring Clark Gable. The villain in the story bore remarkable resemblance to the blustery George Washington Hill of the American Tobacco Company, and the agency depicted sounded a lot like Foote, Cone & Belding, for whom Wakeman once wrote copy. Many years later, Fairfax M. Cone, a principal in the agency, wrote: "With the filming of the story and its repeated showing [on the late, late show] over a period of almost twenty years, it has undoubtedly had more influence on public opinion than either Upton Sinclair's exposé of the unsavory meat packing industry in *The Jungle* or Ida M. Tarbell's *History of the Standard Oil Company,* which focused the country's attention on the evils of monopoly forty years before." He added: "It is doubtful whether Vance Packard's *The Hidden Persuaders* could have achieved anything like the acceptance it did without the lurid setting of the scene by Fred Wakeman."[1]

In the world of make-believe, the advertising executive is as often ruthless and conniving as the whore is loving and generous. Tom Gavin of the *Denver Post* tells of a couple of agency people meeting on the street. One says to the other: "You hear that Joe Parsnip died?" "No, what did he have?" "A few small industrial accounts."[2]

Some advertising people no doubt are insensitive, cynical about what they do, merciless in achieving their goals; but others—surely, most others—have the same standards, the same goals, the same concerns as others who hold down white collar jobs. Some of their work, especially if they are associated with advertising agencies, is invigorating, even glamorous; much of it is routine and dull.

THE LEVELS OF ADVERTISING

The advertising business is organized at four different levels.

1. *Advertising departments of advertisers.* Almost every large company has an advertising department. The department coordinates the company's advertising activities and may produce some of the advertising, especially some of the pieces that are distributed by mail. It represents the company in its dealings with its advertising agency. If the company does not have an advertising agency, the advertising

---

[1]Fairfax M. Cone, *With All Its Faults: A Candid Account of Forty Years in Advertising* (Boston: Little, Brown, 1969), pp. 164, 165.
[2]Retold by Cleveland Amory, "Trade Winds," *Saturday Review,* August 9, 1969, p. 10.

department handles all the jobs an agency would be expected to handle.

2. *Advertising departments of the media.* The media have advertising staffs, too. A newspaper, for instance, has one group handling national or brand-name advertising, another handling classified advertising, still another handling local, or retail, advertising. The retail advertising staff, often called the local display advertising department, is the largest. People in that department solicit advertising from local retailers and then, because most of these advertisers do not have their own ad departments or agencies, write the copy, lay out the ads, and see that they are set in type. Some media employ *representatives* (or *reps*, as they're called), individuals or organizations whose function it is to solicit advertising from the agencies located in distant advertising centers.

3. *Advertising agencies.* An advertising agency plans, produces, and places advertising for advertisers. Advertisers represented by agencies are called *clients* or *accounts*. Clients include nonprofit organizations, like the American Cancer Society or the armed forces, as well as business firms. For nonprofit clients the media sometimes, but not always, donate time and space while agency people volunteer creative services.

4. *Specialty shops.* Advertising, like other businesses, has developed specialties, and some organizations have grown up to handle these specialties. For instance, most advertising agencies buy their illustrations from *art studios.* They have their type set by *type houses.* Some of them engage *research organizations* to test the market and the effectiveness of the ad in reaching the market. Newspapers make use of national *art services,* which supply ready-made illustrations for local advertisers.

Students in advertising tend to think only of advertising agencies when they think of careers, but careers exist at all four of these levels, and jobs in any one of the areas can lead to very different jobs later on. Many newspaper publishers, for instance, came up through advertising and business departments rather than through news and editorial departments.

KINDS OF ADVERTISING

Advertisers make use of eight different kinds of advertising.

1. *National advertising.* This advertising, sometimes called "brand name" advertising, has as its purpose the selling of products to consumers. Most of the advertising that goes into general-circulation magazines and on broadcast networks is national advertising.

2. *Retail advertising.* Its purpose is to get people, some of whom may be presold on particular brands of merchandise, into the stores. Price is almost always prominently displayed. Most newspaper and local radio and television station advertising falls into this category. Sometimes retail advertisers and national advertisers get together to share the costs of the advertising, in which case it is called *cooperative advertising* or *co-op.*

3. *Mail-order advertising.* This kind of advertising often combines elements of national and retail advertising. The retailer, in this case, is far removed from where the purchaser lives, so transactions are conducted by mail. Mail-order advertising makes use of existing media, but it also depends to a great extent on its own publications (leaflets, catalogues, and other direct-mail pieces).

4. *Trade advertising.* The retailer, the wholesaler, and the broker are also "customers," in that they buy products and in turn sell them to others. Manufacturers realize they have to do a selling job on middle men, too, so they advertise to them. Here, instead of stressing the benefits of using the product, the advertisers stress the profits that can be realized from stocking and selling their products. Manufacturers reach the trade largely through trade magazines and direct mail.

5. *Industrial advertising.* Manufacturers are customers, too, when they buy raw materials and machines to use in

*Let us not be remembered
as the generation that saved the whales
and saved the trees
but ignored our own kind.*

ALLEN AND
DORWARD
ADVERTISING
SAN FRANCISCO/HOUSTON

As a public service, and for its own image, Allen and Dorward, a San Francisco-based advertising agency, ran this ad in the advertising trade press. "It generated a great deal of positive feedback," reports Bob Hoffman, senior vice president and creative director. It was a good way for an agency to build an image, for it tells several things about the agency—its outlook, its creative approach, and its style.

their manufacturing processes. The people who supply the raw material and machinery reach their customers through ads in business magazines and direct-mail pieces.

6. *Professional advertising.* Physicians prescribe drugs. Architects recommend building materials. The manufacturers of these products, through ads in professional journals and direct mail, sell doctors, architects, and other professional people on the merits of products. Some of the best-written and designed ads fall into this category, but the average person never sees them.

7. *Institutional advertising.* Advertisers use this kind of advertising to build images or to do public-relations rather than outright product-selling jobs. The first six kinds of advertising go after a share of the sales market. Institutional advertising goes after a share of the mind. Individuals can engage in this kind of advertising, too.

Yoko Ono, wife of John Lennon, took out full-page ads in a number of newspapers around the world January 11, 1981, to thank people for their concern following the shooting death of Lennon. With full pages costing, for instance, more than $20,000 in the *New York Times* and the *Washington Post* and more than $15,000 in the *Los Angeles Times,* the cost of the gesture came to considerably more than the $100,000 that had been sent by the public to the couple's Spirit Foundation.[3]

8. *Advocacy advertising.* Advocacy advertising is institutional advertising grown militant. One of the most visible advocacy advertisers of the 1980s was Mobil Corporation, with its editorial-looking advertising quarreling with media coverage and defending oil profits.

Like institutional advertising, advocacy advertising can be used by nonprofit as well as profit-making organizations. The American Civil Liberties Union, for example, took out a full-page ad in the *New York Times* to attack the Moral Majority, an evangelical-political organization not in favor with

[3]"Thank You Ad Run by Yoko Ono," *Editor & Publisher,* January 24, 1981, p. 44.

the ACLU and its supporters. "If the Moral Majority Has Its Way, You'd Better Start Praying," said the somewhat clever if startling headline. Phil Kerby, writing about the ad in the *Los Angeles Times,* said it was "the first time I can recall that the ACLU, even tongue in liberal cheek, has advocated prayer under any circumstances."[4]

To keep the discussion to a manageable length, this chapter will deal mostly with advertising sponsored by business firms to sell products and services. Idea selling, which includes institutional and advocacy advertising, will be discussed in a follow-up chapter on public relations.

MEDIA OF ADVERTISING

The media of advertising include not only the basic media of communication, the news and opinion media that this book is presenting, but also media created solely to carry advertising. These include billboards, point-of-purchase displays, and direct-mail advertising. Direct-mail advertising (leaflets, booklets, and similar printed matter) as a medium ranks right up with television in dollars spent by advertisers, and just below newspapers, still the number-one advertising medium.

Deciding which media to advertise in is a highly statistical, computer-assisted activity these days. Numbers alone—circulation figures and viewer and listener counts—are only part of it. The quality of the audience is important, too. Is it made up of people likely to buy? One of the strengths of the specialized magazines, to name one medium, lies in their concentration of single-interest readers. The advertiser who caters to that single interest is likely to enjoy a spirited response. Some specialized magazines can point to the high income level of readers. For instance, *Smithsonian,* with 1.8 million subscribers (impressive for a quality magazine), estimates that each one earns an average of $42,000 per year.

[4]Phil Kerby in "ACLU, Evangelicals on Collision Course," reprinted in *The Oregonian,* December 15, 1980, p. B7.

Roughly two-thirds of a newspaper's or magazine's revenue and just about all of a radio or television station's revenue comes from advertising. Advertisers do not normally buy space in print media or time on electronic media to provide support for those media; they buy space and time to do a selling job. That the media are kept alive by such purchases is incidental to the advertising process, but how important those purchases are to the free flow of information in our society! Consider the alternatives.

1. *Government-sponsored media.* While a case could be made for government news and opinion media to use as a yardstick by which existing media can be measured, no serious student of the press advocates public-supported media *in place of* privately owned media. Under such a circumstance news and opinion would surely evolve into propaganda. Who, then, would be in a position to criticize?

2. *Owner-subsidized media.* What we are talking about here is the underwriting of news and opinion media by people with wealth. Readers would either get the publications free, or at cost. Some media already are financed this way, but surely this is not the ideal way to finance the nation's newspapers. The wealthy tend to have similar political affiliations, similar social values. The editorial policy of papers would be monotonously uniform. It can be argued that the press *now* is subsidized by the advertisers who pay most of the costs of publishing and who provide most of the profits, but the control one advertiser exercises over media content is small compared to the control that could be exercised by an ideologue absorbing all the costs and answerable to no one, including the readers.

3. *Reader-financed media.* Among the media as they now exist, only books, a few quality magazines, listener-sponsored radio in several cities, and films (if they are considered as news and opinion media) are paid for completely by the people who use them. The typical hardbound book costs more than ten dollars. If a daily newspaper were to drop all advertising and if it had no financial angel to make up the difference, we would have to pay at least a dollar to get a

copy. For a magazine, the cost would rise to several dollars. Few readers could afford the prices.

ARE WE MEDIA?

There is one other advertising medium. The jeans we buy have a label ingeniously sewn into the back-pocket seam so that it can't be torn away without ripping the pocket. The designer version has a label even more prominently displayed.[5] Our swim suits have a diving girl on the front, instantly identifying the maker. The department store puts our purchases in a bag (handsome enough) that says exactly where the purchase was made. The cars we drive not only have a name affixed in metal script in front and on the trunk; they have license plates framed in advertisements to tell others exactly where we bought the car. If we drive a pickup truck, we are used even more blatantly—the names of our trucks are stamped in the tailgate metal itself in letters a foot high. Then we pay extra for tires with white raised letters shouting the brand name.

Loaded with all this advertising, we drive into one of the tourist traps along the highway, and upon return to the car find our bumper has become a miniature billboard to tell the world we were there. Back on the road, we catch ourselves singing a catchy commercial jingle. We are wearing T-shirts with product names emblazoned across them, or maybe they just make statements.[6] Who but someone with an identity crisis wears a plain T-shirt?

When we get back home we take the car back to where

---

[5] A study at the University of Maryland, reported in *Parade* (November 23, 1980), shed some light on the kinds of people most likely to spend their money on "signature goods." These people were more aggressive than others, more interested in social status. "The signature-goods avoider might be a person who is successful in his own right and who does not need his self-image bolstered," said Dr. Marvin A. Jolson, who headed the study.

[6] When a man was convicted of murder in California in 1981, in celebration two Yolo County sheriff's deputies in their off-duty hours sold T-shirts showing a hangman's noose and the words "Adios Louie." The deputies quit the project after complaints were filed.

we got it for a tuneup and accept a ride in a courtesy car with a sign on the side that tells the neighbors where we have been. If we are called upon to speak at a convention, we endure the explosion of a flash bulb midsentence and then see ourselves in the paper the next day with the name of the hotel etched boldly in the front of the lectern from which we spoke.

We are, each of us, walking, jogging, driving, and bicycle-pedaling billboards.

THE ROLE OF AGENCIES

Advertisers in the United States now spend close to $40 billion a year to reach their audiences. Much of this spending is directed by the several hundred large advertising agencies headquartered mainly in New York City, many of them on or near Madison Avenue. But there are advertising agencies in every medium-size and large city in the country. Even in small towns there will be a person or two who does some kind of advertising work.

Chicago thinks of itself as the birthplace of modern advertising, and it remains the home of *Advertising Age,* the industry's leading trade journal. Among the great advertising agencies making their headquarters in Chicago is the Leo Burnett agency, the originator of such campaigns as "Fly the Friendly Skies of United" and "You're in Good Hands with Allstate." Other great campaigns or slogans out of Chicago include "When You Care Enough to Send the Very Best" (Foote, Cone & Belding, agency) and "You Deserve a Break Today" (Needham Harper & Steers).

Students of advertising can see a difference in the kinds of advertising coming from various agencies, which tend to develop individual styles. For instance, over the years it has been easy to trace many clever, sophisticated, understated ads to Doyle Dane Bernbach, best known for its Volkswagen advertising. It was with some pride, however, that the president of J. Walter Thompson declared once that "there is no such thing as a J. Walter Thompson ad."

There are even regional differences that can be ob-

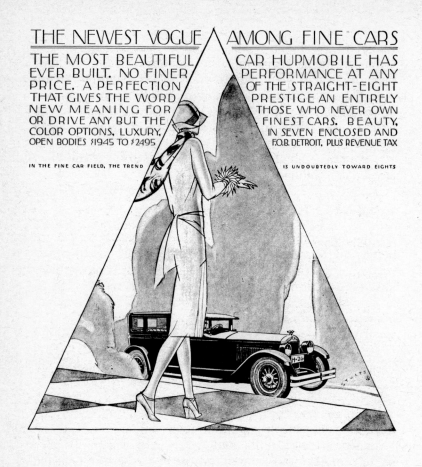

What an automobile ad looked like in 1926. "In the fine car field, the trend is undoubtedly towards eights." The automobile was a straight eight, and the cost varied from $1945 to $2495.

served. Keith Reinhard of Needham Harper & Steers, sees New York–originated advertising as "more cerebral," Chicago advertising as "more visceral." Further, New York advertising is "more street smart," Chicago advertising "more customer-wise. New York advertising is more likely to be frosted with wit; Chicago advertising is more likely to be infused with heart. . . ."[7]

Big agencies maintain branch offices in most large U.S. cities and many foreign ones. A single agency serves scores of clients, usually ones that do not compete with one another. Foote, Cone & Belding in 1979 counted 900 clients in 17 countries. The biggest agency in the U.S. in 1981 was Young & Rubicam, with billings of $2.27 billion. Billings represent the total cost of space and time purchased in various media. Prior to 1981 J. Walter Thompson was the leading agency in billings.

Client–agency associations can span decades, but many, if not most, are shorter-lived. Campbell Soup took a big part of its business away from Batten, Barton, Durstine & Osborn in 1981, ruining a 27-year association, to give it to Backer & Spielvogel, which came up with a highly successful soup-is-nutritious campaign for the West Coast. BBD&O kept the chunky-soup and soup-for-one-serving ends of the business, but the billings taken over by the new agency came to $27 million.[8]

Although agencies are currently arguing the merits and even the ethics of their system of compensation, they still earn most of their money through rebates from the media. The media—newspapers, magazines, and broadcast stations and networks—sell their space or time to agencies at a price 15 percent below the stated price. The agencies in turn bill their clients the stated price. The difference represents the agencies' fee for creative services rendered. "The actual ads

[7]Keith Reinhard, "Chicago Advertising: The Heart of the Matter," *Advertising: Chicago Style,* advertising supplement to *Chicago Tribune/Sun-Times,* October 26, 1980, p. 16.
[8]Donald K. White, "Ad Agency Is in the Soup," *San Francisco Chronicle,* May 29, 1981, p. 29.

are produced almost as a sideline, as if the artist charged for
the frame and threw in the painting as a bonus," grumbles
one critic.[9] The media are content with the arrangement because the agencies supply the ads ready to run. The media
do not have to write copy, do layouts, or produce the commercials.

The arrangement dates to the last century, when agencies were nothing more than space brokers. Media were scattered then, records hard to keep, circulation figures misleading, and it took an expert not only to decide which media
to advertise in but even to figure out where they were. Advertisers went to agencies primarily to get their advertising
placed. It was natural for these agencies to offer copy writing
and design help, and gradually the idea of full-service agencies took hold.

When agencies buy artwork, typesetting, and other services from the outside, they pass these costs on to the clients
with a handling fee. For advertising that is not "commission-
able"—not eligible for the 15 percent rebate from the
media—a special fee is charged. Agencies seem to be moving
in the direction of charging on a fee-for-services rather than
a kickback basis for all advertising.

As was mentioned earlier, an agency measures its size
by the amount of each year's billings. Billings include the
cost, *before* the 15 percent discount, of the space and time
purchased.

Agencies tend to fall into one of two categories: (1) those
that rely more on research than intuition in putting together
a campaign, and (2) those that believe that creativity is king.
Perhaps the distinction is too harsh; most agencies believe
in both research and creativity. It is only a matter of which
one is stressed.

The pendulum swings one way in advertising, and then
swings back. In the 1950s and early 1960s agencies were re-
search-oriented. If figures could not be brought to show a

[9]Dugald Stermer, "Advertising Is No Business for a Grown Man," *Ramparts,*
September 1969, p. 21.

campaign would work, it would not be tried. In the late 1960s creativity made gains. A number of smaller "hot shops" or "boutiques" sprang up to take advantage of the trend. Their selling point was that they were unencumbered by the past. Their principals were young, their ideas wild. Some of the well-established agencies argued that these new shops were less interested in selling than in "doing their thing." It is interesting to note that as the "boutiques" became successful they tended to adopt the more thorough, more businesslike approach of the larger, sounder agencies. In the 1970s all agencies became more cautious and, some say, less creative.

The quarterback in an agency situation is the *account executive* or *account supervisor,* who works directly with the client's advertising manager. The account executive draws on the talents of the agency's *copywriters* and *art directors.* The details of getting the ad in print are handled by a *production manager.* A *media buyer* decides where the ad should appear.

As far as the media are concerned, the media buyer is the key figure in an agency. Advertisements in *Advertising Age* and *Editor & Publisher* and even in *The New Yorker* tell of the virtues of a given publication. These ads are there not to pick up subscribers, but to sell media buyers or their clients on the merits of the publication as an advertising medium. When media buyers lose confidence in a publication, the publication falters, as we saw in Chapter 7. The number of subscribers is not nearly so important to a publication as the number of advertisers, although the number of subscribers determines, to some extent, an advertiser's interest in the publication.

At one time advertisers had no choice but to accept a publication's claim concerning the number of subscribers it had. Later the media, agencies, and advertisers got together to form the Audit Bureau of Circulations, which verifies for newspapers and magazines that circulations are as claimed. Trade journals have a similar organization. Radio and television audiences are not so easily measured, but several organizations attempt to do a job for these media, too.

Advertisers have some rather inflexible ideas on where in a publication their ads should be located for best results. In spite of research conducted by the media to prove them wrong, most advertisers continue to believe that up-front placement is better than back-of-the-book placement and that a right-hand page gets better readership than a left-hand page. They often request such placement and complain when they do not get it. They are willing, and required, to pay premium prices for back cover or *centerfold* position.

All advertisers want their ads next to regular editorial matter, not buried in a sea of ads. This is why newspapers, with their many ads per page, attempt to arrange them in stair-step formations; they are thus able to get at least part of each ad next to a news story.

A desire to go with the medium that offers the most responsive audience for the product logically should motivate the media buyer. Sometimes other considerations intrude. A number of companies, through their agencies, have purchased space in media simply because company management liked the editorial policy.

ADVERTISING AS A PUBLIC SERVICE

Partly because they were concerned about the country's welfare and partly because they wanted to build their image, advertising people representing the advertisers, the media, and the agencies set up the War Advertising Council in the 1940s. The council helped the government sell bonds, build morale, and do some of the other propaganda jobs necessary during wartime. So successful was this volunteer organization that, after the war, it continued as the Advertising Council, creating ads for a number of worthy causes, among them forest-fire prevention, church attendance, and aid to higher education. The media provided free space and time.

On an individual basis, agencies and ad people devote time to a number of other causes. Campbell-Ewald, Detroit, helped the police department there with a recruitment campaign, tripling applications within a month. In a similar campaign the Cleveland Advertising Club brought in 1400 applicants for 500 police jobs there, "the largest group of applicants since the depression years," said then Mayor Carl Stokes. Rock Bergthold & Wright, San Jose, California, signed an ad in *Time* telling "what it's like to be a cop today."

North Advertising Incorporated in Chicago, following the shooting of Robert F. Kennedy, produced and sponsored a series of ads calling for gun legislation. Although the agency's clients had no connection with the campaign, a group of gun lovers and assorted right-wingers organized in an attempt to get the clients to drop their agency or face a boycott of their products.

ADVERTISING RESEARCH

With so much money at stake, agencies increasingly rely on research to help them know an audience and tailor advertising to fit. An agency not originating the research can make use of existing findings.

The U.S. Department of Labor estimates that 59 percent of women between the ages of 18 and 64 work outside the home, and 20 percent of managers are women. These facts are altering the way advertisers appeal to women. Many advertisers are cutting out any references to gender. AMF, for instance, which used to talk about strength in its tennis racket ads, now stresses finesse and control. Other advertisers are depicting women in nontraditional roles, inviting men over for drinks, for instance. Of course, there are some problems. One advertising agency executive told a *U.S. News & World Report* writer that making a woman an executive in a tweed suit "will turn off a lot of women who are not executives and can't relate to that."[10]

Original research conducted by Shulton Inc. in 1981 in connection with the introduction of its Blue Stratos line of men's cologne and after-shave lotion showed that men on the

[10]Michael Doan, "Business Shifts its Sales Pitch for Women," *U.S. News & World Report,* July 6, 1981, p. 46.

West Coast use almost twice as much cologne and after-shave as men elsewhere. The company speculated that one reason for the difference might be that West Coast men are more sports oriented, taking more showers and hence using such products more often. One could expect Shulton to concentrate on areas where a product already has good sales prospects, but its advertising also could be designed to whip up enthusiasm where enthusiasm does not already exist. That kind of advertising, of course, would use a different theme from ads to an established market.

Research conducted to determine sales prospects is *market research.* Research designed to measure advertising effectiveness is *copy testing.*

TELEVISION COMMERCIALS

The average television commercial, seen for 30 seconds, costs $100,000 to produce, which is a lot, but the cost for its one-time exposure during a popular network program can come to more than that. When we consider that a television commercial is meant for repeated exposures, it is clear that air time is where most of the money is spent.

Before a commercial actually goes into production, it undergoes copy testing to determine whether its message is clear enough and interesting enough to do the job. This kind of copy testing involves showing a series of sketches, called a "storyboard," to groups of consumers. The commercial can also be tested at a more advanced stage.

Once the idea is approved, the agency hires a production team to arrange for the talent, do the filming and editing, and coordinate the music. It takes at least a 12-hour day to film enough footage for a 30-second commercial, but for certain effects it can take a lot longer.

Time costs and other considerations limit most television commercials to 30 seconds, but the surge of interest in cable television (by 1981 about one-quarter of television homes were linked to cable) brought about much longer commercials, called "informercials." Advertisers using cable find access to more select audiences and at comparably lower rates. "Informercials" can go on for as long as four hours. A national advertiser, for instance, can go into considerable detail on how to use its product.[11]

CREATIVE ASPECTS OF ADVERTISING

A recent purchaser of Sperry Top-Sider deck shoes is shown in a full-page, full-color ad in *The New Yorker*. She is sitting on a dock, holding a shoe to her ear, looking pleased. "If You Listen Very Carefully, You Can Hear the Ocean," says the ad's headline. Technically, the advertising is false, but there is no record of a disappointed shoe buyer returning her purchase to the store, complaining to the clerk that "I can't hear the ocean." We have learned to accept such advertising, even applaud it for its imaginative approach. It may even be, as some have suggested, that such advertising adds to our enjoyment of the product. If it sets the shoe apart from similar shoes on the market, it is successful as advertising.

This is advertising creativity. Most effective advertising has a dose of it. It starts with a basic idea or theme, a "unique selling proposition," as one advertising executive labeled it.

People are always trying to analyze creativity in the hope of finding some magic formula. When *Advertising Age,* for a feature on creativity, sent out questionnaires to advertising people known for their creativity, Hal Riney, senior vice president–marketing director for Ogilvy & Mather, San Francisco, said he could not provide answers because "far too much damage has already been done to our business by people who seem to want to remove the uncertainties of creative insight and replace them with absolute methodology." Furthermore, Riney, whose humorous commercials for Blitz-Weinhard (a Portland, Oregon, brewery) have won wide

---

[11] "'Informercials,'" *Time,* May 18, 1981, p. 69.

Director George Rosenberg waits as wrangler Don Howe positions a rattlesnake for a scene in the television commercial "Loran C" for the U.S. Coast Guard. The advertising agency was Henry J. Kaufman & Associates, Washington, D.C.

praise in the advertising industry, has "never really known where ideas come from and exactly why they occur to some people and not to others."[12]

What works as advertising in one part of the country, or in one country, does not necessarily work in another. An American-directed campaign in Hong Kong had a green hat on a man's head. The campaign was killed when it was pointed out that a green hat on a man's head to Chinese marked the man as a cuckold. The Marlboro man, who sits tall in the saddle against a sunset, sells cigarettes in the United States, but the campaign fizzled out in Hong Kong because, "It turned out that the Hong Kong Chinese, an increasingly affluent and a totally urban people, didn't see the charm of riding around alone in the hot sun all day." The Hong Kong Marlboro man was changed to a younger, better-dressed version with a truck as well as a horse.[13]

Marlboro's cowboy image failed in Japan, too. The Marlboro smoker there, instead of remaining on a horse, traded it for a shiny pickup and put on a classy suit. Marlboro country took on a different look. "The Japanese . . . couldn't see the point of being like the [original] Marlboro man—dirty and poor—so why would they want to smoke the same kind of cigarette he did?"[14] In Japan, in contrast to the United States, ads do not make direct commands to buy. Such commands would be considered insults. Furthermore, ads prepared for the Japanese do not make direct brand comparisons, for these might cause competitors to lose face.

Often the advertising campaign is built around a slogan. Once adopted, a slogan can go on for years. In fact, it would be wasteful to come up with a good slogan, exploit it briefly, and drop it for another. Some experts in advertising believe that even after the client's and agency's staffs have grown tired of the slogan, it should be kept alive. *Playboy* in 1976

[12]"The Sources of Invention," *Advertising Age,* December 29, 1980, p. S-4.
[13]Nicole Seligman, "Be Sure Not to Wear a Green Hat If You Visit in Hong Kong," *The Wall Street Journal,* May 11, 1979, p. 1.
[14]Tracie Rozhon, "Learning the Differences in the Language of Sell," *The Press,* May 1981, p. 11.

started promoting this line, especially to people who might be interested in buying space in the magazine: "The *Playboy* reader. His lust is for life." In 1981 the slogan was still going strong.

We know an advertiser's slogan or theme has "arrived" when it becomes the subject of public comedy. Kellogg's "Special K" breakfast cereal made the grade in a 1981 *New York* magazine back-of-the-book competition. Readers were asked to complete the expression, "It was so _____ that . . . ." (Johnny Carson uses the routine in his opening monologue on the "Tonight Show.") Marlon Campbell, a *New York* reader from St. Albans, New York, submitted this: "He's so fat that he needs both hands to do the Special K pinch."[15]

Coming up with just the right name is often the key to an effective advertising campaign. The Oakland Athletics of 1981, just before the baseball strike, hired Ogilvy & Mather to produce six commercials to bring in the fans. The agency coined the term "Billy Ball" to describe the team's feisty play and to focus attention on the A's manager, the colorful, dirt-kicking, umpire-baiting Billy Martin.

ADVERTISING AWARDS

Advertising people place great store in awards they can win for the ads they produce. Clio Awards for the best television commercials create quite a stir each year. There are many others, including awards for the best design in ads. All kinds of organizations, national and local, do the judging and make the awards. The awards cannot very well deal with measured effectiveness of ads, only with their cleverness or artfulness. Ad makers pay fees to enter the competitions.

There have been some complaints. Some observers feel that awards only serve to help ad creators impress their clients. Certainly the awards massage the ego. They do not hurt the people who make the awards, either, bringing them lots of good publicity. One winner took out a full-page "open let-

[15]February 16, 1981, p. 111.

ter" ad in *Advertising Age* to say he was burning all his awards "as a protest to the current awards shows." He talked about confusion and proliferation of awards and asked for a single awards committee to be sponsored by the American Association of Advertising Agencies.[16] He was not likely to get his wish.

THE LANGUAGE OF ADVERTISING

Some of the best art and typography in the media today comes from advertising artists and designers. It would not be hard to make a case to show that the excellence of design in magazines was largely inspired by innovative advertising art directors.

The text matter in advertising—the "copy"—has not kept pace. While a few memorable passages can be cited, like those in Volkswagen advertisements, the bulk of what one reads in the ads, especially in retail ads, is not as well reasoned, not as well phrased as what one reads in the editorial columns of the publications in which the ads appear.

Perhaps that is the nature of advertising. For one thing, the advertising copywriter does not seem to stand much in awe of the language. One finds few purists in the ranks of advertising copywriters. They know well enough that "Winstons taste good like a cigarette should" and "Ain't no reason to go anyplace else" are indefensible from a grammatical standpoint, but, they argue, "That's the way people talk." They know that people should not "Shop Macy's," people should "Shop *at* Macy's," but the shorter version moves faster, and that is important to copywriters. They make verbs out of words meant to be nouns. They use phony transitions like "Fact is" and "What's more" to tie sentences together. Above all they often make the tone embarrassingly conversational.

From the customer's standpoint, how the copywriter says it is less important than what the copywriter says. Pro-

[16]Michael Ulick in an ad in *Advertising Age*, July 13, 1981, p. 14.

tected by anonymity, the copywriter makes promises not likely to impress the thoughtful reader or listener. Examples like the following are still too easy to find.

"Hurry! The supply is limited." One suspects the very opposite is true: the hapless store is overstocked. If the supply *is* limited, and if the product *is* as good as the ad says, why did the store not buy more in the first place? If the supply is truly limited, why does the store create a desire for the product only to disappoint late-arriving customers?

"Open evenings and after Church on Sunday." The reader is supposed to think that here is a used car dealer who probably goes to church himself; that is why he cannot open until Sunday afternoon. As a religious man, he will surely treat his customers right.

"Prescribed by four out of five physicians." Can that be possible? Certainly. All the advertiser has to do is get groups of doctors together to find out what they advise for headaches, hemorrhoids, or whatever. If most of the physicians in each group pick some product other than the advertiser's, never mind. Eventually the advertiser gets one group together in which the product in question comes out best, and that is the "survey" talked about in the advertising.

"Half-price sale." Buy the first tire at the regular price and get a second tire at half price. That might be a half-price sale to the copywriter, but to the person actually buying, it is nothing more than a three-quarter-price sale.

"No sales to dealers." The reader is supposed to conclude that somehow the prices are even lower than wholesale. Here is a chance for the ordinary citizen to buy better than even a dealer can buy! Does anyone believe there will be someone at the door checking ID cards? A variation of the "No sales to dealers" line is "Dealers welcome."

"The tars and nicotine trapped in the filter never reach your lungs." Not if they're trapped, but what about the ones that aren't?

"Lasts 25 percent longer." Longer than what? The copywriter does not say. If a reader is obliging enough to complete the sentence with the name of a competing product, the advertiser will appreciate it. If you want instead to assume that the new product lasts longer than an earlier version of it lasted, that is all right, too. It is a sort of do-it-yourself advertisement.

A San Francisco brewery some years ago made clever use of the incomplete comparative when it called its beer "one of America's two great beers." The ads never named the other "great" beer, which was whatever the reader thought it was.

Copywriters have been such spendthrifts in their use of superlatives, real or implied, that the old ones have deflated in value, and there are not many unused ones left. In the public mind now a miracle product is one that merely works. The deluxe line is only ordinary. King size is the smallest size available. When a company comes out with a genuine improvement in its product, there are no words left to describe it, or no words that a conditioned public will not yawn over.

It used to be that advertisers did not mention competitors by name—it was always Brand X that failed in a comparison test—but that restriction no longer holds. Advertisers have rolled up their sleeves to get their share of the market.

POLICING THE ADS

While the federal government, particularly through the Federal Trade Commission, the Food and Drug Administration, and the Federal Communications Commission, has some jurisdiction over advertising, its policing powers are limited. What protection the consumer enjoys comes largely from the media themselves, and from consumer groups.

Industry polices its advertising through several organizations, including the Council of Better Business Bureau's National Advertising Division. When this organization challenges an advertiser, the challenge having been brought on by customer or competitor complaints, the advertiser often modifies or discontinues the offending advertising. To cite one case, Alpo Beef Chunks Dinner in 1981 agreed to delete lines suggesting that the product extends a dog's life span, even though the lines had included a "maybe." "Maybe [Fido] has been around so long because Alpo's been around so long" would be heard no more from the lips of Lorne Greene.

Except in the electronic media, where federally supervised "equal time" provisions dictate to some extent what a station must run, the media can refuse to accept any advertising, so long as they do not violate restraint-of-trade laws. A publication, for instance, can say "No" to an advertiser for a good reason (the product may be inferior or the ad itself may be misleading) or for the flimsiest of reasons (the publisher may not like the design of the ad). The advertiser may be asked to change the ad before it is accepted.

Every newspaper and every magazine has a list of products or appeals it will not tolerate. *The Saturday Evening Post* in the 1930s refused to accept liquor advertising (but when the magazine world became more competitive later it decided liquor was not so bad after all). A number of magazines, including *The New Yorker* and the *Saturday Review,* following the Surgeon General's report on smoking, refused to accept cigarette advertising. *Ms.* turns down ads that might be offensive to its liberated women readers. By mutual agreement, the broadcast industry and the tobacco industry have parted advertising company.

Magazines like *Good Housekeeping* and *Parents Magazine* have worked out seals of approval that guarantee readers that the products are as advertised. Readers of some magazines have found that when a product proves to be faulty, they can get a refund by writing to the advertising department of the magazine in which the ad appeared.

A number of newspapers refuse to accept any ads, no matter how tasteful, for X-rated movies. But newspapers fight a losing battle with the ingenious ad people. Insist that breasts be covered with a bra, and the advertiser will comply by painting it on so crudely that readers will quickly get the idea that it was put there just to get the ad into the paper.

A publication's policy on what it will accept in advertising is not always based on truth and good taste. It is sometimes based on provincialism. In past years some newspapers did not accept advertising from retail establishments in other cities. They bowed to the pressure from local retailers—local advertisers—who cried that local dollars would go out of town.

ADVERTISING AS WHIPPING BOY

Of all the products of journalism, advertising is the most ubiquitous. We see ads wherever we look, we hear them wherever we go. Constantly clamoring for attention, some ads are as likely to build resentment as win converts. By their very nature their excesses and their mistakes lie exposed, waiting for the criticism that is bound to come.

Advertising has always had its critics. Complaints against advertising grew intense during the Depression of the 1930s when its cost became difficult to justify. Economists led the attack. In the 1940s, as we have seen, novelists took over. In the 1950s, sociologists—and their follow-up man, Vance Packard—stepped in. In the 1960s the critics allied themselves with the politicians.

People do not like advertising if for no other reason than that they do not like to admit that they are vulnerable to it.

To Arnold Toynbee, advertising is an evil. To J. Kenneth Galbraith, it is wasteful. To Arthur Schlesinger, Jr., it is awful.[17]

In his spiritual autobiography, Malcolm Muggeridge writes:

> If you happen to cast an eye through the advertisements in your color supplements, you will see displayed there a credulity which would be the envy of every witch doctor in Africa. . . . I never met a man made happy by money or worldly success or sensual indulgence, still less by the stupefaction of drugs

[17]See Victor S. Navasky's article, "Advertising Is a Science? An Art? A Business?" *New York Times Magazine,* November 20, 1966, p. 52.

or alcohol. Yet we all, in one way or another, pursue these ends, as the advertiser well knows. He offers them in Technicolor and stereo sound, and there are many takers.[18]

The syndicated cartoon panel *Graffiti* by Leary shows this message scrawled on a wall: "Abominable Snowmen Dwell on Madison Avenue."

The critics build an impressive case. This chapter has already presented some of it. The case boils down to six basic charges:

1. Advertising makes people buy things they do not need or cannot afford.
2. Advertising confuses customers by stressing trivial differences between brands.
3. Advertising makes things more expensive because manufacturers pass the costs of advertising along to their customers.
4. Advertising encourages monopoly because only big companies can afford to advertise.
5. Advertising is vulgar, tasteless, and misleading.
6. Advertising is not necessary, for if a product is good enough, word of mouth will do the job. Look at the generic brands now on grocers' shelves.

But the proponents of advertising have some answers.

Advertising does not force people to buy. It merely announces, suggests, persuades. Nor can ad people know exactly how a campaign is going to work. "Advertising is not a science with laws, rules, and prescriptions which if followed precisely lead to predictable results each time they are applied," John Crawford wrote in his textbook for advertising students. "It can accelerate the downfall of a poor product as quickly as it can promote the rise of a good one."[19]

Advertising is largely news about products, and readers

---

[18]Malcolm Muggeridge, *Jesus Rediscovered* (New York: Doubleday, 1969), pp. 53, 57, 58.
[19]John W. Crawford, *Advertising,* 2nd ed. (Boston: Allyn and Bacon, 1965), p. 2.

generally treat it as such. Indeed, some of the best-received features in a publication are the advertisements. The person who runs the home, especially, would find the daily newspaper a disappointment without the ads from retail establishments. One of the troubles with the short-lived West Coast edition of the *New York Times* was the fact that it omitted the ads of the stores in Manhattan. People on the West Coast may not have been able to respond to such advertising, but they enjoyed seeing it, nevertheless. Many *New York Times* readers, especially those who read the Sunday paper, preferred to wait the four days for the mail delivery of the more complete New York edition.

Advertising in some product categories may stress trivial differences, but in other categories the differences are considerable. This is especially true of appliances, cars, and other high-ticket items.

At least one authority defends advertising on economic grounds. Dr. Jules Backman, research professor of Economics at New York University, found that advertising is *not* anticompetitive, it does *not* lead to monopoly power, it does *not* generate excessive profit, it does *not* set up a barrier against new companies entering an industry, it does *not* contribute to consumer price increases.[20]

Dr. Backman showed, for instance, that the most intensively advertised products have characteristically increased in price by a smaller amount than have the poorly advertised products. He concluded that expenditures for advertising do not represent a net cost to the economy. If ad costs were eliminated, he pointed out, other marketing costs would go up, possibly making the selling job more costly overall than it is *with* advertising. Of course, the cost of advertising is built into the price of the product, but advertising makes possible greater sales, which means lower production and distribution costs and hence lower prices.

Ad people have two defenses against the criticism that

[20]Jules Backman, *Advertising and Competition* (New York: New York University Press, 1967).

only big companies can afford to advertise. One is that a wide variety of media are available, in every price range, with every kind of audience. The other defense is that with (among other things) the right kind of advertising, a small company can itself become big, as Polaroid, Xerox, and Sony exemplify.

As for the charge that advertising is vulgar, tasteless, and misleading, ad people have to admit that some of it is. Such advertising is usually confined to products facing excessive competition, or, on the local level, stores catering to non-discriminating buyers. The vulgarity and tastelessness is not dissimilar to that found in some of the news and editorial content of the media carrying the advertising.

Ad people are less willing to admit that advertising misleads. At least, they will argue that ads are more truthful today than they have been in the past. Government agencies, the advertising industry, the media, and consumer groups have all stepped up pressure on borderline operators.

Finally, ad people argue that word-of-mouth communication will no longer do the job in today's complex society. Even Hershey Chocolate Corporation, the one big holdout against consumer advertising, went looking for an agency when in the late 1960s Mars candy bars began outselling Hersheys.

In his lectures on advertising to students at the University of Oregon, Dr. Willis L. Winter with this list summarizes what he considers to be the contributions of advertising to "our socioeconomic welfare":

1. Advertising creates mass markets for products, thus raising our standard of living and expanding the job market.
2. Advertising serves as a buyers' guide for consumers, providing information on a wide range of products, both new and established. In the words of Turner Catledge, then managing editor of the *New York Times*, "Advertising is news."[21]

[21]Turner Catledge, Gideon Seymour Lecture, University of Minnesota, 1958.

3. Advertising supports the mass media, contributing two-thirds of the revenues of most newspapers and magazines and virtually all the revenues of radio and television stations.
4. Advertising adds value to products by pointing out previously unrecognized attributes either physically or psychologically inherent in the products.
5. Advertising fosters better products through sharpened competition. It engenders better quality control through clear brand identification and manufacturer accountability.
6. Advertising lowers selling costs by making the sales person's job easier or by replacing the sales person entirely, as in the case of mail order houses, supermarkets, and discount stores.

Arguments over advertising's worth, pro and con, are not conclusive. The trouble with many critics is that they lump the various categories of advertising together, and they fail to consider the various functions that advertising performs. Much of their criticism is really directed at the competitive free-enterprise system, for which advertising is only a means of communication. Fairfax Cone said, "Most of the viewers who fear advertising as an evil force give it too much credit."[22]

The trouble with advertising proponents, who are mostly advertising people themselves, is that they fail to admit, even to themselves, the true nature of their work; they are not philanthropists or advance people for a better social or economic system; they are nothing more, nothing less than sales people. Selling is, or can be, a useful occupation. Those in it should not try to make it appear to be something other than what it is.

[22]Fairfax M. Cone, *With All Its Faults* (Boston: Little, Brown, 1969), p. 8.

Chapter 14
For Immediate Release

When J. R. Ewing on the television program "Dallas" hired the unscrupulous Leslie Stewart to polish his tarnished image, real-life public relations people cried "Foul!" James A. Little, president of the Public Relations Society of America, said in a *Los Angeles Herald Examiner* feature that an ethical public relations (PR) practitioner would not consider serving a client like Ewing. Anyway, "In attempting to make a questionable client look good, [Leslie Stewart] is violating some very basic standards of professional conduct, such as promising results in areas over which she has no control."[1]

[1] "J.R. Ewing Needs PR; Gets Press Agentry," *IABC News*, June 1981, p. 11.

Carol Orsborn, a PR consultant, complained that the show had Stewart in her first meeting with Ewing selling a new corporate logo for an advertising campaign. "Now most people who watch the show are going to think she turns out ads," Orsborn complained to a *San Francisco Examiner* reporter. Orsborn was also critical of the PR woman's setting up interviews without first consulting with her client.[2]

The show created the impression that PR for a major client is a one-person operation where, in reality, a team of people would be involved.

At least one critic of the "Dallas" show saw a bright side. The *PR Reporter,* a newsletter representing the industry, said that the sequence showed that "public relations is powerful, the way to get things done." Also, PR people could take some comfort in the fact that television programs like *Dallas* misrepresent *all* professions and trades, including business itself. The whole entertainment industry tends to engage in exaggeration and stereotyping. Time constrictions do not allow for subtleties, and plotting biases tend to collect on a single side.

PUBLIC RELATIONS: WHAT IT IS

Public relations is both a *condition* and an *activity.* As a condition, public relations is what people think of a company, organization, or public figure—the client. It is the client's image. As an activity, public relations includes everything from publicizing events to moving people to action. It involves public-opinion measuring, advice to management, news-release writing, publications work of all kinds, broadcasting, speech writing and making, film making, corporate design, money raising, personnel work, lobbying, tours, meetings, committee work, advertising, training programs, selling, promotion, entertaining—the list goes on.

Public relations help comes from a department within the company, a consultant, a PR organization, or an advertis-

[2]Loc. cit.

To promote her appearance on Dick Cavett's "Back-lot U.S.A.,"
a CBS-TV special in 1976, Stanley Musgrove, the press agent for
actress Mae West, invested $250 to rent this theater on
Hollywood's busiest street for one night to put an unusual
message on the marquee.

ing agency that maintains a PR department. "Some agencies offer both public relations and advertising as a total communications concept, because they feel that while advertising sells the products, public relations does the equally important job of selling the institution beyond those products," says Jeff Clausen, an executive of Themmel, Marx & Associates, Portland, Oregon.[3]

Donald K. White, business editor of the *San Francisco Chronicle,* noted with some disapproval in 1979 the takeover of public relations firms by major advertising agencies. Carl Byoir and Associates had just become part of Foote, Cone & Belding, Bursten-Marsteller had become part of Young & Rubicam; and Manning, Selvage & Lee had become part of Benton & Bowles. The mergers might be good for "the economies of scale in the communications business," White wrote, but they "will further add to the gray zone that now exists in the public mind about the differences between public relations and advertising."[4]

Public relations is a broad term, broad enough to include both advertising and publicity. People have a tendency to confuse all three terms. Public relations differs from publicity in that publicity represents only the telling of a story, while public relations includes the telling, and also all the activity that made a story possible. Public relations differs from advertising in that it is essentially institution-oriented, whereas advertising is essentially product-oriented; on the surface, at least, PR is more interested in reputation than in sales.

A major difference between PR and advertising is that in advertising the client is always identified. The print media insist that the client be identified somewhere in the ad so that the reader will know it is an advertisement, not news or editorial matter. If the advertiser has designed the ad to simulate news or editorial matter, the medium puts a sort of warn-

[3]Jeff Clausen, "The Role of Public Relations," *Business Success,* September 1979, p. 11.
[4]Donald K. White, "The Marriage of Advertising, PR," *San Francisco Chronicle,* December 11, 1979, p. 25.

ing at the top: "An Advertisement." Even though the medium offers the advertiser help with the wording of the ad and, in some cases, insists that changes be made in order to make the ad conform with certain standards, the space is the advertiser's to use as desired.

On the other hand, what the PR person submits to the medium goes directly into the news and editorial hopper, along with material submitted by the medium's own staff members, to become an integral part of the publication or broadcast, if the editor decides to include it. The PR person exercises no control over how his material is used or *if* it is used.

If the material is used, the reader or listener may not know that a PR person originated it. Not that the PR person minds. The credibility of the information about the client is enhanced if the reader believes that a working journalist rather than a propagandist originated the story and wrote it. (It is better to have a friend tell others how good we are than for us to do it ourselves.)

The various front organizations set up by trade associations and other organizations are an extension of the PR person's acceptance of the idea of anonymity. Give the front an impressive name to mask its true identity, and it will have an easier time with its propaganda. The Tobacco Industry Research Committee, with its stubborn denials of the link between cigarettes and disease, operated more effectively under that name than it could have with a more descriptive name, like, say, the Tobacco Industry Defense Council Against the Surgeon General's Report.

Over the years PR has included "business communications" as part of the field, but business communicators are starting to separate themselves from PR departments. "The business communication profession . . . has gained a solid identity of its own and has earned considerably more recognition from top management," observed John N. Bailey, executive director of the International Association of Business Communicators, following a 1979 survey of its membership. Nearly a third of business communicators work in separate or employee communication departments. Only about 25 percent work in PR departments. Business communicators not only put out company publications; they also produce audiovisual materials, engage in face-to-face communication, develop telephone information systems, and direct bulletin-board programs.

"THE ENGINEERING OF CONSENT"

Bernays calls public relations "the engineering of consent."[5] The term is pretentious, but it does illustrate the broad scope of PR. As an activity, it represents much more now than the "press agentry" of the nineteenth century.

People in PR see their work as falling into three categories.

1. *Publicizing the client.* This they do by mailing or delivering news releases to the various media, by arranging events so the media will assign their own writers to the story, and by publishing their own media.

2. *Sizing up various publics.* The PR person wants to find what the client's image is and how it can be improved. Here PR utilizes the tools the social sciences have developed. Public opinion polling has become a familiar tool. Through its findings, companies have been better able to understand their publics: employees, customers, stockholders, opinion leaders, legislators, and so on.

3. *Helping the client make management decisions.* In this role the public relations person acts as the company conscience, operating under the assumption that before the company can enjoy good public relations it must first *deserve* good public relations. The PR person cannot tell a story unless there is a story to tell.

Society doubtless has enjoyed some benefits from industry's preoccupation with public relations. Industry has begun to believe its own public relations and is acting accordingly.

---

[5]Edward L. Bernays, ed., *The Engineering of Consent* (Norman: University of Oklahoma Press, 1955).

Edward L. Bernays calls this "enlightened self-interest," and notes its surge since the end of World War II. The PR field gained prestige in 1946 when Boston University established a School of Public Relations.

As a career PR becomes more attractive to journalism school graduates each year. The Newspaper Fund Inc. in a survey found that 10.4 percent of the 14,600 persons getting bachelor's degrees in journalism in June 1980 took PR jobs. An estimated 100,000 persons now work as PR practitioners for profit and nonprofit organizations.

In some respects, handling PR for a nonprofit organization, like a university, is easier than handling PR for a corporation. Large segments of the public are likely to be more sympathetic to the goals of the nonprofit organization, but the corporation is more likely to have the funds for full-scale PR activities, including research.

PR people are among the best-paid in the communications field. A study by Marshall Consultants, Inc., an executive search firm, showed in 1980 that top PR people earn as much as $300,000 a year, but most PR persons, who often carry a vice-president title, earn from $30,000 to $150,000 a year.[6]

Women have been especially welcome in PR jobs. *The Corporate Communications Report,* a newsletter, in 1981 reported that women make up 20 percent of the membership of the 9200-member Public Relations Society of America and 54 percent of the 8400-member International Association of Business Communicators.[7]

"It's the best of times for public relations," said the *Public Relations Journal* in a 1980 editorial. "From every quarter, all indicators point to the profession's steady climb up the ladder to greater importance, broader acceptance, and

[6]Compare this with the average of a little more than $50,000 a year paid to the editor of a typical metropolitan daily newspaper. (For a report on a survey of newspaper editors' salaries, see Warren W. Schwed, "Big City Editors Earn Over $50,000 a Year," *Editor & Publisher,* July 4, 1981, pp. 9, 10.)
[7]"Communications Best for Women," *Oregon Business,* February 1981, p. 65.

increased prestige." The magazine predicted a growth in PR activities to meet "external pressures affecting . . . companies."[8]

A *Wall Street Journal* writer said that where once PR might have been considered a dead-end job, it is now seen as "the fast track to top management. . . . Beset by organized consumer and labor groups, antagonistic politicians and the press, companies are channeling more talent into public relations, offering PR people fatter paychecks and handing out loftier titles. They are promoting their public relations executives into other areas of the company—including operations."[9]

A University of Missouri School of Journalism study predicted that in the 1980s public relations would be the fastest growing management function in American business. "By 1990, our society will have become more complex, and more organizations will look to trained communicators to 'tell their story' to others," the published report said.[10]

ANY NUMBER CAN PLAY

Because public relations involves so many different activities, it appeals to a variety of persons as a means of earning a living. Not all are really qualified, and this embarrasses the professionally oriented men and women in the field, but there is little they can do to run the others out. The field of PR has organizations that set standards and even certify people, but any policing within organizations does not affect nonmembers.

In their frequent conventions, PR people make speeches to each other about their professional status. Is public relations a profession, or merely a craft or business? If *profession* is strictly defined, of course, public relations does not qualify;

[8]"Steadily Up the Ladder," *Public Relations Journal,* October 1980, p. 8.
[9]Sue Shellenbarger, "Work in PR Now a Route to Top Jobs," *The Wall Street Journal,* June 24, 1980, p. 31.
[10]"Study Foresees High PR Growth in the '80s," *IABC News,* October 1980, p. 1.

there is no licensing, and there is no body of knowledge that each PR person must master before being allowed to practice. Anyone can rent an office, hire a secretary, get some letterheads printed, and then be in business.

While public relations people build and polish images for clients, they worry about their own image. They have never known exactly what to call themselves. When the first of them became a force in American journalism in the nineteenth century, offering, as was customary then, a bottle of whiskey to a city editor in return for some favorable mention of a client, the representative went by the name "press agent." Later, eschewing bribery, the agent became a "publicist," and still later a "director of information." As the activities expanded to encompass listening as well as talking, making the work, in the phrasing of Edward L. Bernays, a "two-way street," the title stepped up to "public relations counsel."[11] At the corporate level the function now carries the title of vice president. But to many reporters and newspaper editors the person, regardless of income or title, is still a "flack."

REACHING THE PUBLIC

The public relations person develops programs and materials for a number of different audiences divided between two basic publics, an internal public and an external one. The internal public consists of employees, people in management positions, and stockholders. The external public consists of customers, potential customers, dealers, suppliers, citizens in the communities where company facilities are located, civil officials, lawmakers, and others, depending upon the particular client.

An internal PR problem develops, for instance, when a company decides to relocate. Georgia Pacific faced the prob-

[11]Edward L. Bernays, whose PR career spans more than half a century, has written a number of books, including his memoirs, *Biography of an Idea* (New York: Simon and Schuster, 1965).

lem in 1978 when it announced it was moving its Portland, Oregon, offices to Atlanta. The PR department took on the job of convincing employees there were advantages for them in the move. It arranged tours of Atlanta, brought speakers from Atlanta to Portland, and set up a room at the Portland offices to answer questions about Atlanta and the South. Long-time Portland residents were reluctant to leave their favored city, of course (Portland had been ranked as one of the most liveable big cities in America), and making the job even tougher for the PR department was an independent report aired on the network news shows naming Atlanta at the time as the number-one city for crime.

Similarly, when AT&T Long Lines in Washington, D.C., decided to move its headquarters to Oakton, Virginia, it published an elaborate *Oakton in a Nutshell* booklet introducing employees to the area and making their move less unsettling.

Publications issued on a regular basis—company magazines, newspapers, and newsletters—remain popular as tools for maintaining good internal public relations, but other tools are important, too, including bulletin boards, for instance, and films, and in more recent years the electronic media. Another inside medium involves a combination of the telephone and recordings.

Pacific Telephone's "Newsline," a daily "dial company news" recording, was initiated in the early 1960s in preparation for bargaining with the unions. The initial unit, which served telephone employees in the San Francisco Bay Area, provided up-to-the-minute reports on labor negotiations. Today the recording idea serves some 115,000 Pacific and Nevada Bell employees with seven "Newslines," located in San Francisco, Sacramento, San Jose, Los Angeles, Orange County, San Diego, and Reno. In addition, a "Corporate Newsline," available to the field "Newsline" editors, feeds systemwide and companywide telecommunications items of interest on a daily basis. Locally, "Newsline" editors add items of area interest, AT&T and PT&T stock quotations, and weather news. "Newslines" are updated in the event of late-breaking news. The San Francisco "Newsline," which is located in the firm's headquarters city, is equipped with 100 lines, 10 of which are toll-free numbers that can be used by retirees and others living or working out of the city. The other "Newsline" operations have fewer trunks. The "Newsline" concept has been adopted by AT&T, other Bell operating companies, and other firms in a variety of businesses.

The most important tool for reaching stockholders, another internal public, is the annual report, filled with charts, graphs, and tables, along with photographs and writeups about progress made during the year. An annual report is often an elaborate booklet costing several dollars per copy to produce. What it contains is controlled to some extent by the Securities and Exchange Commission. Some companies issue special annual reports for employees. Nonprofit organizations issue annual reports, too, but these are often less structured.

The external public can best be reached through news releases to the media, programs for television, advertisements, publications, and lobbying activities. Every company activity, every gesture deserves notice. For instance, PR considerations prompted a company like Sears, Roebuck and Co., to donate 66 gallons of paint to Glendale, California, in 1981 to help the City Council cover graffiti on park buildings and other public facilities. The *Glendale News-Press* responded by running a photograph of Sears people making the presentation to the mayor.

In the Los Angeles area a PR firm is likely to have, among other departments, one for "planters" and one for "bookers." Planters with movie people as clients send out short items to trade papers and gossip columnists. Bookers arrange appearances for clients on talk shows.[12]

School children form an especially important public for PR people. In her *Hucksters in the Classroom* (1979) Sheila Harty, a member of Ralph Nader's consumer group, estimates that two-thirds of *Fortune* magazine's top 500 corporations and most trade organizations supply free materials to

[12]P.J. Corkery, "For Immediate Release," *Harper's,* March 1982, p. 13.

teachers for use in the classroom. The Chamber of Commerce of the United States issues kits that explain the economic system. Companies and associations producing free school materials naturally portray themselves and their products in a favorable light, but argue that their materials are truthful. Besides, they say, these materials are necessary to balance antibusiness materials students are subjected to.

USING THE MEDIA

Public relations people work with all media. In the case of radio and television, they take advantage of a provision of the Federal Communications Commission that directs these media to devote some time to "public service" broadcasting. If a PR person can produce a film, say, that deals with an issue of public concern and confine the advertising content to simple company mention at the end, a station is likely to run it at no charge—though not, of course, at prime time.

The Atlantic Richfield Co. (Arco), unhappy with the way energy issues were covered on television, in 1979 began producing a monthly half-hour show, *Energy Update,* to be distributed free to television stations and cable operations that requested it. Some stations used the program, or parts of the footage, as filler; some tossed it aside or asked that no more tapes be sent. There was some mention of Arco, of course, but the company attempted to keep the shows, which were like news programs, reasonably balanced.

Alarmed by inroads made by Moral Majority and other ultraconservative groups in 1980, Norman Lear, the television producer (*All in the Family, Maude,* etc.) organized People for the American Way to produce some "freedom of thought" commercials which he hoped television stations would run as public service spots. Lear had built a reputation as one who crowded liberal messages into his popular television comedies.[13]

[13]Alfred H. Edelson, "Advocacy Advertising," *Advertising Age,* March 30, 1981, p. 47.

In working with magazines, PR people try to submit exclusive articles rather than duplicated releases. The PR people may avoid writing the articles themselves and instead supply information to the freelancers or staff members who have drawn the assignments. The PR person's chief contribution often is the suggestion of the article idea to the editor or to the writer. The University of Virginia and Boston University send out printed tip sheets to writers to alert them to article ideas on campus.

We have already seen that many PR people publish their own magazines, for employees or for customers and opinion leaders. They get into the book publishing business through the issuing of company histories, some of which are important enough to be published by major book publishers. They also get into film production. They make films primarily for free showing by schools and service clubs. Outside organizations usually handle the distribution of the films.

One of the most important media to the PR person is direct mail. Unlike other print media, direct mail has no frequency schedule. Each piece is a "one shot." When using direct mail, the PR person in effect becomes a publisher, overseeing the writing and design, picking the printer, arranging for the type to be set, deciding what kind of paper to use, and taking care of many other production details.

Public relations people like direct mail because it is so flexible. It can take any shape, any size. They like it, too, because they consider it an intimate medium. When recipients get it, they presumably read it without any accompanying distraction. It does not have to fight for attention with other items on a printed page, as, for instance, an advertisement in a newspaper would. Furthermore, the medium is highly selective. The PR person can rent a mailing list of exactly the kind of persons he wants to reach.

The various publics, however, have learned to recognize much of direct mail for what it is, junk. It goes into a waste basket as soon as it's delivered. The various devices used to fool readers into opening the envelope deserve the contempt thoughtful readers feel for them. Mail-order insurance companies are chief offenders with their attempt to hide their identity by printing at the top left of the envelope the address only or the name of the president or by making their envelopes look like those used by the government for official business.

Not only do PR people work with all media, they work with different departments of each medium, helping to supply if not shape editorial as well as news content. A call on the editor of the editorial page may result in an editorial being written siding with the PR person's client. The PR person is especially interested in the letters-to-the-editor column. A newspaper faces a constant problem of weeding out PR-written or inspired letters from letters submitted by ordinary citizens. This is not to say that the paper does not give the PR person a hearing in the column, especially if that person's company finds itself at the wrong end of a controversy. It is just that it does not want professionals taking over a section reserved for readers who are not paid propagandists.

From time to time the PR person finds it necessary to complain about coverage rather than help supply it. A textbook, let us say, makes unfavorable reference to the woods operations of lumber companies. Someone at the American Forest Institute, the PR organization of the lumber, pulp, and paper industry, sees the reference, disagrees with it, and points out to the publisher where the author erred. The author may agree to change the reference in the next edition.

Further, PR people get in touch with newspeople whenever they unwittingly use language that tarnishes a client's image. Ethnic groups, religious bodies, and various trades and professions are particularly sensitive to this. The head of a model school some years ago wrote to a London paper protesting what he called "the new and grossly unfair newspaper practice of calling any woman a 'model' who so describes herself." The "model" in question was Christine Keeler, a call girl linked with a top government official. The head of the model school suggested that because Miss Keeler had just sold her memoirs to a newspaper, it made just as much sense to refer to her as "the well-known journalist."

What You Should Know About Chiropractic

HANDBOOK FOR MEDIA

AMERICAN CHIROPRACTIC ASSOCIATION

To help insure that what the media says about the profession is factual, the American Chiropractic Association, Inc., representing more than 16,000 members, offers this handbook to editors. ACA takes out ads in publications like *Editor & Publisher* to announce the availability of the handbook. Some 30 staff members work for ACA.

MANUFACTURING NEWS

Go through each story in a newspaper for a given day and see if you can figure out how the story originated. Was it a story the reporter stumbled onto in the course of covering a beat? Was it a story the city editor uncovered and then assigned? Or was it a story dreamed up by a public relations person in an attempt to draw attention to a client?

Surveys of the origin of news content have found that at least a quarter of the stories in newspapers started with a PR person, who sensed a story about the organization and either alerted a newspaper reporter or wrote it himself, or the PR person staged an event that could not be ignored by the media.

Much of what the PR person turns out is junk, obvious puffery, with no real value to readers—"artificial dissemination," someone has called it—but some of the releases interest editors. Why?

In the first place, no paper can completely cover the whole news scene. No staff is big enough. So a paper's stories and features for every issue are supplemented by material submitted by outsiders.

In the second place, the newspaper is not particularly concerned that some organization or some person (PR activity goes on in behalf of individuals, too) will benefit from a story's being published. The test for a news release must be: Is it news? Is it of interest to the readers, a sizeable segment of the readers, of this newspaper?

Everyone with an axe to grind quickly learns what is reportable and operates accordingly. In the words of one observer, "From the demonstrator on the street to the President of the United States the behavior of the actors in the news is affected by journalism. All the subjects of news tend to conform to journalism's standards of what is reportable."[14]

---

[14]Max Ways, "What's Wrong with News? It Isn't New Enough," *Fortune*, October 1969, p. 111.

NEWS RELEASES

Like the ad maker, the public relations person makes use of news and opinion media to reach an audience and influence it. Unlike the ad maker, the PR person does not pay for the time and space obtained. How successful the PR person is depends upon an ability to supply a publication or broadcast facility with material comparable to that supplied by the medium's own writers and photographers. In effect, the PR person becomes an unpaid member of the staff, grinding out stories in the form of news releases.

The PR person usually duplicates each release and either mails or delivers copies to the various papers. Some papers run the release as is. The better papers do some checking, edit the copy, perhaps combine it with some other story. If the story is important enough, the PR person may send it in before the news has actually taken place and indicate to the editor when the story should be published. If the story is only routine, the PR man marks it "For Immediate Release," meaning the paper is free to run it right away. Since they are under no obligation to PR people, not all editors honor release dates anyway.

An adept PR person tailors the release not only for a particular paper or group of papers, but also for a particular department within the paper. All departments are targets. What the sports department will run will not necessarily be what the regular news side will run. Sometimes the "lifestyle" editor is the editor to appeal to, or the church page editor.

Editors seem more responsive to the releases issued by government agencies and nonprofit organizations.[15] Thus university news bureaus are able to score with releases that, if they were carefully considered, would not see print; a pro-

---

[15]One editor said he preferred government releases to industry releases because they were more carefully printed with no smears on the reverse sides; he could use them for copy paper.

fessor gets included in some obscure *Who's Who,* another one makes a routine speech or writes an article for a miniscule audience, the school paper wins a fancy rating in a contest in which every entrant wins. The PR people themselves realize that much of this is meaningless, but they turn the stuff out because their fellow practitioners do, and the media continue to use it. The PR person is on a treadmill.

Imagine the appreciation of one editor in early 1968 when an organization sent out a release with this note, "We call . . . [this event] to your attention in the hope that we will get some publicity out of it, and that we will make money from the publicity and that it will cost us nothing." *Editor & Publisher* called it "history's first truthful publicity release."

Client mention in a release is sometimes referred to as "poison." The word typifies what some newspapermen think of the PR person. It goes back to early in the century, to the days of Ivy Lee, the newspaperman-turned-PR man whose pronouncements were viewed by other newspapermen with some suspicion. Along the way he picked up a nickname— what else but "Poison" Ivy?

It used to be customary for PR people to send a letter with their release saying they were considering an advertising schedule, implying that if the paper did not run the release, it would not get the advertising. Public relations people are more sophisticated these days.

Still, a survey conducted by Professor Bill Baxter of the University of Oklahoma in 1980 showed that nine out of ten news releases sent out by businesses, industries, and organizations never see print. Editors told Baxter that they did not use the releases because they were not localized, they contained advertising, they were too long, or they arrived too late. Sometimes a PR person will produce a story, feature, or article exclusively for a publication, submitting it as any freelancer would. That kind of item gets a better reception. Some PR people hire outside firms to handle the writing and/or the placement of releases. One organization, Newsmaking International Inc., Santa Monica, California, offers "steady publicity" for corporations through a "quota system" of placing features and news stories in national publications.

The PR person often needs a record of how widely news releases are used, and in what form. A number of "press-clipping" organizations can monitor this. Burrelle's, Livingston, New Jersey, appears to be the largest. It scans all 1750 dailies, 670 Sunday papers, 8000 weeklies, and also some 4600 magazines and trade journals, 215 ethnic and religious newspapers, 85 college papers, 230 newspapers serving blacks, and 70 papers that can be classified as "underground." Stories produced by or involving clients using Burrelle's services are clipped and sent to those clients. The firm also maintains a television monitoring service that watches network news and public affairs programs. Clients get a typed transcript of "all name or subject reference mentions." Burrelle's in the 1980s was starting to provide similar television coverage of local news and public affairs programs in selected large cities.

A listing of press releases placed and speeches written may not be enough. In the years ahead PR people will have to subject themselves to more evaluation and measurement than in the past. Like other aspects of business, PR will have to prove its worth. Until recently, PR was an activity not often and not easily measured. Its sisters, advertising and marketing, depended a lot on research, but PR seemed unconcerned. In recent years PR has grown in importance, its budgets have increased dramatically, and, understandably, PR clients are now interested in monitoring the money spent.

Major PR firms like Hill & Knowlton and Ruder & Finn have maintained research departments or subsidiaries for years, but the big corporations are involved these days, too. One of the most developed of the research programs is the one instigated by AT&T. AT&T got into PR research partly because "state regulating agencies were asking for justification for including public relations costs in rate increase requests."[16]

THE UNQUESTIONING PRESS

Sometimes an organization does not need its own PR person. It gets help directly from the media. Staff-written stories appear that could well have been written by a PR person. The stories question nothing. They praise when perhaps they should question. The sports pages of some newspapers have published such stories, resulting in what has been called "cheerleader journalism." The sportswriter feels, apparently, that the job is to keep up the morale of the players and build pride among the townspeople.

We see a lot less of this kind of journalism today. Hero worship on the sports pages largely gave way to legitimate journalism in the 1960s. Sometimes coaches and students become irate over the hard-hitting, straight coverage they now get on sports pages. Wick Temple, AP general sports editor, says, "It's an exciting time to be involved in what used to be the toy department of the newspapers ... and while we don't want to pick fights, we must make the sports establishment understand that at long last it is going to be covered—really covered—by the press."[17]

Another fixture in American journalism that has come into question is the news conference sponsored by a profit or nonprofit firm or by an individual. Reporters are invited to attend the conferences and ask questions. J. Kyle Goddard, a PR man who arranges them, has suggested that news conferences be abolished. "Most news-conference statements should be confined to commercial time and space because they are strictly attempts to advertise," he says. A PR person

---

[16]Cecelia Lentini, "Demand Ups Research," *Advertising Age*, January 5, 1981, p. S-9.
[17]Quoted by Celeste Huenergard, "No More Cheerleading on the Sports Pages," *Editor & Publisher*, June 16, 1979, p. 11.

sets the bait for a news conference, and media people bite. "The quickest way to end this silly game is for some big shots to call a news conference for which no press gang comes," Goddard adds.[18]

Russ Sadler, a television commentator, told the Oregon High School Press Conference in Eugene in 1979, "The plain truth is that we've become patsies for every public relations firm that's learned to stage a media event."

THE INSTITUTIONAL AD

Industry's concern about its image is a twentieth-century phenomenon. "The public be damned," William Vanderbilt's classic response to a reporter's question about the decline of services on the New York Central, more accurately reflected the nineteenth-century attitude. But, after some 20 antibusiness novels late in that century and after the muckrakers had had their day at the turn of the century, industry became concerned.

The Pennsylvania Railroad, among the first to take action, hired ex-newspaperman Ivy Lee to polish its image. Lee came up with a revolutionary idea: instead of hiding facts about accidents and keeping reporters away, the line should make it easy for the press. Take reporters to the scene. Volunteer information. Lee figured that by cooperating with the press, the railroad would come out looking better when the stories were written.

Industry in general enjoyed a good press in the 1920s, thanks largely to the emerging field of public relations, but with the Depression of the 1930s, the pendulum swung back. Perhaps PR had done its job too well. If industry could be credited for good times, it could also be blamed for bad times. World War II gave industry a chance to redeem itself as the nation united in a common cause, but reaction set in again as the economy made its adjustments after the war.

[18]J. Kyle Goddard, "Abolishing News Conferences," *San Francisco Chronicle,* December 15, 1979, p. 32.

In the 1930s PR men developed the "institutional ad" to fight growing antipathy. Such an ad read a lot like a newspaper editorial and often occupied a full page in a newspaper. Its job was to sell the free-enterprise system, which was being threatened, many in industry believed, by Franklin Roosevelt's New Deal.

Examining industry's free-enterprise campaign after World War II, William H. Whyte, Jr., concluded it was "an insult to the intelligence and, as many businessmen themselves suspected, a prodigious waste of time and money to boot."[19] However, if institutional advertising failed in its initial assignment, it failed because it was badly used. As a tool currently available to the PR person it enjoys widespread use for all kinds of clients and for every conceivable cause.

As explained in the previous chapter, when an institutional ad goes on the attack, when it abandons the "See what a nice guy I am" approach and says "Look what the bad guys are causing," it becomes advocacy advertising. Anheuser-Busch used this kind of advertising in the early 1980s trying to squelch rumors that it had contributed to antihunting and antigun interests. "We would appreciate receiving any information which would help us identify those who are responsible for [the rumors]."

SPEECH WRITING AND SPEECH MAKING

Public relations people write speeches both for themselves and for executives they work for. Writing for others is a challenging job. The writer not only must echo a "party line" but also has to fit the words to the style and personality of the speaker. Sometimes the speaker works closely with the writer on the draft of the speech or makes changes in it after it has been written. In order to make their deadlines, reporters often get copies of speeches prior to the time they are given and work from these. Their stories carry the protective

[19]William H. Whyte, Jr., and the editors of *Fortune, Is Anybody Listening?* Simon and Schuster (New York: 1952), p. vii.

phrase, "in a speech prepared for delivery . . . ," in case the speaker makes a change later.

Bob Orben, who conducts humor workshops for corporate speakers and communicators, tells the story of the frustrated speech writer who, feeling he was not appreciated, quit his job after writing a final speech for his boss. The boss, a pompous sort who did not bother to read his ghost-written speeches before delivering them, started off a meeting with "My friends, in the next five minutes I will tell you how, in the coming fiscal year, we will double our gross, triple our net, and quadruple the price of our stock." The applause was deafening. Turning to page 2, the speaker saw only this: "Okay, you S.O.B. You're on your own!"[20]

The story is no doubt apocryphal. Another Orben Story, showing again the separation of speech writer from speech maker, probably really happened. As Orben tells the story, a speaker "came to the line: 'Which reminds me of a very funny incident.' Then he read the incident. And it was very funny. And he had never heard it before. And he broke up laughing to the point where he couldn't proceed with the speech."[21]

LOBBYING

Lobbying is a highly specialized PR activity. Among the most powerful lobbies operating in Washington is the National Rifle Association. When Congress considers bills the NRA has an interest in, Mailgrams go out to the 1.8 million association members asking them to get in touch with their lawmakers. "Within hours," reports *Time*, "Mailgrams and letters from supporters are on their way to Washington—rallying, cajoling and threatening the legislators." "Ours is a grassroots effort," says an NRA field representative, Lewis Elliot, explaining the organization's success in squelching gun legislation

---

[20]Bob Orben, "The Care and Heeding of Speechwriters," *Enterprise* (National Association of Manufacturers), July 1979, p. 10.
[21]Ibid., p. 11.

in the various states." Instead of paying a lobbyist, we just use the people." At the federal level, the NRA does employ lobbyists, 5 of them. There is a paid staff of 275 that coordinates various state groups and gun clubs and watches over three magazines, including the *American Rifleman.*[22]

The Tobacco Institute merits attention here for the persistency of its work. Whenever the Surgeon General issues another report linking smoking with cancer or whenever another law or ordinance is passed to protect nonsmokers' rights, the Institute swings into action. Six major cigarette companies created the Institute in 1958 to stem the tide against smoking. Since then the Institute has constantly sounded the refrain: the link between smoking and cancer had not been *proven.* In 1978 the Institute employed 70 persons. Among other things, it runs a "Tobacco Action Network." Most of the Institute's efforts these days go to heading off state and local restrictions on smoking. Critics of the Institute charge that it has Congress under its thumb, partly because of the Department of Agriculture's price support program and partly because of the estimated $6 billion in cigarette taxes realized by federal, state, and local governments. "The government is the biggest partner in the tobacco business in this country today," says Horace R. Kornegay, president of the Institute.[23]

Other important lobbying organizations at the national level are the National Education Association and the American Medical Association. National organizations lobby at the state level, too, and at that level all kinds of other organizations get in on the act. For instance, in Oregon lobbyists outnumber the state's legislators six to one. They supply information and literature to legislators and get to know them well. They represent public as well as private and business interests. They represent school districts, counties, cities, and various government agencies. A single lobbyist might repre-

[22]"Magnum-Force Lobby," *Time,* April 20, 1981, pp. 22, 27.
[23]Quoted by Chris Connell, AP dispatch, *Eugene Register-Guard,* January 9, 1979, p. 7C.

sent several, but not competing, clients. As in any state, lobbyists' backgrounds often include terms in the legislature. Defeated for reelection, they turn their talents to influencing, if not originating, legislation. The same holds true for some federal legislators.

Michael McMenamin and Walter McNamara conducted a study of the dairy lobby, "one of the three most influential special interest groups in the country," and published a book with their findings in *Milking the Public* (Chicago: Nelson-Hall, 1980). Some 80,000 dairy farmers contribute $7 million annually to the lobby's political fund.

PR IN TIMES OF CRISIS

Public relations faces its biggest test during times of crisis, as when a company is involved in a major accident, loss, scandal, or recall. What is done during the hours and days afterward can seriously influence the future of the company. The consensus among PR people is that a company should be candid with inquiring news people at such times, that companies should not try to cover up.

Most large companies have a PR plan ready for any emergencies that might come along. Part of the plan deals with ways the company can best cooperate with reporters. This is a far cry from the time when a PR person felt that the first chore, upon learning of, say, the crash of one of his planes, was to paint over the name of the airline. Even today, companies that send up clouds of pollution alongside major highways may leave their names off the sides of their buildings.

Trans World Airlines has published a *Red Book* for its own executives to use after a plane crash. Among its bits of advice is that executives "avoid being led to speculate, even off the record."[24]

24Thomas Petzinger, Jr., "Crisis PR," *The Wall Street Journal,* August 23, 1979, p. 19.

PR FOR THE POLITICIAN

No one is more public-relations conscious than the politician. On going to a meeting to hear a political candidate, then noticing the sparse attendance, one wonders how, under the circumstances, the candidate can seem so unruffled about it and go ahead and make the speech after all. The politician gave the speech, and gladly, knowing it was being reported in the press. It did not make any difference that a mere handful showed up to listen. Thousands would read what the politician said on the front pages, and that is enough of an audience to play to.

Theodore Roosevelt used to make his significant announcements on Sunday afternoon because he knew that Monday morning papers were hard-pressed for news. There would be less competition for headline space. Politicians knew how to use the press. It was a large part of their job.

In the nineteenth and early twentieth centuries politicians acted as their own PR people, but with the proliferation of media and the increasing apathy of readers to their "messages," politicians, bewildered by the enormity of the job, have in recent years turned their press relations, sometimes even their administrative chores, over to journalists. The PR person is firmly established now as an aide to the politician. Stanley Kelley, Jr., pointed out back in the mid-1950s that the politician has an almost naive faith in the magic of public relations.[25]

Kelley, a political scientist, viewed the emergence of PR men in politics with some equanimity. It had, he pointed out, done away with the "boss" system. The machine, the party, the precinct organization now were no longer so important. Now the *media* are what's important, and as far as the political candidate is concerned, it takes a PR person to know how to use them.

In recent years PR for politicians has changed greatly.

[25]Stanley Kelley, Jr., *Professional Public Relations and Political Power* (Baltimore: Johns Hopkins, 1956).

Oregon State Senator John Powell's campaign directors rounded
up some kids at the state capitol and put them and the senator
in front of an appropriate building inscription, and Christine
Craft took the photograph. It was used in campaign literature.

With the party leadership making fewer decisions and with the rank and file making more, especially in the nominating procedures, the PR effort is directed to the masses instead of to the few. That means more use of television. Politicians need "more than . . . simple press releases and stump speeches. . . . They [need] imaginative events, media happenings, to get on the six o'clock news. And they [get] this help not from the traditional press aides (usually journalists), but from public relations professionals," says Daniel M. Gaby, a New Jersey PR man who was a campaign manager for President Carter.[26] With the continued weakness of political parties, greater reliance on the media, and availability of government funding for campaigns and contributions from political action committees, politicians will turn increasingly to PR people for help, Gaby says. He points out, too, that elected officials, once they take office, find they need PR help even more.[27]

Almost all congressmen and senators have press secretaries. Even congressional committees hire them "to coordinate communication with the press." Besides turning out press releases, radio "actualities," and the like, a press secretary or "administrative assistant" conducts rehearsals to get the boss ready to appear in interviews. The press secretary often has to put off the press, incurring its wrath. Gary Hymel, administrative assistant to House Speaker Thomas P. "Tip" O'Neill (D.–Mass.), says, "I work for the Speaker and not for the press. That's a very important thing for every press secretary to understand."[28]

But Saul Friedman, reporter for the Knight-Ridder chain, says that a press secretary should be "first of all, a servant of the taxpayers and not his boss."[29]

---

[26]Daniel M. Gaby, "Politics and Public Relations," *Public Relations Journal,* October 1980, p. 11.

[27]Ibid., p. 12.

[28]Adrian C. Taylor, "The Flacks on the Hill," *Washington Journalism Review,* June/July 1979, p. 39.

[29]"Can Reporters and Flacks Work Together?" *Washington Journalism Review,* June/July 1979, p. 45.

A reporter is not likely to stand in awe of a reporter
turned press secretary. "Anybody who is a press secretary is
regarded, in varying degrees, as a sell-out, somebody who
didn't like reporting or didn't excel at it and decided to take
the easy route," says Mick Rood, reporter for States News
Service. "Not that being a press secretary is easy. But that's
definitely the image conjured up. But eventually, with some
press secretaries, you realize it's not quite the sell-out or cop-
out it appears to be."[30]

PR FOR GOVERNMENT

When Mount St. Helens erupted several times in 1980,
nearby Portland, which got some of the ash, also got more
press attention than it wanted. People in the East and elsewhere, including people who might like to settle in Portland
or establish businesses there, might have thought the city was
dying.

The PR department of the Port of Portland, in a counter-
attack, sent out news releases to show that life went on pretty
much as usual in the Rose City and prepared "Official Mount
St. Helens Anti-Baloney Kits" for shippers, steamship operators, and other commercial groups. "The farther away you
are, the more hot air you're exposed to," was one of the
catchlines. In the kit was a folder telling "how to put all the
hot air about Mount St. Helens to good use," plus a real balloon—for the hot air. To tell its story further, the Port of Portland also took out ads in various magazines read by business
people. All over the Northwest other governmental bodies
and private organizations also conducted similar campaigns.[31]

The federal government engaged in PR when it tried
to get the public to use the Susan B. Anthony dollar coin in-

[30]Adrian C. Taylor, op. cit., p. 44.
[31]W.W. Marsh, "Public Relations and the 'Big Blow Up'," *Public Relations Journal,* October 1980, pp. 19–22.

troduced in 1979. Nobody liked it, and most people refused to accept it as change. Its size and shape were part of the problem; people did not take the coin seriously. The government paid DWJ Associates, New York, a PR firm, $150,000 to build the coin's reputation. The campaign failed because good stories about the coin could not be found. The firm looked hard for stories about the coin, according to an executive of the firm. Maybe there would be a story, for instance, of an organization that paid everyone in Susan B. Anthony coins. "But nothing good ever happened. Anywhere." That was one executive's assessment. The firm was able to get information about the coin into newspapers all over the country, but the publicity did not help. "All the publicity in the world can't sell something people don't want," the executive said.[32]

Working for government, PR people like to call themselves "government communicators." In Washington, D.C., alone, an estimated 19,000 of them do PR jobs for the various departments and agencies. "No one knows [exactly how many are at work]," says a *Wall Street Journal* writer, "because public relations operations aren't normally budgeted separately and public relations people often carry titles that fail to suggest what it is they actually do." The *WSJ* writer points out that the Department of Defense probably has the biggest PR budget. The Department of Agriculture, which includes the U.S. Forest Service, is close behind.

The news release is still popular as a PR vehicle for government agencies, but not as popular as it once was. Advertising campaigns are big in government PR these days, and government agencies seem to want to go directly to the people now instead of getting to them only through existing media, so they publish slick magazines, produce colorful brochures, and produce videotape cassettes, among other things. The Library of Congress reported that in the 18 months between January 1977 and June 1978 federal agen-

[32]Bob Greene, "Heads You Lose, Tails You Lose," *Esquire,* April 1981, p. 14.

cies produced 102,000 different publications. To print its many publications, the government maintains a major printing plant in Washington and 6 regional plants. It authorizes various agencies to operate 300 of their own printing plants and farms out printing to 7000 private firms.[33]

For films and other audiovisual products alone, federal agencies in the 1980s were spending an estimated $100 million a year. President Ronald Reagan in 1981 put a freeze on the production of both film and printed pieces, charging that "The federal government is spending too much money on public relations, publicity, and advertising." The Reagan administration took its action partly because irate citizens had sent in examples of government-issued publications that, according to the complaints, wasted taxpayers' money. Under the freeze, each government agency reviewed its film and publication programs to determine what was really necessary to keep the public informed.

A U.S. PR firm working for a foreign government prepares press kits, arranges field trips for writers and editors, and advises the embassy on how to explain its nation's problems to the U.S. public. Foreign governments that hire U.S. PR help do it in some cases to encourage U.S. investments or U.S. travel or to get U.S. economic aid. In recent years a number of U.S.-based PR firms have tried "to shine the tarnished images of nations accused of human-rights violations" and have suffered attacks, verbal and physical, because of this activity. One PR official complains that "Law firms handle the same clients with no moral judgments being made about them, while we become part of the issue." "Whom you work for is a business decision, not a moral one," another PR person said.[34] The PR people argue that every side of a dispute has a right to tell its side of the story. They even suggest that

[33]James M. Perry, "Federal Flacks," *The Wall Street Journal,* May 23, 1979, pp. 1 and 28.
[34]Quoted by John E. Cooney, *The Wall Street Journal,* January 31, 1979, p. 1.

PR advice can help moderate repressive regimes. Some news media people agree that the new PR activity at least makes the governments more accessible.

PR FOR MARKETING

Marketing PR is PR that is meant to increase sales of a product or service. It may be conducted by individual companies or by trade associations. An example of company-marketing PR is the program put on by Johnson Wax products to sell its Raid bug killers. The program was designed to convince people they need not feel ashamed to admit they have roaches in their houses, that roaches do not signify dirty houses or poor housekeeping, and that they can be eliminated. Manning, Selvage & Lee, the company's PR firm, prepared some public-service broadcast announcements that were distributed through the National Homeowners Association to stations and cable television outlets. The antiroach program also included the publication of folders and booklets and the public performances of 250-lb. actor Josh Mostel dressed as a cockroach.[35]

Marketing PR on the part of an industry, rather than only one company, is exemplified by a 1981 cigar promotion. To counter the continuing decline in cigar sales, that industry, through Carl Byoir & Associates, launched a "friends of the cigar" PR campaign that attempted to show that the cigar is not as offensive as the media so often depict it.[36]

Marketing considerations along with the image of a city prompted the launching of the Miss America Pageant in the early 1920s. The event was designed to extend the tourist season in Atlantic City beyond the Labor Day weekend,

[35]Theodore J. Gage, "PR Ripens Role in Marketing," *Advertising Age,* January 5, 1981, p. S-11.
[36]Sam Harper, "Cigar PR Campaign Ignites Controversy," *Advertising Age,* May 18, 1981, p. 59.

when usually things quieted down for the merchants and innkeepers.

PR FOR MEDIA

The media, though often critical of PR because of its lack of objectivity, themselves engage in PR to build their images, to make themselves more attractive to advertisers, and to win subscribers. Let a paper win a Pulitzer Prize and see if it keeps the prize a secret.

In recent years some of the bigger papers, to improve relations with readers, have hired full-time ombudsmen to act as trouble shooters bringing staff members and readers together. A reader has a complaint about news coverage, and the ombudsman traces down the source of trouble and perhaps sees that changes are made. Some ombudsmen write columns in their papers explaining coverage and procedures.

A newspaper likes to involve its readers through its letters-to-the-editor column and sometimes through contests. Nowhere is this more evident than in the big cities. In 1981 in San Francisco, for instance, the "Scene" section of the *Examiner* ran a write-your-own-novel contest. Once each week a new chapter appeared in *For Whom the Foghorn Blows*, for which a reader–writer received $50 (employees of the paper were, of course, ineligible to enter the contest). Every week there was a different writer. The result was a dreadful, disjointed, and complicated story, not unlike a bad soap opera, about a Des Moines secretary who moved to San Francisco, but people had fun with it and the *Examiner* got talked about.

EUPHEMISM

Just about everybody these days worries about "image." What a person is called is important. A once perfectly honorable name describing an occupation may strike someone as "inappropriate," so the janitor becomes a "custodian," the garbage collector a "sanitary engineer," the hairdresser a "beautician," the undertaker a "mortician" or even a "grief therapist," the journalist a "mass communicator." Printers of high school yearbooks become "publishers."

Words have a way of deteriorating under constant use. What sounds good for a few years changes as people begin reading into a word new and unflattering connotations. Perhaps the word's real meaning finally catches up with it.

A word or phrase substituted for another because somehow it sounds better than the original is known as a *euphemism*. A person uses a euphemism, if not to mislead the audience, then at least to muffle meaning. The late Senator Everett Dirksen told a story of a man filling out an application for an insurance policy who came upon the question, "How old was your father when he died and of what did he die?" It just so happened the father had been hanged. So the applicant wrote: "My father was 65 when he died. He came to his end while participating in a public function when the platform gave way."

In middle-class society, people do not use toilets, they use "bathrooms" or, in some settings, "powder rooms." In their late years they become not old people but "senior citizens." They do not die, they "pass away."

Some of this is necessary, of course. *Time,* in an essay on euphemism, quoted what it called a "familiar saying": "A man who calls a spade a spade is fit only to use one." Bergen Evans, the lexicographer at Northwestern University, suggested that euphemisms are necessary because "lying is an indispensable part of making life tolerable."

Among those who rely heavily on euphemisms are sociologists, teachers, government officials, and even radicals, conservatives, and anyone else with a cause.

To a social worker a slum becomes a "culturally deprived environment." Mentally retarded children are "exceptional children." In many states there is no such thing as divorce; it is, officially, the "dissolution of marriage." To a teacher, students who cheat "depend on others to do their work." A below-average student "works at his own level." A lazy student "can do more when he tries." A library is a "learning resource center."

Birth-control activists began to dislike the negative sound of what they were advocating and changed their goal to "planned parenthood." When the National Organization for the Reform of Marijuana Laws started up, its backers wanted "repeal" not "reform," but "reform" is harder to argue with, so "reform" it was. To bureaucrats, "undocumented workers" sounds better than "aliens," and people on welfare get the classy title "clients."

When the U.S. Information Agency brought out comic books on President John Kennedy for overseas distribution, it called them "illustrated continuities." When members of the Students for a Democratic Society occupied a building on campus they "liberated" it. The politician who puts his foot in his mouth one day calls a hasty press conference the next to "clarify his position."

The true disciples of euphemism are PR and advertising people. A major contribution they make to their clients is putting ordinary or even embarrassing information into attractive terms. The phrasing makes the difference. Store A is "Closed Sundays so our employees can be with their families." Store B across the street is "Open all day Sunday as a service to our customers."

In the world of advertising, a television commercial is "an important word" or "a message" or "Now this . . ."; pimples are "facial blemishes"; false teeth are "dentures"; hair dyes are "tints" or "rinses"; used cars are "preowned cars"; houses are "homes"; colors are "decorator colors"; butter is "creamery butter." Jantzen, Inc., makes special swimsuits not for fat women but for women with "full figures." When a television network schedules reruns for summer, it calls them "encore performances."

One can understand why PR people resort to euphemism in their news releases. They want to create the best possible climate of opinion for their clients. They do not want to offend anyone. But why are newspaper editors not more vigilant in changing the PR euphemisms to words that are more direct? As the *Eugene Register-Guard* said in an editorial on "Nice Nellyisms" (another term for euphemisms):

"Ah, for a society in which a spade is not an agricultural implement!"

PROPAGANDA

The term that best fits the PR person is "propagandist," but that term, especially since World War I days, carries with it unfavorable connotations. People associate "propaganda" with unworthy causes; they think of it as the utilization of dishonest tactics. At one time it was a perfectly respectable word, originating with the Roman Catholic Church and its efforts to propagandize for the faith.

Indeed, one can say that any person who persuades is a propagandist, the clergy included. Certainly advertising people are propagandists. Even editorial writers in a sense propagandize, but because theoretically they write as disinterested observers rather than as ideologues or as paid promoters of causes, one would be stretching a point in referring to them as propagandists.

Propagandists themselves regard what they promote not as propaganda at all but as "information" or even "education." What is the difference between education and propaganda? Again theoretically, education presents both or all sides and permits the listeners to make up their own minds. Propaganda presents only one side and tries to make up the listeners' minds for them. Another observation about propaganda is that if one approves of what is said, it is education; if one does not approve, it is propaganda. The anticigarette campaigns that many Americans consider educational are considered by some—cigarette manufacturers and tobacco farmers—to be strictly propaganda. Some billboards in the South, in North Carolina and Virginia, particularly, where tobacco is so important an industry, read, "Caution: Antismoking Propaganda May Be Hazardous to Your Economic Health."

Educators like to think that what they do makes the propagandist's job harder. An educated person, it is thought, can see through an appeal, recognizing it for propaganda, but to some extent education actually helps set the stage for propaganda.

In his book *Propaganda,* Jacques Ellul calls education "prepropaganda" because it conditions minds with vast amounts of incoherent information. It remains for the propagandist to come around and make some sense out of the morass for those who are susceptible. Ellul goes so far as to suggest that intellectuals are more vulnerable to propaganda than nonintellectuals because they are used to absorbing information second-hand. Furthermore, they feel a need to form some opinion about almost everything. For this they need help.[37]

A more universal opinion, however, holds that the less educated person responds more favorably to propaganda than does the intellectual. That person, propagandists find, also responds more surely to emotional than to rational appeals.

The Institute for Propaganda Analysis in the 1930s came up with a list of propaganda devices: name-calling ("Pig"), glittering generalities ("The American Way"), transfer devices (an American flag used as a backdrop for a rally), testimonials ("Recommended by Duncan Hines"), "plain folks" (the political candidate out fishing), deck stacking (quoting out of context), bandwagon ("everybody's doing it").

Advertising and PR people still make use of these devices, but they use them subtly. Nor do current propaganda devices—"tactics" might be a better word in this context—fall so conveniently into the basic categories set up by the Institute. Tactics include these:

1. *The unstated advantage.* The secret here is to arrange the facts so that the reader will reach a mistaken conclusion—a conclusion that works to the advantage of the client. Example from a real ad of the past: a correspondence school

[37]Jacques Ellul, *Propaganda* (New York: Alfred A. Knopf, 1965). Malcolm Muggeridge in *Jesus Rediscovered* takes a similar view of education: "For the most part, it only serves to enlarge stupidity, inflate conceit, exchange credulity, and put those subjected to it at the mercy of brainwashers with printing presses, radio, and television at their disposal" (p. 101).

specializing in training students for work as insurance claim adjusters runs a picture of a man bent over the prostrate form of a beautiful girl, her dress torn, looking provocative despite the fact she has just been hit by a car. Although the copy does not say so, the male reader is supposed to get the idea that if he takes the course, he will spend the rest of his life getting paid for comforting beautiful, suffering women.

2. *The make-believe advantage.* The secret is to get there first with the disclosure of an ingredient that all products in that category have. If one makes enough noise about it, people will think it is the only one that has it.

3. *The appearance of modesty.* People like to side with the underdog. So some companies, comfortably settled in first place, would just as soon talk about something else. No sense in rubbing it in. Often when a major company is attacked, it ignores the provocation. To fight back is to dignify the attack.

Sometimes a number-two role can work to the advantage of a company, as Avis Rent-a-Car proved with its "We try harder" campaign. Hertz tried to ignore Avis, and did for a long time, but there comes a time when number one can no longer afford modesty. "For years, Avis has been telling you Hertz is No. 1," read one Hertz ad. "Now we're going to tell you why."

A PR person shows the worth of PR when a bad break for a client is turned to an advantage. *The New Yorker* used to advertise it was not edited for the old lady in Dubuque, a reflection on the level of sophistication in that town. The Chamber of Commerce there, seizing the initiative, launched a contest for the ideal "little old lady" and earned some attention for Dubuque.[38]

4. *The long way around.* When a medical clinic decides to charge for phone calls to doctors, it does not announce this in the opening paragraph of a form letter to patients. Instead it announces that it is now possible to get advice by phone

---

[38]She turned out to be Mrs. Delbert Hayford, whose favorite magazine was *Reader's Digest.*

(it always was) and, oh yes, as an afterthought: "Effective October 1 we will institute a policy of charging for such special services rendered over the telephone."

5. *Pick a reason, any reason.* No store conducts a sale just to conduct a sale. Customers like markdowns better if they think the retailer was forced into it. The manager is away and the assistant manager has gone berserk, or a new shipment is coming in and there is no room for it. A dance studio calls and offers a free lesson if we can answer a question only a moron could miss.

6. *Phony authority.* People are impressed by footnotes and scholarship. Never mind who the authority is, as long as the person looks like an authority. A favorite device of right-wing organizations that like to "document" their cases is the citing of the *Congressional Record.* If something is published there, some people believe, it must be important. But how does an item get into the *Congressional Record?* All that is needed is to get a Congressman to request its inclusion, and it will be published. The *Record* contains not only the texts of what is said in debate in Congress but also all kinds of articles and editorials put there by congressmen to flatter or placate constituents back home.

7. *Leave it out.* A university in the West a few years ago, launching its annual drive for contributors to the Development Fund, published a leaflet listing the names of persons who had given previously. The headline read, "Is Your Name on This List?" It went out to all graduates. A not inconsiderable number kicked in with some money that year, not wishing to be left off a published list the following year.

8. *Buck the trend.* When everybody is writing short letters, write long letters. When the soft sell is in, use the hard sell. These are sure ways to be noticed. Bucking a trend often results from an inability to keep up. The company heads in an opposite direction because that is all it *can* do.

9. *Out of character.* Occasionally a company does the unexpected. In 1966, *Scientific American,* in one of the notable promotion stunts in the history of magazines, ran a paper airplane contest. Eleven thousand entries arrived from all over the world. Eight distinguished judges supervised a "fly

off" held in New York's Hall of Science. Winners were duly announced in the press, and Simon & Schuster brought out a book based on the event, showing diagrams of some of the entries.

For a small feeder airline Stan Freberg once produced an ad that shocked the industry. "Hey there! You with the sweat in your palms," said the headline. The ad admitted people were frightened about flying. So were the pilots, and this made them more alert. Freberg drew angry complaints from other airlines because the ad, they said, would frighten all airline passengers, but Freberg argued that by facing up to fears, timorous prospective passengers would take heart and take a plane next time. He even wanted to hand passengers "survival kits," including copies of Norman Vincent Peale's *The Power of Positive Thinking,* and he planned to substitute porters for stewardesses, pipe in the sound of clacking railroad wheels over the sound system, pull the shades, and project pictures of telephone poles going by. During the uproar over the campaign, the line merged with another, and the campaign was quietly dropped.

THE ETHICS OF PERSUASION

Persuasion can be a perfectly honorable and useful activity. Our society is based on the premise that people have a right to make their ideas known and to influence others to accept them. People can do this for themselves, or as hired hands for others or for organizations. To most of us, persuasion is far preferable to coercion.

When people criticize public relations (or advertising) their reason often is that they do not identify with the cause. Such critics may approve a blatant appeal to emotions, for instance, if the purpose is to alleviate hunger among underprivileged children, but not if it is to elect some disagreeable politician to office. Professional persuaders feel that emotion is a legitimate tool to use, provided it does not lead to action or an opinion opposite to what an appeal to reason would lead to.

A prevailing spirit among professional persuaders holds

that every client deserves a hearing in the court of public opinion provided no law prohibits the distribution of the product or service. The persuader owes consideration to the public being served but also loyalty to the client. Such loyalty requires aggressive PR activity.

Some PR and ad people work for causes or products or companies they are enthusiastic about. Others are not as fortunate. People working for a PR agency serving a variety of clients usually are able to stay away from clients they do not approve of. For instance, a confirmed nonsmoker would not be expected to work on a cigarette account. Both PR and advertising agencies frequently turn down clients whose products are inferior or whose ideas do not coincide with those of the agencies.

Chapter 15
Curbs and Limits
on the Media

As has been noted earlier in this book, the news media operate behind the secure shield of a special constitutional guarantee against government interference. The broadcast media are nominally under the jurisdiction of a governmental agency, the Federal Communications Commission, but in recent decades they have with increasing success asserted the same First Amendment freedoms that the print media have enjoyed.

The safeguard of the First Amendment is justified—in fact, necessitated—by the importance of the news media to the system of representative democracy under which we live. Yet the right to publish and broadcast is not an absolute one. It sometimes happens that the news media, in carrying out their essential function of informing the public, infringe upon other guarantees that are also vital to our system; some of them, indeed, have just as impressive constitutional under-pinning as does the concept of press freedom. When such conflicts of rights occur, it is often difficult to sort out the values involved and determine which has priority.

Guidelines exist for resolving these conflicts, sometimes in the form of statutes, sometimes in common law, and some-times only through an evolving consensus, but in all cases the guidelines are imprecise. Substantial expanses of gray areas are left—stretches of no-man's-land across which opposing forces shift back and forth—and the issue remains in doubt.

THE 50 LAWS OF LIBEL

One of those gray areas involves the law of libel and its limit-ing effect on the freedom of the media to disseminate the news without hindrance. That freedom is spelled out in the First Amendment's provision that "Congress shall make no law . . . abridging the freedom of speech, or of the press . . ." and in the extension of that prohibition to the states by means of the Fourteenth Amendment.

As the courts have interpreted it, the First Amendment affords assurance to anyone who publishes (or broadcasts) that the government will not impose prior restraint on that publishing activity; that is, there can be no censor who must approve the content before it is disseminated, and no agency of government can prevent such dissemination by a court in-junction, a sheriff's order, or any other attempt to restrain a potential publisher before the news or information has been published or broadcast. (In this discussion of libel, the term "publish" should be understood to include broadcast in its meaning, and "publisher" means broadcasters as well as those who distribute news in printed form.)

But the courts have also held that the First Amendment does not render the publisher immune from responsibility *after the fact* of publication, if what has been published injures other well-established and safeguarded rights. Among those rights is that of any citizen to a good name and reputation.

The way someone is thought of by others in the community usually depends on the things he has said and done through the years, on a pattern of conduct. A person's standing is gradually built up by this accumulating record, and, the courts have held, this reputation belongs to that person. It has value. If that reputation is damaged by something that appears in the newspaper or something that is broadcast over radio or television, the injured party is entitled to take steps to reestablish a good name and to recover monetary losses that may have been suffered. The laws of libel provide the means to take such steps.

Each of the 50 states has its own set of libel statutes, but there is no federal law of libel. However, the U.S. Supreme Court frequently hears and rules on cases arising out of state libel actions and by its decisions establishes precedents that affect the application of all state libel laws.

Individual state libel codes differ in some respects, and if we want to gain a full understanding of libel codes as they affect us, we must take the trouble to examine in detail the libel laws of our state. It is possible, however, to consider the subject in general terms, since there are more similarities than differences among the various statutes and because the Supreme Court decisions impose some national uniformities.

All of the state laws are in approximate agreement in defining what libel means: the publication of a statement that in some manner damages the reputation of an individual or group of individuals. (A particularly useful definition is that devised by Harold Cross, once counsel for the *New York Herald Tribune*. It well reflects the ambiguity and uncertainty that are so much a part of the laws of libel. "A newspaper publication is libelous of any person if its natural effect is to make those who read it think worse of that person.")

In the several definitions of libel, the term "publication" has broad meaning, as we observed earlier. It embraces not only the obvious ways of publishing, such as in a newspaper, magazine, or book. Publication, so far as libel law is concerned, also includes the dissemination of a statement over radio or television (even though verbal or visual, it has been "published" to hundreds or thousands of listeners and viewers, with the same effect as if it had appeared in print).

In some cases, the courts have held that damaging material that was reproduced on a copying machine for only a few readers represented "publication" as far as the law of libel is concerned; even handwritten letters that were passed around to several persons have been held to be "published" libel. In other words, the damaging or defamatory material need not have been distributed to many persons in order for it to be considered libel.

Moreover, the definition includes material in any form—not only the substance of a newspaper story, but also the headline, an accompanying picture, an advertisement, or a cartoon sketch. Whatever is published and causes injury to a person's good name is by definition libel.

If the statutes stopped there, they would constitute a sweeping limitation on the freedom of the press. A cursory skimming of any newspaper would yield numerous examples of published material that would be damaging to the reputations of the persons mentioned in the stories. An account of an arrest of a man on a charge of burglary certainly is likely to dim his good name among those who read it; the report of a debate in Congress wherein the President's motives and policies are bitterly attacked could well damage his standing; a photograph of a dignified citizen caught in an amusing but embarrassing mishap may expose the person to ridicule and diminish the person's reputation. All of these instances are, under the law, libelous. Why, then, is every publication not constantly under legal siege by aggrieved citizens demanding satisfaction for injuries done them through the news report? Chiefly because the laws of libel, after defining the term, go on to spell out various specific ways by which a publisher can defend against libel suits and escape the damages that might be sought by a reader who felt injured by something that had been published. The defenses thus provided enable the publisher to sidestep some of the hazard represented by the law of libel.

THROUGH THE LOOPHOLES

If we consider the concept of libel law as a kind of limitation on the freedom to publish, then the defenses specified in the statutes must be considered as loopholes or exemptions to that limitation. It should be noted, however, that each such specified exemption rests upon a determination that in this specific instance the public's right to be informed takes precedence over the individual's right to safeguard a good name against unwarranted injury by the media of information.

One of these defenses is that of *privilege*. A journalist invoking this defense claims the right to publish material from official and public records (such as the testimony given in a trial) even if that material is defamatory and damaging to the reputation of some citizen or group of citizens. If the journalist's report taken from such records is a fair and accurate one, this defense of privilege will protect even against a suit for libel damages by someone mentioned unfavorably in the report.

The rationale for this exemption to the general concept of libel responsibility is persuasive. It goes back once again to the First Amendment. The purpose of the guarantee of press freedom contained in that amendment is to ensure that the public will be well and fully informed. It is particularly necessary that the public be kept informed about the way in which its elected and appointed representatives are carrying out their responsibilities as public servants.

It follows, then, that the press should be free to report for the public the ways in which the public's business is being conducted by the legislators, the judges, the administrators, and others who have been given a public charge, and the news of how the public's business is being conducted is found in large part in the proceedings of legislative, judicial, and administrative agencies.

So in reporting material from the records of those proceedings, the press is considered to be the public's agent; it is also considered to have immunity from liability if some of the material it reports from the records happens to be defamatory. It has a privilege, in short, to report public and official records without fear that it might later have to run the post-publication gauntlet of the libel laws.

The defense of privilege is invoked by journalists to shield their reports of congressional or legislative debates, proceedings in the various state and federal courts, and official actions by administrators or administrative agencies.

As a practical matter, this means that if something bad is said about us by a state senator during a debate on the floor of the senate, and a newspaper publishes a story quoting the senator's unpleasant comment, we will very likely be unable to win a libel suit against the newspaper. The senator, of course, has absolute immunity conferred by the state constitution and cannot be reached by suit, either.

But if that same senator were to make exactly the same statement about us in the course of a talk at the local Rotary Club, the senator *would* be open to suit, and if the newspaper quoted the comment in its news story of the club meeting, the newspaper would be vulnerable to libel action as well. The Rotary speech is not an official occasion, and no privilege attaches to what is said or written about it. The defense of privilege applies *only* to public and official proceedings about which the public has a special need to be informed.

If the press were not given the right to invoke the defense of privilege, it would be inhibited from reporting many kinds of news about the public's business that in one way or another involved defamatory material. As a result the public would not be fully informed about the activities of its governmental representatives.

SOME ARE FAIR GAME

A second defense that journalists can use against a libel suit also has constitutional roots. It is the defense of *fair comment and criticism.* The reasoning behind this defense runs thus: Those persons who run for public office, or accept appointment to public office, thereby solicit the public's trust and confidence. They also lay themselves open to criticism of their performances as public representatives; sometimes that criticism may be painful to bear, but they have asked for it. They have, in effect, yielded up some of their rights as private citizens and made themselves subject to scrutiny and comment in their role as representatives of the public, and they cannot expect to be protected by the laws of libel to the same extent as when they were private citizens.

So if a news report quotes a constituent who has some unflattering things to say about a congressman, the legislator will be frustrated by the defense of fair comment and criticism if there is an attempt to sue either the disgruntled voter or the newspaper.

Trends in the law sometimes build case by case, reflecting the philosophy that happens to prevail for the moment in the Supreme Court. During the 1960s that philosophy favored the media, and the once quite narrow defense of fair comment and criticism was broadened again and again by successive Supreme Court decisions.

The pattern began developing with a landmark case in 1964, *New York Times* v. *Sullivan,* in which it was held that a libelous statement about a public official could be defended as fair comment even if parts of it were shown to be false, provided that the publisher had not printed it or broadcast it with malicious intent or foreknowledge that it was false.

Subsequent Supreme Court decisions during the 1960s extended the Sullivan doctrine to apply not only to public officials then holding office but also to persons who had *formerly been* public officials. Then, in the most sweeping extension of the principle, the justices drew into the category persons—including private citizens—who had either involved themselves in or had been drawn into public controversies or matters of public concern and had thus become *public figures.*

This last step had the effect of lumping into the public

figure/public official group such persons as a retired general who took a part in a racial segregation demonstration, a prominent college athletic director, and a widely known newspaper columnist. All were public figures under the Court's definition and thus could not hope to win a libel action unless they could prove that the defendant publisher or broadcaster had shown willful and malicious disregard of the facts, not an easy matter to establish. In some cases in lower courts attempts were made to apply the doctrine to such minor officials as a candidate for mayor and a police patrolman—not a captain or chief, just a cop on the beat.

This chain of decisions, each one more liberalizing than the last, obviously made life easier for publishers and broadcasters. They had acquired protection from the consequences of publishing almost any kind of criticism of persons who fell within the widening circle of public figures.

The rationale for their rulings, the justices indicated, was the need to make sure that the news media were provided with the opportunity to maintain a free and robust discussion of public affairs and of those persons chosen to represent the public. Writing an opinion in one of the series of cases, Justice Hugo L. Black observed that "unconditional freedom to criticize the way such public functions are performed . . . is necessarily included in the guarantees of the First Amendment . . . ."[1]

Not all of the justices then on the bench agreed with this interpretation, however. One of them, Justice Abe Fortas, voiced a concern that was shared also by some observers of the news media: "The First Amendment is not a shelter for the character assassinator, whether his action is heedless or reckless or deliberate. The First Amendment does not require that we license shotgun attacks on public officials in virtually unlimited open season. The occupation of public officeholder does not forfeit one's membership in the human race."[2]

[1] *Rosenblatt* v. *Baer*, 1966.
[2] *St. Amant* v. *Thompson*, 1968.

THE PENDULUM SWINGS

As often happens, the Court a few years later began a new sequence of decisions that had the effect of withdrawing some of the open-season freedoms that had concerned Justice Fortas. By then, of course, there were some new faces on the Court, and a somewhat different general philosophy prevailed, one less friendly to the media.

The first indication that the pendulum was swinging back a bit came in a 1974 decision by the court, *Gertz* v. *Welch.* The court held that the public-figure category did not include the plaintiff in this case, even though he was a well-known Chicago attorney, active in civil rights causes, the author of several books and a member or former member of many committees and commissions in Chicago and the state of Illinois. Back in the 1960s the public figure category had been held to include a college professor who was active in the fight to restrict atomic bomb testing, who had written many books and was widely known in the country. Clearly, the meaning of the term "public figure" was shifting in the eyes of the court.

Two years later, in *Time, Inc.* v. *Firestone,* the court further narrowed the public figure interpretation. It held that a prominent society woman involved in a divorce case should be entitled to sue for libel as a private citizen, not as a public figure, this despite the fact that she had been much publicized for her social and athletic activities (and had even hired a clipping service to keep score on the amount of newspaper space devoted to her).

Two 1979 cases had the effect of underlining the trend in the court's thinking. In *Hutchinson* v. *Proxmire* and *Wolston* v. *Reader's Digest,* the court ruled that someone who has been *involuntarily* drawn into the news does not by that fact become a public figure in the sense set out in the Sullivan decision and in other cases of the 1960s. The plaintiffs involved were in one case a scientist who had received a $500,000 research grant from the federal government—clearly a "public figure" as that term had been defined a decade or so earlier—and in the other case a man who had figured in a major investigation of Soviet spy activities in this country and who had pleaded guilty to a contempt charge for failing to respond to a grand jury subpoena.

That last case was particularly disturbing for the news media. In part of its ruling the court specifically rejected the contention "that any person who engages in criminal conduct automatically becomes a public figure for purposes of comment on a limited range of issues relating to his conviction." A very high percentage of libel actions against the news media are brought by persons charged with or convicted of criminal acts. Now, the court seemed to be saying, such persons were not to be considered public figures, and hence one of the defenses against libel actions brought by such persons was significantly weakened.

As the 1980s began, the defense of fair comment and criticism that had bloomed so dramatically in the 1960s had begun to look more than a little withered. But it had not dried up altogether; it still applied to public officials, and it thus still afforded the press an important protection in reporting news about the public's business.

Nonetheless, some of the same press observers and analysts who had worried ten years earlier that the press was getting too much freedom to criticize without fear of libel actions now were beginning to fret that the situation had been swung too far in the other direction. A chill had fallen on the newsrooms. Publishers and broadcasters were backing off from touchy stories. They were not only concerned about losing libel actions that might have been won under earlier court interpretations; the extensive costs involved in fighting libel suits—even if they were eventually won on appeal to a higher court—were a sufficient deterrent to dampen the investigative zeal of many journalists.

THE TRUTH, THE WHOLE TRUTH, AND . . .

There is a third major defense that a publisher can use to defeat a libel action, that of *truth*. In most state jurisdictions, if a publisher can prove to the satisfaction of a jury that the defamatory material published about the plaintiff was true in all significant respects *and* was published without any malicious intent but only as part of the news report, the newspaper or broadcast company will be able to escape damages.

That latter provision is very important to the success of the defense of truth. If in the course of reporting legitimate news a journalist publishes material that is damaging but true, this is simply carrying out the role contemplated in the First Amendment. If the defamatory story is true, the journalist is not responsible for the injury it causes and the wounded party has no recourse.

Note that this line of reasoning rests on the assumption that the defamatory material is *legitimately* a part of the news report. If it is included frivolously, or if it is dragged into the news story when it really is not a part of the news, then the court is likely to assume that spiteful or malicious intent was involved. In that case, even if the material happens to be true, the journalist will be held accountable for the damage the report has caused. But where it is possible for the publisher to demonstrate the defense of truth, without any malice being shown, this defense is sound and solid and will defeat most libel actions. It can be a solid defense without being based upon literal truth. As long as it can be demonstrated to the jury and court that the *gist* of the report was indeed true, it is not necessary to establish that every word or syllable of the account was factual.

(In one case, a newspaper published a story claiming that an alderman had a terrace constructed in his backyard by city workers, who used city-owned bricks for the job. In fact, such a terrace had been built, but of dismantled paving stone, not bricks. The alderman brought suit against the paper, and his attorney argued that the paper could not offer a defense of truth because the story contained an error, the reference to bricks rather than paving stone. The court ruled that this error was a "triviality," and that the gist of the story was indeed correct and the paper's defense of truth a good one.)

However, even if truth as a defense need not rest on lit-eral accuracy, it must embrace the whole impact of the de-famatory publication. That is, the defense must be as broad as the charge, and if the effect of the defamatory material is in part created by innuendo and suggestion, then the de-fense of truth must extend to the innuendo and suggestion as well as the flat statement. In such cases the use of crutch phrases such as "it was reported," or "it is claimed" does not reduce the liability of the publishing agent. Attribution of the defamatory material to someone else does not relieve the publisher of responsibility for whatever damage the material may cause (unless, of course, the attribution is to a privileged official record, such as a warrant or a grand jury indictment).

"OOPS, SORRY . . ."

These three—privilege, fair comment, and truth—are the principal defenses that journalists can employ to defend themselves and their publications against a libel action. There is one other device, however, that an editor or broad-caster can use in some states to escape at least some of the damages that are assessed when a libel action is lost. In those states the publication of a retraction—an acknowledgement that an error had been made and an apology for having made it—frees the publisher from some damage liability even if there is no defense to offer against the suit.

In most states that have retraction laws, the provision is intended to free the publisher only from responsibility for inadvertent libel, the kind that stems from an accident in the news handling process, such as a typographical error or the transposition of names. Usually a retraction will not ease the liability of a publisher for a libel published with malice. As-suming that the publisher of a libel has no good defense to offer, the newspaper or broadcasting station can be brought to account in court for the damage that the publication has done.

In theory, anyone who has had a significant role in the publication of the defamatory material is vulnerable to suit—the reporter who wrote the story, the copyreader who edited it and put a headline on it, the editor who assigned the reporter to the story, and, of course, the publisher, who bears ultimate responsibility for anything the paper publishes. As a practical matter, however, the chief target of a libel action is usually the ownership, the moneybags that have the means to pay the damage awards, if the jury decides that damages are due.

Often the damages sought by a plaintiff in a libel action sound astronomical. Suits for $5 million and even $30 million have been filed, and rarely does the injured person seek less than $100,000. To a considerable extent these vast claims are window-dressing. Those suing really do not expect that a jury will agree that their reputations have been injured a million dollars' worth, but even the act of filing the suit for such a staggering amount may accomplish at least a part of the plaintiffs' purpose. Persons hearing of the action will think to themselves, "They *really* must have the goods on that paper if they're going after *that* much," and to an extent the plaintiffs' reputations will already have been rehabilitated in that the reader has by implication accepted the guilt of the publisher.

In some instances in recent years, however, the plaintiffs have actually won the vast damages they sought (perhaps much to their surprise). In 1981 actress Carol Burnett won $1.5 million from *National Enquirer,* which had published a story claiming that she had been disorderly in a restaurant. Also, a former Miss Wyoming was awarded a total of $26.5 million by a jury that heard her case against *Penthouse* magazine. The magazine had published a piece of fiction about the sexual exploits of a Wyoming beauty queen; *Penthouse* claimed that similarities between the fictional character and the actual Miss Wyoming were unintentional coincidence. The jury decided otherwise. Such damage awards are customarily appealed in the expectation that they will be reduced by the appellate courts.

Usually a successful plaintiff receives a much more modest sum. The award may be in several parts: "special" damages that are to repay actual monetary loss the plaintiff suffered as a result of the libel (such as in the case of shopkeepers who lost business because it was said that they had a dirty store); "compensatory" or "general" damages that are intended to recompense the injured person for loss of good name and reputation; and "punitive" damages that may be added to the award by the court if the offending publication was particularly outrageous.

Some plaintiffs may win the case as far as the court record is concerned but gain little else. This happens if nominal damages—such as $1 or $100—are awarded when the suit had asked for $500,000. What the court is in effect saying in such cases is that the plaintiff's reputation has indeed been damaged by the publication, but not much, or else that there was not much reputation to damage in the first place. In either instance, the outcome represents a rather sour triumph for the plaintiff and really constitutes a moral victory for the defendant.

A substantial damage award in a libel action can be a crippling blow to a publication or broadcasting station. Moreover, the court costs of defending against a rash of libel suits can themselves be a serious burden, even if every case is won by the publication at the trial or appellate level.

So the libel statutes do represent one type of limitation on the freedom of the press to publish whatever it pleases, and a significant safeguard of the rights of the individual who is in conflict with one of the media of mass communication.

PRIVACY: A CASE-LAW DOCTRINE

There is another area somewhat akin to libel wherein the right of the press to publish the news conflicts with an individual right, that of privacy.

Here there are few statutes to serve as guidelines. In fact, the concept of a "right of privacy" is relatively novel in the law; it was first enunciated in an 1890 *Harvard Law Review* article by Samuel D. Warren and Louis D. Brandeis, later to become a distinguished justice of the Supreme Court, and its evolution since then has been chiefly through court decisions.

The underlying reason is similar to the one underlying

the libel laws. Citizens are presumed to have the right to keep their private lives free from intrusion, just as they are assumed to have a right to their good names and reputations. If their privacy is unwarrantedly invaded by a reporter or photographer bent on getting the news, the citizens ought to have some means of recourse.

Many of the early court cases involving violation of the right of privacy had to do with advertising in which an individual's picture or name had been used for commercial purposes without consent. The findings in favor of the plaintiff in most such cases were clear-cut and uncontroversial.

The privacy issue takes on more complexity, however, when the offending publication involves news rather than advertising, and when the plaintiff who is complaining that privacy has been invaded is someone who has in some fashion become a part of the news. How, then, are we to distinguish between invasion of privacy and legitimate reportage of a newsworthy person?

The decisions have been made on a case-by-case basis, and in the process the concept of invasion of privacy has taken on some general outlines, though not precise ones.

One illustrative case involved a man who in his youth had been a boy genius in mathematics. He had attracted wide attention, and news stories recounted his brilliant and precocious grasp of the field. Then he dropped out of sight for a number of years, until much later a reporter discovered him working in a humdrum job as a minor statistician, his initial promise faded. When the reporter wrote a "where are they now?" kind of story, the man sued the newspaper that published it; the basis for his suit was invasion of privacy. In that case the court held that he could not recover damages. Having once been so much in the news, he had lost his claim to privacy and could not reinstate it, even though circumstances had changed.

In other, somewhat related cases, the courts have held that privacy cannot continue to exist where there is a legitimate public interest in the news. Public officials, for example, have little claim to privacy.

Yet other cases have suggested where the boundaries

may lie. In one of these, decided in the mid-1960s, a woman sued a newspaper after it had published a picture of her with her skirts flying in the updraft of a carnival fun house. She was awarded damages, and the judge observed that "to hold that one who is involuntarily enmeshed in an embarrassing pose forfeits her right to privacy . . . would be illogical, wrong, and unjust."

In another case, the story of a family that had been held hostage for several days by escaped convicts was recounted years later in a magazine account. Members of the family sued for invasion of privacy and won damages in a jury trial, but the Supreme Court later reversed the verdict, holding that the magazine account dealt with legitimately newsworthy matter and that in the circumstances the First Amendment took precedence over the right of privacy.

Some courts have held that persons who are shown in a news picture as part of a crowd gathered at a public place are not entitled to claim that their privacy was invaded (as at a protest scene, when the television camera pans over the crowd), but if a camera singles out an individual for no particular news-connected reason, there may be substance to the invasion claim.

The rules of the game with respect to invasion of privacy are still in the process of evolving, but they already constitute at least a moderate form of restraint on the freedom of the media to seek the news wherever it is to be found. They clearly place on the journalist the duty of distinguishing between acts and events legitimately reported as news and private ones that are invasively made public by being turned into news through reporting. The difference can be subtle, elusive, and expensive.

KEEPING TRIALS FAIR

There is a third point at which the right of the press to publish news clashes with an equally respected constitutional right. This conflict has received a good deal of attention in recent years under the shorthand label of "fair trial *versus* free press."

At seeming odds in this issue are two articles of the Bill of Rights—the First Amendment, with its provision for freedom of the press, and the Sixth, which states that "In all criminal prosecutions, the accused shall enjoy the right to a speedy and public trial, by an impartial jury of the state and district wherein the crime shall have been committed. . . ."

The operative phrase here is "impartial jury," and the argument arises over whether it is in fact possible to empanel a truly impartial jury to try a person if the community's newspapers and newscasts have been filled with accounts of the arrest and the preliminaries to trial. To the lay observer, the argument is a difficult one to follow, since the two sides often seem to be espousing very similar positions, but there are crucial points of disagreement, and they are not likely to be resolved soon or easily.

Consider first the viewpoint held by most lawyers and judges. They contend that only the barest minimum of information should be published about an accused person prior to the time of trial. Legal purists would allow publication only of such items as the fact that someone had been arrested, the nature of the charges filed, and the legal sequence that will be followed in handling the case.

They argue that if additional information is given out— such as a report that the accused has confessed, or a prediction by a prosecutor that a guilty verdict will be returned, or details of the accused person's prior criminal record—the minds of potential jurors in the community will be prejudiced. It will then become difficult to select 12 persons who can honestly say that they have not formed an impression about the accused's guilt or innocence, and the accused will thereby be deprived of the right to a trial by unbiased jurors who are prepared to hear the case with open minds.

In support of their position, spokesmen for the legal profession can cite and document a succession of celebrated cases in which "trial by newspaper" did indeed take place. They can point to headlines in which the guilt of an accused person was assumed ("Police Name Seaman as Slayer of Eight Nurses") and to even more blatant instances in which the press appeared to be trying to direct a verdict ("Why

Isn't Sam Sheppard in Jail?" and "Quit Stalling—Bring Him In"). They can also enumerate various cases in which pictures, such as a staged reenactment of a crime, had implanted in the public's mind an impression of an accused person's guilt long before that person was brought into the courtroom to be tried.

As remedy for what it considers to be an impediment to justice, the legal profession has brought forward a program of restrictions on the release of pretrial information. These restrictions were developed first in the form of a report by an American Bar Association committee, and later were adopted formally as part of the canons that guide the behavior of lawyers and officers of the court. Such canons, once they have been adopted by the individual state and local bar associations and courts as well as by the ABA, become a part of the ground rules of the courts, and a judge has the power to enforce them by citation for contempt-of-court or by instituting disciplinary procedures through a bar association.

In some respects, the position taken by the newsmen in the free press–fair trial debate does not seem markedly different from that of the jurists. Most editors will concede that there have been some spectacular abuses of news coverage of criminal cases; they will not attempt to defend such excesses. Most editors will also acknowledge that the ABA formula for limitation of the release of pretrial information would allow for the reporting of *most* of the facts that the public needs to know in *most* criminal cases.

But the editors balk at the rigidity of the ABA approach. They insist that the public has a need to know how the machinery of justice is working at all of its stages, and that in some instances this requires a close and detailed account of the course of a case from the time that a crime has been committed until a verdict has been reached.

In support they can cite numerous instances in which the rights of an accused person were violated in secrecy by corrupt law enforcement agencies that were able to avoid press scrutiny (black persons in small Southern communities have frequently been the victims of such tactics). They can also point out cases in which bargains were struck behind the scenes by prosecutors and defense attorneys at the expense of the public interest.

The press must have discretion, the editors argue, to consider each case by itself, and to push for full coverage when the public interest would be served by such an approach. The ABA formula, were it to be widely adopted by individual courts and bar associations, would throw a universal blanket over the handling of court cases and in the process would raise the specter of judicial contempt power as a club to keep the press from getting at facts that in some instances should be aired.

The concern of newsmen about the threat of use of the contempt power is a genuine one, based on some unhappy experiences in earlier eras.

The power to cite and punish for contempt is available to all judges. It is a power usually not based on statute but on a common-law assumption that a judge must be able to maintain order in the court so that justice can be administered. When anyone or anything threatens to interfere with the orderly processes by which justice is dealt out, the judge is assumed to have the authority to put an end to that interference and to punish those responsible for it.

Under this doctrine, judges have punished not only outbursts of violence in the courtroom itself, but also statements made or publications disseminated at a distance from the court when the judge concluded that they were likely to affect the attitude of a jury or apply pressure to a judge and thus obstruct the administration of justice.

As it was exercised in early English courts (and American practice derives from the English model), the power was swift and harsh. A judge could cite an offender for actions that constituted interference with the decorum of the court or with the administration of justice. Having cited the contemptuous behavior (or, in effect, stated the charge), the judge could proceed on the spot to find the offender guilty, pronounce sentence, and order a bailiff to haul the hapless attorney, witness, or defendant off to a cell (or to the scaffold, in very early times)—all in the space of a few moments, and with no provision for trial by jury or right of appeal.

While the common-law basis for the contempt power is still recognized in the courts of this country, there have been some limits placed on the exercise of the power. In some cases the limits have been statutory. (For example, the law provides that if a contempt penalty of imprisonment for more than six months is to be assigned, the offender must be given a jury trial. Appeals are also provided for in most cases involving contempt citations.) In other respects the contempt power has been limited by judicial decisions, and these limitations are of particular interest to the press.

In *Bridges* v. *California* in 1941 and later in *Pennekamp* v. *Florida* in 1946, the U.S. Supreme Court held that for a newspaper publication to constitute contempt it must represent a "clear and present danger" that it would have the effect of obstructing justice in the pending case. In these two decisions, the court held that the publication of news articles or editorials could not be held to represent such a clear and present danger, and reversed contempt penalties that had been imposed on newsmen by trial judges and upheld in the lower appellate courts.

To many editors, the American Bar Association recommendations that the contempt power be invoked to assure adherence to the proposed limitations on pretrial publicity raised the prospect of a revival of earlier, pre-*Bridges* interpretations. They feared that individual judges, encouraged by the ABA recommendations, might begin utilizing the contempt power to prevent publication of information about the working of the court system, information that the public should be entitled to have.

In a number of cases, such fears have been realized. Judges have brandished the contempt power to back up their imposition of "gag orders," judicial directives forbidding the release of information about a pending case or one at the trial stage. Other judges have closed pretrial hearings to the press, thus preventing any coverage of a significant phase of the workings of the machinery of justice. Broadcasters and newspapers have consistently resisted gag rules and closed hearings, sometimes getting a measure of backing from Supreme Court decisions and sometimes suffering rebuffs from the highest court. The issue of free press and fair trial has continued into the 1980s unresolved.

One attempt at a partial resolution has been underway for two decades in the form of joint bar–press–broadcast codes drawn up by journalists, lawyers, and judges. These codes set standards of behavior for both the press and the officers of the court and they usually include many of the same kinds of provisions as those embodied in the ABA recommendations. But the codes have been entirely voluntary in character, and they have functioned unevenly. Some of the time journalists have been guided by the code provisions and have avoided clashes with the judiciary over potentially prejudicial publicity, but often, when a particularly spectacular case came along, the codes were forgotten and the old adversary confrontations between press and bar arose once again.

The prospect is that this particular stretch of no-man's-land will continue to be contested for some time to come.

ACCORDING TO _____?

There is still another sector where the issue is similarly unresolved. Here a less momentous problem than the free press–fair trial question is involved. This question is whether under certain circumstances a reporter should be allowed to keep news sources secret, even when ordered by a court to reveal them.

On the face of it, this seems a paradoxical matter. The mission of the press usually is to tell what it knows, not to suppress it, and that includes the source of news; in many instances knowing where a given item of information originated is essential to an understanding of that item. So why would a reporter want to conceal sources? It does not very often happen, but there are times when journalists feel that the claim to secrecy must be made, and when they make it they often find themselves on a collision course with the courts. These infrequent situations almost always involve an investigative story, often an exposé of wrongdoing on the part of some agency of government. The Watergate scandal was a spectacular example, with the mysterious "Deep Throat" feeding tips and leads to the *Washington Post* team of Robert Woodward and Carl Bernstein.

In less momentous situations the break in an investigative story may come from an informant willing to blow the whistle on superiors as long as the informant's name will not be brought into the case. The tipster may fear, often with reason, that loss of job or even personal injury might be the consequences if it became known how the newspaper got on the trail of the story. So the reporter promises anonymity, gets the needed tips, and proceeds to develop the story. If it involves laying bare illegal activities, the chances are pretty good that sometime later on the reporter may be called before a judge or grand jury and asked to provide evidence in the matter under investigation, including the names of the persons who leaked the original tips.

In making such a request, the authorities are only doing their job, of course. Most of us, as citizens, subscribe to the doctrine that law enforcement officials are entitled to the cooperation of the public, and that they ought to be able to seek and obtain information that they need to carry out their responsibilities. When citizens are summoned to court to give evidence, they are expected to give what help they can, as long as their rights are not jeopardized in the process.

The journalists' contention, however, is that they should in certain cases be exempted from this obligation. Other categories of citizens are commonly allowed such exemption— doctors and lawyers are permitted to maintain client and patient confidentiality, and in some states other designated persons (such as priests and ministers, or private secretaries) have the same privilege.

Journalists argue that they should be permitted to remain silent about the identities of news sources because to expose them would jeopardize future access to the kind of information that could be obtained only in this way. The journalists maintain that the public is better served by keeping such channels open than it would be if the press were compelled to expose informants and thus dry up the only avenues through which certain kinds of news can find their way to the attention of the press and thereby to the public.

Thus the issue is drawn. The court and the prosecutor contend that journalists as citizens must give evidence that is needed to further the ends of justice; the journalists as representatives of the press respond that they must withhold the evidence in order to be faithful to their obligation to inform the public. Each side claims that righteousness and the public interest are in its corner.

In about half the states, resolution of the matter has been attempted by statute, the so-called shield laws. By law in those jurisdictions reporters may refuse to reveal news sources under certain specified circumstances, but these shields have proven porous. Even in states where they have been erected, judges have nonetheless insisted that journalists give evidence about sources and have imposed penalties—including jail sentences—on reporters who refused.

Some journalists have sought to press the claim that the First Amendment gives them the right to claim source confidentiality, but this thesis has found little favor with either lower-court judges or the Supreme Court. As in other gray areas where the right of the press to find and publish the news is in some fashion at odds with other rights that are also vital to our way of life, the issues are not yet resolved. The drawing of simple boundary lines is very difficult, and the continuation of a see-saw shifting of forces seems likely to be the pattern for the foreseeable future.[3]

[3]Complicating the debate over shield laws and journalists' claims of source confidentiality is the widespread and sometimes abused practice of relying on unnamed sources in news stories about government or in background stories about social ills. The damage often inflicted on media credibility by this practice was discussed in Chapters 2 and 5.

THOSE DOCTRINES AGAIN

Earlier in this book (Chapter 3) we noted that the broadcast media are subject to one form of limitation or control that the print media do not have to contend with. The Federal Communications Commission licenses radio and television broadcasters and, by its regulations, to some extent influences the content of their broadcasts.

That influence is less significant today than it once was. During broadcasting's early years, the FCC discouraged any expression of editorial opinion on the air; now it is not only permitted but encouraged. At one time the FCC requirement that broadcasters devote a specified percentage of air time to public service categories of programming represented a prescriptive influence on the broadcasters. Today, with the ever-growing importance of news in broadcast content, few stations have any problem demonstrating that they meet minimum public service standards, since newscasts satisfy much of the requirement.

In an earlier era, the broadcast media were second-class citizens, as far as First Amendment protections were concerned. Their print media competitors did not worry much about the existence of a government licensing and supervisory system for broadcasting, but let anyone even hint at setting up a similar arrangement for the newspaper press and that industry was at once bristling and denunciatory.

As the years went by, however, and first radio and then television came to be significant news media as well as entertainment channels, the publishers began to recognize that everyone was in the same boat in regard to First Amendment freedoms. With print media support, the broadcasters asserted and gradually made good their claim to share in those freedoms.

Some indirect constraints remained, however. The two FCC doctrines of fairness and equal time still represented a form of control over the content of broadcast news. (In 1981 the FCC recommended repeal of the two doctrines, but it was uncertain whether Congress would agree.)

The equal-time provision requires that broadcasters who give or sell air time to one candidate or party in an election campaign must make similar blocks of time available on the same terms to the opposing candidate or candidates. The fairness doctrine holds that if a person, organization, or cause is attacked on a broadcast medium, an opportunity must be made for a response presenting the viewpoint of the other side or sides. The fairness doctrine does not specify air time equality; its purpose is to make sure that all aspects of a controversy are fairly presented.

The two doctrines can influence broadcast news content in an inhibitory sense; broadcasters may consciously avoid certain dimensions of the news, since reporting them might trigger demands for balancing coverage that would consume air time and staff resources. It is obviously impossible to measure the effect this has on the content of broadcast news coverage, but individual broadcasters will acknowledge that it sometimes plays a part.

The most obvious element of FCC control over broadcasting, the licensing power, has not often been wielded in an attempt to influence news content. During the Watergate scandal of the 1970s officials of the Nixon administration did threaten to "make trouble" for the television station owned by the *Washington Post* the next time its license came up for renewal, but they were out of office before they could make good the threat.

"A PRECIOUS RIGHT . . ."

In summary, while the freedom of the media to seek out and disseminate the news is not absolute, it is nonetheless extremely broad and sweeping.

There are indeed curbs and limits set by the various laws of libel, by the right of privacy, by the powers of judges, by the Sixth Amendment protections for persons accused under the law, and even by the indirect influence of the FCC's fairness and equal-time doctrines.

Yet even encumbered with such restrictions, the news

media have great latitude as long as they are pursuing their mission of informing the people as fully and fairly as possible.

Vermont Royster, former editor of the *Wall Street Journal,* put it eloquently in a speech to a group of his colleagues:

> "But what a precious right that is [the people] have granted us. So long as the First Amendment stands, the American press, each part choosing what it will, can publish what it will. When we think it necessary to the public weal we can seize upon documents taken from government archives and broadcast them to the world. We can strip privacy from the councils of state and from grand juries. We are free to heap criticism not only upon our elected governors but upon all whom chance has made an object of public attention. We can, if we wish, publish even the lascivious and the sadistic. And we can advance any opinion on any subject."[4]

[4]From his comments on accepting the Fourth Estate Award from the National Press Club, as quoted in *Quill,* April 1979, pp. 28–29.

Chapter 16
The Pear-Shaped
Silhouette

During the 1970s and early 1980s, numerous futurists and analysts made predictions about the shape of things to come in communication technology. Some of their visions and prognostications were fanciful and utopian; some could most charitably be described as bizarre. But some others were more credible and hard-headed, based on trends that were already evident and technology already in place.

If we accept only the forecasts of the least far-out of the futurists, it seems that we should be prepared for some far-reaching changes in the ways in which we relate to others and the ways in which we conduct the various activities that make up our life and work.

For example, by the 1990s or perhaps a few years later, school-age children may well be getting their education at home rather than at the schoolhouse. They will sit before video consoles while master teachers guide them through courses, employing electronic wizardry to make anthropology an immediate and involving experience and mathematics a universally achievable skill. Interactive devices will make it possible for students to proceed at varying paces, punching the console to ask questions or to request repetition of complex passages. There will be no sprawling educational campuses and complexes, only compact centers with testing capacity to serve those who have completed home programs of study and now want accreditation.

Much business activity will also be conducted through the home communication center. Two-way television will allow for conferences of individuals scattered across the country, exchanging on their video and computer terminals information ranging from sales graphs to architectural drawings.

The same home screens and consoles that serve for business activities will be used for shopping. The homemaker in the market for a new appliance will be able to call up on the screen advertising presentations from various manufacturers or purveyors. Salespersons will demonstrate their competing models, stressing advantages; the shopper can simultaneously call up consumer group ratings of the products, complete with repair and breakdown histories. When the shopper finds the right buy, a few more punches on the console will record the order and direct the bank to transfer the purchase price to the dealer—but only after a later signal has been punched in to indicate that the appliance actually has arrived in satisfactory condition.

Most family financial transactions, from banking to paying bills to investing, will be done electronically through the home communication center or by credit cards with built-in microcomputers that keep running balances to alert both spender and vendor. Money—coins and paper bills—may by then be something to be viewed in museums.

The entertainment uses of the home communication center will expand dramatically by the 1990s, the futurists tell us. With cable and satellite potentialities fully realized, the catalog of offerings available will be exhaustingly comprehensive. It will include live and taped coverage of sports events from around the world, supplemented by banks of film and tape of notable games and matches of yesteryear, all available to be called up on the wall-sized home screen with three-dimensional reception. Equally as available will be entertainment of every variety—movies, new and old; Broadway plays and musicals; variety and cabaret shows; magic acts, animal acts, grand opera, soap opera, concerts, and ballets.

So, too, with news and opinion, our chief concern in this book. Summaries of local, national, and international events will be on tap 24 hours a day, fully indexed and constantly updated. We will be able to punch a few buttons and learn all that we want to know about any facet of current news, together with explanations and admonitions from our favorite commentators and columnists.

The information we are now accustomed to getting from newspapers and magazines will be delivered electronically, both visually and in text form (with a printer device to provide hard copy for later re-reading). A massive central computer will store the equivalent of the millions of books and documents that now fill the archives of the world; we'll be able to call up on the screen *War and Peace* or the *Congressional Record,* page by page, without a trip to the library.

Many of the practices and artifacts of our present era may be no more in this future world. For example, there may by then be no great newspaper presses and no armies of small "independent dealers" fanning out each evening to toss packages of newsprint into the rain-soaked bushes in the approximate vicinity of the front door; millions of trees that might have been cut down to become newspapers and magazines will still stand in the forest.

The home communication center perhaps will not be able to meet all of the needs of the family of the future, but it may come close. More sophisticated versions of present-day electronic games will allow for vicarious participation in virtually any competitive activity without the strain and bother of taking to the field in person. Citizens will be able to discharge their voting responsibilities at home, electronically, by inserting a coded voter card in the console to register choices. (Election night parties may be drastically shortened.) The home center will alert the family to disasters, near or far, and automatically summon help when needed, since there will be electronic links to public safety centers.

The two-way video capacity of the home center will even allow for family reunions and visits with friends without anyone having to stir from the hearth (which by then will probably be a remarkably lifelike representation of the real thing, with the satisfying crackle of logs and the gradual dying of the flames to glowing embers—and never any ashes to clean out).

Whether the futurists who have been sketching these visions of the decades to come are seeing ahead accurately won't be known, of course, for quite a few years. (That's why long-range forecasting is such a risk-free and exhilarating sport; the hapless souls who deal in short-term predictions— tomorrow's weather or next week's Dow Jones averages— lead much more anxious lives.)

If we are willing to buy the futurists' scenario, we may also want to be concerned about possible evolutionary adaptation over the generations to come. The human shape may take on pear-shaped contours, from much sitting before various screens. Heads may have to expand to allow for increasing brain capacity, and eyes will become more prominent. Fingers will be stronger (all that button-pushing) but overall muscle tone may run to flab. Heavy work and dirty jobs will of course be handled by robots, so no one will work up a sweat except those archaic zealots who persist in exercising out of doors, away from the all-giving screen.

It is entertaining (and sometimes depressing) to muse on about visions of the future. It may be more to the point, however, to consider what evidence there is that the prognosticators may be on the right track, and if they are right, what implications there will be for the dissemination of information and ideas in the future and what actions we ought to be taking right now to ensure that we make the best of whatever changes are to come.

THE HARDWARE IS THERE

As far as technology is concerned, most of the components of the all-purpose home communication center were already in use in one form or another before the end of the 1970s.

One of those components, cable television systems, had been wired into about a quarter of the nation's homes that were equipped with television sets, as we noted in Chapter 3. When a third of those homes have been wired, cable will have the economic base to push ahead rapidly, despite the considerable cost of wiring the remaining homes (in some cities, installing a mile of cable along the street can cost between $100,000 and $150,000).

Cable has been expanding city by city, neighborhood by neighborhood. Each advance has been accompanied by sometimes bitter and cut-throat competition between rival systems bidding for a local franchise. The franchise is typically awarded by a City Council or an ad hoc commission, which tries to get the best possible deal for the community (public service channels, with citizen access guaranteed, for example), but often politics and bribery influence the awards, for each franchise amounts to a potentially lucrative monopoly for the winner.

By 1980 some cable systems were already bringing into subscribers' homes programming on as many as 36 channels, and expansion of these systems to 80 or even 100 or more channels was technologically feasible. Experiments were also underway with interactive channels. In Columbus, Ohio, subscribers to QUBE cable systems had attached to their sets small keyboards with which they could register their views on poll questions or order merchandise pictured on their home screens.

Another approach to "videoshopping" was being tried in 6 cable television markets scattered across the country. There was no interactive aspect involved, but viewers in the 6 communities could place orders for merchandise by calling a toll-free telephone number. Their "Shopping Channel" operated 16 hours a day, 7 days a week, showing a wide range of products displayed in simulated home settings with models demonstrating the virtues of fine china, small appliances, or television sets. Sponsors of the shopping channel were a credit-card company and a department-store conglomerate.

In another such venture, aimed at a New York audience, a "Home Shopping Show" offered a succession of ten-minute segments, each devoted to a single product or service. Advertisers paid $6000 to get their wares on a home shopping segment.

These all represented first steps toward the futurists' vision of the home center. With satellites playing an increasing role in video communications, programmers can bounce their signals off one of a number of satellites poised over the earth and back down to cable systems carrying the programs into subscribers' homes. This greatly increases the diversity of fare a cable system can offer its customers. "Cable" now means not just a clearer picture of local channels, not just a couple of distant signals piped in, but a range of original programming from around the nation.

The next logical step had also already been taken in a few instances by the early 1980s. The cost of the antenna systems that would enable an individual viewer to take signals directly from the satellites, without any cable intermediary, had been coming down rapidly. They had originally been huge, multiton structures costing hundreds of thousands of dollars, but by the beginning of the 1980s the cost was down to about $10,000 for a compact backyard installation, and a few well-heeled viewers had hooked them up and were sampling the wide variety of programming up there "on the birds."

Electronic transmission of newspaper contents began in the 1970s in about 100 communities across the country. They were experimental ventures and in some cases were not very sophisticated. In Murray, Kentucky, for example, the *Ledger & Times* leased a local cable television channel and used it to transmit news items, sports results, weather forecasts, and some kinds of advertising. Lines of type moved across the screen at a fixed pace and viewers could tune in anytime, but could sample, of course, only what was running at that moment; there was no call-up feature and no bank of stored material.

The *New York Times* and *The Wall Street Journal* were furnishing much larger quantities of such news-related items as financial and stock market reports to selected clients willing to pay to have that material available on a retrieval basis. Clients had to pay the computer-time costs involved, and they were steep enough to limit the market for the services to brokerage houses and large businesses. The Knight-Ridder newspaper chain was experimenting with a system that would permit viewers in their homes to use a keyboard attached to their television sets to bring in wanted consumer information such as airline schedules, movie theater times, advertising, and regularly updated news summaries. Both individual newspapers and chains were making investments in cable companies in order to have access to the channels if the experiments demonstrated that the market was there for the electronic newspaper offerings.

Those aspects of the home communication center of the future not concerned primarily with information programming were also in the developmental stages through the 1970s and into the 1980s.

Television had been used in education for several decades, chiefly to extend the classroom to wider and more diverse student populations than could be served by standard campuses. Computers had been programmed to provide self-paced instruction for individual students; courses in disciplines ranging from mathematics to writing were available for students from elementary grades to college level. Combining the two—television and computer—was a perfectly feasible development.

Electronic voting was foreshadowed by the QUBE experiments in Columbus; that system had also pioneered with some limited television shopping. Transmission of news and information text material via television or cable at viewer demand and from established data banks had been underway in Great Britain since the mid-1970s, and in several other nations, including Canada and France. In this country, one version, Teletext, had been tested in Salt Lake City in the late 1970s by KSL-TV.

BUT WOULD IT PAY?

Just about all of the pieces that might eventually be assembled in the futurists' all-purpose home center were thus available by the early 1980s. It only remained for someone to come up with financing formulas that would make the whole vision economically feasible. That, however, was a formidable assignment.

Commercial through-the-air television had followed the pattern set by the print media and radio, and all depended on advertising revenue. Most cable systems operated on a subscription basis—homes hooked to the cable paid a monthly fee for the service. Special programming offered either through the air via scramblers or on cable channels (sports events, first-run movies, concerts and plays) was financed by fees charged for each individual offering selected by the viewer. Early data-retrieval experiments also depended on user fees to cover the computer costs and turn a profit for the operators. Public broadcasting survived on the basis of government funds, subscriber contributions, and corporate grants.

It seemed likely that some complex combination of all of these approaches would have to be worked out to cover the forbidding costs in both hardware and software that would be involved if the futurists' home communication center were to become a reality.

User fees, for example, might cover the home-education aspects of the service, as tuition does for private education today. Advertisers would presumably foot the bill for the electronic equivalent of classified and display advertising, and would probably also be willing to continue to pay for some entertainment offerings in return for sponsor identification and commercial pitches. Other entertainment programs might carry individual price tags, as on such systems as Home Box Office. Information retrieval would be initially costly, at least until the data banks had been filled with the electronic versions of books, documents, and magazines; after that, user fees might be nominal.

Putting together this complex jigsaw puzzle of approaches to financing could be a challenge that would take years—even decades—to meet. After all, many of the component parts of the home communication center had already been around for a good many years without anyone finding an economically viable way to exploit their possibilities. Facsimile transmission of newspapers had been touted as the wave of the future back in the 1940s and 1950s but caught on in only a limited way until the 1970s; two-way television had been demonstrated at mid-century; education via television and computer was possible for years, but its use was stymied by the resistance of educators and students and by hardware costs.

But once the existence of a market for such services can be established, it seems highly likely that ways will be found to put the financing package together and pave the way for the era of the home communication center. Because so many components are already in place, it could develop with astonishing, confusing speed.

A TEMPTING POWER CONCENTRATION

A related problem—deciding who will be in charge of this vast new information-disseminating system—may be more difficult to resolve, and more momentous as far as the public interest is concerned.

With home communication centers finally in place and functioning there would be, in effect, a vast information mo-

nopoly. News, education, basic information retrieval, entertainment—in short, *all* information—would be routed to the
American consuming public over one pervasive electronic
network. It takes little imagination to picture how greedily
such a network would be eyed by power-hungry elements
of society, and how much power its control would bestow.

Some of the components that would eventually be
merged into the overall network are now under a form of
control by an agency of the federal government; other components (local cable systems) are franchised by local government; still others (the news-gathering organizations of the
newspapers and the wire services) are entirely independent;
and still others (the entertainment programming packages)
are subject to advertiser influence.

How, when they are all rolled together in one great "ball
of wax," will control be exercised over the resulting amalga-
mation?

The prospect that government, at whatever level, might
be in charge of the system through which the public gets all
of its information and conducts most educational and business activities evokes fearsome Orwellian visions. It would
be a dictator's dream come true.

Even nondictatorial governments would be tempted
sorely with such a power concentration under their control.
Consider, for example, how President Richard M. Nixon
might have availed himself of the opportunity to keep out
of the information pipelines the damaging tidings about
Watergate. Or how President Lyndon Johnson, committed
to pursuit of the Vietnam War, might have convinced himself
that the American people should be allowed to know only
one side of the Southeast Asia story.

The all-purpose information network, if it ever comes,
simply cannot be allowed to fall under government control
if America's liberties are to have a chance to survive.

It is nearly as dismaying to contemplate the possibility
that a supercorporation—say, AT&T—might dominate the
brave new world's information lifelines.

All this suggests the imperative need for planning. The

1980s very likely will see the molds being fashioned for the communication system that will be in place sometime in the twenty-first century. There must be blue-ribbon commissions and presidential task forces. There must be participation by all elements of society in the drafting process, to insure that a check-and-balance control of that system will be guaranteed. Apart from planning to prevent nuclear warfare, no task will be more pressing than this one: shaping the system that will so sweepingly affect the quality of life for the next several generations.

GOODBYE TO THE GLOBAL VILLAGE?

Even if the issue of control can be resolved on terms that will not endanger democratic freedoms, the advent of the home communication center may have other disturbing implications.

The news and information available over the universal network will, as we have noted, come to consumers on a call-up basis. Individuals will be able to bring to their viewing screens the kinds of news they want to have—and *only* those kinds, if they wish.

At first blush that seems an appealing rather than a disturbing prospect. Discriminating viewers would be able to tune out sensational news and trashy entertainment and concentrate instead on significant and uplifting tidings. Persons who today cannot get as much specialized information about particular topics as they would like to have could be accommodated with a nonstop diet of sports news, or Wall Street analyses, or ethnic news, or congenial editorial opinion—whatever they might want.

But consider further what that would mean.

The mass media of the present day are generalized. They cover a very broad range of news, information, and opinion; the formula is something for everyone. As consumers of these media we cannot help being exposed to that broad range of ideas and information, even if as individuals we tend to focus on pet interests as we scan the newspaper or watch the evening newscast. Whatever our specialized concerns may be, we cannot avoid exposure to the generalist mix of the mass media.

But in the era of the home communication center, each person will be able to fashion his own newspaper or newscast, punching the console to call up only topics of personal interest. Those who want to will be able to build their own individualized pictures of the world—narrow pictures, or lopsided ones, without much resemblance to the broad, multifaceted reality. The result could well be a severe fragmenting of society. The common data base represented by today's mass media would no longer inform understanding and condition interaction among people.

If that sounds alarmist, think for a moment of the remarkable proliferation of specialized magazines in recent years, catering to intense, narrow, and blinkered interests. That proliferation suggests what might happen when it becomes possible for everyone to summon up design-it-yourself news media on the home information center screen.

The generalized media have served to link groups and individuals by providing them with a shared experience of many kinds of information. As Dominique Wolten put it, "what will remain of this democratic function when each person reads—or punches up on the console—only what his or her information needs require?" Wolten, a French journalist, in the late 1970s surveyed the progress in America toward the realization of the futurists' communications vision. "It may be that, despite their shortcomings, today's mass media will turn out to have been more democratic than the *à la carte* media of the future. For these, in the long run, may only serve to reinforce existing social divisions."[1]

Will that be the legacy of the new tomorrow? Not a global village, but increasingly segmented and isolated tribes identified only with their separate concerns?

Not everyone expects that. There are some observers of

[1]Wolten, Dominique, "Do You Love Your VDT?" *Columbia Journalism Review,* July/August 1979, pp. 36–39.

the media (the authors of this book among them) who are confident that the need for a common information base will continue to be recognized in the era of the home communication center. Whatever their individual interests, the inhabitants of the twenty-first century will want the sentinel function performed by some reasonably impartial agency. They will recognize their need to be informed about issues and happenings outside their immediate personal or professional circles of interest.

It may well be that the mass media we know today will indeed be replaced by an all-purpose electronic network—perhaps even sooner than the futurists predict—but the *functions* that the familiar media have performed in our society will still be needed. The services of news gatherers will still be valued, and so will the expertise of editors in sorting out the significant elements from the vast array of information bits available.

In the years of change that are certain to come through the rest of this century and into the next, the shape of the journalistic enterprise is likely to alter significantly. But the concept, the central ethic—informing the people as fully and accurately as possible about events in the world—*that* will endure. Or so it seems to us.

Index